W9-AKU-595

"This is much more than a boxing book. In an attempt to accurately describe Depression-era life and the characters of Brooklyn, New York (and its Brownsville section in particular), Ross has succeeded marvelously. . . . Ross deftly captures the atmosphere of this time and place with a dialogue written in Runyonesque style, dripping with phrases and syntax reminiscent of the Bowery Boys, Chester Reilly, or any "film noir" movies about boxing, New York, or both. The era has also been covered well in some of the films of Woody Allen and Neil Simon, but Ross's characters were real, and life was more pessimistic and dangerous. . . . All of this history is so well presented by Ross that even though most boxing historians, as well as hardcore fans are familiar with the story of Bummy Davis, you still find yourself unable to put this book down, and one becomes so emotionally invested in the main character that one keeps hoping the tearful conclusion somehow ends differently, even though you know it will not."

—Mike Greenhill, *Boxing Insider*

"Ron Ross's *Bummy Davis vs. Murder, Inc.* provide[s] a portrait of urban Jews in the Brownsville section of Brooklyn during the 1930s and 1940s who were anything but 'nice Jewish boys.' . . . Weaving together the lives of boxer and gangster, Ross makes Brownsville a study in contrasts. . . . The members of Murder, Inc. raised homicide and mayhem to a level of professionalism virtually unmatched in the annals of American crime. And in spite of his Runyonesque prose, Ross conveys the full horror of the organization's casual approach to murder. . . . Ross has given us a good read, one that is a knowledgeable evocation of the Jews who became *bulvons* and boxers rather than doctors and lawyers."

—Leonard Kriegel, *The Forward*

"Ross vividly brings to life Brownsville's colorful streets with their push-cart peddlers, candy stores, and rough characters. He provides us with the characters both 'civilian' and criminal whose ornate and flowery speech, peppered with Yiddish argot, sounds like a cross between Damon Runyon and Henny Youngman."

—Alan Abbey, *Jerusalem Post*

"It is with exuberance that I review a second book by Ron Ross. . . . For those who relish a good read . . . I strongly suggest Ron Ross's *Bummy Davis vs. Murder, Inc.*"

—Dr. Nikos Michalis Spanakos, *Brooklyn Daily Eagle*

"My heartfelt thanks to Ron Ross for bringing excitement back into my reading time. I couldn't separate myself from *Bummy Davis vs. Murder, Inc.*"

—Angelo Dundee, trainer of Muhammad Ali and Sugar Ray Leonard

ALSO BY RON ROSS

The Tomato Can: A Novel

Ron Ross

BUMMY DAVIS VS. MURDER, INC.

The Rise and Fall of the Jewish Mafia and an Ill-Fated Prizefighter

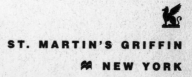

ST. MARTIN'S GRIFFIN

NEW YORK

www.stmartins.com

Design by Kathryn Parise

LIBRARY OF CONGRESS CATALOGING-IN-PUBLICATION DATA

Ross, Ron
    Bummy Davis vs. Murder, Inc. : the rise and fall of the Jewish Mafia and an ill-fated prizefighter / Ron Ross.
      p. cm.
    ISBN 0-312-30638-5 (hc)
    ISBN 0-312-33571-7 (pbk)
    EAN 978-0312-33571-7
    1. Jewish criminals—New York (State)—New York. 2. Organized crime—New York (State)—New York—History—20th century. 3. Davis, Bummy, 1920–1945. 4. Boxers (Sports)—Biography. 5. Jews—New York (State)—New York—Social conditions. 6. Brownsville (New York, N.Y.)—Social conditions. 7. New York (N.Y.)—Social conditions. I. Title
HV6194.J4R67 2003
364.1'06'0899240747—dc21

                              2003052903

First St. Martin's Griffin Edition: December 2004

10 9 8 7 6 5 4 3 2 1

To my greatest fan, my inspiration,
my driving force,
the sum total of all the good things in life,
my beloved wife, Susan.

And to

my dear friend, a true prince of the boxing world
and the person who opened the doors that made
this work possible—Vic Zimet. What is supposed to
be is not always the way things turn out. Vic Zimet
passed away on January 13, 2003, but center stage
will always be his—in my heart and Susan's.

PROLOGUE

Mottel Scharansky lived to die. To him, the pinnacle of a person's life came the day after it ended.

Mottel was a daily visitor (except on Shabbes) to the I. J. Morris Funeral Parlor. As a night sandwich-and-salad counterman at the Concord Cafeteria on Pitkin Avenue, he was quite willing to forgo sleep in favor of this pursuit. Shortly after his beloved Yetta passed on, he moved from their large apartment on Hopkinson Avenue to a cramped flat over the Tuxedo Store on Stone Avenue, just to be within easy walking distance of I. J. Morris, where he spent more time than in his apartment anyhow. Everyone in Brownsville eventually wound up in I. J. Morris, Mottel said, so in truth it was home to all. When Mottel walked the streets of Brownsville, passersby believed him to be a distant relative, and there were many wavings of hands and bemused smiles of recognition.

In the potato bin under his kitchen window Mottel kept three Hegeman Farms milk bottles, each gradually filling with coins and bills, and carefully labeled with a Johnson & Johnson Band-Aid. The first bottle, "Mine Kuffin," presented a dilemma, as Mottel could not decide between the dictates of his religion, which called for a simple pine box, and the comfort he craved from a silk-lined mahogany casket. The second bottle, "Fyunorel," carried the savings for a fine funeral service, complete with a chazzen and a wonderful eulogy that Mottel had prepared and stuffed in the bottle along with the money. The third bottle, "Pushke," was a sort of guarantee of safe passage. It contained money to be donated to charities. Certainly God would look upon this with much favor.

So it was that on the Friday morning of November 23, 1945, Mottel Scharansky stood before his cracked medicine cabinet mirror, rubbing spit on his one and only brown print tie in an effort to remove a stain that was part of the design. There were plenty of stains that Mottel could have worked to remove, but this was not one of them. He checked himself in the mirror, gave a grunt of approval, and then, with lopsided tie, half-unbuttoned fly, curling jacket collar, and shoes that looked like they had been dredged from the Louisiana swamps, he made his way, light of heart and with a smile upon his face, to his daily destination.

The sidewalk in front of I. J. Morris was crowded with mourners and men with cameras and other men with writing pads. When newspapermen came to Brownsville to cover a funeral, it was obvious that the guest of honor was not the butcher, the baker, or the candlestick maker. Only a big shot from Murder, Inc. or the rabbi of a very large and prestigious congregation drew such attention.

Mottel squirmed, wriggled, and pushed through the assemblage, trying hard not to wrinkle his clothes, a task that was superfluous at best. Just as he got to the entrance, Yoodie the caretaker was coming out.

"Yoodie, not that I care, but I got to know, who's having such a funeral?"

"Today it's Davidoff," Yoodie answered, like it was the current movie at the Loew's Pitkin.

"Max Davidoff? The nice candy store man?" Mottel asked, truly upset.

"No," Yoodie corrected, "his son."

Mottel slowly nodded his head, as though giving his approval. Patting Yoodie on the shoulder, he went inside. From a basket on a vestibule table he took a yarmulke, placed it atop his head, and tucked a half dozen more in his jacket pocket. In his bedroom bureau was one drawer completely filled with yarmulkes. When he sat down to negotiate the cost of his own funeral, he would make sure they credited him for supplying the yarmulkes, and he had a note to that effect in one of his milk bottles.

Mottel made his way directly to the chapel, passing by the receiving room. He prided himself on being a most respectful person who did not intrude upon the privacy of the lamenting family. He grieved tangentially and in unison with the family, not officiously.

Not five minutes from the time he seated himself, the entire chapel was filled. Everyone rose as the immediate family entered, and this was when Mottel gave a gasp. Just moments before, he had prepared himself to bid farewell, better yet, good riddance, to Willie Davidoff, the bulvon Hitler they called Big Gangy. It was a funeral in which he was going to partake with much enthusiasm. Instead, there was Willie, together with his brother, Harry, the two of them supporting their grieving parents. This was not the Willie Davidoff whose face hung like a picture on the wall of Mottel's mind. That Willie Davidoff could never have tears running down his cheeks or lips that trembled. That Willie Davidoff had eyes that could burn through you and lips that curled at the corners, just like a mad dog when it's ready to bite a chunk out of you.

Mottel didn't see Rabbi Borodkin enter the chapel and gently embrace Max and Rose Davidoff before going to the lectern. He didn't see because his eyes were closed as he relived, from almost twenty years ago, actually it was eighteen, how he was bitten by the mad dog.

It was a time in Mottel's life when happiness inspired him to learn how to whistle. How many people blow the first melody from their pursed lips in their late forties? Yetta couldn't get over her husband's newfound talent. It was not that Mottel was a young man, but he was still young enough to have the burning desire of ambition. Besides working nights as a counterman—then it was at Dubrow's on Utica Avenue—he took advantage of the thriving pushcart market in hopes of achieving his American Dream before he was too old to appreciate it. Sleep, Mottel knew, was important, but someday he would have an eternity of it.

He struck up a partnership with Reuven, Dubrow's day manager, who let him take from the kitchen any leftovers or overstocked food items. These he sold from a spot he had purchased on Belmont Avenue, half a block from Pennsylvania Avenue, as choice a location as one could desire. To Reuven he paid 10 percent of his profits, a good deal for both. All day long he would stand at his pushcart selling "restaurant-quality pastries, fruit, and daily specials," and whistling every Yiddish melody known to man, occasionally throwing in his specialty, "Danny Boy," before a babushka-adorned throng of women with hands clasped and tears spilling from red-rimmed eyes. Sales were always brisk after such a rendition. Eventually, most of the Belmont Avenue shopping crowd was certain that "Danny Boy" was a Jewish folk song.

All the pushcart peddlers knew the rules and regulations of the street, and they knew what to do when Willie Davidoff came around. Willie provided a service—a very important service, to be sure. He kept Willie away. In return, once a week or twice a week or whenever he cared to, he would bestow upon certain pushcarts the honor and privilege of permitting him to take whatever he wanted.

One day Mottel had just finished setting up his pushcart display and was whistling "Joseph! Joseph!" when Willie Davidoff walked up and without so much as a hello started loading a large basket with jars of stuffed cabbage. Mottel could never be mistaken for a hero, but for whatever reason—and till this day he doesn't know why—he pointed at the stuffed cabbage and said, "It's the special, ten cents a jar, a bargain." It was then that he noticed Willie's brother, Harry, standing at his side, along with a little boy of six, maybe seven, wearing knickers with argyle socks.

Willie turned to Harry. "Hey, Heshy, how's this guy's account?" Harry didn't say a word. He didn't have to. Willie played all the parts.

"It's been brought to my attention that you are way behind on your dues."

Mottel was so frightened that he thought he would soon have to change his pants, but something compelled him to stand up to this little squirt of a gonif. "I don't know about no dues. I bought this cart from Zimmerman. . . ."

The cart Mottel had purchased from Zimmerman was now being turned into firewood by a kicking and ranting Willie Davidoff. There was a shattering of glass as jars broke. This, together with the squish of fruits and the plunk of pastries, was all there was to be heard. Harry smiled as Willie wheezed and snarled, pumping his finger into Mottel's chest.

"You sonuvabitch! You see how busted up that wagon is? If I ever see you back here, you're gonna look a fucken lot worse!"

After that day, Mottel never dared venture beyond his job as a counterman, and he was never heard to whistle again.

Mottel opened his eyes. He barely listened as the rabbi intoned his prayers and gave his eulogy. For the parents and the wife and the little boy she was holding in her arms Mottel felt a true heartache, but should he feel any less enthusiastic about this funeral if it was another Davidoff brother instead of Willie who had left this world? Is one so different from the other? He recalled some of the terrible things he had heard about the one they called the Brownsville Bum.

Sergeant William Schroeder of the 69th Precinct sat in the last row of the chapel, listening intently as Rabbi Borodkin delivered his eulogy in Yiddish. Schroeder absorbed its full meaning although he couldn't understand more than two or three words of the language. The message came from the eyes, from the heart, from the melodious and pathetic break in the voice.

When he'd come off duty after working straight through Thanksgiving on a forty-eight-hour shift—most of it spent at Dudy's Bar & Grill, scene of the shooting—his wife thought he was going to catch a few hours of sleep, but instead he showered, changed into his blue serge suit, and asked her to join him at a funeral in Brownsville. At first Helen Schroeder was reluctant, knowing nothing about the deceased and never having been to a Jewish funeral service, but her husband had never made such a request before, and it seemed so important to him that she couldn't refuse. She tried to straighten his tie and smooth his jacket, but it was hopeless. The only clothing that ever fit Bill Schroeder properly was his uniform.

Schroeder sat very still, staring at the casket at the front of the chapel. He didn't consider his presence here a duty or an obligation. It was a need; he had to be here. He didn't know why he wanted his wife to be here too, except that he wanted her to know something about Albert Avrum Davidoff, known to the world as Al "Bummy" Davis. She felt him squeeze her hand, which was clasped in his, and looked at his square-jawed, impassive face. He had just shaved this morning, but the gray specks of stubble were already peeking out from their pores.

Helen Schroeder knew that bravery came in many forms, and on this day she considered her husband a hero. She had never heard of and certainly never met Willie Davidoff, but she knew who and what he was the moment she saw him. The swollen, reddened eyes and occasional sniffle did not camouflage his look of loathing when he saw her husband.

"What do you want?" he snarled. "Don't you have any respect?"

Schroeder didn't flinch. "Respect? I came to pay my respect to your brother," he said, looking directly into Willie's eyes.

"Who ya kidding? I know what you think of me."

"Your brother's not you, Willie. I'm here for him." He turned toward Rose Davidoff, who was swaying in the arms of her daughters, lost in a nightmare of despair. Sergeant Schroeder took her hand and pressed it. She raised her eyes and fell into his arms, heaving with sobs.

Max Davidoff was leaning on his son Harry. It was as though his soul and his mind had been removed and all that remained was a sightless, senseless shell. Schroeder gently touched his shoulder. It was like touching a stone. As he and Helen started for the chapel, Willie grasped his arm. The tears had stopped. There was a hard look to Willie's face now.

"You gonna get those sonsabitches?"

"We got guys working around the clock," Schroeder said.

"Do me a favor," Willie whispered hoarsely, "lay back a little. I wanna get those scumbags before you do."

"I'm just a cop from Canarsie, Willie, I don't call the shots." But Schroeder was thinking to himself that for once he would truly enjoy Willie and his boys getting there first.

For two hours Rose Davidoff plowed the streets of Brownsville with her body, forging through the snowdrifts on New Jersey Avenue, on Dumont, Livonia, and the blocks in between, all the while calling out "Avrumeleh!" until her voice failed and her hands and feet were numb. "He'll be upstairs. I know he'll be upstairs," she told herself when she got back home to New Jersey Avenue.

As she opened the door to the apartment, little tingles danced on the soles of her feet and the palms of her hands. Willie was sitting at the kitchen table biting into a thick slab of rye bread covered with shmaltz and washing it down with a glass of seltzer.

"How come I have the honor of your company?" Rose asked, pulling off her babushka. "In this weather nobody's outside for you to beat up?"

Willie took another bite of rye bread. "What are you doing outside on a day like this? You wanna catch pneumonia?"

Rose took cautious steps towards the sink, filled her teakettle with tap water, and put it on the stove to boil. "Avrumeleh is gone all day. With this weather God knows what happens to him."

"Ah, the kid can take care of himself," Willie said with a wave of his hand. "He's probably at the store with Poppa."

"What am I, a numbskull? Don't you think that's the first place I checked? Heshy is there with Poppa, and the girls are at the Community Center."

"So you think he's kidnaped or something? Who'd want him?"

"Go ahead, baboon, laugh. Yesterday he comes home with a farshtinkener hund, carrying it like an infant in his arms. It had such a smell to make a sewer seem like a perfume factory. He says, 'Momma, I want to keep it,' and I tell him not in this house. So he has one of his red-in-the-face temper tantrums and swears he's going to run away from home. A seven-year-old hobo I got."

There was a whistling from the kettle and a knocking at the front door. Momma Davidoff ran to the stove, but when she realized that you can't answer a stove she turned and ran to the door.

"Mrs. Davidoff? I'm Officer Schroeder, ma'am." The policeman removed his cap respectfully.

"Oy! Don't tell me! It's my baby!" she cried, raising her eyes upward as though looking to God for relief.

"No, no!" Schroeder held his arms out in a gesture of reassurance. "Little Vroomy's okay. I have him waiting downstairs until I spoke to you."

"I'm telling you, I got palpitations." Rose groaned, covering her breast with her right hand. "What is he doing downstairs when he lives upstairs?"

"He's standing next to a radiator to warm up. The poor kid's half-frozen, but the dog's warm as toast."

Rose pursed her mouth and nodded, tapping her foot. "So the dog is warm and he's frozen. Tell me something, Mr. Policeman, how come?"

"You have a very sensitive, compassionate boy, Mrs. Davidoff." Schroeder glanced at Willie. "Maybe a unique quality among his brothers. Anyhow, I'm walking my beat on Pennsylvania Avenue, right around the corner, and the snow is coming down in sheets when I hear a whimper."

"My Avrum? Sure, I walked in the other direction."

"It was the dog, not Vroomy," Schroeder continued. "I find him squatting in an alley, cradling the mutt in his arms. That's when the kid tells me he ran away from home."

There was a snicker from Willie. "He ran away from home—right around the corner."

Schroeder ignored him. "Vroomy told me that he's not allowed to cross Pennsylvania Avenue until he's eight," he said to Rose.

She beamed. "Did you ever see such an obedient child? An angel I have."

Schroeder turned toward the stairwell. "Vroomy, come on up," he called. "I think we can work everything out."

There was the slapping sound of wet galoshes on marble stairs, and then Vroomy's head peeked around the door.

"Vrumeleh, you ever give me such a scare again," Rose scolded, wagging her finger at him, "and I'll break every bone in your body." She ran over and hugged him with the dog in his arms, almost breaking every bone in both their bodies as the brown mutt wailed "Woo-oo!"

"Oy! Oy! Oy! The stink from that hund," she gagged.

Schroeder patted her on the shoulder and smiled. "For one night you can take it. That's the deal I made with him. He keeps the dog for one night and no more running away."

"If I live through that smell for one night, I'll live forever." Rose clasped her hands together, shaking her head. "The sweater we'll burn. It's the only way to get the smell out."

"Kid," Willie laughed, "where were ya when they were giving out brains? Ya know I love ya, but how dumb can ya be? Ya freeze your tuchis off while ya give your sweater to a mutt . . ."

"I got my sweater," Vroomy said meekly.

Willie looked at his brother. Vroomy was wearing a sweater. Willie looked down at the dog. The dog was wearing a sweater. It was a large sweater, the sleeves extending well over the dog's paws. For a long moment Willie just stared. Finally it all clicked into place, and his nostrils flared. All he could do was sputter as he recognized the pricey collegiate-style wool sweater with the big turn-up collar that he'd bought at Jaffe Brothers just last week.

Rose Davidoff thought it was a very good thing that Officer Schroeder was there that evening. Vroomy thought so too.

No matter which way he turned his body, no matter how hard he pushed and twisted and huffed, Fat Yerna could not squeeze himself into the row of seats. Rabbi Borodkin paused in the midst of his eulogy and looked out over the chapel to see who was making such a disturbance on this solemn occasion.

Everyone in the Davidoff family was looking straight ahead at the rabbi and the plain pine coffin, but they all knew Fat Yerna was there. They smelled him. At first Willie was angry when he realized who was causing the commotion, but then he remembered that this was a guy who generally did not pay his respects. Yerna didn't even attend his own mother's funeral because he was busy making book on a big-stake race at Belmont.

Finally Yerna gave up. If they were going to finish this service and bury the kid, there was one rule that would have to be broken. He plodded over and sat down heavily at the end of the first row, reserved for the immediate family.

Ordinarily Yerna didn't go to funerals because he couldn't see the point, unless some bum owed him money and he wanted to make sure the guy was in the box. Being stiffed by a stiff was something he did not wish to deal with. In all truth he had no intention of coming here today, but when he sets up his chair in front of the candy store this morning he finds he has nobody to talk to. He goes over to Mike's Barbershop, but it is just another place where silence prevails. The prospect of a totally silent day is just enough motivation for Fat Yerna to pick himself up and join the rest of Brownsville at I. J. Morris.

Fat Yerna comes barreling through the locker room door, huffing and puffing like a locomotive that is chugging uphill for a very long time. He takes a look at the Amateur Athletic Union man in the striped shirt yelling out, "Pesconi! Pesconi, G.!" which is what sets Yerna in motion in the first place. It is a voice loud enough to be heard over the din of two dozen jabbering, overexcited kids. It is a very loud voice, accustomed to the conditions of its job.

"Pesconi! Please answer to your name."

There is no response.

The AAU man is now pretty exasperated, running his fingers through strands of hair that he lost years ago. Fat Yerna, red in the face and shaking from exertion, waddles over to him and grabs hold of his elbow.

"You looked in the crapper, Pete?"

"I was going to do that."

"Some of these kids are so nervous they spend the whole night in there. Go ahead, check."

As soon as Pete leaves the locker room, Yerna walks over to the corner where Boomy is sitting on a bench reading a comic book, which Yerna unceremoniously plucks from his hands.

"Hey! Whatcha doin'?" Boomy yells.

"Listen, Davidoff, just because you're a guinea now don't mean you have to act like one." He gives Boomy a light tap on the top of his head. "You gotta remember your goddamn name. Don't go makin' trouble for me now."

"I remember my name. Pesconi. P-E-S-C-O-N-I."

"So why don't you answer when someone calls it out?"

"Oh, *that's* what the guy was yellin'." Boomy's eyes light up, then he shrugs. "I guess I ain't used to it yet. Gimme a break, Yerna."

"You got your break, kid"—Yerna is jabbing his finger in Boomy's face—"when I got you the AAU card. You came to me, remember, I didn't go to you."

Yerna thinks back—it is not exactly a trip down memory lane as it is only a few weeks ago—to when Stutz, the ball-rack boy at the Livonia Pool Room, comes looking for him at Beecher's Gym with Boomy, telling him the kid wants to be a fighter but he is only fourteen. Boomy is not exactly unknown to Yerna, not just because he is the kid brother of Big Gangy, which immediately takes him out of the ranks of the invisible, but because he gets into enough scrapes and jams on the streets and is such a holy terror with his temper and fists that his name gets bandied around pretty good.

People do not come to Fat Yerna because he drips with the milk of human kindness, but it is known here and about that he is a guy who gets things done—when there is something in it for him. One of the somethings that Yerna depends on to keep him in overstuffed club sandwiches is working with young fighters. He puts on occasional amateur shows and develops a fighter here and there of whom he becomes a thirty-three-and-a-third percenter, not a bad something. The way Yerna figures it, if he has six fighters he is making 100 percent of two fighters, without taking a punch.

But he is too smart to get on the wrong side of Big Gangy, so he goes to him first. Willie is not thrown into a state of shock. He already knows that Boomy is pretty handy with his fists, and he tells Yerna to let the kid see what it's all about. But to fight, a kid needs an AAU card, and to get an AAU card a kid has to be sixteen, so Yerna fixes Boomy up with some other kid's card, which is how Pete the AAU man comes to be hollering for Giovanni Pesconi.

When Pete returns to the locker room, Fat Yerna tells him that Giovanni Pesconi was sitting on this bench all along but didn't understand when his name was called out because everybody talks with their hands in the part of Italy he comes from. "The kid hears you," Yerna explains, "but he don't understand because you are not expressing yourself properly. This kid gotta see what you say, not just hear."

It is quite surprising how much attention Pete gets when he tells Boomy that he is fighting in the fourth bout of the night. You would think he was talking to Geronimo or Chief Sitting Bull in sign language. Pointing his finger at Boomy, he speaks in a very deep voice. "You, soon fight." He pummels the air with his fists in make-believe punches. "Fight number four," with which he holds out four fingers of his right hand and ticks them off with the index finger of his left hand. Pete is greatly surprised to see that just about every kid in the room has gathered around to get a look at his performance, and wonders whether it is possible that they all come from the same part of Italy as Giovanni Pesconi.

It sounded like a bugle. The mourners jumped in their seats, Rabbi Borodkin paused again, and Fat Yerna turned to see who would disrupt such a funeral. Huddled self-consciously in a row near the back was Sammy Aaronson. Sammy was some nose blower. He couldn't help it any more than he could help the tears that welled in his eyes as he pictured Boomy bouncing around in that twenty-foot square at Beecher's Gym. The kid was a real charmer, Sammy remembered, always had a smile for everyone. Then Sammy remembered one time when the kid didn't smile.

It was the week of July Fourth, 1934. The kid was working on the heavy bag, and this small-time bookie, Puggy Feinstein, an ex-fighter who was never much of a fighter, as his mashed-in nose let you know, was standing nearby shouting words of encouragement.

All of a sudden, all you hear is the *pock-pock* of the kid's punches whacking the big Everlast bag, because all other sounds have stopped. The sawed-off runt who has just walked into Beecher's and heads directly for where the kid is working casts a big spell. He is wearing a short-sleeved white shirt, and his forearms, with tattoos of a dagger, are as thick as any fighter's in the gym. He is Abe "Kid Twist" Reles, Brownsville kingpin of Murder, Inc.

Reles looks at Puggy and points his finger at the door. "What'd I tell you about placing bets in this neighborhood? Out! Now!"

Puggy makes tracks for the door without a word. Everybody else makes a point of not watching.

"You oughta be a little more selective about who you hang out with," Reles tells Boomy.

"You're right." And the kid turns his back and walks away.

If Abe is smoking right now he does not show it. He slowly struts over to the speed bag, where the kid is peppering a staccato *rat-a-tat-tat*.

Young Al spins and again walks away, heading to the locker room. "I gotta go grab a shower."

Reles smiles. "You hardly worked up a sweat so far."

"Yeah," Boomy agrees, "but for some reason I feel dirty."

The smile is gone from Reles's face. There is only the sound of his shoes slapping on the hardwood floor as he leaves the gym. Sammy Aaronson remembers how everyone in Beecher's Gym that day put their hands in their pockets to check, like some kind of reflex, though they didn't have to. They all knew nobody had as big a pair of balls as this kid Al Davidoff.

A couple weeks after the funeral, Mottel Scharansky learned, at his age, how easy it is to forget and how hard it is to remember. He bumped into his old partner, Reuven, who now owned a grocery store on Sutter Avenue, and told him about the lack of compassion he felt while listening to Rabbi Borodkin's eulogy. It was then that Reuven reminded him of what he had forgotten.

After Willie destroyed the pushcart, Mottel had called Reuven. After all, shouldn't a partner share in the tsuris also? Reuven arrived to find a young boy in knickers and argyle socks helping Mottel clean up the debris. As Mottel was describing Willie's attack to Reuven in detail, the boy looked up, and said, "He doesn't mean all the things he does. He's usually sorry after." They both looked at the youngster.

"How do you know so much, little boy?" Reuven asked.

"I'm his brother."

"You remember?" Reuven asked now, patting his ex-partner's arm.

Mottel Scharansky stared at his old friend for a long moment. Then he went home and mourned for the soul of Al "Bummy" Davis.

1

Albert Abraham Davidoff arrived in Brownsville a nickel to the better as he expended no fare with the New York City Transit Authority. That is not to say that his method was not a traditional one. His arrival was punctuated by a resounding slap on the ass, which he seemed to take as a personal affront. He wailed fiercely, his little arms flailing in anger—a sign of things to come.

It was a new world he was born into on January 26, 1920, though that meant little to Avrumeleh because it was the only world he knew. Brownsville was a vibrant, rapidly changing community inundated by waves of desperate but hopeful Jewish immigrants from Eastern Europe, spilling over from Manhattan's Lower East Side in search of die goldeneh medina, the golden land. This influx was made possible by the construction of the Williamsburg Bridge in 1903, a funnel drawing the compressed hordes from across the East River. Farmland and open spaces disappeared in eye blinks, replaced by block after block of bleak, hastily constructed row houses. It was Eden. It was Gomorrah. To some it was a dream, to others, a nightmare.

Though Brownsville was no more than two and a half square miles of concrete wasteland, to those who lived there, its borders seemed always out of reach, tantalizingly unattainable. Bounded on the west by

Rockaway Parkway and Buffalo Avenue, on the east by Pennsylvania Avenue, on the north by Atlantic Avenue, and on the south by Linden Boulevard, it lay sequestered more by perception than by any physical barrier.

On or near almost every street corner was a candy store, not far from which would be a small grocery store, a fruit and vegetable store, and a delicatessen. Butcher shops with their kosher trademarks on the front windows were within shouting distance of one another, and the smell of freshly baked bread and bagels wafted on every air current. But it was the large avenues and thoroughfares that gave Brownsville its character. Pitkin Avenue was a combination of the rue de la Paix and Delancey Street. Sunday afternoons saw shoppers from Park Avenue and Central Park West rubbing elbows with visitors from Canarsie and Flatbush, all bargain hunting at the tony shops in a carnival atmosphere, capping off the day with delicacies such as freshly baked sweet potatoes, peppery potato knishes, and pickles so sour you couldn't eat them without a pucker.

Nowhere were gray days grayer than in Brownsville, and nowhere did sunny days seem more golden and uplifting. Perhaps that is the way with people of great appetites and yearnings. On the third day of February, 1920, the sun melted the cold edge of the winds and bathed the streets in a glow. It was an ideal day for a celebration.

You couldn't hear the IRT train rumbling overhead on Livonia Avenue less than half a block away. You couldn't hear that the Victrola playing "A Pretty Girl Is Like a Melody" had been repeating "like a mel . . . like a mel . . ." for God knows how long. You couldn't hear anything above the tumult in the Davidoff apartment except the sound of food coming out of the kitchen. All the men were busy gorging themselves on platters of boiled specials, sauerkraut, kishka, baked beans, and potato salad, washed down by occasional shpritzes from the seltzer bottles strategically placed throughout the apartment. The subsequent belching and burping was mostly drowned out by the rest of the noise. For appetizers and dessert, sponge cake and strudel were chased by shots of sinus-clearing schnapps.

While the men downed the food, the women toiled in the steamy, odorous kitchen as though on an assembly line. Every woman was very good at giving orders. None was too good at receiving them. Each had her own way of doing things and was busy trying to convince the others that her way was best. Rose Davidoff stared into the huge pot of boiling specials, trying to blot out everything around her, daydreaming that maybe the whole kitchen floor, except for the part that she was standing on, would collapse and everyone would disappear.

Poppa Davidoff was not eating. He was drinking, though. At this moment he was happier than anyone in this world had ever seen him. For one thing, he had closed his candy store for the day. This in itself was an event. And to look at him, you could not believe that he was the same wiry little man who stood behind the soda counter all day, wearing a white apron and hardly ever smiling, mainly because he did not have too much reason to smile. Here he was, shot glass in hand, making toast after toast in honor of his newborn child, singing praises to the Lord in English, in Yiddish, in Lithuanian, imploring his guests to join him in impassioned ballads. To hoarse cries of "Huzzah!" and "Mazel, mazel, mazel tov!" he whirled like a dervish around the room, knocking into people, furniture, and food, but no one minded the bumps or the grease stains. Everyone was caught up in the spirit of the moment.

Everyone except Willie Davidoff, who at the age of fourteen had already learned to take advantage of an opportunity when one presented itself. While everyone was watching his father, Willie sauntered into the bedroom, where the coats and jackets of the guests were piled upon his parents' bed. He took his time going through all the pockets, shrewdly leaving some of the contents. He was a veteran at this stuff. Whistling softly, he went about his business.

Willie was learning his business well. He didn't understand how his father could be satisfied with a job where your customers paid you in pennies and it was a shocker when someone plunked down a quarter. In Willie's eyes his father was okay, he just didn't know which end was up—but none of the older guys did.

Just as he was about to leave the bedroom, the door opened. He took a deep breath, then let it out when he saw it was little Harry waddling in. At three and a half, Harry adored his older brother and tried to follow wherever he went.

"Heshy," Willie whispered, "bring Poppa's socks over to me."

Obediently Harry picked up the pair of black socks draped on top of the radiator and handed them to his brother. Willie put half his take in one sock and half in the other, then stuffed both inside his shirt. Holding hands, the two brothers walked angelically into the crowded living room, where all eyes were upon the bearded, skullcapped man in the white smock.

"Dat butchy, Willie?" Harry backed up hesitantly at the sight of this stranger.

Willie was a linguist when it came to his kid brother. He understood every word that came out of his mouth. "Yeah, that's the butcher all right, Hesh. Just watch. He's gonna cut off a slice of the baby's salami."

The white-smocked elder, who was a mohel, not a butcher, smacked his lips with relish after downing two shots of whiskey handed to him by one of the many uncles in the living room. "So, where's the little shtik naches?" he asked.

The mohel's cue line brought on Poppa Davidoff, who was now doing his version of a Moldavian gopak, a vigorous, high-stepping reel, while hoisting the baby over his head. Wheezing, he halted in front of the mohel and raised his youngest son to his flushed cheeks. This would be the third Brith Milah the mohel had performed for the Davidoff family, but it was the first time he had seen such a display of tenderness from the father. He was impressed.

Max Davidoff had prayed for a son who would not only honor and respect him but who would one day say kaddish for him. To be remembered and prayed for by a loved one after departing this world was very important. He didn't think it was too much to ask. He loved his four daughters and his first two sons, and he believed that they loved him too, in their own way. He just had a feeling that this Avrumeleh would be different. For him he had much hope.

Gently he placed his newborn son faceup on the sheet-covered coffee table. The mohel shooed the women back into the kitchen, then turned to Max and asked him to name his child.

"Albert Abraham . . . Avrum," Max intoned solemnly.

"Avrum," the mohel repeated in a clear, loud voice. "The name of Abraham is of very special meaning, and a person bearing such a name should be honored. Our Holy Bible tells us that the Brith Milah, the ceremony of the circumcision, began with Abraham, the Father of Jewry, who was the very first to be circumcised. And this first circumcision was performed at the age of ninety-nine."

"Oy," cried one of the men, "I got sympathy pains."

As the mohel was rocking back and forth chanting "*Baruch ata Adonai—*" his mouth was suddenly filled with a wet, warm sourness. An eternally long instant of silence hung over the room as the little yellow droplets clung, then fell from his beard. A spontaneous explosion of laughter shook the walls and windows of the apartment.

Poppa Davidoff stared in disbelief. What if the mohel was so upset that he packed his tools of the trade and left? Willie Davidoff pounded away on Harry's noggin as he roared in glee. "The kid's gonna be okay, Heshy! The kid's gonna be okay!"

The mohel stood stoically dripping as Momma Davidoff worked her way through the throng with a damp towel. Wiping his glasses, he pronounced, "Nisch g' felach. You think it's the first time I get a faceful of pishachs? It comes with the territory."

Max sighed with relief, and the mohel smiled for everyone to see how good-natured he was. He finished cleansing his tools with alcohol and readied himself for the circumcision, thinking to himself how his goddamn beard would stink from piss until he went to the mikva just before Shabbes.

Albert Abraham Davidoff stared at what was above and sensed that this day might not be as good as his first seven. Where was that nice lady whose breast had kept him so happy until now? A light was blinding him, and then he saw what was reflecting the light—a glistening steel blade moving directly toward him.

The knife whistled through the air, ripping flesh, spraying blood. Salvio screamed. The swarthy brewery operator had a reputation as a pretty tough number, but he'd been caught completely off guard. One minute he's talking quietly, although not on an exactly eye-to-eye basis, to the three nutsy Shapiro brothers, and the next minute Meyer, who's peeling away on a Macintosh apple, starts slicing him instead.

"What the fuck's the matter with ya!" he bellows. "Ya crazy or somethin'? Ya cut my fucken nose off!"

"It ain't off, it's only in two pieces now," Meyer explains matter-offactly, "and it ain't my fault anyhow. It's your fault for being an asshole." His voice rises steadily. "We come to you like gentlemen. We talk nice to you and put a deal on the table that's so fair my mother I wouldn't give more. And you, you stupid guinea sonuvabitch, all you do is say no, no, no! If your fucken nose falls off, blame yourself!"

Meyer Shapiro was of the opinion that Brownsville belonged to him. It was an opinion that nobody cared to dispute to his face, because he was a sadistic bully built along the lines of a tank, with lips curled in a perpetual sneer. He permitted no one and nothing to stand in his way. Irving, the middle brother, was more the studious type and didn't possess the nerve or toughness of Meyer, but he was tough enough. Poor Willie, the youngest, was a frail wisp of a man who would have been just another street-corner kibitzer if he hadn't been born into the Shapiro clan, whose chief enterprises, until recently, were prostitution and gambling machines. Meyer had whorehouses sprinkled throughout Brownsville, and like a proud entrepreneur, he enjoyed sampling all his merchandise. He would point out how fortunate he was in his chosen field of endeavor; if he were a restaurateur, sampling the merchandise would mean eating away at the profits.

While Salvio cups his nose in his hands as though maybe he can catch the blood and recycle it, Willie is doubled over heaving his guts on the brewery floor, which produces a most unusual odor in combination with the smell of malt, hops, and yeast. Irving is patting Willie on the back while gingerly dancing out of the way of the splashing puke.

"You outta your fucken skull?" Salvio is looking at Meyer in wide-eyed disbelief. "You come in here and horseshit me that a business it took me a lifetime to build up you're gonna push yourself in and become a partner, and you expect hugs and kisses from me!"

Irv, knowing Meyer's touchy nature, figures it is time for a little intervention on his part. He points his finger in Salvio's bloody face. "A word to the wise. Watch how you talk to my brother. He's an extremely generous person who is very sensitive to criticism."

"I don't need no help, Irving," Meyer says in a controlled voice, gently moving his brother out of the way. "I got news for you, shmuck. You *got* no business anymore. Uncle Sam put you out to pasture two weeks ago. The Eighteenth Amendment's in, you're out."

Salvio laughs, which is a big mistake because it forces a spray of blood to shoot from his nose. "If I got no business anymore, then I got nothin', and according to my arithmetic, half of nothin' is nothin'. If that's what you want, you got it!"

The next thing Salvio knows is how a roast pig feels, because there he is, flat on his back on the floor with an apple shoved in his mouth and Meyer's right foot on his windpipe.

Smiling down at the blue-tinged Salvio, whose eyes seem ready to pop out of their sockets, Meyer makes a very attractive proposal. "If you just behave and shut up and listen, I will permit you to live." Salvio realizes that this is not the time for counteroffers, and raises his hand in acceptance.

Meyer is a man of his word. Not only does he remove his foot from Salvio's throat but he helps him up and removes the Macintosh from his mouth, which he then examines but decides it has lost its appeal and tosses it aside. Salvio is now giving Meyer his full attention while holding his nose together with the thumb and forefinger of his left hand.

Meyer spreads out his arms as though to encompass the entire brewery. "We oughta thank God for Prohibition. It's the best thing that coulda happened for the business community."

Salvio shakes his head. "Yeah, I'm gonna go light a candle for it. Meanwhile, I ain't been allowed to make or sell any beer for over half a year now."

"That's why, with a goyisher kop, you need partners like us," Meyer says. "You sell this building to us—"

"For how much?" Suddenly there is great interest on Salvio's part.

"For nothin', shmuck, it's strictly camouflage. We give you back a partnership agreement on the side. Then we change this to an auto repair shop or a seltzer distributor, all this fucken equipment goes underground, and—"

"So how come I gotta sign the building over to you? Camouflage is camouflage."

"Because if Tony Salvio starts sellin' seltzer from the same place where he's been pushin' out beer for ten years, the feds'll be sniffin' around like a mutt at a pile of horseshit. But if a new owner takes over and opens another business, that's fucken kosher."

Irv, who has been walking around the place sneaking looks here and there, calls out from the far corner, "Do you know how much suds are packaged over here?"

"It's been sittin' there since July when they closed me down," Salvio says.

"We'll move out the whole shitload, and at premium price," barks Meyer. "This stuff'll be worth more than gold now."

"Yeah, yeah." Salvio laughs. "I wanna see how far out the front door you get the stuff without the feds jumpin' up your ass. You think I'd be sittin' with it if there's a way out?"

"New team, different ballplayers, putz." Meyer's face drips with contempt. "We'll get it out, every last drop of it, if we have to pump it into eggshells or carry it out in your wife's drawers. Prohibition, we love you!" he shouts, shaking his fist in the air for emphasis.

Salvio feels that the best thing he can do now is be quiet, even though he wonders what part he's going to play in this partnership other than providing everything.

"I gotta tell you something, Salvio. You got one fucken ugly nose. You really oughta do something about it." Meyer reaches toward Salvio, who jerks his head back, but to his great relief all Meyer does is pinch his cheek.

"What the fuck am I gonna tell my wife? She'll take one look at me an' she'll throw up her guts."

Meyer shrugs. "She has a lot in common with my kid brother. Explain to her that usually such a thing would come about for puttin' your nose in other people's business but in your case it was just the opposite—it was an accident caused by you not puttin' your nose in business with other people."

As it turns out, neither the nose nor the partnership becomes a problem for Salvio, because less than a week after deeding over his property he is probably in such a euphoric state of mind that he isn't concentrating on such mundane things as crossing Linden Boulevard, which he becomes imbedded in as the direct result of a bone-shattering encounter with a Mack truck.

There was no need to cry anymore. The worst was over, little Avrum sensed. A short while ago he had been suckled by the nice lady again.

That always made him feel happy and secure. Also, the large hairy face was gone. The sound of the el train rumbling at the corner soothed him, and soon he was asleep.

The Davidoff family was still celebrating the birth of their Avrumeleh. Elsewhere, upstanding citizens were celebrating the birth of Prohibition, a long-awaited and most laborious birth. But with Prohibition, joined as closely as a Siamese twin, came one of the most feared gatherings of cold-blooded killers to grace the annals of crime. Albert Abraham Davidoff and Murder, Inc. were born in Brownsville within ten days of each other. It was his lifelong effort to avoid the gravitational pull of this loathsome entity.

The Brownsville where Albert Davidoff grew up was two different worlds. One was from sundown on Saturday until sundown on Friday, a world of tumult, constant jabbering, men hawking their wares from stores and pushcarts, a constant parade of horse-drawn wagons, delivery trucks, seltzer trucks, women in housecoats and shaytls and kerchiefs running from store to store not to miss out on any bargains, and on every block a gaggle of kids, the younger ones playing potsy, skelly, and skip-rope on the sidewalks, the older boys playing punchball or stickball in the middle of the street.

Brownsville's other world began at sundown on Friday and lasted until sundown on Saturday. It was as though all the clocks stopped and all sounds ceased to exist. The stores were shuttered, and the cats could stroll along without fear of rumbling delivery trucks or traffic of any kind. The streets were deserted except for the men and young boys walking to and from shul, carrying their Siddurs and talaysim under their arms and wearing the only suits they possessed. On Saturday morning they would be joined by the women, who would sit in a separate section of the shul, but on Friday nights the women generally remained at home preparing the Shabbes table while the men prayed. The mingled smells of potato kugel, freshly baked gefilte fish, simmering chicken soup, and gribbenes blanketed the entire neighborhood.

For these twenty-four hours, the Sabbath, Max Davidoff was a man completely at rest, except for going to shul and eating. Although he was a smallish man with a wiry body, Max consumed huge quantities of food, and he did so with a passion. Little Avrum would sit and stare in wide-eyed admiration of his father's ability to shovel forkful after forkful of food into his expectant, almost quivering mouth, propelling it down his gullet with a fistful of gravy-sopped challah bread. Willie did pretty good too, but he was hardly ever home with the family on Shabbes anymore.

To Max, going to shul was a very serious matter. He strongly believed that much of your success in this life depended on your devotion to God. Also, every now and then he would do something a little wrong—actually it was more like doing something that was not absolutely right—and so it was even more important to make your peace with God. Like when he occasionally sold a little whiskey under the counter, though that was not really wrong. After all, with Prohibition, the government had made it very difficult for a lot of people to meet their medicinal needs.

Praying in shul was even more important in Max's mind because he was also covering for Willie. Hopefully, in His infinite wisdom, God recognized that Willie, not yet twenty, was just suffering from the mishegoss of a young head, but sometimes Max found himself davening in double time because of his oldest son. He took great comfort in the fact that at least his little Avrum accompanied him to shul. He would walk down the street beaming with a warm delight as the youngster skipped beside him, holding his poppa's hand and trying to keep pace.

One Shabbes morning, Garfinkel the tailor sat down on the bench next to Max and Avrum. He removed his tallis from its case, blessed it, kissed it reverently, and placed it upon his shoulders. Max, to his almost immediate sorrow, leaned over and whispered most sociably, "Good Shabbes, Garfinkel, how's life treating you?"

Garfinkel stared at Max for a moment, and said with a sigh, "Now that you asked, Davidoff, it could be treating me a little better."

Max smiled reassuringly. "It will. You'll see. What could be so bad that a little praying and a little hard work won't cure?"

"Actually, the hard work and the praying would not be so necessary if your boy Willie would leave me alone and go into another line of business."

"Ssh, everybody's davening," Max hissed, to shut Garfinkel up. This, God did not have to hear.

Garfinkel lowered his voice. "Look, I'm not the kind of person what complains, Davidoff, and I know boys are boys. They're not girls. But I think maybe it's not such a bad idea that you get a good lokshen strap. It's never too late to make a few red stripes on the tuchis. A broken tuchis now is better than a broken kop later."

Avrum was staring up at the long hairs in Garfinkel's nose. He wasn't sure what this was all about, but he did understand that his big brother Willie was not Garfinkel's favorite person.

Max started davening again, then turned back to the tailor, trying to end the conversation on a more satisfactory note. "You gotta understand, Garfinkel, kids today are wilder. Don't be such a greener. Keep up with the times."

"A second, please. A second." Garfinkel was no longer whispering. "I didn't bring it up. You brung it up. So I'm telling you, but understand, I got nothing against you. I see by the little boychik here that he's an angel and God should only always look after him. But your Willie, you should know he hangs out with a bunch of trombeniks. They squeeze money from all the stores, and we give them because everybody is afraid of them, me included. And that's it, the gontzeh megillah."

Max forced a weak smile. "What are you talking about, Garfinkel? My Willie's a little wild, maybe, but believe me, he wouldn't hurt a fly!"

Garfinkel's smile was no stronger. "Unfortunately, Davidoff, I am not a fly."

Sometimes Rose Davidoff would go to the butcher or the fish store and a neighbor would look at her like she had two noses instead of one. Rose would inquire what was wrong, which she immediately regretted when she was enlightened by an answer she already knew.

"A young man like your Willie, what's the matter? He doesn't have enough pockets in his pants? He has to put his hands in everybody else's pockets?"

Willie was her son, which was reason enough for Rose to love him and rationalize his actions—there was no defending them. She would blame the ghetto life, the maddening pace and new ideals of the postwar world. It was a crazy world with crazy, farblondjet people. Wild young people, girls with dresses so short you could almost see their pupiks—flappers, they were called, and they did dances, the Charleston, the

Peabody, that were more like something you would see from clowns and acrobats. And the music—only shvartzers could play such music. Ragtime, jazz—a person couldn't even sing to such music. People came to Pitkin Avenue to shop not just on Sunday but every day of the week. Everybody had money to buy whatever they wanted and do any meshuggeneh thing they dreamed about. Wherever you turned they were building theaters more beautiful and magnificent than palaces. They were showing movies in places where kings and queens should live.

With the exception of Pitkin Avenue, the spillover of wealth and good times did not touch Brownsville, but Rose saw the yearning and reaching out for it by the younger generation. Right inside the walls of her own apartment—that was as far as she had to look to find a reacher and taker. If putting dollar bills on the kitchen table made for a good son, then Willie was a good son, but Rose hoped, she prayed, that her other sons did not follow the same path.

Sunday was a day that took getting used to by Max. It was like putting all the gears back in motion again. He grumbled as he hauled the stacks of morning papers from the curb to the green wooden newsstand outside the candy store. But he couldn't help smiling as from the corner of his eye he saw Avrum, not quite five, red-faced and grimacing as he struggled to slide a pile of *The New York Times* along the sidewalk.

"Come, Avrumeleh, let me take it."

"I got it! I got it, Poppa!" Vroomy said, fending Max off with an outstretched arm.

Max shrugged and went into the candy store. A real mazik, that one. A stubborn little devil if ever there was one. There was simply no quit in him. By the time Max returned with his wire cutter to snip the bindings on the newspapers, *The New York Times* was stacked on top of the newsstand.

Vroomy loved going to the candy store with his father. He would spread out on the floor with crayons and a nickel coloring book, jumping from page to page without ever finishing a picture. Then he would play with a set of tin soldiers, moving on to jacks and pickup sticks, all the while stuffing his pockets and his face with so much penny candy that if he'd been a customer Max Davidoff would have had a most profitable day.

To Max the candy store was a refuge, the one place where he was the boss. Home was Rose's domain. He didn't have the kishkas to settle arguments, discipline the kids, or make wise decisions. King Solomon he wasn't. But all the things he couldn't or didn't do at home he did very well in his candy store. He took no guff from anyone. No punks or wise guys made trouble there. Anyone who bought so much as a two-cent plain or a penny pretzel was welcome to hang out the whole day if he wanted, as long as he behaved. If he didn't, he was likely to become acquainted with the business end of Max's broom or the point of his wingtip shoes.

Like its counterparts all over the city, Max's candy store served as combination town hall, library, and meeting place. Outside, to the right of the door, was the newsstand, which carried more than a dozen different papers. The traditional ones, like the *Times, Tribune, Sun,* and *Jewish Daily Forward,* lay faceup, while the newer-style tabloids—the *News,* the *Mirror*—were displayed on racks at the rear. Next to the newsstand was a red Pulver gum machine with three big silver selection buttons. A large plate-glass window displayed a row of cigarette cartons, a row of boxed children's games, and two or three advertising posters that changed every week or so. All the cartons and boxes were faded from the sun.

Inside, the front left wall was one big magazine rack. Opposite was a long marble-topped counter with many chips and gouges. The dozen stools were sorely in need of new cushions. At the far end of the counter, a red tin can filled with long pretzel sticks sat on the floor. The centerpiece of the store was the all-glass four-tiered display case filled with a huge assortment of candies ranging in price from a penny to a nickel. Across from it were four tables with wire-backed chairs. This was Max's empire.

To Max, being the ruler of anything did not come naturally. In the old country one did not even dare dream of such things. Max knew that his sons were growing up in another world. To survive, you had to be a fox. This he was learning, this he would pass on to his children. It was not exactly the way of a pious man, but on Yom Kippur he would atone.

Vroomy was over by the counter playing one of his favorite games—getting all the stools to spin at the same time. Max smiled indulgently. "Vrumeleh, you'll watch the front, please," he said, removing his apron. "Poppa gotta go to the toilet."

Vroomy was so engrossed in spinning his stools and chewing on a cherry licorice stick that he never noticed the pig-faced punk walk in.

"Hey, kid, is Willie around?"

"I don't know." Willie had instructed him never to tell anyone where he was.

"Whaddya mean, ya don't know? Either he's here or he ain't here, you little vonce," the punk said in what would have been a snarl except for his lisp. He picked a chocolate twist from a box on the counter, shoved the whole thing in his mouth, and swallowed it in one gulp. "Where's your old man? You ain't here alone, are you?"

Vroomy couldn't stop staring at the punk's long arms. They reminded him of the gorilla he saw when Aunt Yetta took him to the Prospect Park Zoo last summer.

"There's no old man here—only me and my father, and he's in the toilet."

"What's he doin', pullin' his chain?"

Just then the door at the rear of the store opened, and Max came out adjusting his belt. Seeing who was there, he grunted. "What do you want, Abie? I can do you something?"

"I thought maybe Willie was around. When you see him, tell him I'm lookin' for him." Abe Reles started toward the door.

"He ate a twist, Poppa," Vroomy sang out.

Abie stopped and turned around, smiling. "The kid's right. I almost forgot. What do I owe ya?"

Max smiled right back. "Usually, for a friend of Willie's, I'd say nothing, but in this case, let's make it two cents."

The smile faded from Abie's face as he reached into his pocket, pulled out a handful of change, and dropped two copper pieces on the counter. He glared at little Vroomy and walked out of Max Davidoff's candy store with his strange ducklike gait.

Max stared at the departing stump of a figure and shook his head in despair, feeling a twinge of guilt for all the times he'd told Willie and Harry how important it was to fight for what was yours and to take because if you didn't someone else would. In the old country you had to fight just to survive, but here Willie and his friends were the young cossacks. Max had learned that it was not so important for his eyes and ears to be always at work, but as much as he made an effort to ignore, he could not completely fool himself. Worse, at times he felt what seemed to be a sort of pride in what Willie did and how he was spoken of and feared in the neighborhood. But to love a son, no matter what, was the mark of a decent man—wasn't it?

Max tried to recall some of the stories he had heard about this Reles kid. Good stories they weren't, of that much he was sure.

Abie Reles, who never went further than the eighth grade in public school, made an art form of extortion. His college courses were in robbery and murder. His evasion of the law was not a matter of intelligence or subtlety but of brazenness and disdain. To say that he was a product of his environment and his times is to slight the rest of his family, all decent, hardworking people.

In March of 1921 Abie, fifteen, was caught in an attempted mugging. When he went before the judge, his mother went with him in her housecoat and apron, wringing her hands and wailing tearfully in Yiddish and broken English: "Please, please, don't send my little boy away. He's not a bad boy. Where he lives, who can help such a thing? We'll watch him, Judge, we'll watch him." The judge gave Abie an almost apologetic, fatherly lecture and fined him two dollars. Patrolman Frederick Murray, the arresting officer, waited expectantly for him to lean over and rumple Abie's hair. From the little black purse strung around her neck Mrs. Reles extracted a crumpled dollar bill and five quarters, one of which she tried giving to the judge as a tip. He smilingly declined, even though Patrolman Murray felt that he'd earned it.

Just two months later Abie was arrested for breaking into a vending machine, and wound up back before the same judge. This time no amount of pleading or cajoling worked. Abie got four months at the Dobbs Ferry Children's Village and became a big shot to his neighborhood cronies. Getting in trouble was part of growing up in Brownsville, but having a record made you a prominent individual.

One of these cronies was Martin "Buggsy" Goldstein, who may have been of the opinion that there were too many flies in Brownsville, since he spent so much time reducing their population by pulling off their wings. Enjoying similar sadistic pursuits was Herschel "Pep" Strauss, also known as Pittsburgh Phil, a nickname borrowed from an earlier mobster dandy. Herschel loved to study himself in a mirror, preferably a full-length mirror. He was always dressed to the nines and was the darling of the Pitkin Avenue clothiers. Nobody had a more extensive wardrobe of sixty-dollar suits, and nobody was sure what gave Pittsburgh Phil greater pleasure, his penchant for clothes or his penchant for creative murder.

Abie and Buggsy and Herschel learned at an early age that Brownsville was divided into the somewhat sophisticated English-speaking avenues (east-west Pitkin and Sutter, north-south Rockaway), where the big stores catered to customers from all of New York and Long Island, and the side streets, where the stores were small and family operated, the spoken language was generally Yiddish, and the customers rarely came from more than a block or two away. Business was conducted to meet the needs and pocketbooks of customer and store owner alike. The baker would sell you a quarter loaf of bread, the grocer would let you buy two eggs. Transactions were often done on credit, which meant writing down on a brown paper bag that so-and-so owed sixteen cents and tacking the bag to the wall behind the counter. Most of the shop owners were Jewish immigrants who had fled Russia and Poland. They had a built-in fear of government and law, and paying tribute for the right to live and work was a way of life. Was it any wonder that they were such easy marks for the young hoodlums who preyed on them in their new homeland?

Every once in a while, Abie and his pals were easy prey themselves. Ask Vito Carbone. Vito did not come over with Columbus, a fact you would not be certain of by looking at him. His age was unknown but was variously said to be anywhere from 90 to a 125. What was known was that his grandchildren, who had long ago taken over the family salumeria and adjoining Italian ice shop on the corner of Saratoga and St. Marks in Ocean Hill, were now doddering old men.

Every morning at the crack of dawn, except on rainy days, Vito was set out on a canvas beach chair in front of the family store. He no longer had the strength to throw a bocci ball, and all his card-playing comrades had long since left this world, so his exciting moments in life were limited to a an occasional good bowel movement, a very occasional erection, which dissipated as soon as he peed, a good loud fender-bender, and—best of all—the gang fights between the Italians and Jews.

Harry "Happy" Maione and Frank "Dasher" Abbandando terrorized the Ocean Hill merchants in much the same manner as Abe Reles and Co. did in Brownsville. Ocean Hill, which bordered on Brownsville, was mostly Italian, but in background and mentality its inhabitants were very similar to their Jewish neighbors. In the old country, the Jews were victimized by public officials and a virulently anti-Semitic citizenry, while the Italians suffered under the mafia and the padrones. In both cases the teenage mobsters found little or no resistance to their demands.

Although some say that Vito Carbone was stone deaf and had been for years, there are those who swear he heard so well you would think he was a Comanche brave. They say he could hear a delivery horse fart from a block away, and that his eyes lit up at the gurgling splish of someone pouring a glass of Chianti behind the closed door of the salumeria. But what is attested to by everyone in the neighborhood is that minutes before a gang fight was on the way, Vito leaned forward in his chair, shaking both fists in the air—at any other time an impossible feat for him—and began cheering the impending battle that no one else was aware of yet.

Vito's greatest joy was that a stranger, someone not from the neighborhood, should happen by at such a time. As soon as the two gangs came into sight, Vito would reach out and inveigle the stranger into betting against the Italians. At that moment, Happy Maione and his cohorts would be in full flight from the much larger Jewish gang, with Abie at the forefront screaming, "Get the guineas!"

Vito would now be cackling gleefully and stamping his feet in anticipation as the gang of bedraggled Italians raced down Saratoga Avenue toward Atlantic and suddenly screeched to a halt. "Come on, ya sheenie bastards, see what we got for ya!" Happy Maione would whoop as his band bent down over freshly deposited piles of horse manure. This was a commodity the streets of Brownsville and the rest of the city abounded in. From early morning until after the sun went down, horse-drawn delivery wagons made their daily rounds and left their distinctive calling cards.

It was the Jewish gang's turn to lose a full layer of the soles of their Keds as they skidded to a halt. In unison, the Italian kids scooped up a handful of horseshit, lovingly molded it like a snowball, and reared back to release the pitch like a chorus line of Christy Mathewsons.

Vito rocked and laughed until his frail body shook. Tears cascaded down his withered cheeks as he held out his hand to collect his bet. Vito knew, Happy Maione knew, even Abie Reles and his gang knew: Jewish kids gag, melt, and crumble at the thought of touching horseshit. It is like a crucifix to a vampire or a flaming torch to a jungle beast. No matter how hard or how often they tried, they could never steel themselves to stand up to it.

It was taken for granted, as no one lives forever, that someday Vito would pass peacefully away, but that was not how things turned out. One day Vito was sitting in front of the salumeria in his usual near-catatonic state when he suddenly arose with a start. Obviously, he had heard the distant pounding of approaching footsteps, one gang chasing the other. But there in the middle of Saratoga Avenue was a New York City street sweeper who had just removed his broom and shovel from his two-wheeled hand wagon to scoop up the morning's accumulation of horse manure. Vito lunged at him in a final heroic effort to maintain the prevailing balance of power. The exertion proved too much.

There are no statues in Ocean Hill to commemorate the valor of Vito Carbone, but those who remember him also remember that Abie Reles did not always have his way.

2

The Davidoff girls hated Prohibition. Vroomy thought it had definite advantages. His views had nothing to do with moral or political beliefs.

Prohibition freed Vroomy from a barbaric ritual that deprived him of good solid street time every Saturday night. His sisters, on the other hand, were reduced to cringing wrecks, furtively sniffing their armpits. The fact that their father was able to provide much better for the family because of his bathtub gin did not impress them.

Surprisingly, it was Willie who was responsible for reinstating the bathtub and bringing joy to his sisters, as he was able to supply Max with all the bootleg booze he could handle. Vroomy was sorely disappointed, but at least he was still gainfully employed. Not that other eight-year-olds weren't part of the workforce, but they were delivery boys or stock boys, whereas Vroomy was a lookout for his father, more of an executive position. His job was to stand in front of the candy store and cry out "Chickie, the fuzz!"—Brooklyn slang for "Look out, cops!"—if he saw the police or the feds approach. Then he would scurry into the candy store and crawl under the counter. His father would hastily stuff under Vroomy's shirt the one or two bottles of moshkeh he kept hidden there, and the youngster would do a twenty-three skidoo out the rear door. It was a lot like ringaleevio, Vroomy's favorite game, except that in the fuzz-versus-Vroomy version, the Pursuers never once caught the Pursued.

Irving Shapiro was seated at the counter of Midnight Rose's candy store one overcast Thursday morning, looking at a cup of coffee. He wasn't drinking it because it smelled like his mother's sink before she washed the dinner dishes.

They called her Midnight Rose because it seemed that she never slept. Her store, on Saratoga Avenue just off Livonia, was open all hours of the day and night. She was a plump, frumpy woman with stringy gray hair knotted in a bun at the back. In a floral print housecoat covered by a soiled white apron, she swept the floor ceaselessly, moving the dirt from one corner of the store to another. Her one son, Sam, apparently didn't satisfy her maternal instincts, for she had adopted as her brood the boys who came to be known as Murder, Inc. It was not uncommon for the containers in Rose's counter freezer to be filled with vanilla ice cream, chocolate ice cream, and a couple of pistols cooling down.

Irving Shapiro was still looking at his coffee when Abie Reles and Buggsy Goldstein walked into the store. Abie helped himself to a chocolate twist—his favorite candy, and the reason for his street name, Kid Twist—while Buggsy browsed through a girlie magazine.

Irving told them how disappointing it was to his brother Meyer that Itzik's Delicatessen on Stone Avenue hadn't ordered any beer or whiskey in a very long time. He then handed each of them a ten-dollar bill, placed a nickel on the counter, and headed for the door.

"Whatsa matter? You didn't touch your coffee," Rose barked.

"I really wasn't hungry," Irving said. "Why fill up for no reason?"

Before Prohibition got them into bootlegging, the Shapiro brothers were pretty much able to run their operation by themselves, but now it was a much more complex world filled with dishonest and fickle people. Two or even three pair of eyes were not enough to make sure their customers didn't roam and buy their booze elsewhere. So Meyer needed workers. Educational background and résumés were not necessary, just a natural aptitude for the job and a willingness to work cheap. Abie

Reles and his gang fit the bill, and so did Happy Maione and his gang. Not that there was a shortage of punks eager to work for the notorious Shapiros, but none had the toughness or cunning or ambition of the Reles and Maione crews. Peace prevailed, and the mounds of horse manure were left undisturbed on the streets of Brownsville and Ocean Hill.

Abie and Buggsy parked their battered black Ford at the Socony station at the corner of Stone and Sutter, where they had a clear view of Itzik's Deli. As Buggsy lost game after game of gin rummy in the cramped front seat, he grew irritable. He didn't enjoy wasting his talents on a jerkwater operation like a delicatessen. Itzik may have been big time when it came to Dr. Brown's celery soda, but Buggsy had no intention of freezing his ass off over maybe a dozen bottles of whiskey a week. When Kid Twist knocked with three, Buggsy almost knocked the side window out with his fist. This he followed up by flinging his cards all over the car.

"What are you, a fucken sore loser over a penny a point?" Abie yelled.

"This is shit, ya know! This is pure, total, unadulterated shit!" Buggsy shouted back. "The sonuvabitch ain't ordered in weeks—ya know he's buyin' outside. I ain't spendin' my life on no two-bit shtick!"

Itzik Koslowitz grunted with the effort of moving the push broom across the ceramic tile floor of his delicatessen store as Chana, his wife, laboriously scrubbed the grill.

"Itzik, you want to sit, sit. Tomorrow's another day," she counseled him.

"For some," he sighed. "For me, who knows. Today the floor is dirty, I'll clean it. Tomorrow the floor is dirty, I may not be here to clean it."

"Don't talk like such an imbecile, you hear me? 'Tomorrow I may not be here,' " she mimicked. "You feel like being sorry for yourself, be sorry by yourself. It don't take two of us to be sorry for you. Otherwise, be a mensh, shut up and I'll be sorry for you. You should thank God you're still here after the operation you went through, but who needs a gallbladder that don't work?"

Itzik stopped sweeping and meekly nodded his head. "You're right, Chana, I'm sorry. Did you ever hear me complain before? I'm just not used to feeling like a feather."

Chana relaxed and turned lovingly toward her husband. "Come, ta-teleh, let's sit down and have a nice hot glass of tea, then we'll close up and go to bed."

Chana knew the first day back would be hard. God should only take pity and make easier days for Itzik. The gallbladder that he didn't need he still had. Her face was soft but her heart was heavy as she thought of the past weeks.

They'd gone to visit their daughter Muriel, who had to marry a lumberjack and live in the forest in Richmond—or Staten Island, as Muriel called it. That's a job, to live with the animals and take care of the trees, like the trees all of a sudden don't know how to take care of themselves? It's such a trip you think you're going back to Europe. You get on a boat and go past the Statue of Liberty just like when you first came over.

When they got off the boat Itzik was green and nauseous, so naturally they thought he was seasick. Marvin the lumberjack was there with his car to drive them to the house in the forest called Clove Lake Park. By the time they arrived, Itzik was in so much pain he couldn't stand up straight, and Muriel, who was always the smartest one in the family, except when it came to getting married, said he should go straight to the hospital. But Marvin the lumberjack said, "Just give him an enema."

Chana folded her arms and gave a nod of her head. "You think that's what he needs, an enema? Okay, you give him an enema."

Poof! Itzik was in the hospital. For almost a month he was there. First they gave him tests and X rays and decided it was his gallbladder. They opened him up to take out a stone, but what they found wasn't a stone. They closed him right up again and told Chana there was nothing they could do; maybe for a while he would be okay. Sometimes this type of tumor grew slowly. They gave him painkillers, and Chana told him it was vitamins. This kind of burden two people didn't have to share. It was enough that she knew. As far as Itzik was concerned, they took out his gallbladder. In a little over a month she saw him shrivel up and become a tired old man.

While Itzik was in the hospital, they left the store in the care of their son, Samuel—Kozzy, everyone called him. They told him to offer a very basic menu like frankfurters, corned beef, pastrami, brisket, and potato knishes; cooking on the grill was the only cooking he should do so there was a good chance the store wouldn't burn down. Whiskey he was not to buy or sell. Such a chance they wouldn't take with their son. Not that he wasn't a good boy, but his head was so empty that on a breezy day you could hear the wind whistling through his ears. This morning, on their first day back, it had seemed like ten years worth of dirt was waiting for them.

Itzik poured some tea into his saucer and blew on it, then sucked in a mouthful through the sugar cube clenched between his front teeth. He closed his eyes as the sweet, warm liquid spread through his weary body. Chana, herself worn out from the day's arduous labor, smiled at the rare look of pleasure she saw upon her husband's face. As the front door opened and closed, she sensed that it was a look to be stored in a memory vault.

"I'm sorry, we're closed," she stated politely to the two men in slouch hats as they looked around the store and saw that there were no customers. The taller one turned and walked to the door, locking it and pulling down the night shade, at which Chana involuntarily gasped.

Itzik surprised her. He was composed and spoke in a voice stronger than she had heard from him in weeks. "Look, fellas, we ain't got much in the register, but what we have you can take. Also, what's in my pockets, that you can have too. Shnorrers we're not."

Abie walked up to him, raised the glass of tea, sniffed it, and put it down. "Who says you're not a shnorrer? Meyer Shapiro says you are a shnorrer. His feelings are very hurt, Itzik."

Itzik's face creased in bewilderment. "What are you talking about? I got no idea about what you're saying."

Chana started to get up, but Buggsy placed a hand upon her shoulder and roughly forced her back in her seat. From the pocket of his camel's-hair coat he pulled out a billy and started slapping it in the palm of his hand. He was smiling. It felt good to be out of that car.

Abie spoke slowly, accenting his words by tapping the stubby middle finger of his right hand on the table next to Itzik's glass of tea. "To save a couple of cents you turn your back on a good friend like Meyer? Meyer Shapiro, who took care of you through thick and thin? You don't call that being a shnorrer?"

"What did I ever do to Meyer Shapiro? You got me so farchadat I can't think straight no more."

Chana pushed up from her chair. "Can't you see he's a sick man? Leave him alone already!"

Reles continued as though Chana didn't even exist. "How do you stab a friend like that in the back? Who are you buyin' your whiskey from, Itzik?"

"Nobody. Just Meyer!"

"You fucken old bullshit artist!" Abie grabbed Itzik by the collar and shook him violently. "There's only one person you buy from in this whole world, you understand?"

Chana closed her eyes, trying to blot out reality. "You crazy gozlen!" she shrieked. "The man is just out of the hospital! He's dying! Drop dead and go to hell, you grauber yung!"

Buggsy Goldstein couldn't contain himself. "What're we wastin' time for?" he said, shoving Reles out of the way. "When I get through teachin' him his lesson, he ain't never gonna buy from anybody else again."

Buggsy was right. Itzik never bought whiskey from anyone else, including Meyer Shapiro. Buggsy punched, prodded, and pounded the little man with his fists and his blackjack. Ribs cracked like dry twigs, organs ruptured. Only the pain of the first two or three blows was felt by Itzik. After that he was blanketed in a cocoon where sound and feeling did not exist.

Buggsy Goldstein did what the medical men could not do. He released Itzik Koslowitz from his cancer-driven pain.

Chana shrieked and screamed to an empty world. First she tore the shaytl from her head. Then she tore at the short strands of her real hair. She pounded upon her slack breasts and ripped her fingernails across her face until she drew rivulets of blood. It was almost as an act of mercy when Buggsy turned his blackjack on the base of her skull, sending her into peaceful unconsciousness.

There was pain and a headache, but Chana awoke. Itzik never did. He slept in a painless coma for almost half a year, Chana never leaving his side for more than a few minutes. She told the police nothing. God would be the judge. That was her way.

Soon after earning their twenty dollars for the lesson they taught Itzik, Abe and Buggsy learned that he had been in the hospital for more than a month and had not ordered whiskey from anyone. It was too bad, they agreed, but after all, mistakes happen.

Max was standing on a stepladder arranging cartons of cigarettes on a shelf when Vroomy vaulted over the counter and cried in a frightened whisper, "Poppa, chickie, the fuzz!"

Max didn't panic. This was not the first time they had been visited and searched by the feds, and he was sure it wouldn't be the last. They had their routine down pat. Vroomy could pick out a cop as easily as you could pick out a lemon in a bushel of apples.

"Okay, take it easy, I'm coming."

"No, Poppa, there's no time. Stay there!" The words were hardly out of Vroomy's mouth when the door opened and the two agents entered.

"Get down, please, Mr. Davidoff. We'd like to have a little look around if you don't mind."

From the corner of his eye Max stole a glance at Vroomy, who had crawled under the counter on his stomach and was sliding open the door where the two bottles were hidden.

"Mind? Why should I mind? But what do you need me for?" Vroomy had stuffed both bottles under his shirt and was inching toward the rear screen door on his back. "By now you guys know the place as good as I do."

"Where's the kid who just came in here?" one of the agents asked.

"What kid?" Max climbed slowly down the ladder. "Now you're seeing kids? You sure you guys aren't drinking on the job? I didn't see no kid."

There was a bang as Vroomy shoved open the screen door and bolted for the alley, clutching the bottles. On Blake Avenue he heard the two feds in pursuit, half a block behind, and started zigzagging like the soldiers in the war movies at the Supreme. He scooted across Pennsylvania Avenue and compounded the sin by not even bothering to look. He took side streets all the way to Sutter, then cut around and back to Blake, praying he'd lost the fuzz. At Hopkinson Avenue, lungs on fire, he turned and was heading toward Sutter again when something sent him sprawling to the sidewalk. The two bottles fell free of his shirt and shattered across the cement. He heard somebody laughing like a horse spooked by a truck, and then more horses joined in.

"Hey, shitass, look what a mess you made. Clean it up."

Vroomy raised his head. He was in front of the candy store across the street from the Hebrew Educational Society Community Center, where his sisters hung out. Kozzy Koslowitz and Porky Kramer, the guy who was telling him to clean up the sidewalk, were standing over him with a gang of four or five other guys. Even though everyone said Kozzy was a real jerk, Vroomy felt sorry for him because of what happened to his father at the deli. One of the reasons people said he was a jerk was that he had friends like this fat slob Porky.

"Okay, you did enough," Kozzy said. "Leave the kid alone already." That's when Vroomy realized that Porky had tripped him.

"Whatsa matter with you?" Porky gave Kozzy a shove. "This brat is Big Gangy's brother. After what they did to your old man, you're tellin' me to leave him alone?"

"It was Reles and Buggsy. Big Gangy had nothin' to do with it," Kozzy mumbled.

"Bullshit! Birds of a feather." And with that Porky kicked Vroomy in the stomach. "You guys think we should send a message back to those yellow bastards for what they did to poor Itzik?"

Fists pumping in the air, Porky, who needed no urging at all, was urged on by a chorus of cheers from the group of candy-store jockeys. Vroomy saw a larger crowd gathering now. People spilled out of all the neighboring stores and houses, hearing the commotion.

"Go on, lick it up, you little fucker," Porky shouted, ramming his shoe into Vroomy's side.

"After you squeeze your pimples, you fat tub of lard," Vroomy shouted back, each word causing a stab of pain to his ribs. "Or maybe you're afraid you'll drown in your pus."

A wave of snickers ran through the crowd. Porky reached down, grabbed Vroomy by the hair, and slapped him hard across the face. The sting was like an electric shock. All the colors of the rainbow tore through Vroomy's head.

Another kick from Porky, followed by an "Ooh!" from the crowd and some calls of "Leave the kid alone."

While Vroomy was trying hard to disperse the clouds that were filling his head, he remembered a lesson his brother Willie had taught him. "When you're fightin' down and dirty, go for the balls, kid. That's the weak spot of any and every guy you'll ever be up against."

Vroomy felt his head wrenched up as Porky all but lifted him from the ground by his hair. With a cry of rage that pierced the crowd like a knife, he grabbed Porky's crotch and squeezed what felt like a pouch with two marbles. Another cry tore through the air. It was different, though. This was a cry of fear and pain. Porky screamed and flailed, and Vroomy squeezed tighter and tighter. A couple of Porky's buddies jumped in, but before more than two or three punches landed, the crowd came to Vroomy's aid and pulled them off.

Vroomy felt blood running from his nose. He looked at Kozzy and still felt sorry for him, but people were right—he was a jerk.

As he hurried home, Vroomy didn't pay much attention to his scrapes and bruises. The real hurt was what Porky said about Willie. It wasn't the first time Vroomy had heard terrible things about his brother, but he had always been able to shut them out or convince himself that whoever said them was some kind of screwball. Now the truth had been pounded into him. Worse, Vroomy knew that no matter what, he would always love Willie and stand up for him simply because he was family.

By the next day Vroomy was an eight-year-old legend. All of Brownsville and East New York had heard how little Albert Davidoff brought the giant Porky Kramer to his knees by squeezing his balls until he was ready to sing an aria from *Aida*.

It was springtime, and Vroomy stood before the bedroom mirror running a comb through his hair, painstakingly building a large wavy curl in the front and shaping it with the heel of his right hand. This was not an easy task. He was dealing with a pile of hair that had been pretty much on its own for over nine years, and suddenly, with no warning, it's going through a training program. But Vroomy, with more patience than is usually found in someone his age, plus a bottle of Vaseline hair tonic he'd appropriated from Willie's side of the medicine cabinet, was nearing a semblance of success. He was concentrating so hard on his hair that he didn't realize his mother had been calling to him from the kitchen for the past five minutes.

"Avrum?" Spatula in hand, she pushed open the bedroom door. "Your ears didn't wake up yet?" She stopped and stood staring at her son with an expression somewhere between shocked approval and disbelief.

"Come on, Ma, what're you lookin' at?" Vroomy said, his face starting to redden.

"Looking? Who's looking? Because you don't hear, I shouldn't see? Anyhow, what's to see? I got four daughters with hair as straight as sticks, and all of a sudden I got a son who got such a curl it should only happen to a movie star." Rose reached out to pat his head.

Vroomy ducked. "You think it looks funny?"

"Funny? Why should it look funny? You know what? If I were a bird I would probably want to live in it."

"Cut it out, Ma. You're makin' fun of me. All the guys are combin' their hair like this. It's called a pompadour. You wouldn't want me to look like a freak, would you?"

"Tell me, better, where are you going with your hair all done up with a whole bottle of your brother's hair shpritz that he'll kill you for when he finds out?"

"Where do you think I'm going? I'm going to school."

"Oh, so that's what I should think? From what your principal says, when you show up in school they're going to have a celebration. Only he's not getting the cake yet because he's afraid it will go stale."

It was not reading, writing, and arithmetic that did draw Vroomy to school, nor was it the punchball games in the schoolyard at recess. What he wouldn't tell his mother, his brothers, or even his friends—sometimes he didn't even admit it to himself—was that he liked being able to look at Sheila Goren, who sat two rows over from him in their 5B class. Just look at her—he wasn't ready for talking yet. Vroomy had no trouble talking to anyone else, but for some reason he never knew what to say to Sheila.

Sheila was small and very thin, with large brown eyes that seemed to take up most of a pale face framed by jet black hair. Except for Mrs. Farrell, his teacher, she was the only one who called him Albert. To everyone else he was Vroomy or Boomy, and that's what he liked. When Sheila Goren called him Albert he didn't like it—he loved it. It gave him a funny feeling. It made him feel warm, like when it's a cold winter night but he's tucked in his bed under a heavy wool blanket, and at the same time it gave him a chilly tingle, the kind that runs up and down your spine and makes you shiver and shake.

But Vroomy had to watch his step. It was okay to be friends with a girl, but to really like her—he knew that's when you get it up the old kazoo, so he tried to make sure that Shorty, Mousey, and the other guys didn't get wise. One day he tried a little too hard.

It was three o'clock, and they were just leaving school when someone started calling Sheila the farmer's daughter—which she was—and soon everyone was joining in. Sheila just kept walking, ignoring them but looking pretty upset. That's when Vroomy said, "How much time do you spend in the haystack?"

The words were barely out of his mouth when three things happened. First, he tried to grab them and shove them back down his throat. Second, Sheila, who had been walking the gauntlet without breaking stride, head high, turned and looked at him as though he had slapped her in the face. He felt the red heat of shame crawl from his neck to the roots of his hair.

The third thing that happened was that Carlie Packman's sense of chivalry came into play. Carlie was very good at spelling, arithmetic, history, and geography. Nobody remembered his ever getting less than a ninety-seven in any subject, and that was not because of short memories; it was because he never did get less than a ninety-seven.

At that instant in time when Vroomy was trying helplessly to retrieve his words and Sheila stopped in her tracks, Carlie Packman wagged his finger in Vroomy's face, and said, "Why don't you act like a gentleman, Davidoff?"

The next thing Carlie said was "Ouch!" He said it loudly and with much sincerity. He also said it from a horizontal position, staring up at Vroomy with his good left eye—good in comparison to his right eye, which was now swollen shut and turning a deep shade of purple from its collision with Vroomy's fist. Here Vroomy got the ninety-seven.

Although it may be difficult to believe at such a time, Vroomy liked Carlie Packman. He did not want to hit him, but more and more often lately his temper worked faster than he was able to think. He was angry at himself and ashamed of what he'd said to Sheila, and Carlie's reproach just added to his embarrassment. It was like turning the key on a windup toy.

"Albert Davidoff, you are a big bully!" Sheila shouted as she stood over her fallen defender, staring at Vroomy with her hands on her hips and red dots of anger speckling her milky cheeks. All the kids were gathering around now, and Vroomy felt as though he were under a microscope as everyone watched to see his response. Carlie, still on his back, was shielding his face with his left forearm, prepared for the worst.

Vroomy felt terrible. The last person in the whole world that he would want to upset was now furious with him. And he had just beat up one of the nicest kids in his class for no reason at all. Carlie Packman always helped Vroomy with his homework or an assignment he didn't understand. So what if he was a lousy punchball player and made everyone else look bad by getting the highest marks in everything. He never bent over his paper or covered it with his arm during a test. Anyone with good eyes was able to sneak a look at Carlie Packman's answers. He was an okay guy, and Vroomy only wished that he knew how to apologize. His brother Willie had told him over and over that you never say you're sorry because you can't change things once they're done. But who said Willie was such a know-it-all?

As Vroomy leaned down to offer Carlie his hand, they were engulfed by disappointed groans of "Aw, nuts!" and "Heck!"

"I didn't mean it, Carlie. I guess when you yelled at me it was like a reflect."

For a second Carlie shied, and then he looked up at Vroomy and shook his head condescendingly. "You mean 'reflex,' not 'reflect.'"

"Yeah, that's what I mean." Vroomy was not about to disagree now that things were getting back to normal, except for Carlie's eye. The circle of disappointed kids had broken up and drifted away, leaving only Vroomy, Sheila, the wounded Carlie, Shorty, Mousey, and the schoolyard vendors—the knish man, the jelly apple man, and the charlotte russe man. Vroomy was desperate to make amends. He couldn't let Sheila Goren leave here thinking of him as a bully.

"I want you to sock me as hard as you can, Carlie," he grandstanded, sneaking a look at Sheila.

"I don't want to sock you," Carlie said suspiciously. "Why should I?"

"It'll make me feel better, that's why."

"You socked me, and it didn't make me feel better. Not at all."

Sheila had gathered her schoolbooks and was turning to leave. She was sniffling and wheezing.

"Well, if you ain't gonna hit me, then I'll treat you to a jelly apple, okay? You too, Sheila," Vroomy said with a sheepish smile.

"Hey, I'll take one," Mousey piped up.

"You don't get one," Vroomy snapped.

"How come?"

"I didn't sock you, that's how come."

"You didn't sock the farmer's daughter either," Mousey pointed out.

That's when Shorty comes to Vroomy's rescue by announcing, "Hey, guys, they're choosing up for a punchball game in the schoolyard," with which he grabs Mousey by the elbow and drags him away. This makes Vroomy feel greatly relieved, as he knows that there is a lone, single nickel in his pocket with which he has the buying power for two jelly apples with a penny left over.

As it develops, he winds up with the whole nickel, as neither Carlie nor Sheila wants a jelly apple. Carlie gets cavities just by being within ten feet of candy, and he is in much more need of something sugarless and cold to put on his eye. Sheila, who is now breathing a little easier, just wants to go home and rest. Vroomy is very happy because she is no longer angry with him. Carefully he looks toward the schoolyard to make certain that Mousey and Shorty aren't watching him, but they are so caught up in an argument about someone on the other team running up over the lead line that he knows he doesn't have to worry.

It is at this moment that Vroomy gathers up his courage and does what he believes is the bravest thing he has ever done in his whole nine years of life. He tells Sheila Goren that he will walk her home. This he does not do, as his feet never touch the ground. He floats all the way to Linden Boulevard.

Vroomy had seen pictures of farms in books and magazines, and he had seen farms in movies at the Supreme, but standing with Sheila at the broken wooden gate that was barely hanging by one hinge, he was looking at a real farm for the first time. And although he was not an agricultural authority, he knew that he was looking at something most unusual. In places with names like Oshkosh or Kokomo you would look at a farm and not give it a second thought, but a farm was not what you expected to see in Brooklyn, New York, of which Brownsville is part.

He scratched his head, although it didn't itch, and said, "Some farm."

As farms go, the Goren farm was not a large one. It was less than a small city block in size, and there was no barn because there were no animals, except for a collie and a few sickly-looking chickens. In the center of the property was a two-story white clapboard house that looked as though it hadn't been painted since the Civil War, and on all four sides of the house were neatly hoed rows of crops. Vroomy couldn't figure out why anyone would want to be a farmer when you could get all the vegetables you wanted at any pushcart.

Sheila's father, Milton Goren, was a man of few words, which was not a very Jewish trait. Vroomy remembered hearing his father say that Goren the farmer wasn't really a Jew. Besides the fact that he was never seen in shul and a conversation to him consisted of one or two words, he wore flannel shirts and smoked a corncob pipe. "Who ever saw a Jew in a flannel shirt?" Max asked. "People in Scotland and Yankees in Maine, they wear flannel shirts. Jews wear white shirts or shirts with a thin pinstripe. And to smoke a corncob pipe? Hillbillies in the Ozarks smoke corncob pipes. Jews smoke cigarettes, sometimes a cigar. Once in a while you'll see a Jewish doctor or college professor smoke a pipe— a real pipe!"

Vroomy, accepting that his father was a very wise man, carefully weighed and considered his logic, then put it up against the fact that Sheila Goren wore a Star of David necklace, and decided that once in a while his father could be wrong.

One of the points that Milton Goren made with his few words was that no one related to Big Gangy Davidoff would ever be welcome in his home. Though this was nothing new to Vroomy—he had been spit at and beaten up and given "horns" on behalf of Willie—this was the most painful rejection of all. Goren's dislike even rubbed off on the collie, who would growl and lunge whenever Vroomy came within ten feet of the gate, though Sheila was right at his side.

In spite of Farmer Goren and his dog, Vroomy's spirits soared. He walked Sheila home from school almost every day and set a personal best for attendance. In fact, because Sheila was constantly plagued by colds, he soon had a better attendance record than she did.

On the way home to Linden Boulevard one day, Sheila told Vroomy that her father often sold his vegetables from her uncle's pushcart on Blake Avenue. "My poppa says that your brother Willie steals from the peddlers and forces them to pay him money or else he doesn't let them sell."

"Naw, it's not like that. My brother has an insurance business," Vroomy said, though he didn't really believe Willie's explanation himself. "They buy insurance from him, and he protects them so nobody can just move in on them."

"But if they don't pay, he beats them up. My father says he's a thug."

Vroomy looked down at the sidewalk, not quite sure what a thug was. "You know, you can't make an exception for one guy. Everyone has to pay or else it ain't fair. My brother's got a really tough job. Anyhow, I ain't my brother. I'm me and he's him."

Sheila turned around and skipped backward, facing him, her eyes lighting up in a way that made Vroomy want to shout and do cartwheels. "That's exactly what I told my father, Albert. Almost word for word." She stopped skipping and stood there with her head tilted, her excitement suddenly replaced by a frown that made Vroomy think of a cloud blotting out the sun. "But he said that when the same blood runs through the veins, the heart and the mind work alike."

Vroomy knew that wasn't true. It couldn't be. There was no way he would join Willie in his work. There was no way he would be a lookout for his father's candy store anymore. And there was no way he would ever be a farmer. He was going on ten, and he was pretty definite about what he didn't want to be. Now he just had to figure out what he did want to be.

"What do you want to be, a two-bit punk your whole stinkin' life?" Abe Reles sneered as he crushed Indian nuts between his thumb and forefinger, popping them in his mouth and dropping the shells to the floor. "Show me you got a pair of fucken balls, for cryin' out loud!"

At this moment there was nothing happy about Happy Maione. He sat on his stool, hands clasped in front of him on the counter, unable to look at Reles, who was pacing like a caged lion.

"Will ya stop throwin' those goddamn shells all over my floor," Midnight Rose grumbled. "What am I, a shvartzeh that has to run around and clean up after you all day?"

Abe ignored her. "You know what? You and your k'nocker friend Dasher are the last guys I ever thought were stuffed with bullshit. You got a feast spread out on the table in front of you, and you're afraid to pick up the fucken fork an' dig in."

Buggsy, who was leaning against the counter moving a toothpick around in his mouth, decided that it was a good time to throw his two cents in. "Whaddya expect from these friggen dagos? Soon as the sun comes out and they see their shadows they're ready to crap in their pants."

Happy raised his head and spun around on his stool. What Abe Reles could get away with, Buggsy Goldstein couldn't. "Hey, asshole, you think you're so brave? You're just too stupid to be scared."

There was a loud bang as Rose slammed her hand on the counter. "If this sawed-off paskudnyak don't wanna go along, throw him the hell out, Abie. Just let him pay me for the coffee and bialy first."

Happy Maione is very sensitive about his five-foot-four-inch stature, and he gives Rose a look that if she were any other woman she would probably go into cardiac arrest right then and there. But being that she is Rose, she waves her dirty dishrag at him and laughs in his face.

At that moment the door opens, and Frank "Dasher" Abbandando walks in carrying a well-worn fielder's glove. A pair of baseball spikes tied together by their laces is thrown over his shoulder. He is a husky guy who looks like he can run through a brick wall.

"Hiya doin', fellas?" He is beaming with a four-for-four ear-to-ear grin. "Sorry I'm late, but I get a call this morning askin' me to fill in for the Powerhouse at Dexter Park."

The Dasher is barely out of his teens but has already taken two trips up the river. Word is that he is a good enough ballplayer to make it as a pro. In fact, he gets the name Dasher because of his hustling, spikes-first style of play for the Elmira reformatory team. Whether he truly has pro potential is never discovered, because he follows his idol and eventual partner, Happy Maione, into another field of endeavor where his slugging prowess is just as evident.

It is more than three years now that Happy and Dasher are hooked up with Reles's gang as the strongarm squad for the Shapiro brothers and the Amberg brothers, the two major liquor distributors in Brownsville. Between them the Shapiros and the Ambergs control all the bootleg alcohol, flesh parlors, and gambling machines in the neighborhood. They are totally independent, and that Reles's boys are on the payrolls of both creates no conflict of interest.

But now Reles wants to stage a coup against the Shapiros, and Happy and Dasher can't make up their minds whether to go along. They do not share Reles's ambition. They feel very safe and secure with the status quo, but Reles has been leaning on them hard.

Dasher now notices the scowls being exchanged by Happy Maione and Midnight Rose. He has no idea what brings this about, so he winks at both of them. "Hey, you two in love or something?"

"Okay, everybody, cut the crap!" Reles orders, thinking to himself that the League of Nations has more productive meetings.

Abe's firm approach has a dramatic effect on Happy and Dasher, who are most comfortable being told, not asked. They listen with interest as he points out the terrible inequity of the prevailing pay scale, with the Shapiros raking in the big bucks while the guys under them hardly take home enough to keep them in bullets. Buggsy gets so caught up in Kid Twist's eloquent denunciation of the ruling class that his nostrils flare and his fists coil into tight balls of anger.

"So we do all their fucken work," Reles concludes, "and these whores toss us spitballs and laugh watchin' us grovel at their feet while they stuff their pockets till they bulge like their fat asses."

Happy and Frank look each other in the eye. There is a silent, subtle nodding of heads: they are in.

Rose, without anyone noticing, has quietly slipped into the back room, and now she returns holding a bottle of real scotch, not the bathtub variety. She picks up the dirty dishrag and methodically dries five coffee mugs that are sitting in the sink unwashed. Buggsy watches her with a most dubious look upon his face.

"Don't you use no soap and water?"

"What for, are ya stupid or something? Don't ya know alcohol kills germs?"

So saying, Rose pours a double shot all around. They raise their cups in a good-luck toast and down their drinks in one gulp.

"Salud!" says Happy Maione.

"L'chaim!" says Abe Reles.

Boomy loved hanging out on Blake Avenue. He loved the noise, the action, the smell of fruits, vegetables, pickles, fish. He loved the crowds, and he loved to watch the haggling and bargaining between peddler and customer. To Boomy, this was Brownsville.

When he was seven or eight, Boomy used to make it part of his daily routine to race down the street with Shorty and Mousey and Snake and swipe something from one of the pushcarts, just for the sheer joy and adventure of it. Now, at ten, he was much more settled in his ways. After all, he was just three years shy of becoming a fully certified man, wasn't he?

Boomy was sauntering along Blake one day after school when an "Oy, oy, oy!" pierced the air. He turned to see an old pushcart peddler holding his back and trying to rise from his little wooden crate so he could wait on a customer. Boomy observed the struggle for a while, then went over and placed a hand on the old man's shoulder.

"Sit down, mister. Let me help you."

The peddler watched as Boomy carefully bagged and weighed the fruits that the woman picked out. Moistening his pencil with his tongue, the peddler wrote the price on each bag, totaled everything, and made change for the woman. When she left, he squinted up at the boy and pursed his lips.

"You're Vrumeleh, huh? The younger brother from Big Gangy?"

"Yah, Vroomy, Boomy, but don't call me Vrumeleh. That's for a little kid."

"Excuse me, excuse me, please," the peddler said with mock reverence. "Moishe forgot who he's talking with. So, what is it you want? You're making a collection for your brother?"

"I don't want nothing, it just looked like you could use a hand. I don't work with my brother, and he don't work with me."

Seeing the hurt in the boy, Moishe reached out and gave him a pat on the arm. "I'm sorry, my young friend. What I should have said was thank you. Old is not necessarily wise."

"Aw, forget it. It happens all the time. I'm used to it."

"Maybe being Big Gangy's brother don't win you popularity contests, but never let yourself get used to it, Vroomy. People should know better."

This was not a subject Boomy enjoyed, so he changed it. "I could come over and help you out after school if you want. You shouldn't be working so hard."

"No, I'm fine, Vroomy," Moishe said with a smile. "It's just this lumbago—you should never know from it, God willing—and I couldn't afford to pay you anything. It's not such a profitable business that it needs a supervisor with an apprentice."

"That's okay, I didn't ask you to pay me anything. You'll teach me how to be a fruit peddler. That's just as good as getting paid, and maybe I'll make some tips. Ladies love little kids."

Moishe picked an apple from his wagon and pulled a heavy-handled pocketknife from his jacket. Carefully he opened the blade and pared the apple until a red spiral of skin dangled from the stem to the tips of his shoes. Boomy watched, spellbound by the old man's deftness. As the corkscrew of peel fluttered to the sidewalk, Moishe raised the fruit, opened his mouth, and looked at Vroomy as though remembering a very important fact. He lowered the apple, sliced it in two with one swift stroke, and handed the bigger half to Vroomy.

"See, payment in advance."

Shorty cannot believe he is doing what he is doing. Here he is with Boomy on a Saturday morning, standing like a putz on Linden Boulevard picking up rotten fruit while all the guys are at the schoolyard playing ball. Shorty and Boomy are pretending to drop the fruit from their orange-crate wagon so they can pick it up and put it back on the wagon and pretend to drop it again.

Shorty is playing this game as a very big favor to Boomy, who has to

make it look like he has a reason to be here, half a block from Milton
Goren's farm. Why he needs a reason to be here when it is a free country Shorty cannot understand. He knows it has something to do with
Sheila going to stay with her aunt in Arizona because the cold winter
air in New York is no good for her asthma. She is absent from school
so much that Mrs. Farrell doesn't even call out her name for the attendance check each morning, but even so she gets the highest marks in
the class next to Carlie Packman.

Everybody knows that Boomy and Sheila are friends now, so Shorty
can't figure out why Boomy doesn't just admit he wants to say good-bye.
But one thing Shorty is definitely not going to do, even though he and
and Boomy are best buddies, is needle him. Shorty remembers what
happens when one of the older kids from the 7A class starts spreading
it around in the schoolyard that he sees Boomy and Sheila kissing. Not
just kissing, but French kissing. Then this jerk says something Shorty is
not too sure about, but it has to do with Boomy's middle finger smelling
like tunafish. Nobody would believe that a kid from 5B could possibly
beat up a kid in the seventh grade, but if this jerk was an egg you'd say
he was scrambled, and if he was a potato you'd say he was mashed, and
if he was a cow you'd say he was hamburger.

Happiness is said to be different things to different people, and so
it is with Boomy and Shorty when Sheila Goren finally comes out of her
house with her mother and father. Happiness abounds. Boomy is happy
because this is why he is here in the first place: to see Sheila, even if it
is to say good-bye. Shorty is happy because he is very, very tired of throwing rotten fruit down just so he will be able to pick it up.

Boomy, who is very good at hiding his feelings, does not let on how
happy he really is, which is good because the happiness doesn't last long.
Milton Goren opens the back door of his Model-T Ford, helps Sheila
in, and tucks a blanket around her shoulders to keep her warm. Mrs.
Goren, almost as tall and straight-backed as her husband, opens the
passenger door and primly seats herself while he walks to the front of
the car and cranks the handle. As the engine coughs and sputters and
rattles to life, Sheila sees Boomy and Shorty down the street and tries
to wave, but Farmer Goren takes a deep suck on his corncob pipe and
drives away in the opposite direction.

Shorty turns to look at his friend. Boomy is standing there, no expression on his face, watching the Model-T and saying nothing. Shorty, who is no good at all at hiding his feelings, picks up a soft tomato and heaves it at the car, missing by only two blocks.

3

S top! Stop! I can't take it anymore!" Willie Davidoff is being tortured. His eyes are red and his face is haggard. From the depths of the apartment comes the earsplitting wailing of "Dayenu."

"Stop with the burtching already," Rose shouts, stamping her foot. "It would be so terrible if he grows up to be a chazzen?"

Willie cups his head in his hands. "Ma, who says he'll live to grow up?"

"Bite off your tongue, you lummox. About such a sweet child who sings with God, that's how you talk?"

It is three days since Boomy went to the Supreme with Shorty and Mousey to see *The Jazz Singer.* Only Shorty and Mousey stayed for the end of the movie. Boomy got kicked out for forming a duet with Al Jolson, although he received no billing or credits. His eviction broke up the duet, but he sang solo all the way home, and hadn't stopped yet.

Willie runs to the bathroom, where Boomy is soaking in the tub and warbling his heart out. Rose runs after him, tugging at his shirt as he gives the locked door a mighty kick that tears the eye-hook fastener right off the molding.

"You little momzer! You trying to drive me crazy?" Willie screams.

"Whatsa matter with you?" Boomy says calmly. "Can'tcha see a guy's takin' a bath?"

Rose lets go of Willie's shirt and looks at Boomy in the tub. "Max, come here, give a cuk, he got little hairs already." She clasps her hands in awe.

Boomy's hands shoot to his crotch. "Ain't I entitled to a little privacy, for Chrissake?"

"You want privacy? I want peace and quiet," Willie says. "You wanna trade? Let's you and me go to the Radio and Phonograph Store on Rockaway, and I will buy you all the cantors' records they have, but you gotta give me your word—no playin' them or singin' when I'm here."

"You got it, Willie." Boomy knows a deal when he hears one.

"But I gotta ask ya, kid," Willie says. "You won't go to Hebrew school, you won't study for your bar mitzvah, so how come you wanna learn this kinda music?"

"Because I wanna be a cantor, that's how come."

"I knew it!" Rose crows. "I knew it!"

Boomy ran up the stairs of a four-story walkup on Dumont Avenue just off Thatford, and stood panting at the door of apartment 4C. He couldn't picture Moishe climbing those stairs.

Moishe hadn't been at his pushcart for four days now, and Boomy was worried. Over the past three months he'd grown very attached to the old man. They would go to the Brooklyn Terminal Market in Canarsie at the crack of dawn each day to buy the produce right off the trucks bringing it in from Jersey, Pennsylvania, and Delaware. Moishe taught him how to check for freshness and quality, ripeness and blight, all the little secrets of the trade. Except that he missed Sheila, it was as good a time as he could remember. He'd received two letters from her. Actually, she mailed them to her father, as she didn't know Boomy's address, and to Boomy's great surprise and joy Farmer Goren passed them along. Not to Boomy personally, to Moishe, but that was okay with Boomy.

He knocked twice on the door, but there was no answer, so he tried the knob. The door opened, and Boomy gasped in horror. There at the end of the long foyer was Moishe, dangling from a rope in the bedroom doorway. Boomy raced to the kitchen and ransacked the drawers until he found a large knife. He ran back down the foyer, climbed up on the chair Moishe must have used to hang himself, and started hacking at the rope.

"Are you a lunatic?" Moishe was swaying and thrashing, trying to shove the knife away, wide-eyed with fright.

"Moishe, you're alive!"

"Not for long if you keep stabbing me, you crazy bonditt!" he bellowed, still swinging away.

"I ain't stabbing you, Moishe. I'm cutting the rope."

"Very nice, boychik! You're cutting the rope so I should fall down and break every bone in my body?"

"What did you go and hang yourself for?" Boomy was flustered and confused.

"Hang myself? For hanging you gotta put a rope around your neck. You see a rope around my neck?"

Boomy took a good look at Moishe and exhaled. He hadn't noticed that the rope was tied under Moishe's armpits in a kind of harness. He helped Moishe step gingerly to the chair and down to the floor, and together they went to the kitchen, the old man limping in obvious pain, leaning heavily on the boy.

"Listen, Boomy, you think I'm meshuggah altogether?" Moishe said, sitting down at a metal-topped table covered with a print oilcloth. "Somebody with a good profitable business like I got and a hotshot assistant I'm learning it to should kill himself? What I was doing was traction. You know what's traction, Boomy?"

"Sure I do. It's a moving picture."

"Traction is a moving picture?" Moishe nodded his head in wonderment. "Where do you learn so much about traction, please tell me?"

"Whenever I go to the Supreme I always see the coming tractions. You know, it's the movie that's coming next week."

"I'm only glad it's something you didn't learn in school. When somebody hangs themselves, Boomy, but not from the neck, that's traction too. It's supposed to maybe fix up my lumbago, but it don't always work so good. Old bones like I got have a mind of their own. Traction and nothing else is going to make them do what they don't want to do. Boomy, I can't get around anymore. I can't go up the stairs, I can't go down the stairs, and I can't walk to Blake Avenue."

"But I can come over every morning and help you."

The old man smiled wearily. "Do you know how old I am, Boomy?"

"No," Boomy said, almost in a whisper.

"Then that makes two of us. But from what I'm told, I am so old that if a horse was so old, the horse would be living in a beautiful green pasture, doing whatever he wanted to do and having the best time of his life. So it's all decided. I'm moving in with my daughter who got a big house with soft chairs and a nice soft bed for me and no stairs to walk. Is a horse any better than I am?"

"Can I come over and visit you once in a while?"

Moishe shrugged. "If you were a hobo and you hopped on a train and took the train to the end of the railroad tracks and walked for a few more days, maybe you'd get there. But I'll write and send you a picture. She got a Kodak." Actually, Moishe's daughter, who was a grandmother, lived in East Flatbush, maybe a fifteen-minute bus ride away, but Moishe sensed it was better this way.

"What about the business?" Boomy asked. "What are you going to do with the pushcart?"

"I'll tell you the truth. With so many things happening I didn't think too much about it."

Boomy's eyes lit up. "Can I take it over?"

"I should give it to you? Who are you? What kind of a father do you think I am? Besides a daughter I got two sons. I don't even know how they're doing now. You know, since the market crashed last year—"

Boomy was startled. "I didn't know the market crashed. We been buying our fruit and vegetables there all along, and everything looked okay. They musta fixed it all up before I started working with you, right?"

What a world, Moishe thought. "Forget it, Boomy. It's a different market. Forget it." He put his finger to his forehead as though in deep thought. "As a good father I should leave the pushcart to my sons so they—"

"You think they're gonna know how to run the business?" Boomy interrupted.

"Ssh, I'm thinking for a minute. On the other hand, like I told you from the start, I didn't pay you no salary, so there is back pay due to you."

Boomy thought the old man's mind must be slipping. "You've been giving me some money every day, Moishe. You did say you wasn't going to, but you did."

"What are you confusing me for?" Moishe snapped, waving his hands irritably. "That's not salary. Salary I didn't pay you. What you got was commission. You sold, you got commission. That's got nothing to do with salary. It's the law. It was your money." Pursing his lips, the old man continued. "So if we take for three months' back salary . . . figure interest . . . I guess we gotta compound it, right, Boomy?"

"I . . . Yeah, I guess so." Boomy had no idea what Moishe was talking about.

"I'll tell you what." Moishe smiled, trying to look cagy. "I taught you the business, you make it easy on me. You give me a full release from any debts or obligations that I may owe you and you got the pushcart. You think about it and let me know if we got a deal."

"You're giving me the pushcart?" Boomy yelled.

"What is this 'giving'? Giving, shmiving! I ain't giving you nothing. What we're doing, it's called a negotiation. So, give me an answer. We got a deal?"

Boomy tried to contain himself, but his feet were drumming a staccato beat under the table. "I guess so." He shrugged, but he really wanted to jump up and give old Moishe the biggest hug he could manage.

Moishe reached over and took a sheet of white notepaper and a pen from the wooden kitchen cabinet next to the table. When he finished scribbling, he handed the paper to Boomy, who squinted and read it haltingly out loud.

" 'Moishe Levinsky who still got a pretty good mind gives to Albert Davidoff one pushcart that's on Blake Avenue that he bought in 1915 from Simon in the Fish Store. On the other hand Albert Davidoff who also got a pretty good mind releases Moishe Levinsky who he says don't owe him anything anymore. This is very official.' "

Moishe signed the document, rubbed some ink on his thumb, and put his thumbprint under his signature. Boomy was very, very impressed.

"It's important you put this in a safe place, Boomy. I don't want my pushcart—your pushcart—falling into the wrong hands," Moishe instructed seriously.

Boomy ran all the way home. In spite of his excitement he felt an emptiness at the thought that Moishe wouldn't be at the pushcart tomorrow, or any day after. Moishe did write to him and did send him a snapshot, as he'd promised. Boomy never noticed the East Flatbush postmark, and after a year the letters stopped.

There were those who said Joey Silvers could have been anything he wanted to be. Joey Silvers wanted to be a punk. Most people in the neighborhood thought he was an okay sort of a guy because it didn't cost him anything to smile and say hello, but Joey had about as much substance as he had loyalty, integrity, and change in his pocket.

When he wasn't hanging out on street corners or running an errand for the Shapiros, Joey could usually be found in Beecher's Gym, a Brownsville institution. Joey was actually a pretty decent boxer. He was one of four brothers, all fighters, and he was the best of the bunch. He had the ability and natural instincts of a fighter, but he didn't like to train because training was too much like work. They called him a six-minute wonder because for two rounds he would move around the ring like a gazelle, snapping out his punches in crisp combinations, and then he would die. As there were no two-round fights, Joey Silvers had no future in the ring.

A few minutes past six one evening, Joey turns the corner of Georgia Avenue onto Livonia and is about to enter Beecher's Gym when he hears someone call his name.

"Hey, Joey, what a coincidence. I'm just thinking about you recently."

It's Abe Reles, and it is not a coincidence at all. He has been planning this little "bumping into" ever since his meeting last week with Happy and the Dasher.

"Come on, let me buy you a corned beef on club."

Joey is always suspicious of anything out of Abe Reles's mouth, but he has no intention of missing out on a free meal, especially when it affords him a good reason to skip a workout. So they step into Alpert's Kosher Deli, right under Beecher's, and Abe starts the ball rolling regarding the deposing of the Shapiros. He has heard from here and around that Joey has been somewhat grumpy lately about the way the Shapiros show their appreciation for him. There have been more pats on the back than green in the palm, and Abe explains to Joey on which side his bread should be buttered, even though they are in a kosher establishment.

"I don't know, Abe, things are pretty good for me right now," Joey says, biting into his corned beef sandwich.

"Then you must be independently wealthy, Joey, because from what I hear, Meyer gives you bubkes."

Joey stops chewing. "What makes you so sure you can knock him over? And if you did, where do I fit in?"

Abe knows he is closing the deal as he walks around the table and crouches down, putting his arm around Joey's shoulder and his mouth by his ear. "It's our time, Joey," he whispers in a most confidential way. "We got the muscle and the organization to bury these fuckers. And when we do, baby, you'll be right up there with me, Buggsy, Strauss, and Maione, just like the board of directors. Whaddya say, kid, you're in?"

Joey picks up his sandwich, takes two big bites, and washes them down with a gulp of cream soda. "That fat sonuvabitch got it coming to him. What do I gotta do?"

"Nothing big or heavy, Joey, nothing big or heavy. All you gotta do is finger where and when they're going to be by themselves. And it gotta be someplace a little outta the way—you know, not in the middle of Pitkin Avenue on a Sunday afternoon. The heavy stuff we do. You can go see a movie."

Joey Silvers did not work out that day, or the next.

Big Gangy sat on a bench in the middle of Kitzel Park, shelling peanuts and tossing them to the pigeons. Usually you were not by yourself in Kitzel Park, which was the area of Lincoln Terrace Park noted for its nighttime necking and related activities, and Willie did not expect to be by himself much longer. He was here because Abe Reles asked him to meet him here at twelve noon.

Willie knew it was Abe as soon as he heard the footsteps. No one else walked like Reles. He turned the bag over and dumped the remaining peanuts on the ground. "Shell 'em yourself, dirtbags."

Abe draped his arm around Willie's shoulders and they strolled down lover's lane together. The pigeons cooed in the background. The talk was not of love, but it was about till death do us part.

He was courted with promises of having the world—or at least Brownsville—thrown at his feet, flattered to be joined in a union with an unbreakable bond and he would honor and obey and be honored and obeyed in return.

"It's our time, Willie," Reles said in a rasping whisper. "I'm telling you, it's our time. No more taking handouts or orders from that whore Meyer and his two nitwit brothers. It's all sitting there just waiting for us to rake it in. We don't have to settle for crumbs when we can have the whole loaf."

"It sounds like too much of a fucken gamble to me, Abie. What makes you think the Shapiros are such easy pickings, anyhow?" Willie turned and looked over his shoulder. The pigeons were gone, and the peanuts lay scattered on the ground, untouched. "After all, they're pretty well connected. Some people may not want to sit back and let this happen."

"Bullshit!" Reles wasn't whispering anymore. "Lepke don't give a shit. He got no use for those assholes. We got his blessing. It'll be like knockin' the milk bottles off the table in Coney Island, only the prize ain't going to be no fucken stuffed doll."

"I still wanna know why you think it's gonna be so easy."

"Because we got the guy who's setting the milk bottles up on the table for us. Joey Silvers is on my payroll now."

Willie looked Kid Twist in the eye. "Joey Silvers? Meyer Shapiro wears that little prick like a pinky ring."

"Well, the ring don't wanna stay on the pinky no more. Shapiro treats the kid like shit—like he treats everyone. Joey hates his guts, and that's why he's throwin' in with us. Tomorrow night the Shapiros are gonna be in a corner with no way out. Hey, I'm offering you something you oughta be kissing my feet for. You're in?"

"You don't give a guy a chance to think, Abie. You throw this at me with no warning and you want an answer right away?"

"Whatsa matter? You ain't got no balls, Willie?" Reles taunted.

"Yeah, I got balls, and I wanna keep them."

Reles took a deep breath. "Look, I'm gonna level with you. Strauss is up in Monticello doing Lepke a favor. I got plenty of cannons, you know that, but I want someone I can trust. It'll be me, Buggsy, and you. You wanna think about it? Okay, go home, put your head on straight, and think, but I want an answer by seven tonight, you understand? And listen, Willie, not a fucken word to no one—no one!"

Every Saturday night there was a big line in front of the Loew's Pitkin, Brownsville's magnificent art deco movie emporium that drew people from all parts of Brooklyn—except Brownsville. With rare exceptions, people from Brownsville could not afford to go to the Pitkin. They settled for theaters like the Supreme, the Oriole, the Stone, the Palace, or the People's Cinema.

To Boomy, the Pitkin was not was not really Brownsville at all. Boomy loved the Supreme Theater on Livonia Avenue. He spent all his Saturday afternoons there. At the Supreme, you didn't have to be afraid to spit your chewing gum out on the floor. The ushers didn't look like bellhops in a fancy hotel, and the patrons were people you knew, not foreigners from Flatbush or Crown Heights or even Queens. So he was not exactly overjoyed about the idea of going to the Pitkin, but he knew how much it would impress Sheila.

She hadn't written for about a month, but in her last letter she'd said that she was coming back to Brownsville now that winter was over. Since getting his address she'd been writing to him every week, and sometimes Boomy even wrote back, though it didn't come easy. He figured he hadn't heard from her in a while because Arizona was so far away and it was a long trip from there to Brownsville. He kept picturing the look on her face when he told her he was taking her to the Pitkin, and he kept practicing how he was going to say it so it didn't sound like a date.

He had it down pretty good when he went to Blake Avenue one day to tend his pushcart and saw that Farmer Goren was back. Boomy had the idea that Sheila's father didn't dislike him so much anymore, but he still had to summon his courage to go over and ask when Sheila would be returning.

Boomy cleared his throat. "Hi, Mr. Goren."

Milton Goren sat motionless on his chair by Sheila's uncle's pushcart, staring straight ahead.

"I'm Boomy Davidoff . . . Albert, I mean . . . Sheila's friend from school?"

Farmer Goren's lips barely moved when he finally said, "I know who you are."

Boomy was so worked up by now that he could only plunge on. "I got a real surprise for Sheila. I wanna take her to the Pitkin Theater, but I'm not sure what day she's getting back."

"She's not going to the Pitkin Theater."

Boomy was shattered, but he couldn't quit now. He felt a big smile might help. "Just for Saturday afternoon, Mr. Goren. She'll be back home by three o'clock, I promise."

Milton Goren kept staring straight ahead. "It's a promise you cannot keep. Go away, please."

And Boomy knew that he would never see Sheila Goren again.

Chotchke Charlie sat on the curb, cradling what looked like a woolly white mop in his arms, rocking back and forth. Occasionally he would flick out his tongue and lick at the salty droplets rolling down his cheeks. Eyes clouded with grief, he didn't see his friend Boomy walking down the street until Boomy almost tripped over him.

Chotchke Charlie was all over the place, in every neighborhood. Every few blocks he could be seen bouncing around on a street corner with his hands in his pockets and his head tilting from side to side. It wasn't the same Chotchke Charlie as the one sitting on the curb, but to those who didn't care to notice the differences—and in the Brownsville of the 1930s that meant most people—the ageless kids with the big heads who wandered aimlessly to their own unheard tune were one and the same. Hardly anyone understood Down's syndrome, and hardly anyone thought twice about referring to those who had it as Mongolian idiots.

Charlie looked up as Boomy stepped around him and kept walking. He wondered how come Boomy didn't say anything to him. He liked Boomy. He had a jumbled memory of Boomy, a long time ago, taking away a bad drink the other kids gave him. It was a hot summer day, and the kids went in an alleyway and urinated in an empty milk bottle. They added a few ice cubes, then walked innocently over to their friend Charlie and offered him a real treat for a hot summer afternoon. That's when Boomy came along. It wasn't that Boomy was a goody-goody who couldn't play a trick on someone, but having someone drink pee wasn't Boomy's idea of a trick.

At first Charlie was upset when Boomy grabbed the bottle from him, but he knew it was a bad drink when Boomy made like he was going to throw it at the kids and they all held up their hands and went "Yech!" Then Boomy took him to Max's candy store and gave him a real chocolate soda. And whenever Charlie would walk down that street he would look in the candy store, and if Boomy was there he would always give Charlie his favorite candy, those little penny tin cups of paraffinlike stuff that came with a tiny tin spoon. The candy was okay, but what Charlie really loved were the tin cups and spoons. Nobody had a larger collection of tin cups and spoons than Chotchke Charlie.

Charlie had a home, but he was seldom there. His father was a pious, learned man—a scholar—who sat in front of the holy books from dawn to dusk and never put in a day of physical work in his life. His wisdom was the wisdom of the bobbe-mysehs, for he was convinced that a dybbuk or demon possessed his son and that it was his sacred duty to make this demon submit, or else he would lose favor in the eyes of God. The torments Charlie suffered on the streets were easier to bear than the canings and whippings he suffered at the hands of his father. On the streets he could collect string, rubber bands, cigarette butts, tinfoil wrappers, pebbles, dead insects—any and every little chotchke—and add them to his treasure trove.

Chotchke Charlie rocked harder as he watched Boomy walk down the street. Boomy always had a wave and a "Hiya!" for Charlie, but not today. Charlie couldn't think about that, though. He was so miserable all he could do was cry. But maybe Boomy could help him.

"Boomy, Boomy," he called in choked sobs. "Looka Shvartzie. He won't go with me no more and he won't listena me." He cradled the white ball of fluff tighter and rocked back and forth.

Boomy stopped and turned around. He didn't know how long he had been walking, or why, or where. Chotchke Charlie was crying and telling Boomy something about Shvartzie, the black cat who had been his steady companion for more than three years. At night Charlie slept with Shvartzie cuddled in his arms near the furnace of the apartment building on Sutter Avenue where he camped out and stored his collection. During the day Shvartzie hung around the street corners with Charlie, rubbing against his legs and purring.

Boomy walked back down the block and sat down on the curb next to Chotchke Charlie. "Whatsa matter, Charlie? I can't understand you. Stop cryin' and talk to me."

Charlie tried very hard to stop crying. He sniffled in staggered little bursts and lifted the limp white cat toward Boomy. "Make Shvartzie listena me. Please, Boomy."

Boomy wanted to cry himself. "That's not Shvartzie, Charlie."

"Uh-huh. 'At's so Shvartzie, Boomy, 'at's so."

"Shvartzie's black, Charlie. This cat is white."

Charlie shook his head violently. "It's Shvartzie! It's Shvartzie, Boomy! Butchie helps me make him white."

"Whaddya mean? How did you make Shvartzie white?"

"I paint Shvartzie, Boomy." Charlie started to cry again. The words spilled out between sobs. "Butchie give . . . me a whole bucket . . . white paint an' a . . . an' a brush."

"But why, Charlie?" Boomy yelled angrily, which only made Charlie cry harder. "Why did you paint Shvartzie?"

"Butchie . . . Butchie tol' me black cats aren't happy . . .'cause nobody likes black cats." Charlie was wailing now, and Boomy was sorry for yelling. "Everybody run away from black cats 'cause . . .'cause it's bad luck, that's what black cats is."

"Why do you listen to those jerks, Charlie?" Boomy knew it was a useless question; poor Charlie believed whatever he was told.

"Because Butchie tol' me Shvartzie was very sad." Charlie was trying desperately to explain and just as desperately to understand. "Butchie said if Shvartzie's white he's very happy, Boomy."

Butchie Brodsky was a fat little roughneck with a puffy face. He was a nephew of the Silvers brothers, which he seemed to think entitled him to special treatment. Boomy remembered now that it was Butchie who organized the "lemonade" prank. He got up from the curb, smudging dirt across his face as he wiped away his tears and headed to the candy store on the corner of Sackman Street where he knew Butchie Brodsky hung around answering the public telephone and taking messages for tenants in the neighboring apartment buildings who tipped him any-thing from a penny to a nickel. Charlie, clinging tightly to his dead cat, was right on Boomy's heels, waiting to see what his friend was going to do to bring Shvartzie back to life.

A couple of kids were pitching pennies in front of the candy store. Boomy was just about to ask them where Butchie was when he came running out of the store to deliver a message. Boomy didn't say a word. He just squared off and hit Butchie flush in the mush. Two sky-splitting screams startled everyone in a two-block radius—Boomy's a mixture of adrenaline, hate, and anguish, Butchie's a squeal of pain and shock as he covered his nose with his hands.

"Ooooh, you broke my face, you dirty sonuvabitch!"

Boomy flew through the air, wrapping his hands around Butchie's fat little neck, and they tumbled to the ground, flailing away. Penny pitching, punchball, soda drinking, and stoop sitting all came to a halt as everyone raced over and formed a ring around them. Boomy was about to land a punch when a hand grabbed each of them by their collars and hoisted them to their feet so that Boomy's arm whooshed harmlessly at the air. He looked up at the good Samaritan who had appointed himself referee.

Joey Silvers looked down at his nephew. Butchie's nose was spraying blood like a fire hydrant on the Fourth of July, and Joey decided quite impartially that for the good of the family it was time to stop the fight.

"Whaddya you two think you're doin'? Go on, shake hands before I kick both of your asses!"

Chotchke Charlie pushed through the crowd and held the lifeless carcass up for Joey to see. "Looka what Butchie dida my Shvartzie."

"G'wan, get outta here, you fucken little imbecile!" As both of his hands were occupied, Joey kicked out with his foot and spat at Charlie.

Boomy was still in a frenzy, lunging at Butchie and twisting in Joey's grasp, when a horn sounded from outside the ring of cheering specta-tors.

"Hey, Joey," a gravelly voice called out, "let the little fuckers alone and get over here."

Joey turned and looked at the Packard sedan. When he saw Meyer Shapiro's head poking out the driver's window he dropped Boomy and

Butchie, who immediately tore into each other, yelping and snarling and winging away. Butchie was better at yelping; Boomy was better at everything else.

Joey obediently trotted over to Meyer's car and got in. Nobody watched them drive off, and nobody else broke up the fight. Boomy raged and cursed at the fates, and Butchie Brodsky became one of those persons for whom all the king's horses and all the king's men could do very little. It might not have been the memorial that Sheila would have chosen, but it was what Boomy did best.

Willie chalked his cue stick and leaned over the table, not concentrating at all on the lay of balls on the green felt. He was thinking about what he was going to say to Kid Twist. As he drew back on the cue stick Fat Yerna waddled over, gnawing on a garlicky salami sandwich.

"Your kid brother just beat the livin' shit outta Joey Silvers' sister's kid. I mean, he gives him a fucken beating, Willie."

"Every time I turn around that little pisspot is gettin' in a fight with someone. I think he's had it out with every pushcart peddler on Blake Avenue by now."

Fat Yerna takes a big bite and swallows without chewing. "Well, this time it ain't over no pushcart. From what I hear it's about some Mongolian's cat."

"Who gives a shit?" Willie snaps as he thrusts the stick into the cue ball, caroming it off the cushion into the six ball, which is supposed to fall in the far right corner pocket but doesn't. "The kid takes care of himself pretty good."

"I'll tell you who'll give a shit." Fat Yerna expels the words with a big belch that makes Willie's nose curl. "Joey's sister'll give two shits when she hears Joey was right there and doesn't stop it. Well, actually the putz does stop it, but then Meyer Shapiro comes by and tootles his honker at him and the little ass kisser don't give a shit about his nephew no more. He turns his back on him, knowing the kid's gonna get all chewed up, and runs off with Meyer, that fucken brown-nosing prick."

Willie puts his stick down and turns to Yerna, "You saw this yourself?"

"What do I look like, a fucken race horse? I don't go over to Sackman Street unless I'm in a car."

"Well then," Willie growls, "how do you know it happened that way?"

"Fuck you, Willie! How do I know it happened that way! I didn't see Tunney beat Dempsey neither, but I fucken well know it happened." Fat Yerna turns his back to Willie. "I'm gonna go get a hot dog."

It was six-thirty when the phone rang in Midnight Rose's candy store on Saratoga Avenue.

"It's for you, Abie."

Reles put down the *Daily News* he was reading for about the tenth time. "Who is it?"

"Big Gangy."

Reles pointed to the door. Rose walked over and locked it.

"I been thinkin' it over, Abie. It ain't for me. I appreciate you—"

"You're wastin' my time, Willie. All you do is ask a million friggin' questions—you wanna know this, you wanna know that—but you're full of shit! You're strictly a no-action guy, Willie."

"Hey, you came to me, I didn't come to you. You ask me if I want in. It is a question which means I can say yes, I can say no. The truth is, I got nothin' against Meyer. I got no score to settle. I don't like the guy, but I got nothin' personal against him. Anyhow, goin' after someone with a rod . . . it's not my shtik, Abie."

"Willie, you're a fucken pussy. Just make sure you keep your trap shut. And I think maybe you should stay outta my way for a while. I'm not feeling too good about you right now." Abe Reles slammed down the phone.

Willie stared at the buzzing receiver in his hand, then placed it slowly back on the hook. It was sort of like a rattlesnake telling you to stay away from it. He smiled.

George DeFeo decided to go straight sometime around the beginning of 1928, give or take a month. Actually, he didn't decide it—his wife did—but he agreed to it, and he meant it. He felt it would be nice if his kid had a father who was like other kids' fathers, someone who left the house early every morning to catch a trolley car or train that took him to a place where he would punch a time clock and load crates or operate a machine until a whistle blew at noon, when he would have a half hour to open a lunch box, eat the sandwich in it, unscrew a thermos and swallow some coffee, then go back to the crates or the machine, work until dark, punch the time clock again, and go home with a newspaper tucked under his arm. Naturally, when he gets home the kid is sound asleep and the old lady is too worn out to talk to him, but being a good woman she has left a by-now cold plate of stew or franks and beans on the table that does not look any more appealing than she does, so he flops down on the battered living room couch and falls asleep there until all this is repeated the next morning. And every Friday he comes home with a small envelope that has his week's pay, which he drops on the kitchen table, and then his wife puts the bills on the same table, and presto, the money is gone. It is called the good life, and George appreciates it.

However, he does not appreciate it for too long because it does not last for too long. Comes the Big Crash on Wall Street and the Great Depression, and the good life becomes a distant memory. At first George reads the newspaper he brings home every evening and feels that he is one lucky stiff. Here are all these big businessmen and society hotshots taking swan dives from windows while he continues going to work each day and punching his time clock. Whenever he reads about another bank failing, George DeFeo congratulates himself on being a guy sharp enough not to keep any money in a bank or make any investments other than an occasional deuce on a nag. The guy who owns his factory should only have such good common sense. He does not do a Steve Brodie, but pretty soon he is forced to close down, and George DeFeo, if he so desires, can now sleep later in the morning.

It's not that George doesn't have credentials and good references for any other line of work. It happens that he is a very handy guy with a rod and knows how to do what he's told with no griping and no dumb questions. He is highly regarded in his previous profession, but he's determined to stay on the straight and narrow.

When George goes hunting for work, loneliness is not his problem. Whenever he applies for a job, he is shoulder to shoulder with an army of other guys lined up at a door that closes before he ever reaches it.

After a while he starts working without being asked to work. He gets a broom and sweeps the street in front of the fruit store or the butcher shop. Then he goes inside and sweeps. He hauls crates of milk bottles from the curb and lugs them inside the grocery store and puts the bottles in the dairy cases. He figures if they can't pay him maybe they'll give him some food for his family. Once in a while they do.

Now and again Abe Reles comes by to catch George in his role as a hardworking family man. He and George go back a ways. He watches for a few minutes, then slips George a fin without saying a word.

One bright and sunny, or possibly dark and dreary day, George DeFeo decides that his old lady isn't encouraging him, she's nagging him, that his son, his little bundle of joy, is a burden on his back too heavy to bear, and that the good life is a fool's paradise. Abe Reles's investment is definitely riding a bullish market.

Buggsy's nose crinkled at the odor of raw sewage. The south side of Linden Boulevard was one big swampy cesspool, and Buggsy was already sorry he'd chosen to wear his new Florsheim wingtips. Then he figured that after tonight he could buy himself a closetful of new shoes.

He was crouched behind a small delivery truck in the yard of the Shapiros' brewery. His entire body was tingling with anticipation. To Buggsy, this was what life was all about—dealing out death. He looked over at Abie, who was kneeling behind a large wooden barrel a few yards to his left. He would go to hell and back for Abie; nobody ever had a better friend. George DeFeo was duckwalking over to Buggsy from their car. When Abie told him he'd decided to drop Big Gangy and use George instead, Buggsy was quick to agree. He felt comfortable with George.

They were waiting for the moon to disappear behind the thick cloud bank that was floating slowly toward it. Everything was just like Joey Silvers said. The three Shapiro brothers were inside by themselves, checking their inventory, and the place was quieter than a cemetery, which it soon was going to be. The lights and traffic from Linden Boulevard were completely cut off by the ten-foot-high corrugated tin fence the Shapiros had put up to keep prying eyes away.

Buggsy felt something brush against his leg. He looked down and saw a swamp rat the size of an alley cat. It sent shivers running from the soles of his feet right up through his scalp. "Hey, Abe," he called, cupping his hands around his mouth to muffle his voice, "let's get the fucken show on the road already, huh?"

Reles frowned. The moon had not yet tucked itself in, but he gave the signal with a wave of his hand. The three of them, stooping low, scuttled toward Meyer's Packard, which was parked next to two large Dumpsters about ten yards from the brewery door. George was supposed to pop the hood and disconnect the distributor while Abe and Buggsy punctured the tires with ice picks so the Shapiros would have no chance to get away. As George raised himself to a half crouch and reached for the hood latch, he thought about what he'd say to his wife when he walked into their apartment carrying an armful of groceries and a stuffed teddy bear for the kid. No explanation was necessary.

There was the grating sound of a Dumpster sliding on rusted wheels, and then a sharp, cracking pop and a flash of light. George DeFeo was thinking about his little boy reaching out for his teddy bear with a huge grin lighting up his face when the bullet tore through his forehead and all thoughts ceased. He fell like a sack of cement, toppling over Buggsy Goldstein, who was leaning on one knee over the front left tire with an ice pick in his hand.

"Holy shit!" he yowled.

As the Dumpster rolled bumpily toward the building, Meyer, Irving, and Willie Shapiro stood silhouetted by the sliver of moon, pistols blazing. "Motherfucken punks! Surprise! You're dead!"

Abie threw his ice pick at Meyer, then reached under his jacket for the gun that was holstered under his armpit. He let loose a scream so primal that Willie Shapiro looked at his two brothers, turned around, and retreated to the brewery. As Reles charged straight for Meyer, his gun spitting tongues of fire in front of him, a hot pain seared his gut, stopping him in his tracks. For a second his eyes blurred. Luckily, Meyer was reloading and Irving's hands were shaking too much to get off a clean shot.

Buggsy was at Abie's side. His gun barked, but he had no idea where he was firing. He just wanted to hold off the Shapiros and get Abie and himself out of there alive. Grabbing Reles around the waist and hooking his arm over his own shoulder, he turned and staggered toward the car with the near deadweight of his buddy. Owing to a combination of bad shooting and good luck, they made it.

Buggsy propped Abe in the passenger seat and sped off down Linden Boulevard with the Shapiros firing wildly after them. Abe was suddenly rocked wide awake by a scream. "Oh, shit! My nose! I'm bleeding blood! I am bleeding fucken blood." Buggsy had taken a slug that managed to miss all of him except for his right nostril.

Dr. Alter Helzeiger bent over Abe Reles's belly and extracted a bullet with a tweezer. He cleaned the wound, sewed Abie up with a couple of stitches, and covered the area with a nice clean bandage.

A few days later he came back to look at the wound. Abie was sitting shirtless at the kitchen table, slurping at a bowl of chicken soup and reading the newspaper. He grunted but didn't move when the doctor set down his black satchel and went about removing the bandage, cleaning the area with peroxide, and checking the stitches. After putting on a fresh bandage, with Abie still not saying a word, he took out a pad, scribbled his bill on the top sheet, and left it in the center of the table.

He was putting on his topcoat in the small foyer when he heard a scream that made him drop his satchel and rush back to the kitchen. Abie hadn't moved a muscle. He was still sitting at the table reading the newspaper. His mother was leaning against the icebox, her right hand clutching her heart, her left waving Dr. Helzeiger's bill back and forth.

"Oy! A heart attack you're going to have to add on this bill because that's what it's giving me. How could a human being put such a burden on a young boy?" She went over and patted Abie on the head. "He hasn't been through enough? Now he has to worry about how he's going to pay off such an amount?"

Dr. Helzeiger stood there looking at her for a long moment. There wasn't a bill he'd ever given her that she hadn't haggled over, but this was real chutzpah. Then again, he thought, for such a performance maybe she should charge him.

"A burden? You call twenty dollars a burden when I drag myself out of bed after midnight on an emergency and I come back a second time to check the wound and I'm coming a third time to remove the stitches?"

"You were so busy at midnight that my Abie cost you business?" Mrs. Reles countered. "That hour of night whatever we put in your pocket is like a gift. Don't be such a chozzer." She rummaged through her house-coat and placed a wrinkled ten-dollar bill in his coat pocket. "And send mine best to Mrs. Helzeiger—such a lovely lady."

"If I could, I would. She's dead four years now."

Dr. Helzeiger walked down the two and a half flights of stairs to the ground floor, wondering if God would ever forgive him for bringing that bum Reles into the world.

It was Saturday night, and Abe Reles was taking Kitty Kirsch to the early show at the Pitkin. Kitty was to Brownsville what an ocean liner was to New York Harbor. An ocean liner could not dock in New York without a whole lot of whistling and excitement. It was the same when Kitty Kirsch walked down the street. She had dark-haired, eye-fetching good looks and a traffic-stopping gait. When a squat, ugly guy who walks like a duck has a beautiful girlfriend, it is generally assumed that he must have personality or a great sense of humor or a big heart, but Abe was zero for three. What he did have was power—that was the turn-on for Kitty. And Abe, who was used to having his way in his brothels with everyone, could not have his way with Kitty. That was the turn-on for Abe.

Abe and Kitty were going to the early show because he was getting together with the boys later in East Flatbush. As usual there was a long line, but lines were not for Abe Reles; he always went straight to the front, and nobody said a word. At the box office window he pulled from his pocket a roll of bills big enough to choke a horse, and everyone who was able to see this was greatly impressed. What they didn't see was that although there were enough bills to choke a horse, there were not enough to buy a horse. The Brooklyn mob never made the big bucks. Abe always carried a big roll of singles and topped it off with two tens.

It was still light out after the show, and Kitty decided to walk home while Abe went off to his meeting. All the shops were open late, and she loved the activity of Pitkin Avenue. It was always aglow with lights. She walked along, window shopping, and didn't realize that the sun had gone down until she came to the big intersection at Stone and Pitkin and happened to look up at the night sky. She had spent the better part of an hour at the bridal shop near Hopkinson and was giddy from trying on gowns and letting it be known that she would soon be the bride of Abe Reles, a man known and respected throughout Brownsville. It did not register with Kitty, despite the flustered reactions of the salesgirls, that to be respected was not the same as being liked and admired, and that some people were respected out of fear and loathing. She reveled in being the sweetheart of a big shot like Abe.

She considered taking a cab the rest of the way home, but her parents weren't expecting her for hours, and it was such a beautiful night that she kept walking. She turned on Stone and strolled along happily, stopping to look at an occasional store window.

Two of Happy Maione's boys stood in front of the Silver Rod Drugstore and Soda Fountain on Utica Avenue and Church, leaning up against the doorway as though the building would fall down if they weren't there. What they were there for was to make sure that none of the wrong people decided to drop in for an ice cream cone. Inside, a young lady was picking out a lipstick at the cosmetics counter, and a couple of elderly people sat near the drug counter waiting for prescriptions to be filled.

Things were not going too well at the soda fountain counter, where Abe, Buggsy, Pittsburgh Phil, Happy, and the Dasher were sitting with five untouched cups of coffee in front of them. Happy and Reles were glaring at each other. Reles had convinced Happy that they shouldn't have to settle for handouts when they could have the whole loaf, but now it was Reles who thought they had to bide their time. He knew that every punk in Brownsville was a potential gun in the Shapiros' army. He and his crew needed more manpower before making their move.

All Happy could do was continue to glare. Reles was calling the shots. They would keep fighting the Shapiros from the trenches, as they had been doing since they made the break. They would knock off their cathouses, steal their slot machines, mess up their speakeasies. And they would build up their army until they were sure they could ring down the curtain on Meyer and his brothers. Kid Twist could taste the blood, but he was going to be patient. What happened that night at the brewery was never going to happen again.

The meeting broke up. Happy, Dasher, and their two watchdogs went

75

to the poolroom a few doors away. Abe, Buggsy, and Pittsburgh Phil got into their car and went back to Brownsville. They were in no mood to play games.

Until now, Meyer Shapiro was not too sure that there was a God. What he saw as he crossed Stone Avenue made him a believer.

Meyer loved tuchises and titties. They actually made him salivate. Though he would go after any available tuchis, he was a connoisseur. He knew and appreciated a great tuchis when he saw one. And there, in front of the jewelry store window, was a great tuchis. He slowed the Packard down to get a good look at the shapely, rounded behind pressed so tantalizingly against the tight-fitting beige wool dress that tapered at the knees, then billowed to the midcalf. He was edging the car closer when he hit the brake so hard he almost vaulted through the windshield. It was her! It was that no-good bastard Abe Reles's girl. He had seen them together a few times and could never understand how a living wart like Reles had such a beautiful girl. Could you believe such mazel!

Meyer closed his eyes hard to make sure he wasn't dreaming. His pulse was racing. He looked around. The street was deserted. The elevated train rumbled overhead, and some sparks drifted down to the street. Meyer Shapiro thought that this might very well be the high point of his life—fucking two people at the same time, Abe Reles and his girl. He surprised himself with the catlike agility of his movements as he slipped from his car and slid stealthily behind Kitty, who was studying a sparkling ring in the window.

She jumped as his arm encircled her waist. She squealed with mistaken delight, as she was certain it could only be her Abe. Meyer lifted her off the ground and roared "Gotcha!" She turned her head, and her face froze into a mask of shock and fear. A scream was rising inside her, but it never made its way out of her mouth because Meyer clamped his hand over it. She kicked, she squirmed, she swung her fists in panic, but Meyer was unstoppable as he dragged her to the Packard.

He had left the car running, with the driver's-side door open. Flinging Kitty facedown across the front seat with her head toward the passenger side, he sat down heavily on her calves to keep her pinned in place. He stepped on the clutch, threw the shift stick into first, and pulled away from the curb with the screech of rubber drowning out Kitty's cries. He slowed down as he turned off Livonia Avenue and headed toward Linden Boulevard.

"I'm Abe Reles's girl! He'll kill you if you don't let me go!" Kitty screamed, her fingers desperately reaching for the door handle.

"Ooh! Ooh! I'm scared shitless, Mameleh!" Meyer sneered as he clapped his hand on her jutting behind and squeezed with all his might.

"Get your dirty hands off me, you lousy bum!" She twisted violently, and she felt his hand release her behind and smash into her left cheek. The force of the blow stunned her into a motionless silence, but then she lashed out blindly and felt a satisfying splat as her blow landed somewhere upon Meyer's jowly face. She cowered, waiting for retaliation, but Meyer grinned. Such excitement he could never get with Cock-eyed Jenny.

He drove a few more blocks until he saw what he was looking for. On the south side of Linden, Bristol Street was a huge, deserted dumping ground. There were no houses, no people, no lights. Kitty was frantic. How could this be happening to her? No one in his right mind would dare mess with Abe Reles's girl. Her own mind braked, and she sucked in a large gulp of air: she was not dealing with someone in his right mind.

Abe Reles slouched in the passenger seat of his car. He was in an ugly mood after the meeting at Silver Rods because he didn't want anyone to think he was afraid of the Shapiros. Pittsburgh Phil was stretched out on the backseat catching a catnap, and Buggsy was driving.

Buggsy stopped for a red light at Bristol Street. They didn't see the black Packard parked halfway down the street. There was no reason to look in that direction.

The small yellow canary was chirping and flapping its wings, never moving from the perch in its cage. Usually the cage stood in the corner near Kitty's bedroom window, but now it hung in a corner of her mind.

Somewhere she had heard that if you focused all your attention on a single object you found restful and pleasurable, you could actually suspend yourself somewhere outside of your body and feel no pain.

"You fucken little bitch! You're bleedin' all over my seat!"

Kitty floated with the canary, sang with it, *was* it, because there was nothing else, nothing but this delicately beautiful fluttering yellow bird.

Kitty's eyes opened as Meyer was buttoning his pants. Her canary was gone. She screamed, and he hit her across the mouth with all his might. She thought this was surely going to be her last moment of life, and she didn't care.

Sneering, Meyer shoved open the car door on her side and pointed his finger at her. "Go on, get out! Go home and tell your fucken punk of a boyfriend what I did. Tell him how it felt getting it from a real man. And you tell him that the fucking I gave you is nothing compared to the fucking I'm going to give him. Tell him this is just the beginning, and the end is right around the corner."

Little Sollie Hoffman did all the painting and plastering in Gruber's buildings. He was cheap, he was quick—and he was Gruber's sister's brother-in-law. Gruber paid him to paint the "empties," apartments that had to be spruced up when tenants moved out. If other tenants in the building wanted their apartments painted, Little Sollie would do that too, but for this the tenant had to pay. Sollie kicked back half to Gruber, who never lifted a paintbrush in his life but made almost as much from painting as Little Sollie did.

So when Sollie rings the super's bell and is told there's a big plastering and paint job on the second floor but not to charge the tenant—Gruber will pay—he finds this most unusual, although not as unusual as what he finds in the apartment. Most families do not have their own personal demolition ball, but Sollie can't think of anything else that could do so much damage. He figures with all the plastering it will be a three-day job. It takes five, because that night as he leaves the building he looks at the name on the bell plate—Reles—and the next day he is shaking so much he can't smooth out the plaster.

Sollie never learns what happened. None of the neighbors know. All anyone knows is that one night there was screaming and shouting and banging and breaking like they never heard before. Little Sollie hears from the super who says he hears from Abie's mother that it was a terrible case of piles so painful it almost drove her boy crazy.

Abe Reles is not exactly unacquainted with pain. True, he is much more intimate with the doling out of pain than the receiving, but when a guy catches a bullet in the gut with not much more than a grunt, you gotta give him some credit. When he pushes open the door to his apartment and sees Kitty lying on the couch in the small living room, surrounded by his parents, her parents, and his brother and sister, what he walks into is a far different kind of pain than he has ever known before. Kitty's pain is a terrible physical and emotional pain, but the pain Abe Reles is suffering is the pain of a wounded ego. He comforts her, but his eyes are vacant.

Kitty's heartbroken parents take her home, escorted by the Reles family, leaving Abe to brood alone in the darkened apartment. Everything that makes up Abe Reles, every fiber of his being, is now being driven by demons of rage, hatred, and frustration, all concentrated on one purpose—the destruction of Meyer Shapiro. He cannot contain his consuming fury, but since there is no Meyer Shapiro present, he strikes at anything and everything in reach. Screaming and cursing, he pounds the walls and the furniture until his knuckles are cut to the bone, his forehead is gashed at the scalp line, and his shoes are covered with plaster.

Little Sollie the painter and some secondhand stores mend the Reles apartment. Tender loving care eventually mends Kitty Kirsch. Nothing will mend Abe Reles but the death of Meyer Shapiro.

4

Shorty was more than just a little nervous. What the hell did he know about watermelons anyhow? He should have told Boomy to go shove it when his good buddy offered to make him a full partner for a week, but Boomy was always selling him a bill of goods he couldn't say no to until it was too late.

So there he was with this guy squeezing this watermelon the size of a zeppelin, holding it up to the sun like he was trying to look inside it. "How do you know it ain't overripe?" the guy said.

That was a very good question, to which Shorty did not know the answer. "My partner, he's the expert—see, I'm like the bookkeeper—he told me so, definitely."

The guy hesitated for a couple of seconds. "Well, how much?"

"Thirty-five cents." That was the thing Shorty was best at, memorizing the prices of everything, which was why Boomy said he was a natural for this business. "Special for you," he added, remembering the little touch Boomy taught him.

"You gotta be kiddin' me. I can buy one this size for twenty cents from the shvartzer's truck on Linden."

"But how do you know that one won't be overripe? My partner gives a guarantee." Shorty was very proud of himself. No wonder Boomy wanted him as a partner.

The guy smiled and raised the watermelon again. "All right, kid. It better be good, though."

It was. It absolutely was, as they found out immediately. There was a *bang-bang!* and something slammed into the watermelon, knocking it out of the guy's hamlike hands. It spun to the ground and split wide open. The pulpy red meat was firm and fresh, as good a watermelon as anyone would want to have.

"Holy shit!" the guy roared, ducking under the pushcart, a spot already taken by Shorty and two old women in babushkas who had moved so fast you'd think arthritis and rheumatism could be cured by loud, sudden noises.

A block away, waddling toward them with a pistol, was Abe Reles. "Come on, you fat sonuvabitch! You're dead fucken meat, Shapiro!"

Meyer's eyes were about the size of the tomatoes sitting on the top shelf of the pushcart as he looked around wildly for a place to hide. Fruits and vegetables were spilling all along Blake Avenue as a hysterical throng of shoppers dropped their bags and raced for cover. Meyer screamed and reached inside his waistband for his rod, but when he saw Abe Reles coming toward him full tilt, gun barking and spitting slugs, he turned and ran for his life.

Reles stopped, pulled out a fresh pistol, and fired off six rounds. He winged two perfect strangers, and Meyer Shapiro wound up purchasing a rubber tube to sit on because he caught a slug in the ass just as he rounded the corner. Three for six. On the boardwalk at Coney Island Abie would have won a Kewpie doll.

Kid Twist came to a panting halt. With the crowd of people on the street he was not going to catch up with Shapiro, but he saw him give a jump and grab his backside. Smiling, he blew the smoke from the barrel of his pistol and returned it to the holster under his jacket. He went over to the two people sitting on the curb dabbing at their flesh wounds and gave both of them a couple of bucks. Then he turned and walked back up the street, the crowds of shoppers parting silently to make way for the heir apparent to the Brownsville mob.

Shorty, meanwhile, couldn't believe he hadn't recognized Meyer Shapiro, and he couldn't believe his bad luck. First day as a partner in the business and he screws up a sure sale. Boomy was going to be hopping mad.

Abe Reles had the sense that someone was following him. Suddenly, Blake Avenue had become very quiet. He couldn't believe that Meyer Shapiro would have the balls to come after him, but he reached for his pistol as he spun around. He saw nothing but people gaping in disbelief. Then he looked down, and there was this snot-nosed kid in corduroy knickers and a stained white shirt. The kid was holding a soggy brown paper bag in his hand, and his face was as white as a bed sheet.

"What's with you, kid?" Reles growled.

"Look what ya did to my watermelon." Shorty opened the bag to show Reles what was inside.

"So whaddya expect me to do about it?"

"Me? I don't expect nothin', I'm just a junior partner. But my senior partner, I don't know about him. He's pretty tough about things like this."

"Tougher than me?"

Shorty gulped. "Please, mister, I had this watermelon sold for thirty-five cents when you came along and ruined it."

Reles laughed. "Who's gonna pay thirty-five cents for a watermelon ya can get for a quarter on Linden Boulevard?"

"Meyer Shapiro."

Abe Reles reached in his pocket, fished out a quarter and a dime, and dropped the coins into Shorty's palm. You could hear a hundred people sighing all together at that moment.

Rose Davidoff was a woman of her times, a baleboosteh who devoted herself to keeping a good clean home and feeding a large family. Most of her life was spent in the kitchen. But when she heard on the radio and read in the *Jewish Daily Forward* about the money troubles of Yossele Rosenblatt, Rose came out of her kitchen.

Yossele Rosenblatt was the greatest and most revered cantor of his generation. He sang in the great concert halls of the world, he performed the cantorial hymns in *The Jazz Singer*, he made nostalgic recordings evoking shtetl life in the old country. He invested his earnings, hoping for a life of comfort, but the late 1920s was not the best of times to invest, and the King of Cantors found himself deep in debt. Offers came in from theaters across the country, but Yossele Rosenblatt was a man of deep religious conviction, and his calling as an Orthodox cantor took him to a small congregation in the Borough Park section of Brooklyn.

Rosenblatt's pain was not his to suffer alone. It was shared by many because his voice belonged to the people. It was shared by Rose Davidoff.

"A disgrace!" she shouted, waving the *Forward* in Max's face as the rich sounds of Yossele Rosenblatt's voice rolled through the apartment from Boomy's Victrola in the bedroom. "Such a man should have to worry about money?" She shoved a few coins into the pushke, making sure they clinked loudly to drive home her point.

"Charity begins at home," Max reminded her, shoving a forkful of gefilte fish into his mouth. "First you got a family to think about."

Another forkful of fish he did not get. He was there and the fork was there but the fish was gone, on its way back to the kitchen with his wife. To Rose Davidoff, Yossele Rosenblatt *was* family.

When Willie walked through the front door he got more than a Shabbes meal.

"A gontzeh k'nocker like you, from everybody you get money for any reason at all, but for such a shayner Yid you don't lift even a finger, Mr. Big Shot!"

Willie couldn't believe his mother was so worked up about something that had nothing to do with taking care of the house, but he didn't laugh at her. Even with the Depression hanging heavily over everyone, there was so much concern for Rosenblatt in the Jewish community that it was becoming contagious.

At the time, Louis "Lepke" Buchalter was consolidating his control of the New York mob. The core of his operations was the garment center and the unions he had established to dominate this multimillion-dollar industry. Brownsville had its own counterpart—actually, a forerunner of the Manhattan industry—and Big Gangy controlled a good slice of the Brownsville operation. Seeing the distress over Rosenblatt in the garment center, Lepke sensed the opportunity for a major public relations coup, but he decided that he was too prominent a person to meet with the cantor personally, so he had a talk with Willie Davidoff, who was still a guy most people didn't know without a scorecard.

Willie was on solid ground as long as he was making the rounds of his dues-paying shops and factories and allowing them the privilege of giving an additional contribution to the "Rosenblatt Fund." But when it came time to turn the funds over, Willie was at sea, as this was not an activity known to him. He wanted company, someone who could speak the cantor's language. He tried to think of a friend. His mind drew a blank. When he asked Boomy if he'd like to come along and meet Yossele Rosenblatt, the kid jumped at the chance.

Boomy liked the way the cantor drank his tea, holding the sugar cube between his front teeth and somehow managing to get the tea to his lips without spilling any. It reminded Boomy of his zayde, only his zayde slurped from a glass, while Cantor Rosenblatt sipped from a cup with his pinky sticking all the way out. When Boomy got home he was definitely going to ask for his tea in a cup.

Also, the cantor had a full beard like his zayde's, except his zayde's was white and bushy, with hairs standing out in all directions, whereas the cantor's was very neat and mostly black, with a few strands of gray. He offered them tea and little cakes, but Boomy and Willie politely declined. Willie was being very, very polite, Boomy noticed.

Willie told the cantor that he was a representative of the Garment Workers Union and was speaking on behalf of the whole community. Squirming in his seat, he said that the union had raised money so the cantor could pay off his debts and continue his work with a clear head.

"There will be no tzedaka for Josef Rosenblatt," the cantor said, a soft smile noticeable through his beard. "If charity is your intention I would be honored if such a tzedaka were made for the children of Palestine. Their burden they were born with. Mine I created, and mine I will live with."

Boomy had never heard anyone refuse money before. As for Willie, this was exactly what he feared. What was he supposed to do, grab the guy by the lapels, shove him against the wall, and yell, "Take this money—or else"?

"It's just that you're very important to all the people and they want to make sure you're able to perform. Look at it that way. It ain't charity. In fact, it's selfish on our part."

"You are obviously a very kind, generous person, Mr. Davidoff," the cantor said, and Boomy was glad he hadn't been eating one of the tea cakes, because he would have choked. "I will not accept such a gift, but I am willing to earn money. If you wish I will perform at your synagogue and other synagogues, my schedule permitting, but only at my usual rates. Strictly business, no charity."

And so it was arranged that Yossele Rosenblatt would perform the evening service on the second day of Rosh Hashanah at the Oheb Shalom Synagogue in Brownsville. Meanwhile, Big Gangy was left with the philanthropic dilemma of what to do with all the money in the Rosenblatt Fund.

Just as they were at the door to the cantor's study, ready to leave, Boomy turned. "You going to do 'Tefillot Yosef'?"

Rosenblatt stopped in his tracks. A question about *The Jazz Singer* would have been no shock, but how did a kleine kind know from 'Tefillot Yosef,' the last original composition the cantor had published? He leaned over so that he could speak with Boomy on more of an eye-to-eye level.

Willie was squirming again, and the cantor suggested that maybe he would like to go for a little walk and get some fresh air. As soon as Willie left, Rosenblatt pointed his finger at Boomy and said, "I don't always guess right—in fact, it's for that reason that your brother came here— but if I had to make a guess, I would guess you are not a yeshiva bucher and you are not in a cantor's choir, so tell me how you know 'Tefillot Yosef.' "

In less time than it took Boomy to watch the cantor sift two cups of tea through the sugar cube between his teeth, Yossele Rosenblatt knew more about Albert Abraham Davidoff—his hopes, his pain, the questions plaguing him—than either his family or his friends. When the little mazik told him how badly he wanted to be a cantor but he didn't want to go to cheder, Rosenblatt explained that a cantor must have a full religious schooling. Boomy'd had it all figured out; he'd just do his singing on the street and all the ladies would throw pennies and nickels—or if he ever learned to sing like Cantor Rosenblatt, maybe even dimes—from their apartment windows. The synagogue's loss would be the street's gain, the cantor thought to himself.

And then Boomy told Yossele Rosenblatt about Sheila Goren. He had never spoken of her to another person. Maybe Shorty had some inkling of his feelings because he was Boomy's closest friend and was with him dropping fruit on Linden Boulevard the last time he ever saw Sheila, and maybe Carlie Packman because he was so smart and perceptive, but Boomy had never so much as mentioned her name in the six months since she'd died. Now his head hung low as he told the cantor about the afternoon at the Pitkin, the gift of friendship and affection that he was never able to give her, and about the strange feeling he had for Sheila that he never had about anyone else: he wanted to take care of her. He looked up and tried to explain to the cantor that he still wanted to do that. He wanted to say kaddish for her; he wanted to perform El Maleh Rachamim, a prayer asking God to grant peace and eternal life to departed souls.

Cantor Rosenblatt put his hand on Boomy's shoulder. "Albert Davidoff, let me tell you something. There are men who live a lifetime but never become a mensh. You, young man, are what—ten, eleven years old? But you are a real mensh. Albert, you can do whatever you want to do if you set your mind on it. Do not let anything stand in your way. You want to say kaddish? God knows at your age you shouldn't have to, but if you must, do it. You want to be a cantor? Forget what I said before, don't let anything stop you. Just do it!"

Willie was very surprised at what he saw when he returned from his walk. There was Boomy, sitting with Yossele Rosenblatt, sipping a cup of tea through a sugar cube.

If Cantor Isaac Tepperman had just paid a little attention to Boomy, and if Shorty's Aunt Sophie hadn't left the cream cheese sitting on the kitchen table all night, everything that happened might not have happened at all.

It was the morning of the second day of Rosh Hashanah, and Boomy was sitting outside his building on New Jersey Avenue wondering how to go about converting to another religion. At this moment he was not enjoying being a Jew. It had taken all the courage he could summon to approach Cantor Tepperman in the shammus's office at the shul the day before yesterday. He had come to plead for a place in the cantor's choir, but before he could say two words Tepperman shooed him off, declaring that he was busy preparing for the holiday services.

Every year during the High Holy Days, the community opened its doors to the boys and young men of the visiting choirs from Williamsburg and Borough Park, and this year it was Cantor Tepperman's ensemble. Boomy had never had any use for these yeshiva buchers in their black suits and white shirts, payess curling from under black felt hats and strands of tzitzit hanging from their waists. Bodies for playing games they didn't need so therefore they didn't have, and their skin was pasty and paper thin, as though sun and wind never visited their world. But now Boomy desperately wanted to join them because he wanted to perform El Maleh Rachamim for Sheila. He had not stopped dwelling on this idea ever since his afternoon with Yossele Rosenblatt.

As he sat there on his stoop Boomy made up his mind. He was not going to convert, and he was not going to let Sheila down. He didn't know what, but he would think of something. He stood up and brushed off the seat of his light brown suit, and that's when he saw Shorty's Uncle Shim hurrying down the street with Mischa Schainheit, the little eight-year-old from the choir who was staying in Shim and Sophie's spare room as an honored guest.

Uncle Shim waved at Boomy and was starting to smile when his mouth sealed shut and his cheeks bulged, fighting to contain the contents of his body. Strange rumblings were heard. Shim sounded like a volcano ready to erupt. Who would believe that his morning bagel with a little shmear of cream cheese could make for such an internal upheaval? After all, it was the same cream cheese Sophie put on her date-nut loaf last night for her midnight snack and left out on the kitchen table like a big petri dish breeding colonies of microscopic clawed demons.

Shim, Shorty's only green uncle, gurgled some words, of which Boomy recognized three—"Take . . . kid . . . shul"—from which he was able to build an understandable thought. Not only didn't Boomy ever realize before that Shorty's Uncle Shim was green, he never realized how fast he was.

Uncle Shim was gone.

But Boomy was not going to ignore his gurgled plea—at least, not entirely.

The night before, Boomy was hanging out in front of Shorty's house with Shorty and Mousy when Mischa came down and sat on the stoop. As long as he sat with his mouth shut he looked pretty much like an eight-year-old is expected to look. Only his clothes and payess made him look different. He had a small, upturned nose, very distinctive in this neighborhood, wide brown eyes that seemed to always be searching for something, and his skin, although pale, was set off by a flock of light freckles high upon his cheeks. His hair hung in long, dark ringlets, interrupted by the stick-straight payess, dangling well below his jawline.

Mischa was not troubled by shyness. No matter what the topic, he was there with an unasked-for opinion, an embellishment or a correction. Only when they tired of talk and started playing box ball, then kick-the-can, did Mischa sit with eyes open and mouth shut.

Boomy's plan was already hatched; Cantor Tepperman's choir would be missing their lead soprano today.

They were just about to cross Pennsylvania Avenue when Boomy said, "Hey, kid, I bet I know what you'd like."

"You don't have to bet. I'll tell you. I'd like to learn how to play that game Johnny-on-the-pony that you were playing last night." Horns ooga-oogaed as Mischa stepped down from the curb against the light. Boomy grabbed him by his collar and pulled him back roughly, more out of annoyance for his messing up his game plan than to save his life.

"Nah, you can't play that with only two people. What you'd really like is some candy, though, huh?"

Suddenly, Mischa was eight years old. "Yeah! I like candy. How did you know?" Candy was an absolute taboo in Mischa's house. His parents spoke of it just as they would of poison.

"Hey, kid, what'ya think, I was never eight?" Boomy swaggered. "I been there." Boomy couldn't help thinking about that kid's poem Aunt Yetta liked to read to him: " 'Come into my parlor,' said the Spider to the Fly." He used to think the spider was inviting the fly to his poolroom, because the only kind of parlor he ever heard of was a billiard parlor.

"So, where's the candy?" Mischa asked, tugging at Boomy's sleeve.

"Kid, today's your lucky day," Boomy said as he spun around and started walking quickly in the opposite direction, dragging Mischa along.

For a moment, Boomy began having some second thoughts about what he was doing. He knew it was wrong, but then, when he thought of why he was doing it, he felt better.

Chotchke Charlie was sitting on the sidewalk in front of Max Davidoff's candy store winding some new rubber bands onto his rubber band ball when Boomy arrived there with Mischa. "Hi, Boomy, you got a new friend?"

Boomy was not unprepared for the job at hand. He was unlocking the door with the key he had taken from his father's night table drawer. "He's a little kid I'm helping out, Charlie. His name is Mischa."

"Hey," Mischa squealed, "Now we can play Johnny-on-the-pony."

Boomy pushed the heavy door open. "T'ree still ain't enough. Anyhow, Charlie don't know how to play."

"I do so, Boomy! I do so!" Charlie was bouncing up and down excitedly, shaking both his hands like a seal at feeding time. "I always watching youse guys, so I know good."

"Let's make a deal, Mischie." Boomy thought that sounded very friendly and sociable.

"If you want me to pay you for the candy," Mischa was shaking his head, "I don't have any money."

"Hey, what do ya take me for?" Boomy tried to sound wounded.

"You don' take Boomy!" Charlie chimed in.

He walked Mischa over to the large four-shelved candy showcase and the kid's eyes opened wide and, unconsciously, his tongue began licking his lips. "You can eat as much as you want from the penny shelves," Boomy said, pointing at the three lower shelves, "but you don't touch the nickel shelf," he emphasized by jabbing at the top shelf, "because I get killed if you do. An' take my word for it, they don't even taste so good."

"What about Johnny-on-the-pony?"

"Whatever you want, kid, but you gotta do something for me in return."

Staring hungrily at the showcase, little Mischa was ready to trade his soul. "You wanna learn Johnny-on-the-pony and you wanna eat all the candy you can and I want to sing with Tepperman's choir," Boomy started. The kid didn't answer, still hypnotized by the candy selection.

"We got a deal?" Boomy held out his hand. "Let's shake on it an' switch clothes."

"How come we have to switch clothes?"

"You can't play Johnny-on-the-pony in your good clothes when you're first learnin'. I'm good at it so I won't mess 'em up." Then, softly, "Anyhow, I'm gonna need them to sing with the choir." Mischa's eyes narrowed as he started mulling over what he just heard.

"I have to sing with the choir, too," Mischa announced.

"Okay with me. Forget the candy," Boomy was playing his big bluff now, but he knew it didn't matter. One way or the other, Mischa was staying at the candy store.

Mischa gave a long stare at the candy, then sighed. "You sure it will be okay? I don't want to get in trouble."

"Kid, everybody in the shul knows me and loves the way I sing."

Chotchke Charlie saw Boomy wearing the kid's clothes and the kid in Boomy's. He wasn't sure of what was happening so he came to his own conclusion. "There's gonna be a circus, huh, Boomy? I never seen a real circus before."

Giving a tug at both Charlie and Mischa, who was lost somewhere in Boomy's clothes, Boomy led them to the street. "Okay, Charlie, you lean up against the wall an' Mischa, you bend over an' lean your head against his back, around waist high. I'll show you how you jump on."

Charlie, beaming with delight at the prospect of playing a game, did as he was instructed, with Boomy helping him get in the right position. Mischa took a look at where he was to place his head and curled up his nose. "I'm not putting my face in his tuchis."

"I thought you wanted to learn to play Johnny-on-the-pony?" Boomy asked. "If you wanna play, that's part of the game."

"You take my part and I'll do the jumping."

"How come he don' like my tookis, Boomy?" Charlie's feelings were wounded.

It didn't really matter because the game lesson lasted exactly one jump. Mischa missed landing on Boomy's back completely and it was some sort of poetic justice that his tuchis wound up becoming the injured party.

Back in the candy store, Boomy slid back the rear glass door to the candy showcase. "Okay, kid, it's a deal, right? You enjoy the candy. I'm gonna sing 'El Maleh Rachamim.' It's important to me." Boomy bit down nervously on his lip. He was thinking that even though he was doing something he felt he had to do, he wasn't sure he was doing it the right way. "I'll come back for you soon as I'm finished. A deal?" Boomy held out his hand. Mischa shook it. He didn't think it was important to tell Boomy that they didn't sing the Rachamim on Rosh Hashanah.

Boomy instructed Charlie to stand guard outside the candy store to make sure Mischa didn't get out until he returned. Boomy, not taking any chances, locked the kid in. Just before he closed the door, he turned back and said to Mischa somewhat reluctantly, "Okay, one candy from the nickel shelf. Just one."

Chotchke Charlie's face was pressed up against the glass panel of the door. He didn't think Boomy was going to like this. The kid was at the drawer where Boomy's father kept the money. Charlie banged on the door but couldn't do anything because it was locked.

Realizing that he might get into a lot of trouble—first, for eating candy, but mostly for missing services at the shul, although he made a deal—Mischa knew that eight-year-old kids were not bound by legal contracts.

Bill Schroeder was a good cop. He didn't panic and he didn't jump to conclusions. When Officer D'Onofrio came charging in, ready to unholster his .38, Schroeder told him to simmer down and called the desk sergeant to get the report firsthand.

"Eight-year-old kid named Mischa Schainheit was forcibly abducted by a juvenile friend of the family he was staying with as a houseguest," said the desk sergeant in a bored monotone. "He knows the abductor as Boomy, the nickname for one Albert Davidoff, who locked him in the Davidoff candy store on Blake Avenue. The abductee was able to use a telephone in the store and call his parents in Williamsburg. The parents want us to know that they're willing to pay any ransom and don't want us to take any chances with the child's safety."

"Was a ransom demand made?" Schroeder asked.

"Not that I heard."

Schroeder slammed the phone down. "Bullshit!" was all he said as he grabbed his cap and headed for the door with D'Onofrio on his heels.

When the "buh-buh-buh" emerges from somewhere in the middle of the choir, Garfinkel the tailor leans forward to see from where and from whom such a sound is coming. The voice is untrained but passionate, and the rest of the congregants are peering too, looking for the singer who doesn't know the words to his song. Rabbi Borodkin has a restraining hand on Cantor Tepperman, who is beside himself. In the balcony, Boomy's Aunt Yetta is vigorously fanning Rose Davidoff. Downstairs in the main temple, recognition dawns on Garfinkel, who is sitting next to Max Davidoff.

"Some boychik! A real little chazzen you got there, Davidoff," Garfinkel whispers, shaking his head in admiration. "A complete surprise to me, I'm telling you, a complete surprise."

The tailor doesn't hear Max's mumbled response. "To me too, Garfinkel, to me too." Neither man notices the two policemen standing at the back of the shul, between them a little boy wearing long payess and a light brown suit much too large for him.

Rabbi Borodkin's office had never been so crowded. Half the congregation was there, watching their rabbi and Cantor Tepperman circle the desk like two wrestlers waiting for an opening to pounce. They seemed to be having a slight difference of opinion. The cantor, if he had a rope, would call for a lynching. The rabbi, on the other hand, was not going to let anyone harm a hair on the head of one of his cheder students, even if it was the one with the highest absentee record in the history of the school. Max and Rose Davidoff were wringing their hands and shaking their heads. A sniffling Mischa kept pointing his finger at Boomy, who was standing with his hands clasped behind his back, staring at the ground.

"Okay, you little punk, I'm gonna book you!" barked Officer D'Onofrio.

"Jail's too good for him!" yelled Cantor Tepperman.

Rabbi Borodkin, who felt that a cantor was maybe a notch above a court jester anyhow, could take no more. "You want to do everyone a favor, Tepperman, mostly yourself? Shut your mouth already. You're lucky God gave you a little bit of a voice. If not for that, you'd be lucky to be a shammus in a pickle factory! That's what you'd be lucky to be."

"Quiet, everyone!" Sergeant Schroeder bellowed. "I'm giving the orders here."

D'Onofrio couldn't contain himself. "He's a rotten little gangster, just like his two punk brothers!"

Max Davidoff lunged at him, and it took three men in prayer shawls to hold him back.

Schroeder glared at his mad-dog partner. "You're in a house of worship and this is a ten-year-old kid."

Tepperman glowered. "A trombenik is a trombenik, ten or a hundred and ten!"

With that, Boomy flew into a roaring rage, and Schroeder had to squash the kid in a bear hug to keep him from going for the cantor. He winced as he caught a flying heel on his anklebone.

"Lemme go! Lemme go!" Boomy hollered, kicking and thrashing. He was prepared to face the music for disrupting the Rosh Hashanah service, and nothing could make him feel worse than he already did because he hadn't been able to perform El Maleh Rachamim for Sheila, but nobody was going to make up lies about him and get away with it, especially not on account of that little piss-head Mischa.

"Settle down, now!" Schroeder said to the thrashing Boomy, turning him over to Max and the three prayer-shawled men while D'Onofrio grumbled under his breath about kid-glove treatment for these Brownsville punks. Testing out his bruised ankle, Schroeder walked over to the sniveling Mischa and knelt down to speak to him.

"Okay, sonny, can you tell me what happened?"

"Sure I can. My name is Mischa Schainheit. I'm eight years old. I'll be nine on February nineteenth, 1931—"

"That's fine, but can you just tell us what happened today?"

Mischa pointed at Boomy and started crying fat juicy tears. "He dragged me and locked me up in a store and said he would kill me if my parents didn't give him a lot of money. . . ."

D'Onofrio's face darkened, but before he could say a word Boomy screamed, "You no-good friggin' little liar. You're lying in a shul, you'll burn in hell!"

Just then a rubber-band ball bounced across the floor. A frightened Chotchke Charlie tiptoed in after it and ran to Boomy. "I sorry, Boomy. They let him out even when I tell them he can't come out."

"Hey," said D'Onofrio, "that's the Mongo that was trying to keep us outta the store. He's in on it!"

Schroeder pointed a warning finger at him and turned back to Mischa. "Did Boomy call your parents and ask for money?"

"No. He made me call them," Mischa sniffled.

"And how come he's wearing your clothes and you're wearing his?"

First there was a giggle, then a loud hoarse guffaw. Chotchke Charlie recalled a very funny incident. " 'Cause he wanteda play Johnny-ona-pony an' he couldn't get his clothes schmootsy and den he wouldn't wanna smell my tookis." Charlie laughed and laughed. There was no more laughing for bright little Mischa, though. First, Charlie pointed to Mischa's pockets which were stuffed with candy and rolls of coins that Mischa had taken from the cash drawer. And from a series of short, easy questions they were able to ply all the answers from Chotchke Charlie and as hard as Mischa Schainheit tried to refute them, it was no use. It was no use because there was one thing that poor Chotchke Charlie never learned to do—and everyone knew that—he'd never learned how to lie.

D'Onofrio was still grumbling, but now about running the little brat in for assault. "You think you're off the hook, kid?" he snarled. "Think again. You kicked a police officer."

"Go fuck yourself! You can all go fuck yourselves!" Boomy cried, twisting out of his father's arms and heading for the door.

Cantor Tepperman raised his eyes to the ceiling. "Such language! In a synagogue to speak such language!"

Boomy raced down the hallway to the incongruous sound of applause and ran head-on into the imposing figure of Cantor Yossele Rosenblatt, trailed by a small legion of adoring well-wishers.

"My little comrade Albert," said Cantor Rosenblatt, but he never finished his greeting because Boomy spun away and raced up the stairs to the street.

Boomy lay on his bed, staring at the ceiling. He had been shut up in his room for hours, and neither Rose nor Max could coax him out.

There was a knocking at his door. Even in his dejection, Boomy figured there must be company. Nobody in this house ever bothered knocking. They just barged in.

There was another knock. "Vroomy, you got a visitor," his father said in a singsong. It couldn't be Shorty, because him they wouldn't announce and his father wouldn't be talking like a woman.

"Let me speak to him," he heard from the kitchen. It was a voice that was unmistakable in this household.

The door opened a crack. "May I come in, my young friend?" said Cantor Rosenblatt.

Boomy couldn't say no. He wasn't sure he really wanted to. "It's kinda messy," he said, sitting up. Actually, the room was neater than usual. Rose had cleaned the entire apartment this morning for the holiday. Harry's bed still had the spread over it.

"Listen, if you apologize for this room, then I'll never be able to invite you back to my home." Cantor Rosenblatt smiled warmly. "Do you mind if I sit on your bed?" There weren't too many options as there were no chairs in the room.

"So, I hear you're singing in shul instead of on the streets for pennies and nickels. I'm told I got some real competition."

It was Boomy's turn to smile now, something he hadn't been doing much of recently. "Yeah, I was so good they had to call the police to hold back the crowds." And then it all poured out, all the frustration and anger, and worst, Boomy's shame over failing in his mission to perform El Maleh Rachamim.

"Albert, El Maleh Rachamim is not done on Rosh Hashanah," said Cantor Rosenblatt softly, and saw first bewilderment, then defeat register on the boy's face. "It is part of Yizkor, the memorial service for the dead. Next week, at Yom Kippur, it will be recited. But there is no one to say you cannot do it on your own. Albert, God is always available."

Rose stood outside the bedroom door, trying to catch snatches of the conversation.

"Come away from there, it's not nice," Max whispered from the kitchen table.

"You think he wants to take him away to a school for chazzens? I don't know if we should allow it, Max." Rose joined her husband at the table, pouring herself a cup of tea from the kettle on the stove.

"I'll tell you, Rose, the day our Vrumeleh becomes a chazzen will be the day after Willie is elected President."

Max and Rose looked up as the cantor stepped into the kitchen with Boomy. "Is it all right if we take a little walk in the neighborhood?" he asked.

"Of course," Rose gushed, "but can't I offer you some tea and rugeleh first? You must have had such a day already, Cantor."

Rosenblatt politely declined, and he and Boomy walked out together, heading toward the shul in silence. The shammus was cleaning up when they arrived, and Cantor Rosenblatt asked him to please give them some privacy, to which he very respectfully agreed. They stepped up to the altar and stood before the ark that housed the Holy Torah. The cantor had placed a skullcap upon Boomy's head as soon as they entered the building. Now he draped a prayer shawl over his shoulder.

Downstairs, the shammus was arranging the wineglasses in the kiddush room. He stopped. Never had he heard El Maleh Rachamim recited with more feeling—and the voice was not the great cantor's. Then again, the shammus thought, maybe it was.

El maleh rachamim shochain bahmromim . . . O God, full of mercy, Thou who dwellest in Heaven, grant perfect rest beneath the sheltering wings of thy presence, among the holy and pure who shine as the brightness of the firmament, unto the soul of Sheila Goren.

Boomy was at loose ends. He'd lost his sense of purpose now that he'd accomplished the mission that had been driving him since the day he sipped tea from a cup with Yossele Rosenblatt. Just for something to do, he started hanging out with the Cowboys, a gang that kept the pawnshops and fences along Sutter Avenue well stocked. Though he was a good three or four years away from the Cowboys' minimum age requirement, his growing reputation as a kid who was more than handy with his fists apparently qualified him for honorary membership, and the fact that he was Big Gangy's brother didn't hurt either.

Boomy and the Cowboys were not a match made in heaven. For one thing, Boomy wasn't a thief. To him, the Cowboys' basement clubhouse was a place to hang out with the "older guys" and wash down stale potato chips with cream soda while reading comic books but he wasn't old enough to go to their Saturday night parties—which was how he happened to be home playing gin rummy with his mother when the police, with Officer D'Onofrio leading the charge, raided a Cowboys party and closed the gang down. Boomy was still at loose ends, until Shorty and Snake dragged him to the Hebrew Educational Society Community Center on Hopkinson Avenue, where, among other things, they had free cookies and milk. That was okay with Boomy, but not enough reason to keep him there. Then he found out about the boxing program, and in less than two weeks he was at the head of his class.

Springtime in Brownsville. It is when the naked tree branches that have been reaching to the sky all winter like the bony-fingered hands of a withered crone are suddenly infused with new life and their tender green leaves begin dancing in the April breeze. It is when the klezmer fiddlers perform in the tenement courtyards and the hurdy-gurdy man with the handlebar mustache endlessly grinds out "The Sidewalks of New York" while the children dance around, trying to outperform his capuchin monkey. It is when the pushcart vendors squirt some fresh oil on the wheels of their carts and set out like an invading army, each searching out his strategic position. It is when the birds return from their winter haunts.

Joey Silvers could not take the heat in Miami. He thought he could take the heat in Brownsville.

Right after he set up Reles and the boys for Meyer Shapiro, Joey thought there was a chance that Brownsville might not be too healthy for him. So he takes a few bucks from Meyer and catches the first train to Miami, expecting that the climate there will be much healthier. Maybe the place is livable in winter, but when he gets there in the summer of 1930, it's a furnace. Joey has to change clothes five times a day. He is desperate to go home, but there are problems. One problem is how the hell Meyer let Reles and Buggsy get away that night at the brewery. What was he shooting, spitballs? Another problem is that Joey is completely without funds. It seems that every nag in Florida, as soon as Joey plunks down his deuce, gets a personal call from the pari-mutuel clerk: "Okay, horsie, let's fuck Joey Silvers." He figures he'll earn some dough by working as a sparring partner in the gym on the beach, but he can't even raise his hands in that steam bath.

Desperation prevails, and Joey starts hanging around in the cavernous lobby of the Roney Plaza, the crown jewel of Miami Beach hotels, where he has counted a combined total of seventy-two sofas and easy chairs. It is astonishing how much loose change finds its way from the pockets of relaxing hotel guests into the furniture. Joey does so well at the Roney Plaza that he decides to corner the market, and pretty soon he is the number one cushion fluffer along Hotel Row. By the spring of 1931 Joey Silvers has enough money to get him back to Brownsville.

Albert Anastasia's right hand was shoved deep into his pocket on April 15, 1931, when he walked into the Nuova Villa Tammaro restaurant in Coney Island, flanked by Vito Genovese and Joe Adonis. The Boss of Bosses, Joe Masseria, was sitting at a table thinking that nobody makes linguine with white clam sauce like his good friend Gerardo Scarpato. Why couldn't he have a restaurant in Little Italy so Masseria didn't have to leave his fortress on the Lower East Side? Sitting next to Masseria was Lucky Luciano, whose idea this lunch date was, and who was not touching his food. As the door opened and closed he took a last sip from his glass of Chianti and slid his chair a little farther from Joe the Boss. Nobody said a word.

When it was over Masseria's face was lying in a bowl of the linguine he loved so much and the back of his head was gone. Gerardo Scarpato had lost a devoted customer. The old order was dead and the Syndicate was born.

For a guy who was spending so much time in restaurants, Albert Anastasia wasn't eating much. It was April 17, and he was sitting in Grabstein's Delicatessen on Sutter Avenue in Brownsville with Louis "Lepke" Buchalter and Abe Reles. He wasn't eating because he was on watch to make sure that no unwanted dinner guests joined the party. Reles, generally a very enthusiastic diner, wasn't eating either, because he had only one thought on his mind, a thought that obsessed him from the time he opened his eyes each morning until he closed them at the end of each day.

Lepke, whose scrawny body housed a huge brain, was a very organized, structured individual. It was time to eat, so he was eating. It did not bother him in the least, as he worked over his hot open-faced roast beef sandwich, that his two companions chose to subsist on toothpicks and water. Usually, when someone wanted to speak with Lepke, as Reles did now, he would visit him in his midtown Manhattan office, but Lepke hadn't been to Brownsville in quite a while, and he'd decided it was a good time to see how things were going, especially since there was a new "board of directors." Albert Anastasia worked under Lepke, and he was director of the branch of the syndicate that carried out the "contract" work—the Brooklyn mob led by Abe Reles. What Reles was putting on the table now was that he wanted to erase the Shapiro brothers and take over their Brownsville operation.

Lepke looked over at Anastasia, who gave a slight nod of approval. It was the Reles-Maione crew that did all the work for them. The Shapiros were nothing more than pains in the ass.

"I just hope you don't run out of ammunition before you finish the job," Lepke said to Reles, and took a gulp of his celery soda.

Reles's face reddened. After his three-for-six fiasco on Blake Avenue last summer, it was like a Keystone Cops comedy. He and the boys had had at least a dozen opportunities to shoot Meyer Shapiro, but they might as well have been firing Ping-Pong balls in a hurricane. He stared at Lepke.

"If I do, I will tear him apart with my bare hands."

The Shapiro brothers hadn't been getting out much. Mostly they stayed cooped up in the basement of their home on Blake Avenue, dining on canned goods. The Fourth of July found them eating sardines with applesauce and shuddering every time a kid shot off a firecracker. So a week later, when Irving mentioned that a friend of theirs who ran a slot machine empire in Upstate New York was going on trial in Monticello, and suggested they drive up to take in the proceedings, the spooked Meyer jumped at the chance. At the time, a day's outing in a place where no one would be looking for him sounded almost as good as a trip to Ebbets Field or a fight at the Garden.

Now Meyer and Irving were on their way back from their frolic in the country—a two-hour drive each way and an afternoon on a hard wooden bench in a stuffy courtroom with a broken fan—and Meyer was bone-tired. The thought of going home and trying to fall asleep on a soggy pillow was no more appealing than the rest of the day had been, so he says to Irving, who is just about to turn onto Blake Avenue, "Whaddya say we go to the shvitz?"

Irving, who isn't enjoying the day any more than his brother, brakes the car and thinks for a minute. "You know, it's not a bad idea, but I got an appointment at the brewery in the morning. If you want, I'll drop you off."

There were five guys sitting on the stairs in the vestibule of 691 Blake Avenue. They were sitting in the dark because Abe Reles had just removed the vestibule lightbulb ten minutes ago. Reles sucked in a whistling gulp of air as he heard a car door slam.

Irving Shapiro was muttering to himself as he walked toward the building. There must be a short in the wiring somewhere. He had just changed that damn lightbulb a week ago.

When Reles saw the single head silhouetted against the entrance, he swore under his breath. It was not the bullet-shaped head of the man he wanted so badly. Out of undying loyalty Buggsy Goldstein commiserated, but Pittsburgh Phil couldn't have cared less that the guy coming through the front door was not Meyer Shapiro. A hit was a hit. This sentiment was shared by Happy Maione and Dasher Abbandando.

The last thought Irving Shapiro had was that there was nothing wrong with the wiring after all.

One of the upstairs tenants was completely fed up. The Fourth of

July was a week ago and still these bonditten were making with the firecrackers. And in the hallway, no less. Eighteen of them she counted. Eighteen! No respect!

When Joey Silvers returned to Brownsville, he thought he was coming home. It's three months now since he's back—but he is not home. Instead, he's groveling in the mud at Pig Town.

Joey figures there are probably worse places than Pig Town, but he doesn't know of any. When he leaves for Miami there is no such place, but as the Depression takes root so does Pig Town. It is a tent city situated on the fringe of Brownsville, bordered by East New York Avenue, Rutland Road, Utica Avenue, and Rockaway Parkway, an open field that soon becomes a muddy marsh filled with rivulets of rainwater and urine. As people lose their homes to eviction, foreclosure, or disaster of any kind, Pig Town is there.

Joey is not thrilled with his new digs, but he tries to put a positive spin on things—plenty of fresh air and the price is right. Out of burlap and oilcloth he puts together a reasonable facsimile of a tent that becomes his home on the range. Although Brownsville is close enough to reach with a good spit with the wind behind you, Pig Towners and Brownsvillites do not march to the same tune, just as Molly Malone and Secondhand Rose cater to a very different clientele. There is no such thing as Shabbes in Pig Town, which doesn't bother Joey in the least because he doesn't observe it anyhow. Friday night is a time for downing a few pints and singing a song or two about the old sod and capping it all off with a lively difference of opinion that generally results in a couple of broken noses. As there is not too much else in the way of entertainment, the same good time is had on the other evenings of the week as well. Joey soon finds it expedient simply to ignore the almost nightly muggings, especially since he has nothing to be mugged of except an occasional Chicklet. Now and then he receives a halfhearted kick from the disappointed pickpocket.

Joey is certain that things will get better because they cannot get worse. He tries hard not to cry over a situation he brought upon himself, but he can't help being envious when he hears that his brother Pal has signed to fight Benny Leonard in October. Pal, who everyone said was the second best of the Silvers brothers, is getting a shot that should be Joey's. He resolves that he will somehow make his peace with Reles and get back in the gym. Who knows, maybe he'll even do roadwork.

Joey continues to learn about the customs and mores of Pig Town. He learns that Sunday is a day of great festivities there—cock fights followed by a buffet dinner of canned beans. He learns something new every day, it seems, and then all of a sudden he can't believe all the things he learns in one night. First he learns from a newspaper he picks out of the garbage how Irving Shapiro cashed in his chips. Next he learns that it is possible to spend a whole night doubled over with a churning gut, nausea, and chills. Finally he learns that his life has become one great big crap shoot.

That being the case and alternatives being scarce, Joey figures he may as well keep gambling to take his mind off his troubles. He soon becomes a true aficionado of the Pig Town cock fights, and on Labor Day weekend, as luck would have it, he gets a personal look at a big strong rooster with an extra-sharp beak and a ferocious cock-a-doodle-doo. Joey knows that this is an opportunity he cannot let slip by, so he borrows a few dollars from his sister. She does not lend them, because she is in the bathtub when he takes the money from her purse.

Joey walks down Sackman Street on his way back to Pig Town, reconsidering his options. He really likes this big chicken, but so does everyone else who got a look, and the real way to make money is to ride in with the long shot. He is busily engaged in thinking of ways to dope a chicken when he arrives at the corner of Saratoga and Sutter, at 9:05 P.M., the exact minute that Happy Maione and Abe Reles arrive there. Considering that there are hundreds of streets in Brownsville and 1,444 minutes in a day, not too many people would have taken book on such a convergence.

"Abe," Joey says, sweating like he's back in Miami. "I been wanting to get together with you."

Reles smiles as he and Happy ease Joey toward the alley. "Me too, Joey. I owe you something."

Abe Reles shows that he is a guy who pays his debts. And Joey Silvers finally shows the world that he is a guy with brains, which get splattered on an alley wall on Saratoga Avenue for all to see. Joey Silvers, whose life was one great crapshoot, has finally rolled snake eyes.

The next day, in Pig Town, the cock fight goes the way most people figured. The big strong rooster with the extra-sharp beak is just too much fowl for his opponent. There is a lot of partying afterward, because quite a few people win quite a bit of money. Large amounts of booze go down the hatch, and sometime during the night somebody gets the bright idea to toast the new champion, only rather than being put on their shoulders and cheered he is put on a spit and seared, and the great fighting rooster goes down as great barbecue.

The day after that, shopping with her boy on Sackman Street, Joey's grieving sister reaches into her pocketbook. "You rotten little brat!" she yells at Butchie. "Where's my thirty dollars?"

It was a mid-September Saturday night, and the sun had just gone down, signaling the end of Shabbes, which made no difference to Meyer. He had no need for a specially designated day of rest as lately every day was a day of rest for Meyer Shapiro. His mother was clearing the dinner dishes, and Willie, good son that he was, was helping her. Meyer lit up a Camel and said he was going down the street to Marcus's candy store to get the early editions of the Sunday *News* and *Mirror*.

"Come on," he said to Willie, who looked at him like he was crazy. Willie hadn't set foot outside the apartment since Irving got his face blown away.

"But you could be a nice guy and bring back a pint of vanilla ice cream." Knowing his brother, Willie was pretty certain that the slice of cherry pie he had sitting in the icebox was not going to be eaten à la mode.

Meyer walked the half block to the candy store, checking the street carefully. He picked the two newspapers off the stand, dug into his pockets for change, and found none, so he went inside and put a dollar bill on the counter. As soon as he saw the look in Marcus's eyes, he knew something was wrong. The old man was shaking as he went to the cash register for Meyer's change, which he very deliberately placed right next to the countertop box of chocolate twists.

Meyer turned to the door, then came back and whispered a few words to Marcus, handing him the coins and the newspapers. He noticed a couple of people standing in front of their houses as he left the store, but Meyer knew that wouldn't make any difference. Besides leaving his change in his dresser drawer, he'd also left his rod there.

A short while ago, Meyer had been very tired. That's what sitting around doing nothing did to a person. Now he felt a strange surge of energy, like a shot of adrenaline. He decided to make a game of this walk to wherever. How many steps would he take before a bullet tore into him or a gun barrel was pressed to his head? For some reason he picked twenty-two, as good a number as any, and was pretty crestfallen when he felt pressure against his back after only fifteen steps.

"If you go for your pocket you're a fucken dead man."

"What are you doing on my block, Buggsy?" Meyer said without changing his pace. He was thinking that if he'd walked a bit faster he probably would've gotten in his twenty-two steps. It would've been nice going out with a winner.

"I knew you were a clown, but I never knew you were a comedian, Meyer. Maybe we'll get you to perform at Sanger's Hall." It was Reles's voice. Remarkably, it filled Meyer with a sense of pure joy.

"Only if the opening act is a sawed-off putz that walks like a duck and acts like a shmuck."

Abe Reles was ready to pull the trigger then and there, but he bit down hard as he and Buggsy shoved Meyer roughly toward the brown Ford parked just around the corner. Meyer sat in the backseat between Buggsy and Reles, on his left. Happy Maione was at the wheel.

Meyer turned to Abe. "You putz, you really need some lessons. After the shtupping I gave your little faygeleh you'll never be able to make her happy."

Buggsy reached across the seat and tore Reles's hand away from Meyer's throat. "Come on, Abie, we're gonna do this like we said."

They had staked out the Shapiros's block for a week now, deciding to take him up close, not in a shootout. It was a sensible decision, since Meyer had survived all eighteen of their attempts on his life in the last year or so. If they didn't want to make it nineteen, they had to keep their cool, which was why they hadn't invited Pittsburgh Phil along.

Meyer smiled, his two gold teeth flashing like stars in a moonless sky. "You can't blame him, Buggsy. Every time he kisses his wife, he's sucking my dick by proxy!"

. . .

On Sunday morning they found Meyer Shapiro in the hallway of a run-down tenement building on the Lower East Side, a single bullet through the left ear. Everyone knew who did it, including the police. They brought in Reles, Buggsy, and Happy but didn't even keep them over-night. Sam Leibowitz, Lepke's lawyer, met them at the precinct, and they all left together. Not one witness ever stepped forward.

5

Wagging his hands and pointing to the locker-room door, Pete the AAU man speaks loudly and slowly. "Pesconi! Time-to-go!"

Boomy is very excited as he skips out of the locker room. He hears shouts from his friends who made the long trip from Brownsville to the Golden City Park Arena in Canarsie—"Boomy!" "Vroomy!" "Al!" "Giovanni!" He isn't nervous, and that surprises him. He'd thought that coming out before a crowd for the first time would tie him up in knots, but instead he's exhilarated and anxious to show everyone how good he is. After all, he mopped up the floor with all the guys he fought at the Community Center.

"Kid, quit skippin' like that. It don't look good," whispers his second, supplied by the house.

Immediately Boomy begins bouncing on the balls of his feet and punching the air; skipping does not project the right image. When he climbs up the ring steps, he grabs the top rope with both gloves and vaults over. The crowd goes crazy at such showmanship. Boomy is glowing like he already won the fight. He's been practicing this vault ever since seeing Sid "The Pearl" Perlow make his entrance that way when he showed up for a sparring session at the Community Center about the time Boomy started there. Sid, who got to the finals of the Golden

Gloves, is supposed to be the best fighter to come out of the center. Boomy hasn't seen him again because the Pearl does most of his training at Beecher's Gym, where many of the top fighters in the area are to be found.

Boomy is busy looking around for his friends when the crowd goes wild again. From the corner of his eye he sees a guy bound up the ring steps, place just one hand on the top rope, and do this unbelievable vault where it looks like he may go through the roof and land in Jamaica Bay. It is obvious that he too has a lot of people who came to root for him, because they are all chanting "Poil! Poil! Poil!"

"Kid, you gotta watch this guy," his second warns him. "He's been around, and he knows all the right moves. I don't know why they take a novice like you and throw you in against an experienced kid like Perlow."

It's not that Boomy is ignoring him, but he catches sight of his father and two brothers in the crowd. He hasn't told them about the match, and he's wondering how they found out—and how his father feels about it.

"He got height and reach," the second continues, trying to get Boomy's focus off the crowd and onto his taller, older opponent, "and he knows to make use of it with his jab. You gotta bring it to him inside, you hear me?"

Whether Boomy hears him almost makes no difference, because when the ring announcer introduces Giovanni Pesconi, nobody steps forward—not until Boomy sees Fat Yerna actually pulling clumps of hair from his head and Pete the AAU man coming to the ring apron to explain to the announcer that he has to speak with more expression and use his hands.

Once the bell rings, Boomy puts his strategy to work. The way Yerna describes it the next day to some of the guys in Alpert's Deli, the judges do not take into account what is termed ring generalship. From the opening bell, Boomy creates a situation where he whacks away at Sid Perlow with his face. The kid is constantly charging, coming in, making big swishing breezes as he wings away with both hands. His face is definitely his most effective weapon, continually landing on Perlow's fists, which must be quite sore from the pounding it is being administered every time Boomy connects solidly with his chin or his nose or the top of his head.

From his ringside seat, Pete the AAU man tries to figure if there is any way for the bell to be rung with more expression, as it seems this kid Giovanni does not understand when it just goes *clang!* After the bell ending the third and final round, the seconds for both fighters have to run in and pull Boomy back to his corner, where he hears the judges give the decision to Perlow.

The Pearl is very happy that the evening's festivities are over. All he wants is to take a shower and leave Canarsie. For Boomy the night is much too short; he's ready to go right back at Sid. He's like a chihuahua snapping and barking at a great Dane. Perlow, tired and sweaty, climbs between the ropes and steps down from the ring to make his way back to the locker room. Boomy is about to do the same when he stops. He places his gloved hands on the top rope, vaults out of the ring, and trots up the aisle as the crowd rises to its feet, cheering and whistling for him. There are more ways than one to come out a winner.

The cheers for Boomy are a show of appreciation for his grit and heart and dogged determination, not a sign that the fans think he should have won the decision. Except for one fan. Willie has to forcibly restrain his father from going after the ring announcer, who in Max's mind is the culprit, not just the person who reads the judges' cards.

"Robber! What is he, crazy?" Max rages. "Would you believe such a gonif lives and breathes?"

Willie, who can't help laughing, is pulling at his father's arm to keep him from climbing up the ring apron. "Okay, Pa, cut it out! The kid fought a great fight. That's all that matters."

Max shakes his fist at the ring. "Fahr vuss, because he's a Telyaineh?"

"Pa, what the hell is the matter with you? You're accusing them of jobbing Boomy because he's Italian? Boomy's Jewish."

"So?" Max turns on Willie as though he is the worst kind of traitor. "They don't know that, those goddamn gangsters!"

Boomy loved to hear the crowd roaring for him. He loved the head-to-head, one-on-one competition. He loved the feeling of freedom that filled him in the ring as he moved to corner, ambush, and destroy. Fighting was what he was born for. And Beecher's Gym was where he was headed, because he had outgrown the program at the Community Center.

There were many people in Brownsville who were of the opinion that Beecher's was where boys went after their bar mitzvahs. Actually, plenty of the young fighters training there weren't Jewish, but in the '20s and '30s word was that if you needed a minyan all you had to do was go to Beecher's Gym. It was a small, clean place that smelled the way a bunch of bodies working out is supposed to smell—a pungent mixture of wintergreen and sweat. Its fixtures were a regulation ring, a couple of heavy bags, one rack of speed bags, a full-length training mirror, a calisthenics and rope-skipping area, a locker room with showers, and Froike.

If Froike had been born a dog, without question he would have been a basset hound. He had big sad eyes with drooping lids, his loyalty and devotion were unmatched, and teaching fighters how to fight was his gift. Of all the gym's fixtures, only Froike was indispensable.

It was a straight line that Willie Davidoff walked when he brought his kid brother to Beecher's: right to Froike. "See what you can do," he said.

Froike knew Willie Davidoff, and he knew Harry Davidoff too because he was training at Beecher's under the ring name Harry Davison, though all the neighborhood guys called him Little Gangy or Duff. So Froike knew what to expect from the kid. But at night he went home scratching his head, and when his wife asked, "What's the matter, you got an itch?" Froike tried to explain. "It's no itch, it's this kid. He calls me sir. Whatever needs doing, he's there to help out, and everything with a smile." Froike started scratching again.

Boomy had been at Beecher's less than a month when Sid Perlow pranced into the ring one day like a king lording it over his subjects and asked if anyone one would spar with him for three rounds—if they could last the distance. It was the moment of Boomy's deliverance. This was the reason he'd come to Beecher's in the first place: to meet up with the Pearl again. At first Froike was against it, but when he saw the glow in Boomy's eye he didn't have the heart to say no. He'd been working with the kid for just a few weeks, turning him around to the right side, but Boomy was a willing pupil and a quick learner. Willie hadn't liked the idea of messing with natural style, but Froike pointed out to him the difficulty of finding opponents for southpaws and stressed that since Boomy was actually a head-on, come-straight-at-you fighter who punched from underneath, it was not really a job of turning him completely around.

When Perlow saw who his sparring partner was going to be, he gave a long, deep sigh. Froike figured if things got out of hand he'd just step in and take the kid out of harm's way. The Pearl should have had such a considerate trainer. Actually, it's possible that he did, but it all happened too fast to tell. The bell clanged, and Perlow moved toward the center of the ring, staring at his opponent, wondering how come the kid is coming to him behind a lead left when he distinctly remembers a rough-and-tumble southpaw. That's when his eyeballs come together in a spontaneous meeting at the bridge of his nose. All the regulars who sit around the gym sipping coffee give an involuntary communal sputter of hot java as Boomy pivots his whole body into a short left hook that comes off his hip and drills into Perlow just under the rib cage.

After removing his various parts from the canvas, the Pearl does not make any excuses for his dismantling. He merely explains how the strained muscle in his back restricted his movement and how his upset stomach drained him of strength and how his hay fever caused his eyes to swell and water, impairing his vision. Charlie Beecher soon has an empty locker on his hands as the Pearl moves his belongings to Sammy Aaronson's gym on Rockaway Avenue, where the pollen count is apparently lower.

Vic Zimet lived around the corner from Beecher's on Georgia Avenue and became the kid's assistant trainer. Whether it was Vic's proximity to the gym that fanned the burning flame of desire for the fight game or his innate love of fighting that drove him to the gym is one of those chicken-or-egg questions, but the result was that he evolved from a ring rat to a polished amateur and intercollegiate boxer and had that rare talent of being able to impart his knowledge to others. Vic could not decide whether he was a more proficient fighter or teacher, so for the time being he was following both paths. Eventually he is able to make his decision when, looking in the mirror each morning as he shaves, he realizes that he is used to and very much likes the straight line of his nose, a fondness which paves the way for his illustrious career as a trainer and coach.

Vic admired Boomy's natural ability and sheer determination, the way he kept wading in and throwing punches even against seasoned veterans. What impressed him most, though, was that Boomy learned from every fight and would invariably win if he was rematched with a kid who'd beat him. But as game and gritty as he was, he was still a raw fourteen-year-old going in against tough, experienced fighters, and he had plenty to learn. Vic would watch him shadowboxing in front of the mirror as he worked on shortening his punches, keeping his hands up after he punched or jabbed, and mastering the subtleties of feinting. Boomy would throw punches at his reflection until the sweat flew every time his fist slashed through the air. He'd continue until the lights were turned off if Froike didn't come over and move him to the heavy bag to work on his overhand right. The kid's left knew what to do all by itself. Froike taught him lateral movement, which was totally unnatural to this young bull who knew only to come to his man, and how to slip and slide punches, and how to cut off the ring and corner his prey. Boomy sopped it all up like a sponge.

"Who is that kid?" Bernie "Schoolboy" Friedkin asked Vic one day as he was watching Boomy work out. Bernie was in his senior year at Thomas Jefferson High School, where he had a reputation as an excellent student who worked hard, got good grades, and respected everyone. He was an even better student of the sport of boxing and was probably the classiest amateur boxer in the lightweight division in all of New York City.

"Al Davidoff," Vic answered. "He's fourteen. Just a novice."

"Oh, yeah," Bernie said, tossing off the towel that was draped around his shoulders. "I know him—Big Gangy's brother. The kid's a pushcart peddler," he said as he bounced toward the ring.

"Bernie," Vic called after him. "The kid's a fighter."

"I am sure! I am sure!"

Shorty is most emphatic in turning down Boomy's deal of a lifetime. He has no desire to peddle fruits and vegetables on Blake Avenue even if Boomy is willing to turn over his business lock, stock, and pushcart at absolutely no charge. The two friends are walking down Pennsylvania Avenue toward Blake, and Boomy is waving and shouting while Shorty hangs his head low, digging his hands deep in his pockets and dragging his feet.

"You got no ambition. That's your problem, Shorty," Boomy scolds. "You ain't never gonna amount to nothin'!"

Shorty stops trudging and looks up to see Boomy racing toward his spot on Blake Avenue. Since he began training at Beecher's three weeks ago, Boomy hasn't been back to check on his wagon, which he left covered with a big tarpaulin. But now here it is, open and fully stocked: someone has stolen his business.

"It's gotta be that goddamn Polack Zelke," Boomy yells to Shorty, his anger rising. He can't believe that none of the other peddlers got in touch with him. They all know him. He's worked beside them for four years, ever since Moishe retired and deeded his pushcart over to Boomy, which was how Boomy got to know the proprietor of Rappaport's Hardware on Sutter Avenue and became his best customer.

Rappaport looked like a teddy bear and acted like a pussycat. He loved shmoozing with his customers, tickling little babies under the chin, and killing every joke that was told to him by reciting the punch line before the teller was halfway through his spiel. His place was always packed with shoppers, and after Boomy took over Moishe's cart, he joined their ranks. After three days of buying nails and angle irons in volume, Boomy decided to ask Rappaport for store credit. Rappaport wasn't sure whether this was a joke or not. He assumed it wasn't because he did not know the punch line.

"Listen, kid," he said. "Abe Kaplan the builder is my customer. Last year he put up over a hundred and fifty houses in East New York. You know what? He doesn't buy as many nails as you do. What are you doing, building a skyscraper?"

The youngster frowned and shook his head. "I'm fixing my pushcart, and every time I fix it, it gets busted up again."

Rappaport gave Boomy more than store credit. He told him to come in and just take the nails he needed.

Unfortunately for Boomy, the peddlers around him were nothing like Rappaport. Not that they were all bad people, but at a time when the country was spiraling deeper and deeper into a depression, it was only natural that there should be resentment over a ten-year-old kid moving in on a spot and working a cart when men who were trying desperately to support families had no such good fortune. It was one thing when Boomy was helping Moishe, but this was different. Then too, some of the peddlers saw a chance to strike back at Big Gangy through his brother.

One of the worst of them was Zelke, who not only demolished Boomy's cart but made a party of bashing the kid himself, laughing with every blow he landed. When Boomy retaliated with a singsong "You're nothin' but a fat old tub of shit!" Zelke, sputtering and foaming, grabbed him by the throat. "You 'pologize or I break neck!" The kick Boomy landed on Zelke's shin sounded like the crack of a rifle. As the huge Pole started doing something between a polka and an Irish jig, Boomy tore free and backed away, yelling in a conciliatory fashion, "Okay, I'm sorry. Maybe you're not so old . . . you fat tub of shit."

The next day, for a change, Boomy was fixing his pushcart. Swinging his hammer, he thought the sound it made as it hit the nailhead was much louder than usual. Then he realized that Blake Avenue was much quieter than usual. Turning, he saw his brothers walking toward Zelke's pushcart. Zelke was almost twice the size of Willie and Harry, but he seemed to be melting faster than a snowman on the equator.

The snarl on Willie's lips looked almost like a question mark. "Which hand did you hit my kid brother with? For your sake I hope it wasn't both of them."

Zelke looked around, terrified, to see if anyone was coming to his aid. He saw statues. His heart had the right idea. It was trying to burst free of his chest and get the hell out of there.

"Hey, Willie, what are you two doin', huh?"

Suddenly there was movement. All heads turned as one to look at Boomy, who had walked up to his brothers and was standing there in what was becoming a very familiar pose for him: feet spread apart, hands balled into fists and resting on his hips, chin jutting out, and eyes blazing.

"Why don't you come to me and tell me what's going on here?" Willie said, waving his finger at the crowd. "I want you should show me anyone who messed around with you, you hear me?"

"Fuck you, Willie, and you too, Heshy. This is my street. I don't butt in on you, do I?"

Whose eyes open wider—Willie's and Harry's or all the peddlers' on the avenue—no one will ever know, but there are a whole bunch of very shocked people in the neighborhood at that moment. It is not the first time that somebody mouths off to Willie, but usually it is a mouth that does not work again for a long time.

Caught between pride and embarrassment, Willie turned and scanned the peddlers. To save face, he moved his finger in an arc, pointing at all of them, and said, "If I hear about anyone ever layin' a hand on this kid again, I'll—"

"I told ya—keep your nose outta my business!" Boomy cut in. "Don't make me look like no Girl Scout. I can take care of myself, Willie."

At that Harry reached out to take an openhanded swipe at Boomy, but Willie blocked him. "You can take care of yourself?" Willie said to Boomy, laughing. "Okay, I only hope I don't have to scrape you off the street."

"With the friends you got, you better worry about scrapin' yourself off the street first."

Willie drilled his kid brother with a hard, angry look, but he couldn't keep the corners of his mouth from twitching upward. He tugged at Harry's elbow, and they walked off down Blake toward Pennsylvania Avenue. Zelke breathed his first breath in the past five minutes.

Boomy went back to his pushcart, or what was left of his pushcart, picked up the hammer, and began driving nails again. This time the sound of his work was drowned out by the noise of peddlers hawking, customers haggling, paper bags crinkling, babies crying. None of the peddlers were looking at Boomy, but they all saw him, and they all knew that there was a new man on the street.

Now Boomy looks across the same street and sees Zelke staring at him, eyes wide with surprise: proof that he is the thief! Boomy clenches his hands and looks around for a stick because he knows fists alone are no match for that ox. Shorty watches Zelke slowly cross the street and wants to fly out of there, but his feet feel as though they are cemented in place.

Label, who has the pushcart next to Boomy's, comes over and places a hand on the kid's shoulder. "Like a big sick puppy he is when you left. Everybody he asks, 'Where is little Davidoff? Where is little Davidoff?' Soon when he goes to the Terminal Market he brings back for your wagon too. All day, every day, he runs back and forth working both wagons."

Zelke is holding a brown paper bag in his hand. "Look! Yours," he grunts. The bag is filled with bills and coins. Boomy later counts out $42.20. He stares up at the hulking Pole.

"It ain't mine. I ain't worked my cart in a month."

Zelke shoves the bag at him. "Take it. I took out what I spend. Tomorrow I start new bag."

Two winters before, Zelke had come down with pneumonia. His wife sent her younger brother Bronislaw, who had just come over from Poland, to tend the pushcart. He couldn't speak two words of English. Boomy helped him with everything, from purchasing to selling. When Zelke came back to work, he was still too weak to do anything but sit. Boomy would get him containers of hot coffee or tea a few times a day. Zelke never said thank you, he just grunted.

By the time Boomy and Shorty leave to go back to Beecher's, a deal has been carved out between Boomy and his old nemesis. Zelke offers to continue taking care of Boomy's wagon, but Boomy says he can't let him do that, so they decide that Bronislaw, who has a night job as a porter, will take over, and if Boomy decides he has to make a comeback as a peddler, he and Bronislaw will work together.

Boomy points his finger at Zelke. "You know what? You're probably the best Polack I ever knew." Zelke leans over and squeezes Boomy in a colossal bear hug.

"Holy shit!" Boomy gasps as he and Shorty head toward the gym. "I think the big lug finally did what he always wanted to do—break every bone in my body."

"I thought you two hated each other," Shorty says.

Boomy frowns. "We do, Shorty, but this was strictly business. You have absolutely no understanding of the business world."

It was a time of changes, and not just for Boomy Davidoff. Franklin Delano Roosevelt took office as President of the United States in March of 1933, and his New Deal changed the social and economic face of

America forever. The Depression deepened and took root, changing the madcap, boisterous lifestyle of the Roaring Twenties to the somber, struggling-to-survive civilization of the thirties. And the repeal of Prohibition in February 1933 changed the mentality and methods of mobsters as well as the structure of crime. The moans and groans of "What's a poor gangster to do?" could be heard far and wide.

With the end of Prohibition the American gangster attempted to transform himself from a caterpillar to a butterfly. The cocoon was spun by a self-delegated group of men who intended to make their power self-perpetuating and unchallenged. These men were responsible for the birth in 1934 of a new syndicate that became one of the largest and most lucrative organizations ever put together. From that day forward crime was to become an organized business, moving into every strata of society. It was to be a democracy run by dictators, a business that catered to everyone.

The idea of consolidating criminal activity under the umbrella of one giant corporation was an idea that Louis "Lepke" Buchalter had been tossing around for years, but it was chubby little Johnny Torrio, the guy who handed Chicago to Al Capone on a silver platter, who drew up the master plan and presented it to the eventual board of directors at a meeting held in a swanky midtown Manhattan hotel. This all-star lineup of the FBI's Most Wanted included Lucky Luciano, Frank Costello, Joe Adonis, Meyer Lansky, Bugsy Siegel, Vito Genovese, Abner "Longy" Zwillman, Lepke and his partner Jake "Gurrah" Shapiro, and Dutch Schultz. Blue-gray rings of cigar smoke hovered above the long conference table, and the only drinks served were water, tea, and coffee. Nothing was to interfere with lucid thinking. Only after Torrio's manifesto became the order of the day and all days to follow were bottles of whiskey and scotch brought into the room and glasses raised in salute. From now on, the mobs and the mobsters were united under new rules and regulations, a discipline that was the only law of the land. Brownsville was part of the land.

Willie Davidoff walked out of the Ambassador Theater on the corner of Saratoga and Livonia, just down the block from Midnight Rose's candy store. He knew he had seen a Western, but he had no idea what it was about because all he was doing was killing time. His mind was not on watching a bunch of stubbly-cheeked cowboys fight over whatever cowboys fought over. It was still too early to go over and have his talk with Reles, so he crossed the street and climbed the stairs to Won Low's for some egg drop soup and chow mein. Willie was raised to believe that one always thinks better on a full stomach, and Fat Yerna had told him that was the absolute truth.

Not that they missed him or anything like that, but the neighborhood's restaurateurs and shopkeepers and union members hadn't been seeing as much of Willie Davidoff as they were accustomed to. Actually, they could see him—all they had to do was look outside, and there would be Willie walking along with Boomy—but he just was not paying them as many visits. Boomy had taken center stage with Willie, who would glow every time the kid climbed into the ring and grimace every time Boomy took a punch, as though he were sharing the pain with him. Big Gangy was not a guy given to kvelling, but he adored his baby brother and hovered over him like a mother hen.

Grabbing a handful of fortune cookies, Willie went back downstairs and crossed the street to the candy store. When he entered, Rose disappeared into the back room, leaving him alone with Buggsy Goldstein and Abe Reles. Buggsy was dunking a doughnut into a cup of coffee while Reles gnawed away on a chocolate twist. Willie thought to himself that Rose's twists never went stale like his father's did. Reles smiled and motioned for Willie to sit down and make himself comfortable.

Willie sat, but he was not comfortable. He knew what this talk was going to be about. Reles had always wanted Willie to throw in with him on a formal basis, which would mean that Reles became a partner on Willie's territory but he did not become a partner on Reles's. Now that the Syndicate was in, lone wolves were on the way out.

Reles does this whole spiel about unity and the new game plan like he's been practicing it in front of a mirror. All along Buggsy is moving his head up and down like a chicken pecking for seeds.

"I'm all for it, one hundred and ten percent," Willie finally interrupts. He is becoming worried that Reles's recitation might be longer than the Constitution, about which Willie knows nothing other than that it is very long. "I'm all for it, but I happened to have a little talk with Lepke, and he spoke with Anastasia and Joey A., and they all agreed that because I have sort of a specialty operation I can run my little territory all by myself and I do not push into anyone else's. It's what Lepke calls a lazy fair operation."

The chicken stops pecking. Buggsy is ambitious not for himself but for his buddy Abe, for whom he takes this as a personal insult. His emotions cause him to crumble up his doughnut and grind it into the counter, which causes Rose to hobble from the back, scoop the crumbs up in a soiled dishrag—the only kind she seems to have—and drop them into Buggsy's cup of coffee while he is busy giving Willie the evil eye, whereupon she returns to the back room without uttering a word.

Reles has a considerably calmer look about him, as though he expected as much. After getting rid of the Shapiro brothers—or two-thirds of them, anyway—Kid Twist is pretty much the king of Brownsville, except for the Amberg brothers, who cheered him on all the way in his vendetta against the Shapiros. They do not cheer him any longer. Anything Reles can add to his territory gives him that much more prestige, but he knows that Willie, who will work with him on certain joint ventures, likes to run his own ship. Also, even though Abe is pretty tight with Lepke and Albert Anastasia as he and his boys are their number-one hit squad, he knows that ever since Willie helped Lepke pull off a public relations coup by bailing out Yossele Rosenblatt, King of the Cantors, they too are on more than just talking terms.

"Think about it, Willie," Abe says calmly. "It may be to your advantage."

"Yeah, I'll do that, Abe."

Willie gets up from his seat and puts his hat on. He shakes Reles's hand, and then he looks at Buggsy, who turns away, lifts his coffee cup to his mouth, and drains it. Willie scowls at him and is gone by the time Buggsy shouts, "Hey, Rose, I think you should put up a fresh pot of coffee. This one's stale as dishwater."

Willie Shapiro jumped, startled by the sudden movement of a large figure slightly behind him, coming from the alley. With a long sigh of relief he stood shaking in front of his sister's building, realizing that the low evening sun, with an assist from his own tortured mind, had transformed his shadow into a giant lurking demon.

Willie had barely been out of his poor old mother's apartment since his brothers died, but now he was desperate to change the story making the rounds that he was going to avenge their murders. His brave words about getting Reles and his gang were meant only for his mother's ears, but somehow they got out and about. Willie was so frightened that he'd actually ventured to his sister's place tonight because he thought maybe she could get word to Reles, who was very visible and very reachable in Brownsville, that Willie was not looking for trouble.

"I want out, Rosie. The rackets ain't for me, never was."

Rose patted her only remaining brother on the back as he sat cupping his head in his hands at her kitchen table.

When Abe Reles stopped in at the drugstore the next day to pick up his antacid tablets, Seidman the druggist handed him his change and said in a confidential tone, "Abe, it's none of my business, but Rosie Shapiro wants you to know that Willie doesn't want trouble and he doesn't want to make trouble. The truth is, he's a shmendrick, he's not like the other two."

Kid Twist popped a Chicklet in his mouth and smiled. "You tell Rosie to let Willie know he has nothing to worry about. Tell her Abe Reles said so."

Vito Gurino knew how to have a good time. One of his favorite diversions was sipping on a cold beer in his backyard in Ocean Hill while shooting the heads off chickens. He could have saved himself a lot of bullets, because Vito was so ugly the chickens would have croaked just looking at him. Two hundred seventy pounds of sadistic animal, Vito became one of Abe Reles's most competent employees, eventually blowing away at least eight people—nowhere near his chicken count, but still entitling him to a high degree of celebrity status among his peers.

So Vito is driving down Eastern Parkway one afternoon, crossing Atlantic Avenue, when he observes an individual whom he believes Abe and the boys would be very interested in. He decides to check out a few places where Abe might be. At the corner of Pitkin and Stone, he sees Pittsburgh Phil standing with Happy and Dasher at the street counter of the Kishka King, gulping down hot dogs and ogling all the pretty girls strolling by. Vito pulls over to the curb, lowers his window, and gives a shrill whistle.

"Hey, Vito, you want some kishka?" Pittsburgh Phil calls out with a laugh, over the counterman's chant of "A nickel a shtikl! A nickel a shtikl!"

"I don't eat none of that greasy shit," Vito calls back. "Unless you're payin' for it, that is." He climbs out of his car, which immediately rises a few inches, and leaves it jutting into the intersection as he walks over to the boys. "Hey, guess who I just seen on Atlantic Avenue."

Right then a young cop, walking his beat and twirling his nightstick, strolls over and asks, "That car belong to one of you gentlemen?" They all turn and look at him like he is a bug under a magnifying glass.

"Yeah, why? You wanna buy it?" Vito answers with a straight face.

It is at that moment that the officer recognizes to whom he is speaking. "No, no," he stammers. "I just want to make sure you know that you left the motor running. I wouldn't want to see anyone jump in and drive off with it."

"Well, if anyone would do such a terrible thing, I am sure you would take off and catch them." Vito smiles at the mortified officer, who smiles back, does a hasty about-face, and continues on his way.

When Vito tells the boys who it was that he spotted, Pittsburgh Phil, smelling an enjoyable night, suggests they walk down the block to the Concord Cafeteria, where Abe and Buggsy are having some danish and coffee. It is times such as this that make Pittsburgh Phil want to sing and dance.

Boomy is sitting on his stoop on New Jersey Avenue, laughing his head off with the rest of the guys as Mousey rattles off joke after joke like he is top banana at the burley show. What with radio being so big, Mousey has decided that this will be his future. His old man, Mr. Cohen the butcher, is not nearly so enthusiastic. Every time he goes to the bathroom he winds up yelling, "Where's the goddamn terlet paper?" because Mousey uses the rolls to write down the punch lines of every joke he hears or reads. Mousey walks around with his pockets stuffed with toilet paper while his father has deep red grooves in his behind from sitting on a hard toilet seat all day.

So when Stutz comes running down the street with his tongue hanging out, what he sees is Mousey bouncing around goggle-eyed with an unraveled roll of toilet paper dragging on the ground and all the guys doubled over like they all just drank a bottle of castor oil.

"... So this guy walks into a bar—Hey, Stutz, where's your fucken manners?" Mousey cries, highly offended when Stutz runs right up to Boomy and starts talking to him while Mousey is performing. "You don't just barge in and interrupt when a guy is doin' his thing!"

Stutz looks at Mousey and shrugs. "I didn't know you was jerkin' off, Mouse." Then he grabs Boomy by the arm, tugging at him. "I gotta tell you something real important, kid. Actually I was thinkin' maybe it's better I don't tell ya, but then if I didn't—"

"Well, just tell me and let me decide," Boomy says, getting up from the stoop and walking over to the next building with Stutz, which inspires a good deal of ambivalence on the part of Mousey, who does not appreciate losing a member of his audience but on the other hand now has the undivided attention of those remaining.

"Look, kid, I'm pretty shook up myself," Stutz tells Boomy a little cryptically. "About four-thirty every day I take a half hour break. Usually I just go down to the deli across from the poolroom, but today I got this urge. I love tapioca pudding, and nobody makes better tapioca than the Concord. You like tapioca, Boomy?"

"Tapioca?" Boomy contorts his face. "Yech! Custard with pimples!"

"Okay, you can't please everybody. Anyhow, I'm in the Concord, and I'm carryin' two cups of tapioca pudding—you don't think I'm gonna go that far for just one cup, do ya?"

"Don't ask me. You won't see me goin' anywhere for any amount of tapioca," Boomy says as he hears Mousey reeling off another joke and the guys on the stoop cracking up. "Come on, get to it, Stutz. What's the important news?"

"Yeah, sure, kid. I grab a seat at an empty table, and who do you think is sittin' next to me?" Stutz does not expect an answer, nor does he wait for one. "It's Abie Reles and Buggsy, and whaddya think they're talkin' about? The movies, would ya believe it? They're jabberin' away like a coupla old yentas—'Did ya see this? Did ya see that? Wasn't so-'n'-so terrific?' I hadda bite my lip to keep from laughin'. Then the other boys come marchin' in . . . and that's what I wanna tell ya about, kid."

By now Boomy is more than just a little anxious. Stutz is playing this thing out like *The Perils of Pauline.*

"Pittsburgh Phil walks in with Chickenhead Gurino and his two goombahs—and I gotta ask ya somethin', kid. They got a hard-on for your brother Willie?"

Boomy turns very serious, and for a long moment he is in deep thought. He remembers Willie telling his father and Harry how Reles and Buggsy try putting the squeeze on him to throw in with them and how he leaves them standing with their mouths open when he explains how Lepke gives him the okay to tell them to go fly a kite. But in Willie's version of the story there's no hard feelings.

"I don't know, Stutz. Why?"

"Now remember," Stutz says, "I'm a table away. I don't hear every- thing, but I hear enough to know Willie's in big trouble—and maybe you and Duff too."

"What kinda big trouble?" Boomy's heart is pounding in his chest.

"I dunno, but Chickenhead tells Reles he sees Willie somewhere around Atlantic Avenue, and the whole bunch of them are so excited I think they're gonna come in their pants."

"You sure it's my brother they're talkin' about?" Boomy is hoping against hope.

"Buggsy said, 'Three fucken brothers, and one's as bad as the other.' That's why I'm worried about you, kid. I want you to be careful."

It was the first week of July, and firecrackers were exploding all over Brownsville, providing a most appropriate background. Boomy did no more walking for the rest of the evening. All he did for the next few hours was run. First he ran to his father's candy store. Willie hadn't been there all day. He called Willie's apartment in East Flatbush, and his sister-in-law told him that when Willie left this morning he said he wouldn't be home until late. He ran to all the shops he knew of that Willie "represented." He ran down the length of Pitkin Avenue, poking his head in all the stores and restaurants. Next he ran down Sutter. He visited the poolrooms and backroom betting parlors. No one had seen Willie.

Boomy decided that if he couldn't locate his brother, he would track down Reles. First he went to the Concord Cafeteria, where he found out that Reles had left with his boys around five o'clock, which jibed with what Stutz had told him. From the Concord, he half ran and half staggered down Pitkin to Saratoga, and when he saw the Kings Highway bus stop at the corner, he hopped onto the rear bumper and hitched a ride down Saratoga to Livonia.

Boomy walked into the candy store and looked around, but no one was there. Then he heard loud snoring and saw Rose sound asleep on a beach chair behind the counter.

"Hey, hello!"

Rose jumped with a snort. "Okay, hold your horses, hold your horses, I'm only one person." She stretched, rested her elbows on the counter, and yawned. "Whaddya want?"

"Do you know where Abe Reles is?"

Rose eyeballed Boomy with a smirk. She didn't answer.

"I want you to give him a message for me."

"What do I look like, the mailman?" she snapped. "Give him your own message. And get outta here. Wakin' me up like that!"

Boomy was undaunted. He glared at Rose, and said, "You tell Abe Reles that Al Davidoff, Willie's brother, is looking for him."

"Willie's brother? Willie Davidoff, huh. He wanted to be king, so now he'll be dreck!"

Rose said it one way, meaning that by not throwing in with Reles, Willie would always be small-time, but Boomy heard it another way. He slammed the door, already running.

Rose looked after him. "Can you imagine a little pisspot like that. . . ."

Sweat poured from Boomy, and his lungs were burning. Fury and frustration took turns coursing through his body, each unlocking another valve that unloosed its own flow of adrenaline. He was exhausted, but he felt as though he could fly; his muscles were weary, yet he knew he could tear through a brick wall if need be; his arms and legs felt like pillars of lead, but he was ready to take on an army.

Saratoga Avenue was a little more than a mile from where Boomy lived on New Jersey, but he wasn't counting distance, time, or anything else. He had already clocked untold miles through Brownsville searching for his brother. Tears made the streets a misty blur, but he would know his way around this neighborhood blind. He just let his feet rise and fall in cadence and carry him through the dark. Rage and fear had joined forces to inspire the unimaginable. He was going home to get Harry's gun. If he couldn't find it, he'd take a knife, a hammer—anything he could lay his hands on—and go to Reles's house on Avenue A to avenge Willie. He didn't even hear his own choked sobs as he ran down Dumont Avenue.

Willie Shapiro walked down Atlantic Avenue sucking on a paper squeeze cup of lemon Italian ice, happier than he had been in years. He couldn't remember the last time he'd been able to leave his apartment without fearing for his life.

It was five-thirty—plenty of time to catch a movie. Tomorrow he would go to Coney Island, spend the day on the beach, and walk along Surf Avenue in the evening, breathing in the sea air and the smell of frankfurters, corn on the cob, and saltwater taffy—things he hadn't done in three years. He told his mother not to wait up for him. He had a lot of living to catch up with. He was about to cross Hopkinson Avenue when he saw that the light was red. Willie smiled. Even though there was no traffic, he was not going to cross against the light. As it turned out, Willie Shapiro never crossed Hopkinson Avenue at all.

"Hiya doin', Willie."

He felt the hand grip his arm and he froze. He turned to see Happy Maione, whose face was creased by an ear-to-ear smile.

"Hi, hiya, Maione." Willie suddenly felt ill. "Nice seeing you. I'm on my way to the movies. It's getting sort of late."

"Don't worry about being late. We'll drive you." And Happy drags Willie toward Vito's car, parked alongside the curb. Willie tries to resist, but his efforts are futile.

"Abe Reles said everything is okay," Willie pleads, more frightened than he has ever been in his life.

"Abe is right here in the car, Willie. He wants to just say hello."

"Thank God!" Willie heaves a sigh of relief.

The rear door opens, and Abe Reles's hand comes out, smashing right into Willie Shapiro's nose. Willie comes to on the floor of the car with three pairs of shoes holding him down. The pain in his nose is unbearable, and the blood is running freely. He is sure that he is a dead man, and he cannot stop the flow of blood, the flow of tears, the flow of urine. Even his bowels are working on their own. The car is beginning to smell like a cesspool.

They stop on Rockaway Avenue in front of Joe's Bar & Grill, an establishment owned by Dasher Abbandando's cousin Joe Daddonna, and a place very convenient for making chopped meat out of almost anything. As a special guest, Willie is escorted to the basement. He keeps repeating just one word. "Please, please, please . . ." It is here that Willie gets the kind of beating his body was never intended to absorb. Each of the six has a turn with him. Bones are broken and flesh torn as Willie screams for God to take him.

Finally the blows stop raining upon him. He hears Reles say, like a guy who's eaten too much cake at a party, "Okay, enough, the fucken bum's done." He feels himself being trussed up as a rope is wound around his legs and hands. Then Pittsburgh Phil stuffs him feet-first into a laundry bag, and they shove him into the trunk of the car. It's okay now, he thinks as he slips in and out of consciousness. They taught him a lesson for his brothers, and now they'll dump him in front of his house, and in time he will heal. As he bounces around in the trunk of the car, Willie cries uncontrollably. He is alive, and someday he'll laugh at all this like a bad dream.

The car stops. He is home. Thank God. The trunk opens. Four hands grab him and lift him out and carry him from the car. He hopes they won't drop him on a hard sidewalk. They don't. He feels soft ground and waits to hear them drive away. What he hears is a scraping sound. With a painful movement of his shoulder he manages to slide the bag down enough to see out the top. There is a full moon. There are long blades of grass and a sand dune. Suddenly he feels himself lifted again, swung slightly, and dumped into a small depression. He looks up and sees Abe Reles lighting a cigarette while Dasher and Buggsy stand above him with shovels in their hands.

"Aw, guys, please," he whimpers. A shovelful of sand hits him in the face. He sputters and tries to clear it from his mouth. Another shovelful and another. The whimpering and crying continue. "Please, please. Not like this . . . please . . ."

Willie Shapiro takes one last look at the world and decides it is not such a great place after all.

Vito Gurino's car is the perfect car for the Fourth of July week. It keeps shooting up sparks because the weight it is carrying has its muffler scraping the ground. As Vito drives slowly down Rockaway Parkway toward Brownsville, everybody is happy, laughing it up, except for Pittsburgh Phil, who is grumbling. "Will you take a look at this. I wore this suit twice. They'll never get this fucken blood out." Meanwhile, Buggsy is doing a Hoot Gibson takeoff while Happy and Dasher accompany him by humming along: "Oh, bury me not in lone Canarsie / were the final words of the late Willie!"

Boomy stopped at the stoop of his house to catch his breath. He knew what he had to do, and he knew that his brother would have done the same for him. As he bounded up the steps, he was glad that his father would still be at the store and that Duff would never be home so early. He turned the key in the door, hoping his mother would be at his sister's apartment down the block.

"Don't you worry, Willie. I'll take care of everything," he swore under his breath as he stepped inside.

"You're even gonna take the garbage out? What a good kid! How come you wasn't at the gym tonight? Froike was havin' kittens waitin' for you."

Boomy froze. There was Willie at the kitchen table eating bobka and slurping coffee while Walter Winchell yakked away on the radio. For a moment, Boomy's head spun. He didn't know whether he was deliriously happy or unbelievably angry. Then, without realizing what he was doing, Boomy was flying. He sailed right over the kitchen table. The coffee, the bobka, and Willie all went splattering to the floor. Willie lay there twisting and turning, trying to ward off the blows as Boomy pummeled him with both fists. "What the hell's the matter with you? Are you loony or somethin'?" Finally he managed to fight his way to a standing position, and the two of them spun and wrestled around the room, knocking over chairs and a bowl of fruit. While Willie cursed and questioned the kid's sanity, Boomy remained completely silent, concentrating on finishing the job he thought Reles was going to do. Then, drained of all emotion, he sighed deeply, changed his grip on his brother, and to Willie's everlasting astonishment planted a kiss right on his cheek.

"Jesus Christ, kid!" Willie wheezed, wiping the back of his hand across the spot. "I'm going to have the AAU doctor check you out good. I didn't think you took that many head shots."

Just then the door opened and Rose Davidoff walked in. She looked at her two sons standing in an embrace, thought things over for a minute, and said, "It's nice that the two of you get along so good, but you know what? I'm not going to say anything to Poppa. His side of the family, they're very cold. Meanwhile, could you tell me what happened to my kitchen?"

Boomy and Willie released their hold on each other and looked at their mother sheepishly.

"I dropped the bobka," Willie said.

"And I spilled the coffee," added Boomy.

Brownsville did not need a Sherlock Holmes or an Ellery Queen to find out who did poor Willie Shapiro in. It was no mystery. Everyone knew who did it. All the people in the neighborhood, the few people left in the Shapiro family, the big guys in the mob like Lepke and Anastasia, even the cops—they all knew. Reles and his boys were invited to the stationhouse. With top lawyers provided by Lepke and no witnesses stepping forward, it was not a very cordial visit, because they didn't even stay long enough for coffee.

Boomy knew who did it before anyone else—with the exception of Reles's boys and Willie Shapiro himself, of course. From the first time he saw Reles, as a little kid in his father's candy store, he had a feeling about him, that someday their paths would cross. Right now, though, the planting of Willie gave Boomy a perverse feeling of relief over the fact that the Willie in question was not the Willie of Boomy's concern.

It was a relief not shared by the rest of Brownsville, where it seemed that the sun did not shine with the same brilliance. Its warmth was no longer soothing but oppressive, and cool air was not refreshing—it chilled to the bone. The sense of opportunity and excitement was replaced by anxiety and fear. People didn't walk for relaxation or exercise or just for the pure joy of it anymore. Now everyone on the streets had a destination, a purpose, and eyes darted to all sides. There were memories of the villages and shtetls of Eastern Europe, but there the enemy was from without. Here, in Brownsville, the goldeneh medina, the enemy was from within.

For the first time in memory the flow out of the community was greater than the influx. Building came to a halt. Real estate offices moved to other areas, as did many tenants, commercial and residential. Most homeowners remained because they were unable to sell. Murder, Inc. had a stranglehold on the community. From loan sharking to insurance protection, from gambling to labor-management control, Reles and Co. made sure that things ran smoothly. If the word came down from Lepke or Anastasia that someone was creating a problem, the Brooklyn mob was the eraser, the corrector. It made no difference who had to be erased or corrected. No one was exempt.

6

Moe Bradie took a huge bite of his chopped liver sandwich and pushed strands of cole slaw into his mouth with a grease-stained forefinger as he glared at Henry Collins.

"C'mon, Uncle Moe, c'mon. When does I ever ask a favor?" Henry wheedled, standing in front of his boss with his hands clasped. Henry knew and played the 1930s race game as well as anyone.

"When?" Moe said with a spray of cole slaw. "When don't you ask for a favor, for cryin' out loud?"

"Whoooie! Why you talkin' such shit, Moe? You know when I comes to work you can all go home and jes' hang up a sign: 'Henry's here, he'll take care.'"

Moe took a long drink from his bottle of celery soda and wiped his mouth with the back of his hand. "There's eight cars for you to wash tonight, and you're supposed to close up with Morris. You're not leaving me in a fucken mess like that."

"Puh-leese, puh-leese, Uncle Moe," Henry pressed his hands together under his chin. "You knows I wouldn't be aksin' if it wasn't important."

"You buried a dozen aunts, two dozen uncles, and your poor mother and father at least three times each in the past year," Moe barked. "You ain't got nothing else left to be important!"

Henry sighed and dropped the Stepin Fetchit act. "It's important, Moe, and I'll make it up, promise. My nephew, Lester's boy, he's fightin' tonight in Queens, and I just gotta go see him."

Henry and his brother Lester had come up from South Carolina some eighteen years ago, when they were in their early twenties. Their second day in New York they were both hired to pump gas at a Mobil station run by the S & R company, a relatively new family-run operation at the foot of the Williamsburg Bridge on the Brooklyn side. They never changed employers. Henry, who loved playing the clown and living the free and easy life, worked at S & R's flagship station on Stone and Sutter. Lester, the more serious and dependable of the two, settled down, married, and began raising a family while working at the S & R station on Church and East 98th, less than a mile from Henry.

"Little Penrod?" Moe's eyes widened. "Little Penrod's a fighter?" And he started counting on his fingers.

"Little Penny's sixteen, Uncle Moe. He's been fightin' in the amateurs six months now, and I'm tellin' you, he's a good 'un."

Moe shook his head. "That little pisher? It's like yesterday I'm rocking him in my arms and all he does is bawl and cry."

"I told ya not to let him look at your face."

"Go on, get outta here," Moe grunted, waving his hand. "You owe me two overtimes—and tell the kid Uncle Moe wishes him luck."

Boomy is all smiles as he comes back to his corner after the ring announcer introduces him as Giovanni Pesconi, to the loud cheers of the crowd. There is silence, broken by scattered boos and a couple of barely audible cheers, when Penrod Collins is announced.

"Ain't that something?" Boomy laughs as Froike removes the short robe from his shoulders. "Everybody is for me now, the Jews and the wops."

"Forget the crowd," Froike warns, "and concentrate on this kid Collins. He's a smart little fighter and he has fast hands. He comes to fight."

Penny Collins did come to fight, but Boomy kept moving in, bobbing and weaving the way Froike and Vic had taught him, taking punches but landing heavier ones in return. In the second round the crowd was on its feet roaring as the two youngsters stood toe-to-toe trading punches, neither one taking a backward step. Toward the end of the round Boomy scored with a left hook to the body, and Penny shuddered. At the bell Froike told him just to box in the final round, as he had the fight won.

At first Boomy followed Froike's instructions and danced around, flicking out his left jab, but by the middle of the round, with Penny desperately trying to land some good punches, he decided to go back to war. He squared away with his right hand poised and his left lowered, ready to uncoil it, and charged toward his man. Penny sidestepped neatly, and Boomy went sprawling into the ropes.

Suddenly, the crowd was silent. Penny raised his right hand, then held it poised in the air as he let Boomy free himself from the ropes. Boomy moved into a clinch. The referee broke it, and Boomy moved around the ring without throwing a punch for the final thirty seconds of the round. Back in his corner, he kept staring across the ring at Penny while Froike sponged his face and back. Then the referee raised Boomy's hand as the announcer called out, "Winner, Pesconi."

Penny was about to leave the ring when Boomy tapped his shoulder and said, "You fought a good fight, but I don't need no charity."

"I didn't give you none. We'll do it again. Next time you won't be so lucky."

All the guys were standing on the corner whooping it up when Boomy came out of the Ridgewood Grove Arena carrying his gym bag. Stutz slapped the kid on the back as they began walking toward Jahn's to bury themselves in hot fudge sundaes and play the Wurlitzer nickel-odeon.

"Helluva fight, Boomy. You sure laid it onto that shvartzer."

Mousey jumped in front of Boomy and backpedaled as he faced him, shadowboxing. "What a doity little fighter that spade was. He was gettin' ready to hit you from behind when you wasn't able to defend yourself. Man, if he woulda done that I woulda jumped in the ring myself and—"

"The kid didn't do nothin' wrong," Boomy said. "He coulda teed off on me if he wanted. I did somethin' stupid, and he coulda taken advantage of it, but he didn't. Froike bawled the piss outta me."

"Go on," Mousey persisted. "He was just scared shit if he missed. It woulda been doity if he hit you."

"It'll be real dirty if I hit you, Mousey," Boomy warned. "Come on, let's go eat."

In the kitchen of their small apartment on Throop Avenue, Penny was sitting with his father and Uncle Henry eating praline ice cream his mother had made specially for him. Slowly he worked spoonfuls of the velvety dessert through bruised lips, savoring the cold sweetness as it melted on his tongue. His father's ice cream sat on his plate barely touched, melting into a syrupy liquid as Uncle Henry scooped a third helping from the small wooden bucket onto his plate.

"You had that fish with the hook in his mouth, and what do you do? You throw him back in the water." Henry waved his spoon in Penny's face.

"Leave him be, Henry," said Lester. "You got nothing to be ashamed of, Penrod. You did yourself proud tonight."

"But I lost, Pop."

"You got to ask yourself a question, boy." Lester placed his hand on top of his son's. "What is a winner? Somebody who hangs his head low because he's embarrassed by how he comes out on top? Or somebody who can hold his head high 'cause he knows not only did he do his best but he did it the right way?"

Henry took another big scoop of ice cream. "Taught that man everything he knows," he said. "Here, have yourself some more, Penny."

Lester pushed Henry's hand away. "You're gonna turn this boy from a featherweight to a heavyweight if you don't take that fool spoon outta here."

Hyman Kalchinsky liked to show off once in a while. He knew it, but what was so terrible, especially on such an occasion as this? He was busting, kvelling, sitting in shul right up on the altar in front of the ark, watching his grandson, Sidney, his little bar mitzvah bucher, singing out his haftorah in front of the whole congregation. A voice from heaven, and a scholar—not a single word mispronounced!

And tonight, after Shabbes ended, everyone, family and friends, was invited to the Twin Cantors Catering Hall on Eastern Parkway, where there would be singing and dancing and food you shouldn't know from to celebrate little Sidney's becoming a man. Was it worth it? That's what Hyman's son, Milton, the bar mitzvah bucher's father, asked him. That's when Hyman knew that his son must have been a very good accountant before the Depression made him into an apple seller, because only an accountant would ask such a question.

"Hyman Kalchinsky." The rabbi was calling for him to step forward for his aliyah. Was it worth it? he thought to himself as he strode the few steps to the bimah, where he stopped, bent over to kiss little Sidney, and then, without having to look at the Torah, boomed out in proud, measured tones, *"Borchu es Adonai h'am voroch . . ."* A moment such as this was worth it a hundred times over.

"Poppa, Poppa," Milton had pleaded with him—no, he didn't just plead, he shook him, he actually shook him—"a simple ceremony will be fine. These are terrible times. People understand, there's no money. It's not a thing to put yourself in hock for."

"Hock shmock!" Hyman bellowed, pushing his son away. "This is not a 'thing'! It is a bar mitzvah! Only once in a lifetime. These are the pleasures that a person lives for!"

That was how Hyman Kalchinsky really felt. It was a momentous occasion, one of those rare high points of life, and after all, how many grandsons did he have? Which was why, when opportunity knocked, Hyman Kalchinsky opened the door.

For fifteen years the Kalchinskys lived right down the block from the Reles family, and for fifteen years Hyman and Abe's father took the IRT train together almost every day to their jobs as cutters in the garment center. At work Hyman always had a thimble on his middle finger, and the truth is that what he knows personally about Abe Reles would not fill up that thimble as much as his finger does. Sure, he reads things in the papers and hears stories, but with such a quiet mouse of a man for a father, the monster they paint can't exist. And there are other stories too, about an Abe Reles who is like this English bonditt Robin Hood. If a person needs money, he doesn't go to the bank, because the bank needed money even worse. To borrow money you go to Abe Reles. To a poor man, which who isn't today, he is like an angel.

One evening when Hyman Kalchinsky walks to the corner candy store to pick up a newspaper and goes inside for an egg cream with a chocolate-covered jelly ring, who should be there buying a couple of chocolate twists but Abe Reles? So what's so surprising if Hyman should be sociable and strike up a conversation? It was a meeting that was meant to be, because day and night the one thing that fills Hyman's head is what to do about little Sidney's bar mitzvah. And wouldn't you know that as soon as Hyman introduces himself and explains how close he is to Abe's father and tells him about his special problem, there is no problem anymore. He doesn't even have to ask Reles for the money. This man has such a heart.

"No friend of my father's is going to be deprived of his grandson's bar mitzvah," Reles says, gripping Hyman's shoulder. He writes down on a napkin the address of a candy store—779 Saratoga Avenue—where Hyman should ask for Sam Gold, who will arrange to get him the money.

When Hyman reluctantly inquires how much the interest will be, Reles responds with a warm pat on the back. "Herman—"

"Hyman," Kalchinsky corrects.

"Hyman, how do you worry about interest at a time like this? But to make you feel better, it's only six for five."

In Hyman's head, where the numbers didn't spin around like in his son Milton's, six for five sounds almost like a gift. He wants to kiss Reles for such generosity, but he manages to confine himself to saying, "Thank you. From the bottom of my heart, thank you. Your father has something to be proud of."

"There's nothing to thank me for," Reles replies candidly. "It's strictly business—on a friendship basis, of course, Ivan."

"Hyman."

The very next day after his meeting with Abe Reles, Hyman Kalchinsky went to Midnight Rose's candy store and met "Dapper," which was what everyone called Sam Gold, who happened to be Rose's son. Such efficiency Hyman couldn't believe. Dapper had an envelope with his fifteen hundred dollars all ready and waiting for him. Hyman signed a note of which he did not get a copy, even though he asked. He shrugged, figuring what was the big deal.

"How is six weeks for repayment?" Sam asked.

"Well," Hyman said after giving it a little thought, "the bar mitzvah isn't for two months yet . . ."

"No problem," Dapper interrupted. "In nine weeks, our representative, Louis Benson, will stop by your house. That'll save you the inconvenience of coming back here."

"You know what?" Hyman decided, "six weeks should be okay. Let it be six weeks." He wanted to show that he was a triple-A customer. Who knew when he'd have to borrow more money?

Hyman hadn't allowed for the extra costs that go into a bar mitzvah celebration. Fifteen hundred dollars took care of the affair and the band, but then there were invitations, flowers, clothes—so many odds and ends that when Louis "Tiny" Benson knocked on his door in six weeks, Hyman was already prepared to plead for the additional three originally offered to him. No pleading was necessary. Benson tipped his hat and said, "I'll see you the day after the happy occasion." Hyman didn't invite Benson in only because he didn't think he could make it through the front door.

The next morning Hyman smiled at Abe's father on the train, and said, "You know, I'm conducting a little business with your son, and I must say, he is one first-class gentleman." He couldn't understand the strange look Mr. Reles gave him.

The Twin Cantors didn't have too many affairs that were bigger or better than Sidney Kalchinsky's bar mitzvah. There was a smorgasbord that almost caused fistfights to get to the food, a bar where the liquor flowed all night, a sit-down dinner with two appetizers followed by matzoh ball soup and a choice of meat, chicken, or fish entrees, and a never-ending table of desserts. The six-piece band played without a stop. Hyman fell on his behind and split the seam of his pants trying to do a kazotzka, he cried when he was given the honor of blessing the challah bread, and he cried again when he was called up to light the first candle on Sidney's birthday cake.

The next day Hyman was on his way into Irv's Tuxedos and Formal Wear on Sutter Avenue when Tiny Benson pulled up in his specially designed Dodge and squeezed his 420 pounds out the door, a smile on his face and a toothpick dangling from his mouth.

Hyman smiled in return. "Good morning, Mr. Benson. I was expecting you, but at my house, not over here."

"I was in the neighborhood and I seen ya walking, so I figured I'll save us both some time. If ya want another extension, it's okay, but this is the last one."

"For what do I want another extension? I said I pay today so today I pay. Just let me return my tuxedo, but then I gotta go home for the money."

Hyman Kalchinsky was an honorable person. When he told Milton about how he borrowed the money for the bar mitzvah at a rate of six for five, Milton, although he was secretly thrilled at what his father had done, explained to him that he was paying twenty percent or three hundred dollars per annum, which was pretty high. Hyman said never mind per annum, what did that come to for nine weeks, and Milton scribbled numbers on a small pad until he arrived at the correct figure, $51.92. "I know you, Pa. Don't round it out and give him fifty-two dollars," Milton warned. "Not at this rate." Hyman cleaned out his small savings account, borrowed against his life insurance, and pawned his late wife Fanny's diamond ring, and there it was: $1,552. He wasn't going to listen to Milton and look like a shnorrer for eight cents.

Tiny Benson looked surprised. The toothpick fell from his lips. "You mean you got all the money, forty-two hundred dollars? You're okay."

Sutter Avenue began to tilt up and down, and the sky started falling. Hyman felt like he had swallowed a bucket of ice and it was running through all the veins and arteries of his body. He managed to brace himself against the building until the world stopped spinning, and then he realized what was so obvious.

"You got the wrong loan, Mr. Benson," he said, smiling weakly. "Somebody must have borrowed to buy a house. Mine was the loan for only fifteen hundred dollars."

Tiny Benson put Hyman Kalchinsky through school. What he learned was that six for five meant one dollar of interest per week for every five dollars borrowed. Twenty percent *per week*, not per year. Hyman got sick. He threw up and then he cried, he actually cried like a baby. But the arithmetic did not change.

Hyman pleaded with Tiny that the whole thing was a terrible misunderstanding. He begged him to speak with Abe Reles and Abe Reles's father. Tiny choked him, but only slightly. He slapped him around, but not with all his might. He bent his arms, but not enough to break them. Then he gave him a week to come up with the rest of the money. Hyman learned what it was all about to do business with the Robin Hood of Brownsville.

Hyman Kalchinsky came out better than most. By selling his house, which was going to be his nest egg, and borrowing from every friend and relative he could, he eventually paid off his debt. Besides losing his home, he could no longer wear his thimble on the middle finger of his right hand because he no longer had one. Tiny Benson cut it off, nothing personal, strictly business. But Hyman Kalchinsky was still alive, he still had nine fingers, and best of all, he moved in with Milton and was able to spend a lot of time with little Sidney. They played checkers and chess and went to the movies together, and when Hyman went to work each morning, he made it a point to avoid Mr. Reles.

Charlie Battles was so tired he was daydreaming about sleep. It was the third time in two weeks that he was covering for Henry Collins, who'd been acting like another Bojangles ever since he found himself that Carolina peahen up at the Savoy. Henry's saving grace was that he would always pay back the favor and you could always count on him if you needed someone to bail you out.

Charlie would have been a lot happier if he didn't have to fill in right after pulling a double shift at his own job at the S & R station at Junius and Liberty, where there wasn't nearly so much traffic as at Stone and Sutter. At his place a guy could sack out a whole night without being disturbed by a single honking horn. Also, working for Moe Bradie was the same as working for a grizzly bear, except if you gave a grizzly bear some honey chances were he'd warm up to you. Wasn't anything took the grump out of Moe.

First thing Charlie did was make sure the air hose was hooked up, the compressor was on, and there were full water pails at each pump island. That way anyone who just wanted to check their tires or put some water in their radiator could help themselves. Then he went back inside the small office, pulled his chair close to the window so he could keep an eye out front, and tried to relax without falling asleep. After an hour without a single customer, Charlie, bleary-eyed, went into the garage and lay down on the backseat of the roadster sitting on the middle bay. He saw no point in not taking advantage of a quiet night and catching a badly needed snooze. If anyone came up they'd blow their horn and he'd be right out.

Ooga-ooga! Ooga-ooga! Charlie Battles dragged himself out of his first sleep in nearly three days. He had no idea how long this jerk had been blowing, but his hand wasn't letting up on the horn for a second. Ooga-ooga! That was one annoying son of a bitch, Charlie thought, shaking his head to clear out the cobwebs.

"I'm comin', I'm comin'," he called.

"You're comin'? Who do you think you are, Old Black Joe?" Abe Reles sneered through the open car window.

"Hey, have a little rachmones for Charlie, boss. You take it a little bit easy and we all gonna live a lot longer life." Charlie rested his tired body against the gas pump with the rounded top that carried the logo of the Flying Red Horse, Pegasus.

Reles's eyes flashed. "Who the fuck do you think you're talkin' to, you dumb nigger bastard?" he bellowed. "You don't move your black ass and gas up my car this second, I'll grind you up and shove you down the tank!"

Pittsburgh Phil sat up straight in the passenger seat and smiled like a kid watching cartoons at a Saturday matinee. "Okay, Abie baby! Showtime!"

Charlie Battles was no longer playing the game. He turned and walked back toward the office with firm strides. He never made it.

Reles flung his door open and bounded out of the car. He picked up a bottle of motor oil, ran toward Charlie, and hit him from behind with such force that the bottle shattered. Charlie toppled over like a sack of potatoes, the viscous oil mixing with the blood that oozed from his head. Reles kicked him in the ribs, walked casually to the pump, and filled up his tank. As he got back in the car, Pittsburgh Phil shook his head reprovingly.

"You didn't clean the windshield."

. . .

A couple of days later Buggsy Goldstein drove up to the station and placed $1.20 on Moe's battered desk. It was the day the report went out that Charlie Battles had regained consciousness and was in good condition at Beth-El Hospital.

"What's this for?" Moe was no dummy. He already knew.

Buggsy popped a Lifesaver in his mouth. "My friend Abie took some gas the other night and wasn't able to pay for it. You know what an honorable guy Abie is. He don't like owin' nobody money."

"That's why he crowned my man Charlie?"

"Abe says he's a very lazy shvartzer as well as being extremely rude and disrespectful. It was a case of self-defense." Buggsy crunched down on his Lifesaver. "Abe thinks the guy will make a much better recovery if you tell him to shut his mouth and forget what happened."

"The guy don't work for me. He was just filling in. Who says he'll listen to what I say?"

"Try," Buggsy stated in a meaningful fashion.

Moe did try, if not with his whole heart and soul. And it wouldn't have mattered anyway, because Charlie Battles was angry and his mind was made up. It was bad enough that he lived in a world where people called him names like "nigger" and "shvartzer" and treated him like a household pet, but that man meant to kill him, and for no reason other than the color of his skin. Charlie Battles was not going to back off.

Abe Reles sat seething in the courtroom as the judge tore into him, denouncing him as a vicious animal and predicting that he would either rot behind bars or die in a hail of police bullets. Kid Twist laughed and turned to his lawyer, snarling a challenge. "Cops think first before they shoot. I just shoot." For the assault on Charlie Battles the judge sent Reles to Elmira, where he served thirty months, the longest sentence of his life.

Lester Collins replaced the dipstick and closed the hood of the Buick. "Oil's fine." The driver handed him a dollar bill for the gas, and Lester waved as the Buick drove off. The sun had set about an hour ago, but the night air still hadn't cooled. The red sunset meant that tomorrow was going to be a hot one, and that made Lester smile. When one of his customers at the Church Avenue station handed him two grandstand tickets for tomorrow's Dodgers-Giants game at Ebbets Field, Lester's first reaction was to thank him but turn down the offer because of work. Then he thought how fine it would be to spend a day with his boy, something he couldn't remember ever doing before. Besides, the truth was—and he was ashamed to tell it to anyone—that neither he nor Penny had ever seen a major-league game. So here he was, working Henry's night slot and feeling grateful to his brother for trading with him, never mind that Henry was a natural-born tomcat.

Penny had called Lester twice tonight so far. "Mom's packing a picnic basket with chicken sandwiches and a bagful of sweet snap peas," he said the first time. Then he called again about twenty minutes later. "My friend Zeke says if we get there three hours early we can stand by the player's entrance on Sullivan Place and get their autographs, and then we can watch the whole batting practice!"

"Sounds good to me, son," Lester had said into the phone with a smile playing on his face.

Penny couldn't sleep. He was so excited about tomorrow's—no, today's—outing with his father that he just kept tossing around in his bed. In the light of the three-quarter moon filtering through the thin linen curtain he could see by his alarm clock that it was almost four in the morning. Maybe he had fallen asleep for a while, he thought to himself, because he never did hear his father come home. Lester had promised that he would close the station by two so he could grab a few hour's sleep before they left for the game.

Penny slipped out of bed and tiptoed over to his parents' room. As soon as he saw that the door was open his heart sank. His mother always left the door open for his father, and when Lester was ready for bed he always closed it. Penny shook his head. It wouldn't be the first time his father took Uncle Henry's night shift and fell asleep on the job.

There was a phone in the apartment, courtesy of S & R, because the company wanted to make sure it could always reach its workers in case of emergency. Naturally, S & R deducted the bill from his father's salary, so Penny was not supposed to use the phone unless it was important, and he'd already made two calls tonight. Still, he picked up the receiver and dialed the station. After a dozen or so rings with no answer, Penny pulled on a pair of pants and a polo shirt and slipped on his sneakers. His father was probably on his way home now, but Penny didn't have the patience to wait any longer. He left a note for his mother and closed the door softly behind him.

It was about two miles from his house to the station, but running two miles was a piece of cake for a kid who trained as rigorously as he did. He knew that his father would drive up Stone Avenue to Atlantic, then go left on Atlantic, then make his right onto Throop and head for home, so that was the route Penny followed.

As he approached Belmont Avenue Penny Collins came to a halt, shut his eyes, and tried to blot out the world. Although he was more than a block away from the station, he had already seen the police cars and the flashing lights.

"You gonna buy anything today?" Midnight Rose snapped as the two kids walked into the store.

"We jus' wanna look at the joke books," the skinny one said as he pointed at the rack of comics, "and if there's one we ain't read yet, we'll buy it."

"Joke books, my aunt Tillie," she growled, brandishing her dishrag at them. "Go on, scram before I kick your tuchises in. You'll go blind looking at those *Police Gazette* kurvehs."

As the kids hightailed it out of the store, Pittsburgh Phil, who was at the counter washing down a chocolate doughnut with a cup of coffee, reached inside his jacket pocket and pulled out an ice pick caked with blood.

"Stash this for me, will ya, mameleh?"

Rose wiped the pick with the dishrag and bent down to put it under the drainboard that covered the floor behind the counter. "You been enjoying yourself, Pep?"

Pittsburgh Phil Strauss grinned widely. "You know something, Rose, shvartzers really know how to die. They do it with much more style than a white guy."

Rose leaned her elbow on the counter and looked into Pep's twinkling eyes. It warmed the cockles of her heart to hear her boys talk about their work.

"I sneak up on him, see, and then I loop a piano wire around his neck, give a good pull, and hold the ends with my left hand while my right hand makes a pincushion outta him. He's going 'gu-gu-gu' and the blood is shpritzin' out of all the holes, and he crawls up to me and starts hugging my leg, and then—this you ain't gonna believe—he's holding these two tickets up to me like he wants me to have 'em. I take a look when he croaks a few seconds later, and they're for today's game at Ebbets Field."

"You got the tickets?" Rose inquired. "My son Sam would love to go if you ain't gonna use them."

"You think I'm a shmuck altogether? If anyone knows about those tickets don't you think the cops would have the seats staked out?"

"Oh, so you do got a head on your shoulders."

Strauss got up from his stool and yawned. "I'm gonna do a little shopping on Pitkin Avenue. I wanna be wearin' some new threads when I visit Abe and tell him how I whacked this prick Battles for him."

"Battles?" Rose gives him a look. "The one who pointed the finger at Abie? You killed him too?"

"Whaddya mean, 'too'? Who do ya think I been telling ya about?"

"Sweetheart," Rose cooed as she picked up the newspaper she'd been reading behind the counter, "according to the afternoon edition of the *Daily News* the name of the person found stabbed to death at the station on Stone Avenue was"—she wet her finger with her tongue and turned two or three pages—"here it is. Collins, Lester Collins."

It was Moe Bradie's intention to do the right thing. Unfortunately, good intentions often produce lousy results. He sat in the second row of the Ebenezer Baptist Church next to Henry Collins and right behind Ruby and Penrod Collins, spellbound by the entire service, this being the first time he had ever set foot inside a Baptist Church. It wasn't the fiery eulogy, spiced with a mixture of venom, sweetness, hope, despair, hatred, and love; it wasn't the soul-stirring singing of the white-gowned choral group, and it wasn't the involvement and urgings of the congregation with commentaries like "Tell us like it is, Brother" and "Praise be to the Lord". What impressed Moe more than anything else was seeing the emotional venting of Ruby Collins kept in check by her quiet sense of dignity. As the Minister would point out a virtue of Lester Collins or relate a memorable highlight of his life, Ruby would seem prepared to cry and shout for him, with her body involuntarily recoiling and her hands reaching out. But her cry would be a silent one and she would immediately recompose herself and place a comforting, reassuring arm around Penny's shoulders. Moe had known Ruby Collins from the time she was a young girl, when she and Lester first met, nearly twenty years ago. Only now did he realize that he hadn't known her at all until today.

Ruby worked as a domestic. Like her husband, it seemed that she, too, was an employee of S & R. She worked a five day week, one day for each of the two partners and one day each for Moe and two other station managers. She was a handsome, intelligent woman who was efficient at her job but, most important, had a strong sense of responsibility and although quiet, always seemed to say the right thing at the right time. She arranged her schedule whereby her workday would start at seven in the morning so that she would be finished at three and home for Penrod when he returned from school. Moe Bradie had great respect for Ruby Collins, and late that afternoon, when she seemed ready to fall apart, his intentions were the best, but he pressed the wrong button.

After the service and the trip to the cemetery Moe drove to Grabstein's Delicatessen, picked up a platter of food, and went to the Collins's apartment. When he got there, Henry and a few friends and relatives were trying to calm Ruby, who was pacing back and forth wringing her hands in anguish. Moe pulled Henry aside and asked him what was wrong.

"Penny said he was goin' down to the grocery store to pick up a few things for the table," Henry said, "and that's better'n an hour ago. Then we get a call from one of Penny's buddies who tells Ruby that Penny's actin' crazy and he's on his way to even the score for his daddy."

Ruby turned to Moe and stared into his eyes. "Mr. Bradie, please. Penny's all I got left. He don't understand about those people. Please, do something."

"Take it easy," Moe said gently. "The boy'll probably go three or four blocks and turn around. He won't even know where to begin looking. You know how kids are."

"I know how kids are, but you don't know my Penny," Ruby sobbed.

That's when Moe remembered that a year or so ago Abe Reles gave him the telephone number of the candy store where he and the boys hung out; just in case a problem ever arose and Moe needed to contact them. Moe didn't ask for it, he didn't want it, but he knew better than to say so. Now that he had it, he thought, he might as well use it. It was to everyone's best interest. The only problem with Moe's logic was simply that—it was Moe's logic.

Midnight Rose was hanging up the phone when the door opened and Pittsburgh Phil walked in, twirling a gold key chain that was clipped to his pants.

"Good timing," she said. "Wanna be a good Samaritan and save your own life?"

"Sounds like a worthwhile cause to me." He flopped down on a stool and started cleaning his fingernails with the blade of a small pocketknife attached to the key chain.

"I just got a call from the manager of the station where you guys have been doing your artwork, and he wants that you please shouldn't kill this kid who happens to be the son of the shvartzer you carved up and is on his way over here to even the score. Manager says he knows you wouldn't want to hurt a kid, so if you hide out for a while he'll get tired when he can't find you and he'll go home and nobody gets hurt. Ain't that a beautiful story?"

"You're shittin' me, of course, right?" Pep said as he folded the blade and examined his nails.

"Could I make up such a story?"

"Where is this punk? I'll cut his fucken head off and hang it in my living room."

"Oy, don't be a putz." Rose tapped impatiently on the counter. "You go out and do that and you'll be keeping Abie company. Just call up one or two of them kids that's always sniffing at your heels and tell 'em some shvartzers are coming into the neighborhood looking for trouble. Believe me, that'll take care of it."

. . .

Boomy's rematch with Penrod Collins was not a scheduled bout and it wasn't a fight that either one of them planned or wanted to have. It all started when Mousey came into a lot of loose change and was treating everyone to a chozzerai binge.

He came by the dough in a most daring and creative way. Being a freshman at Thomas Jefferson High School, Mousey learned that the only time he was noticed was when he looked in the mirror and noticed himself. He realized that things would be different when he was a junior or senior and a few inches taller but seeking more immediate gratification, Mousey decided that if high school girls did not fall at his feet, then his feet were free to pursue other avenues. Back in P.S. 174 it was pretty much unanimously agreed that Mousey was the very best student when it came to the mirror-on-the-shoe-to-look-under-girls'-dresses game. He felt it was time to reestablish his mastery of this art.

Actually, Jefferson High was much more conducive to this activity than P.S. 174 had been. In high school, every hour a bell would ring signifying the end of one class and giving you ten minutes to get to your next class. As soon as that bell rang, the narrow corridors were bulging with wall-to-wall students, rushing every which way to their various classes. If you happened to be a bit on the short side, you were completely lost and unnoticed among the bustling throngs—from the top of your head to the tips of your shoes.

All the freshmen were talking about Mousey Cohen and his "free shows." But it did not take a very long time for Mousey to learn that if you want to stay on top you've got to upgrade your shtik. Every ten-minute changeover it seemed that half the guys in school piled into the boys' room to sneak a smoke. Nobody peed during the break because pee-time was saved for during regular classtime when you would raise your hand and go, "Ooh, ooh, ooh!"

A very lively debate ensues, the consensus of which is that Mousey's mirror act is old hat now and is no longer a big deal. When Mousey emerges from the smoke in most dramatic fashion and announces that he is there to defend his good name the guys let him know that they no longer have any interest in any schoolgirl's drawers. A voice comes out from somewhere deep in the mist, "I bet you can't grab a peek at

Miss Goldberg's." This is followed by an unbearable silence. It is as though someone had uttered a sacrilege. When you are surrounded by teachers who look as though they were on the original passenger list of the Mayflower, and suddenly you get a new English teacher who looks and sounds like Betty Boop—

The thought of it makes Mousey weak-kneed but a challenge is a challenge! "There ain't a girl or a woman alive whose dress I can't get under." He still couldn't see any of the guys but the sounds of their breathing told him they were impressed. For carrying out such a historic accomplishment, he insisted that every guy is to chip in two bits and he is to get paid upon performing his feat. For two weeks the school was abuzz with the anticipation of the event.

Miss Goldberg, seated atop her desk with her legs crossed, with all the boys' eyes focused on her dimpled kneecaps, was taking attendance in her freshman English class. "Morris Cohen," she sang out in her melodious voice. Just then the door opened and in staggered Mousey carrying a large, thin rectangular object wrapped in brown paper.

"Oh, there you are, Morris," She slid down from her perch and bounced over with short, mincing steps to help Mousey, who seemed about to collapse under the weight of his package. As she grabbed hold of its sides and took it from Mousey, she exclaimed in surprise, "Why, Morris, this isn't heavy at all. You're going to have to exercise a little more. What have we here, anyhow?"

"Being that we're reading Shakespeare," he explained, "I thought it would be a good idea if we hung this picture I found of him on the wall so we can all see the guy who wrote what we're reading." Everyone was leaning forward in their seats, eyes bugging, holding their breaths collectively. They had already looked for and seen that tied onto Mousey's right Keds sneaker was a small compact mirror covered neatly by the loose tongue of the sneaker.

"Where in the world did you come upon such a treasure?" she asked with much animation and enthusiasm as she stripped the paper from the frame.

Mousey shrugged and answered modestly, "I know some collectors."

He wasn't going to explain to her that this kid he knows, Chotchke Charlie, has everything in the world that nobody else wants.

"How about right here?" Miss Goldberg asked, as she raised the framed print above her head near the coat closet. There was William Shakespeare, with a large flared collar, looking down at Miss Goldberg's freshman English class with no one looking back at him. It was at this exact moment that Mousey, with a huge lopsided grin on his face stepped up right behind her and with his left foot, gently kicked the tongue of his right sneaker, uncovering the mirror and then slid his right foot directly under Miss Goldberg's skirt, exclaiming "Let me get a good look!" At the same time he lowered his eyes and stared at his mirrored shoe then, behind her back, thrust his two fists victoriously into the air. "It looks great!" The entire class immediately burst into a chorus of cheers and handclapping.

Miss Goldberg turned and faced her class. "I am truly touched. I would not have believed that you could get so—so excited at part of the educational process. It will always be here for you to look at and enjoy." There was another sustained round of applause.

Just as the guys are forming a ring around Mom's Knish Wagon and Mousey is taking a count to see how many potato knishes and how many kasha, this guy from the Bristol Street Barons comes running up to them, wild-eyed and wheezing.

"The niggers are on their way! They're lookin' for trouble!"

"How come?" Shorty asks.

"How do I know how come," the Baron pants. "Do I look like I think like a shvartzer?"

"Okay," Snake hollers, "let's go get 'em," and all the guys begin whooping to pump themselves up.

"Ain't we gonna eat?" Boomy asks. It seems that only he and the knish vendor are not happy, but Boomy reluctantly runs after his pals as they all follow the guy from the Barons to the Ambassador Theater on Saratoga Avenue.

If every guy belonging to a gang in Brownsville wasn't part of the mob under the marquee of the Ambassador Theater on Saratoga Avenue it was only because they were either in the can, in the sack, or hard of hearing. Everyone is there—the Barons, the Dukes, the Cowboys, and plenty of guys who don't even know what's going on but want to be part of it, whatever it is. When the Barons scout shouts, "They're here!" from a couple of blocks away, Boomy gets caught up in defending his turf the same as everyone else.

As the scout runs toward them from Dumont Avenue, pointing over his shoulder, Boomy strains to see how big a gang is coming down on them. Finally he sees a guy walking along by himself, back ramrod straight, arms swinging at his sides, almost like he's marching.

"Where are they?" a dozen voices cry.

"He's the only one I seen so far," the scout croaks, falling into the arms of a buddy. "The rest of 'em must be a couple blocks behind."

Bats and clubs are being waved in the air, chains are rattling, fists are pumping. The guys are getting sore throats from shouting about how they're going to kill the shvartzers. Boomy's throat is fine because he isn't shouting. He's beginning to feel his longing for a knish return.

Meanwhile, the threat to Brownsville keeps coming, not slowing down at all even though the guys at the front of the crowd are screaming and cursing at him.

"What does that crazy boogie think he's doin'?" Snake yells.

"Hey . . ." Shorty is pulling at Boomy's sleeve to get his attention. "Hey, ain't that—"

But Boomy is already pushing his way to the front of the mob. Just as an army of fists and clubs and chains is ready to go into action, he runs up to Penny Collins and blocks his way.

"Hold on! Where do you think you're goin'?"

Penny stops. His eyes seem to stare right through Boomy. "Get out of my way, Pesconi."

Everyone seems to be in agreement with Penny on this point. "Yeah, g'wan kid, blow! We'll show him the way back to Spooksville!"

"I'm only Pesconi for the AAU, but that don't matter," Boomy says to Penny, his voice low. "You outta your fucken mind?"

"Why? Can't I walk down the street, or is it off limits to us po' colored folk?"

"Yeah, you can walk down the street," Boomy says, "but the word is you're here with a whole gang to make trouble."

"If me and my shadow makes a gang, then I guess I'm a gang, but I don't need no gang for what I'm doing. And I'm not looking to make trouble." Penny holds up a newspaper clipping he's clutching in his fist. "The trouble was already made."

"Come on, kid, why don't you listen to him and get outta the way," snarls Red Kulik, leader of the Barons, giving Boomy a shove. "We know what to do with guys like him that think they can move in here and do whatever they want with Kid Twist gone."

Boomy swings around with his fists balled up. Guys who knew or knew of Boomy knew you do not try pushing him around. He can't figure out what this is all about, but he has this strong feeling that Penny Collins is an okay kid, and he doesn't want to see him get all busted up for the wrong reason.

"I don't want anything except one guy," Penny says levelly. "Harry Strauss, the one they call Pittsburgh Phil. That's who I want."

"You want Pittsburgh Phil? Go get him!" says Kulik. "But first you gotta go through us, Brillo-head."

The mob starts shouting again and closing in on Boomy and Penny. These guys look at Strauss and Reles and Goldstein like kids in the bleachers look at Ruth and Gehrig.

"He killed my daddy." Penny speaks softly. No one else hears him, just Boomy. He's seen in the *Brooklyn Eagle* about the colored guy getting killed at the station on Sutter Avenue and how Pittsburgh Phil was brought in for questioning and released. Until this moment he has no idea it was Penny Collins's old man. He's sure the name was in the paper, but he never tied it together. Arms are reaching over him to grab at Penny, who doesn't flinch. Boomy knows there is no holding these guys back any longer. They're like a pack of mad dogs. "Hold it!" he shouts at the top of his lungs. "He's mine! The sonuvabitch coldcocked me in the amateurs, and I want his ass."

For the first time Penny's expression changes. "You lyin' bas—"

He does not finish his statement because Boomy hauls off and doubles him over with a left hook to the gut.

Mousey, who has squeezed his way to the center of the mob, yells out, "You show that doity bum! My boy Boomy'll show him!"

Mousey never sees the shot that Penny brings up to pay Boomy back. As Boomy's butt hits the ground he begins to wonder if this was such a good idea after all. He remembers only too well what a tough, gutsy kid this Penny Collins is. He gets to his feet, and the two of them start swinging away with everything they've got. As the fight goes on, there is more wrestling and less punching, because their arms begin feeling like they're weighted with cinderblocks.

"I'm sorry I didn't knock your head off when I had the chance," Penny hisses during a clinch. "Calling me a dirty fighter."

"I had to have a reason for belting you."

"You had to have a reason for belting me? That's a good one. And why'd you have to belt me?"

"You wouldn't understand," Boomy gasps, breaking away, not quite understanding it himself.

They continued throwing punches as the sun sank and the crowd of Barons, Dukes, and Cowboys cheered and booed the back-and-forth battle. Boomy kept telling Penny there was no way he was going to find Pittsburgh Phil and if he did he wouldn't live to tell about it. Penny kept telling Boomy it was none of his business. By the time the moon climbed high into the sky there were still a few spectators, but most of the guys got hungry or just plain exhausted. They forgot they were there to protect their neighborhood from an invading horde, and all the venom seemed to evaporate into the night air. Finally Boomy and Penny were expending more strength holding each other up than they were fighting. The only ones left watching were Shorty, Mousey, and Snake, and they were too tired to stand and cheer, so they sat on the curb trying hard to keep their eyes open.

It all ended when a little kid, maybe nine, ten years old, walked over to Boomy and Penny. "I heard there was a big fight around here. You guys know anything about it?"

"Nah, we been busy dancin'," Boomy said. "We ain't seen no one fightin'."

"Guys shouldn't dance with each other," the kid said, waving his finger at them.

Boomy, Mousey, Shorty, and Snake walked Penny Collins most of the way home. Mousey hated to admit it, but he was beginning to think that maybe this Penny Collins was all right after all.

When they got to the other side of Atlantic Avenue, Boomy gave Penny a friendly jab on the shoulder. "I'll catch you in our rematch, okay?"

"Who'll I be fightin', Pesconi or Davidoff?"

He didn't fight either, because once Ruby Collins got her boy back safe and sound, she wasn't taking any more chances. Two days later they moved back to South Carolina.

7

I'm telling you, this Dewey is a fucken maniac!" a red-faced Dutch Schultz roars, slapping his hands down on Lepke's desk. "If we don't do him, he's gonna do us!"

Schultz is referring to Thomas E. Dewey, recently appointed as special prosecutor to bust Murder, Inc. Dewey has already made a reputation for himself during his stint as assistant U.S. Attorney for the Southern District of New York, when he blasted away at organized crime with a zeal and flourish that drew cheers across the nation. So when Governor Herbert H. Lehman taps him for the prosecutor's job in July 1935, the heat is on.

Lepke leans back in his leather swivel chair. "You're upset right now. Calm down, Arthur." Schultz's given name is Arthur Flegenheimer, and Lepke must think it suits him, because he never calls him Dutch.

"Upset? Me? Upset?" Schultz parodies, cocking his head to one side. "Why should I be upset?" Then he goes back to bellowing. "Just because that sonuvabitchin' yahoo is pickin' my bones clean and just about puttin' me outta business?" He slams his fist on the desk, knocking over a glass of milk that's sitting in front of Lepke. The milk soaks the papers on the desk and drips down onto Lepke's pants.

Big Al Anastasia is leaning against a wall of the office, marveling at

Schultz's performance. He is thinking that maybe this kraut does have a screw loose but he is one tough nut job. He takes a handkerchief from his pocket, walks over to Lepke, and hands it to him.

Dutch stands in front of the desk like a vaudevillian who has just finished his routine and is waiting for the audience's reaction. He does not get a standing ovation.

"So tell us, Dutch. Tell us what you want to do." Lucky Luciano, who hasn't spoken until now, breaks the silence.

Schultz stares at the kingpin of the Syndicate as though he cannot believe what he hears. "What do I wanna do? How about a ticker-tape parade down Broadway? Better yet, how about we all bow down and kiss his ass in Macy's window? What do I wanna do? I wanna do what we gotta do—send a fucken message by blowin' the prick's head off!"

Willie Davidoff walks into the poolroom after watching Boomy work out. The place is empty except for a couple of neighborhood punks and Fat Yerna, who is sitting by the Coke cooler gnawing away on a salami sandwich you can smell from Brownsville to Pittsburgh. Willie racks the balls on his favorite table and is just chalking his stick when he feels a tap on his shoulder. He looks around, and there is Albert Anastasia standing behind him, nodding his head at Fat Yerna. There are very few things that can interrupt Fat when he is eating. Big Al is one of them.

Fat picks himself up and waddles toward the door, shooing the kids ahead of him. All that remains in the poolroom are eight tables, two guys, a Coke cooler, and the stink of garlic.

"Rotation or eight ball?" Willie asks as he resumes chalking his stick.

Big Al walks to the wall rack and tests out one poolstick after another. It seems pretty certain that he has played this game before. "Straight pool," he answers, sliding his neatly blocked hat a little farther back on his head. Albert Anastasia has a penchant for hats. He has one for every day of the month, which is how he comes to be known here and about as the Mad Hatter.

Willie breaks and leaves a nicely spread table with nothing going into a pocket. By the time he's ready to take his next turn there are only three balls left.

"If you're going to order flowers for Joey Amberg outta respect," Al growls, sinking a shot, "stinkweeds'll be okay."

Willie knows what that means but doesn't say a word. Like everyone else, he hears that Hymie Kazner, one of Anastasia's guns, was murdered and dumped into a sewer by Joey Amberg.

"We're puttin' the hit on the sonuvabitch, but we want someone tailing his brother Pretty to make sure he ain't around when the boys do the job."

Willie watches the nine ball roll into the pocket. "This ain't my line of work, Al. Don't get me wrong. I know you're right and I respect you, but I don't wanna ruffle no feathers." Like everyone else, Willie also hears that Joey Amberg is under the protection of Joe Adonis and Bugsy Siegel. Besides which, it happens that Willie, to the considerable surprise of everyone who knows him, is now a married man and has a wife to think about.

Anastasia sidles up alongside Willie, whispering even though they are alone in the room. "Everything is cleared. Adonis and Siegel put their thumbs down on him. With Reles in the icebox I got enough heat-packers—it's brains I need. That's why I'm depending on you."

So on the last day of September Willie plays the shadow and winds up spending the night watching two gangster movies at the Palace Theater about five rows behind Louis "Pretty" Amberg, whose name derives from "Pretty Fucken Ugly." At the end of the first movie, which has more gunfire and bloodletting than the Great War, the old lady sitting next to him turns and says, "Would you believe this trash? A disgrace, it's just a disgrace."

"You got to tell yourself it's only make-believe," Willie reassures her.

Mousey knows a great catch when he sees one, and the one he sees on Bay 2 at Brighton Beach he doesn't stop talking about for two months. What really surprises him is that the guy that makes such a grab, his good buddy Boomy, is usually much better with a bat than with a glove. In the field you sometimes get the feeling that his hands are made of plaster of paris. Maybe, Mousey considers, Boomy is inspired by new surroundings, because this is their very first time venturing over to Bay 2.

Coney Island has always been their beach, traditionally and almost by heredity.

And that's where they were headed, their brown bags already packed and leaking with their lunches, each guy shouldering a towel with the name of a different hotel in the Catskills, when Shorty starts saying how Bay 2 is where the real "in" crowd goes and how all the high-class kids from Flatbush and Borough Park go there. Nobody is ready to sell Nathan's and Feltman's down the river until Shorty tells how his cousin Herbie from Canarsie started going to Bay 2 about three weeks ago, and last week he moves his blanket under the boardwalk with this living doll from Bensonhurst who is going to start City College in six months, and they wind up French-kissing before they even know each other's names. At this point the guys figure a hot dog is a hot dog and decide to give Bay 2 a try.

When they get down to the beach, the sand is so hot that they look like a troupe of ballet dancers as they tiptoe along searching for a spot to place their towels. While the rest of the guys are going "Ooh! Aah!" with every step they take, Shorty sees Boomy smoothing out his towel about thirty yards behind them, right next to a blanket on which happens to be maybe the prettiest girl on all of Bay 2, a dark-haired beauty with big green eyes, together with a couple of other girls who also are not too difficult to look at. The guys are tongue-tied, all except Mousey, who keeps much better track of the hour than Cinderella ever did at the Prince's ball. Every time he takes a dip in the ocean, which is constantly, he runs over to their neighbors' blanket to ask Miss Green Eyes the time. As she does not go anywhere near the water, she is the only one around wearing a watch.

While Mousey and Green Eyes know what time it is, everyone else on the beach knows that the tall, lanky guy who seems to be part of her group is going to be a starting pitcher for Erasmus High next spring, because he keeps announcing, as he throws to a buddy catching for him, how he's going to blow the competition away with his fastball and lead Erasmus to the championship.

"I guess Erasmus ain't such a great school," Snake comments, turning on his stomach in order to tan his back. "This shnook can't even read." He points to the big sign that says No Ball Playing Allowed.

Mousey is on his way back from another splash in the ocean, and

Green Eyes is sighing as she sits up and gets ready to check her watch, when Erasmus's pride and joy yells out to his catcher, "Okay, Normie, here comes the super-duper drop ball!" He goes into this exaggerated windup, kicks his foot high in the air, and lets the pitch sail. Mousey stops dead in his tracks and blurts out an "Oh, God!" which is all he can think of as he sees the ball sweeping to the exact spot he was heading for. That's when he sees the catch. Like a bullfrog's tongue capturing a meal, Boomy's hand darts out, and everyone around him hears the resounding *splat!*

Miss Green Eyes has a most un-Brownsvillesque name: Gabrielle Samuelson. She also has a way of saying thank you that would draw blank stares anywhere along Sutter Avenue. "I am eternally indebted to you," she gushes as she glides from her blanket to where Boomy sits staring at the ball embedded in his palm.

"Aw, it was nothin'. I just like your face so much the way it is."

Mousey, Shorty, and Snake sit on their towels eating oysterettes with sauerkraut and relish, which are the free "sides" at the hot dog concession. They are watching their pal Boomy, who is now able to use his towel strictly for drying himself as he is sharing Gabrielle Samuelson's blanket as well as her BLT on toast, which she went up to the boardwalk to buy. She does not bring food to the beach from home because she considers it gauche. Boomy tells her that he agrees 100 percent and he thinks to himself that he will find out for sure as soon as he is able to look in a dictionary.

Willie Davidoff's reward for a job well done—keeping an eye on the back of Pretty Amberg's head in the Palace Theater while Happy Maione and company blew off the back of Joey Amberg's head in a deserted garage—is an assignment to keep an eye on the entire body of Special Prosecutor Tom Dewey. Instead of doing this from a comfortable seat in a dark theater, Willie is supposed to carry the job out in broad daylight on Fifth Avenue in New York City, where Dewey lives. He is to monitor Dewey's every move, from the time he leaves his apartment each morning until he arrives at his office, for a period of one to two weeks.

The day before he is to begin, he gets an early-morning call from

Big Al Anastasia, who tells him he is sorry but Lepke says this job cannot be farmed out and Al must handle it himself. Willie can barely contain his joy, but before he has a chance to savor the moment, *bingo!* he gets another phone call.

"Willie, I need a baby. . . . Willie? You hearin' me?"

Willie is silent because he thinks this is a subject Albert Anastasia would be much better off discussing with Mrs. Anastasia, but then Al gets around to explaining.

When Albert Anastasia talks, people listen, just like Willie Davidoff's next-door neighbor listens when Willie talks. She listens because she is struck dumb, and besides, she's running neck and neck with the old woman who lives in a shoe, so what should she say, even if Willie is the last guy in the world she'd picture as a baby-sitter, when he tells her it would be his pleasure, as his mornings have been freed up, to take her infant daughter for daily walks so she can tend the rest of her brood?

For four consecutive mornings Albert Anastasia wheels Willie Davidoff's neighbor's daughter back and forth in front of Thomas Dewey's apartment building. By the fourth morning he and Dewey are close to being friends, nodding and smiling at each other as Dewey leaves for work with his two bodyguards. Dewey cannot help being impressed by such a doting father. Big Al cannot help being impressed by the unswerving routine of New York's number one crime buster.

Each morning Dewey hits the street at precisely eight-thirty, walks to a drugstore two blocks from his building, and goes inside to make phone calls while his bodyguards wait outside. He uses the drugstore phone booth so as not to awaken his wife. After the fourth morning, Anastasia feels that no more surveillance is needed. He and Lepke, together with Lucky Luciano and Dutch Schultz, plan a hit that will take place right in the drugstore.

When Willie returns the baby after the fourth day, he cannot understand the grief-stricken look on his neighbor's face as he explains that the walks will have to stop because his mornings are no longer free. He never knew that each time he returned with the carriage, his neighbor would find a hundred-dollar bill tucked inside the baby's sweater.

. . .

When Shorty sees the large Victorian homes with the neatly trimmed hedges, manicured lawns, trellised rosebushes, and beds of peekaboo tulips, he does not utter a word. All he does is stare. He cannot believe that each of these houses is lived in by only one family. Shorty has had a bad case of nerves ever since Boomy tells him they're going on a double date with Gabrielle's friend Sylvia, but now he's sweating bullets.

They climb the steps to the porch, and Boomy presses a bell that doesn't ring like a bell but makes music. Shorty has seen chimes in Rappaport's Hardware Store, but he has never heard them in a house before. The door is opened by a lady who Shorty thinks is Gabrielle's older sister but turns out to be her mother. She is wearing a dress, not a housecoat, and she smells like one of the roses from her garden instead of scouring powder. She introduces herself with a big smile and invites them into the living room. Shorty and Boomy are trying so hard to be polite that they both trip over the edge of the large Persian rug because they are looking everywhere but in front of them, which is exactly where Mrs. Samuelson's behind and the rug happen to be.

"Oh, do be careful, boys!" she exclaims, turning and holding out her hands to them. "Are you all right?"

"Fine, Mrs. Samuelson," Boomy assures her. Shorty feels it necessary to add, "We're used to walking on linoleum. You know, you can get electric shocks from walkin' on rugs if you don't lift your feet." He cannot understand the look he gets from Boomy. If he'd spent more time in school, Shorty thinks, he would know that too.

"Boys, this is Sylvia."

Shorty has to sit down immediately. He does not have time to say hello, shake hands, or anything. As soon as he sees what look like two prize-winning cantaloupes in Sylvia's sweater, the front of his pants zooms out like there is a spring inside, and he shocks everyone by doing something resembling a back flip and winding up on the couch. Sylvia, who may not have a face that can launch a thousand ships but is not exactly short on absorbing attributes, looks his way with a sly grin, and Shorty's face turns beet red. She saw.

As Shorty is thinking that this is a moment he will never ever live down, Mrs. Samuelson holds a box of Baricini mixed chocolates in front of him, and like magic he's back to normal. It is while he is trying to let a peanut cluster melt in his mouth rather than cut short the ecstasy by chewing that Gabrielle comes walking—no, it is more like gliding— down the steps to join them. Shorty thinks what a lucky stiff Boomy is, because she is even prettier than he remembers.

Mrs. Samuelson is smoothing her daughter's blouse and patting her pleated skirt when Gabrielle's father comes down the stairs. "Gaby," he says, "home by eleven-thirty, right?"

Boomy clears his throat. "You know, that may be a little hard, sir, because we're going to a party in my neighborhood and it'll take us close to an hour each way."

"I didn't know that, Albert," Gabrielle says.

"Where do you live, young man, Pennsylvania?" Mr. Samuelson jokes.

"You almost hit it on the nose," Boomy teases back with a big smile. "I'm right around the corner from Pennsylvania Avenue."

"Brownsville?" Mr. Samuelson gives a sniff like he's expecting a strange smell. "I know the neighborhood. I have a couple of shops there."

"My father's in business there too."

"Is he in the garment industry?"

Before Boomy has a chance to answer, Gabrielle breaks in. "Albert's a prizefighter, Daddy."

Shorty is beginning to think he made a terrible mistake by not loading up on the Baricini chocolates when he had the chance.

"What's your name, young man? You certainly don't look old enough to be a prizefighter."

Boomy feels the smile slide off his face, and he presses his hands deep into his pockets. "I'm just an amateur. My name is Al Davidoff, but I box under—"

"Davidoff? . . . Davidoff?" At no time since he entered the living room would Mr. Samuelson's expression have been considered jovial, but he now looks as though someone has inserted a vacuum tube into him and drained out all the blood. "Are you by any chance related to Willie Davidoff?"

Shorty looked at Boomy's face and saw that it was almost as white as Gabrielle's father's. Then he took one last look at the three things he wanted so badly. He knew he couldn't have Sylvia's cantaloupes, so he grabbed the Baricini candy and ran like hell.

. . .

Big Al Anastasia walks into the conference room, carrying one of those black-and-white marbled composition books that schoolchildren use, and sits down at the rectangular table. He clasps his hands in front of him and looks expectantly at Lepke, who is sitting at the head of the table. In the notebook Al has entered in copious detail every move that Thomas Dewey made during the four-day baby-walking expedition. There are even diagrams that include a legend for bus, trolley, and train routes, as well as a direction arrow.

With all that preparation, it would be understandable if Big Al displays some annoyance when Lepke declares a hands-off on Dewey, but in Anastasia's mind Lepke can do no wrong. With one lone exception, everyone around the table realizes that to take Dewey out would bring the wrath of the whole nation down on them. Even Lucky Luciano, who's taking a beating from Dewey right now, knows that such a move would be suicide.

The exception is the Dutchman. Dutch Schultz does not believe that laws were made for him, but fortunately he does observe the law of gravity, because otherwise he'd be right through the roof when Lepke makes the pronouncement. There are few guys who can rant and rave the way Dutch can, but on this occasion, even he is a distant second to himself.

"It's bad enough you strip me clean while this fucker Dewey is on my back," he screams, jabbing his fingers at each one of them around the table, "but now you wanna stand back and watch him take me down?"

Luciano, the guy that has more of a reason than anyone to see Dewey iced, tries to calm Dutch down. Johnny Torrio, who is the architect of the Syndicate, tries to calm Dutch down. Joe Adonis, who has taken over much of Schultz's Bronx operations, tries to calm Dutch down. It is Lepke, the brains of the Syndicate, who realizes there is no calming Dutch down.

"I need you guys like I need a hole in the head!" Schultz bellows as he pushes away from the table and storms for the door. He has no idea how prophetic he is. "Today's Monday? By Wednesday, Dewey is worm food!"

With a joint flicking of wrists, the Board of Directors of the Syndicate, who moments earlier gave a thumbs-up to their hated enemy, now gives a thumbs-down to one of their own. As Big Al Anastasia watches Arthur "Dutch Schultz" Flegenheimer head for the front page of the *Daily News*, he decides he will cut out the five or six pages he has used and give the rest of the composition book to his nephew, who has just started second grade.

Willie Davidoff is walking along Livonia Avenue near Saratoga when a black Olds pulls up alongside him and Big Al Anastasia steps out.

"I wanna talk to you, Willie."

"I'm all out of babies, Al."

Anastasia walks over to the two shoeshine boys sitting in front of the tobacco store on the corner. "Come on. We'll talk here."

Al talks, Willie listens, and the kids shine. Al talks about the weather, who's going to run against Roosevelt in '36, and how Lepke thinks so highly of Willie. The kids are finished with the shines, but Al tells them not to stop.

Al talks some more, about when should the Depression end, how he's swearing off betting the ponies, and how he also thinks so highly of Willie. The kids are now on their third or fourth round of polishing, and Willie is hoping his shoe leather holds out.

It takes a while and a lot of saddle soap, but Anastasia finally gets to the point. He asks if Willie knows his way around Newark, because he needs a driver familiar with the area to go out there with Charlie "the Bug" Workman and Mendy Weiss tonight, and he would feel very comfortable if that guy was Willie. Willie is tickled pink because he does not even have to lie: he has been to Newark once in his life and would very definitely get lost if he ever went there again.

By now the two kids are making chalk marks on the sidewalk to keep count of their shoe shines, and this is what jolts Willie to remember Piggy Schechter, a guy who walks around Blake Avenue with a little blackboard slate in his hands to take orders from the peddlers, including Boomy back when he was working his pushcart full-time. Piggy has a truck, and he loves driving. Four, five times a day he hits all the markets—Brooklyn, the Bronx, Jersey, Pennsylvania—and that's how he gets to be called Piggy, when someone asks where he is one day and some guy who remembers his nursery rhymes says, "This little piggy went to market."

Willie used to go around to Blake Avenue pretty often to pick up his "insurance" payments and to check up on his kid brother, and he remembers that Piggy was always asking if Willie knew anyone who needed a good driver, so he imparts this information to Big Al, who does not have all the time in the world to shop around. Anastasia pulls out a bill and hands it to one of the kids, who almost faints when he sees a picture of Abe Lincoln, and then he and Willie get in the Olds and take a drive to search for Piggy.

Pretty Amberg does not shout it from a soapbox, but he lets the whole world know that he is going to get the guys who set up and gunned down his brother Joey. His number-one target is Pittsburgh Phil, whose garage is where Joey's execution took place.

Lepke is surprised when he gets a call from Pittsburgh Phil asking for someone outside of the Brooklyn mob to lend a hand with the Amberg situation, because Lepke knows that this is just the kind of situation that to Pep is like a fresh apple pie sitting on a windowsill. Pep explains that none of the Brooklyn boys can get near Pretty—otherwise he would never be making this call—and that all he wants is for the package to be delivered. He will take care of the rest.

Maybe it is coincidence, maybe it is fate, but whatever it is, it happens to be sitting at that moment in Lepke's office in the hulking form of Emmanuel "Mendy" Weiss. Mendy is there listening to Lepke and Albert Anastasia set the stage for a Dutch Schultz-less world when he hears Pep's dilemma.

"Me and Pretty, we're good friends," he volunteers. "He'll go with me. In fact, I never had a chance to pay a shivah call when Joey goes out. Perfect reason to get together."

Lepke thinks how fortunate Pretty is to have such a friend, but Big Al is quick to remind Mendy that he and Charlie Workman are on line for the hit on Schultz tomorrow night.

"Yeah, but I got nothin' to do in the afternoon," Mendy complains.

So the next afternoon Mendy and his good buddy Pretty drive to a club owned by a friend of Mendy's, at the foot of the Williamburg Bridge, which is far enough from Brownsville to make Pretty feel comfortable. Pretty tells Mendy it is good getting together but he has no appetite because all he can think about is what he's going to do when he meets up with Pittsburgh Phil, Happy Maione, and the rest of Reles's punks.

"It ain't good not to eat, because you are depriving your brain and your heart of nourishment," counsels Mendy, a guy from whose lips homilies never cease pouring forth. "Anyhow, just wait till you see what's on the menu."

At that moment Pretty Amberg really appreciates Mendy Weiss's friendship, even though it turns out to be a friendship that does not last an eternity. In fact, to say it lasts another minute would be stretching it. That is about how long it takes for them to enter the club and be escorted by the owner to a private room where Pretty has the opportunity to regain his appetite because his wish comes true and he meets up with Pittsburgh Phil, Happy Maione, and Dasher Abbandando, who in turn are so thrilled to see him that they tie him up hand and foot and place him on top of a butcher-block table to make sure he does not leave abruptly.

Mendy Weiss looks at his watch and realizes if he does not rush he may be late for a very important date. Apologizing profusely, he explains to Pretty that he truly would love to stay but business comes first.

Although Pretty Amberg is in no mood to speculate on the subject, Pittsburgh Phil Strauss may very well have been a deprived child. With a box of crayons or watercolors from the five-and-ten he might have been another Picasso. But it must be assumed that among his first gifts were a stiletto and a piano wire, because nowhere was there a greater artist with such instruments. To Pittsburgh Phil, murder was mundane unless done with a flair. And on the afternoon of October 23, 1935, Pittsburgh Phil was at his creative zenith. On this day he was inspired. Seeing his enemy trussed up like a prize-winning turkey, Pep, along with Happy and Dasher, decided to carve him up like one, starting from the breastbone.

Mendy Weiss walks into Ratner's on Delancey Street a half hour early for his appointment to meet Charlie Workman, which gives him time to order a plate of blintzes with an extra helping of sour cream. The Bug walks in at the same time that Big Al Anastasia shows up with their wheelman, this guy Piggy, who's trying to be Jimmy Cagney but comes across like Buster Keaton.

Piggy is floating on a cloud. When Albert Anastasia—*the* Albert Anastasia—introduces him to these guys in Ratner's, he has no idea what kind of job he's in on, and he doesn't care. Just to be with them is a dream come true. Six days a week, from early morning until the sun goes down, Piggy does nothing but take orders from peddlers and drive from this market to that market. Every night he goes home and reads to his mother from the *Jewish Daily Forward,* then listens to the radio until ten o'clock. On Saturdays he goes to the Stone or the Supreme or wherever a good gangster movie is playing, and he imagines himself driving the getaway car, weaving in and out of tommy-gun volleys, losing pursuing police cars by negotiating screeching hairpin turns. And now here he is, thanks to Big Gangy. When this is all over Piggy will make sure to get him a belated wedding gift.

Piggy is still beaming as he eases the car to the curb in front of the Palace Chop House in Newark, but he feels as though someone sends a million volts of electricity through him a few seconds later, when the Bug leans over to him across the front seat and whispers, "You know what Dutch Schultz looks like?"

Piggy is shaking so much that his head bobs up and down.

"Well, you go in and check the joint out. You make sure Schultz is there, and I wanna know how many people are in the place." The Bug puts both hands on Piggy's shoulders and looks into his eyes in a way that lets Piggy know he is going to do exactly what he is told. "You're the only one that nobody's gonna recognize. Walk in, look around real good while you head to the can, then use it and walk out so it all looks natural."

Piggy is so nervous that using the bathroom is not a ploy. When he comes back outside he holds up five fingers and nods that Dutch is there. Workman stations Mendy by the door as a lookout and tells Piggy to stay behind the wheel with the motor running. Then he walks in and strolls by the bar, which is separate from the dining area. Except for a very smart bartender, the place is empty. Workman unholsters two .38s, and the bartender shows a lot of intelligence by immediately hitting the floor and staying there. The men's room is at the end of the bar, and Charlie, wanting to make sure that no one is around to surprise him, pulls the door open and is glad he does because there is a chubby guy washing his hands. Not that Charlie Workman has anything against chubby guys with clean hands, but *bang! bang!*—Charlie leaves nothing to chance. Then he pumps himself up and goes tearing into the dining room, where only one table is occupied and the meeting on the execution of Thomas Dewey is taking place. Seated at the table are the three big men in Schultz's organization—his two top lieutenants, Abe Landau and Lulu Rosenkranz, and his ace accountant, Abbadabba Berman. With both guns blazing, Charlie Workman blows them all away.

When the gunfire stops and no one comes outside, Mendy goes in, sees the Bug standing over a pile of bodies, and calls out, "You got Schultz?"

Workman is looking puzzled. Piggy told him there were five guys in the place including Dutch. The three guys bleeding on the floor and the smart bartender make four. That's when he realizes that the first guy he took out, the one in the men's room, must have been Schultz. "I nailed him in the toilet, but I want to double-check." He turns and heads back to the bar.

"Hey, come on, before the fucken cops get here!" Mendy has heard the stories about how Dutch Schultz is always carrying around a large wad of bills, and he is thinking that this sonuvabitch Workman is going back to roll him, so he goes running out to the car and shouts at Piggy, "Hit it before the cops are on top of us."

"W-what about . . . w-what . . ."

"I told you to hit it!"

Charlie "the Bug" Workman is one very angry guy when he comes out and finds he is alone in Newark, New Jersey, with four lead-filled guys well on their way to eternity and police sirens getting louder by the second.

October 23, 1935, is a day that Pittsburgh Phil feels should be memorialized for all time. Happy and Dasher, never guys to miss a party, enthusiastically endorse Pep's plan, and the telephone lines sizzle as invitations are hastily extended for the evening's festivities, to be held at a deserted lot in Williamsburg, not far from Mendy Weiss's friend's club.

The highlight of the celebration comes when all the lady friends of the mob parade in front of the guys, converting the lot into a miniature Atlantic City boardwalk. Pittsburgh Phil has recently latched onto a young beauty, Evelyn Mittleman, who makes a Vargas calendar girl look like Whistler's Mother. She has been dubbed the Kiss of Death Girl because she's been passed from one mob guy to another, each one meeting an untimely end, the most recent of which has been engineered by Pep himself. It is no great surprise to anyone that Evelyn wins the coveted title of the Queen of Ladies' Night, especially as Pittsburgh Phil is the final judge. With the title goes the honor of lighting a torch to a stolen 1932 Packard that Happy and Dasher have liberally doused with gasoline.

Evelyn handles her starring role with relish, first cavorting around the car waving the torch like a baton, then dancing up to the window and blowing a kiss to what remains of Pretty Amberg in the backseat, and finally kneeling to dab daintily at the trail of gasoline with her flaming wand. For a long moment the only sound is the crackling of the flames reaching higher and higher to the heavens. It is as close as Louis "Pretty" Amberg ever comes to being honored.

On October 24, Willie Davidoff almost chokes on his French toast while reading the morning paper; Charlie Workman sleeps until 3:00 P.M. before calling Lepke with a major complaint; Mendy Weiss changes his shirt three times because he is sweating heavily; at Stone and Sutter, Moe Bradie kicks an empty oil can in the direction of the neighboring storefront, which just last week was leased by Buggsy Goldstein as a new office for Abe Reles when he gets out of the joint; at Central Police Headquarters on Bergen Street they decide that the cop with the most sick days in the North Brooklyn precincts will be given the job of packing Pretty Amberg into a morgue bag; on Blake Avenue Piggy Schechter does not remember ever being so happy to take orders for pickup at the Brooklyn Terminal Market; and throughout Brownsville a cloud of revulsion spreads.

Even a hot shower and a shave do not make Charlie Workman feel any better, so Lepke calls a meeting of the Board where the Bug tells how he was deserted by his two partners, an inexcusable offense. When

Mendy explains that the Bug endangered them all by going back to the chophouse to roll a stiff, there is a lot of tsk-tsking even though Workman denies it, and being that Mendy is a longtime stalwart with high marks, he is excused. But somebody has to be made an example of, and who is a better somebody than a nobody? It isn't long before they pick Piggy up on a Brownsville side street. They torture him for a while as he pleads and explains how he was just following orders. Soon they get tired of such a small fish, so they shoot him and set him on fire.

A couple days later Willie Davidoff's doorbell rings and there is a Railway Express deliveryman. Willie's wife opens the package and finds two hurricane lamps with a card: "Mazel Tov to you and the missus, even though I am a little late. Thank you for what you done for me, Seymour Piggy Schechter."

Usually Fat Yerna does not enjoy the fight cards at the Democratic Club because there is nothing to eat there except popcorn and peanuts. Only a squirrel or a bird could be happy with such a menu. But tonight is the Knights of Columbus Annual Championship Boxing Show, which matches the two best Italian amateur boxers in each weight division to battle it out before a very excitable overflow crowd, mostly from Ocean Hill and South Brooklyn.

Pete the AAU man is as excited as anyone in the crowd. There is a large corps of reporters and photographers from the local Italian press, *Il Progresso* and *L'Italia*, who are here not only to cover the bouts but also to do a splashy feature spotlighting one young man who, besides being a championship-caliber fighter, is also most representative of the Italian community. They are relying on Pete to make the selection, and Pete doesn't even have to think about it. He tells them about this kid who is not only a dynamite puncher and gritty scrapper but also has the roots of his motherland ingrained so deeply within him that he does not speak or understand a word of English. He is a kid virtually dripping olive oil! They do not walk—this group of inflamed journalists stampedes to reach this icon of Italian manhood.

When they charge into the dressing room of Giovanni Pesconi, they are immediately aware that what they are hearing is not a dialect of Sicilian or Calabrian. Max Davidoff is not conversant with such dialects, nor with any of the Romance languages, for that matter. Instead he is yelling and sputtering in a scathing Litvak jargon, having heard how his two sons had a fight last night in Won Low's that all of Brownsville is talking about. It is a fight about Piggy Schechter.

Yesterday, when Boomy hears what happens to Piggy, his stomach heaves. The papers are calling it a mob rubout, but Boomy knows that Piggy had no mob ties. He was a hardworking bachelor, a real mama's boy whose biggest thrill was the Saturday matinee at the Supreme. Boomy's stomach heaves again when Sergeant Schroeder comes around asking questions about Piggy and Willie and some lamps, so Boomy tracks Willie down at Won Low's, where he is often to be found as it is his favorite Chinese restaurant. The two brothers have it out, wontons flying, until Willie convinces the kid—who is desperate to be convinced, as he is the one who introduces Piggy to Willie in the first place—that he had nothing to do with Piggy's death. Won Low bans Willie from his establishment for life, and tongues all over Brownsville wag, which is why Max Davidoff is now screaming and swearing in his son's dressing room.

Yiddish is not too familiar a tongue with the particular members of the press covering the Knights of Columbus event, but when they come upon an excitable father tossing around words such as "oysvorf" and "golem," and a son in boxing trunks trying to shush him with "Vos vilst-zu'?" they are all certain of one thing—they are going to save a lot of ink and film. Although the Knights and the AAU give serious thought to disqualifying Boomy-Giovanni, there is no way anyone is going to deprive this Ocean Hill crowd of seeing a fight, so after getting it but good from his father, Boomy Davidoff takes it all out on the poor kid who winds up as his opponent, and wins the Italian-American Amateur Featherweight Championship with a one-round knockout. Boomy is very happy, as he has never been a champ of anything before unless you count selling more tomatoes than any other peddler on Blake Avenue. Also very happy is Max, who has never had a son who was the champ of anything before.

Fat Yerna gets no chance at happiness. It turns out that Pete the AAU man is a spoilsport who does not know how to accept a little adversity in life and makes the outrageous accusation that Yerna has perpetrated a fraud upon the Amateur Athletic Union and the Knights of Columbus.

Yerna feels he is too big a person to have his character assassinated in such a way. He mulls over the idea of bending and twisting Pete into a pretzel and adding him to the popcorn and peanuts at the concession stand, but it remains just an idea as Fat Yerna is wedged tightly into his seat.

8

With Dewey playing hardball, guys are getting plucked off the street and booked for everything from dropping a butt on the sidewalk to parting their hair on the wrong side. The order comes down from Lepke that everyone should play it cool and keep a low profile, and everyone listens.

Everyone except Lepke, who continues his takeover of the garment industry and everything else he is able to dip into. The more he grabs, the more Dewey leans on him, and Lepke is not alone in this regard. Lucky Luciano, it seems, will have to look for another nickname as Dewey piles up evidence against him. Frank Costello, who has cornered the market on gambling machines, becomes a sudden admirer of Huey Long, the entrepreneurially minded governor of Louisiana, and the Louisiana Purchase takes on a new historical meaning as New Orleans becomes the slot machine capital of the world. After a while Costello concedes that although it does not compare to fra diavolo, gumbo is not too bad.

What Lepke really needs is a Lepke to tell him what to do when Dewey taps his phones, issues warrant after warrant to check his records, and keeps up a relentless investigation of his unions. Since Lepke cannot disobey his own order not to strike out against Dewey, he strikes out against everyone else.

Boomy is helping his father rearrange the displays in the candy store one day when Spiegel the business broker walks in with a short, stooped guy named Joseph Rosen. Now that Prohibition is a thing of the past, Max Davidoff is thinking about selling the candy store and opening a bar and grill. As Spiegel shows Rosen around, he makes the store sound like such a gold mine that Boomy can't understand why his father would sell it.

"So tell me," says Rosen to Max, "you make such a living that you're ready to retire?"

"I sell so much ice cream that my hands are frostbitten from being in the freezer all the time. Do you know the candy store business, Rosen?"

"As much as anyone who's been in trucking all his life."

"It's a big change," Max comments.

"Not by choice," says Joseph Rosen, who apparently has a lot to get off his chest, because he goes on to tell how he puts in a lifetime of hard work as a clothing trucker, gathering a solid block of tailoring accounts in Pennsylvania that he parlays into a partnership in a large trucking company—a dream come true until orders come down from Lepke that because most shops in Pennsylvania are nonunion, all trucking to and from that state is permanently banned.

"I plead, believe me, I plead with real tears. I tell Lepke and his bulvon of a partner, Gurrah, that such an order wipes me out, that everything I own in this world is invested in this company, but all I get are shakings of the heads and promises as empty as their hearts. I feel like I'm going out of my mind. I tell Lepke that if I am not compensated, I am going to talk to Dewey, that's how desperate I feel."

This gets Max's attention. "Rosen, you don't talk like that to those people."

"All I want is that they should listen to me and not treat me like garbage."

Spiegel interrupts, urging Rosen to contemplate the wonderful future awaiting him once he buys Max's store. It is a transaction that does not take place, because Max is not ready to sell until he is certain of having a new business to step into. Max and Rosen shake hands and part, wishing each other good luck.

Joseph Rosen eventually buys a small candy store on Sutter Avenue, where he works from morning to night. He takes his case to Lepke's union liaison man, Max Rubin, once more repeating his plea to Lepke and closing with a threat to go up and see Dewey. Rubin calls back and says that Lepke, just as on previous occasions, is promising to take care of Rosen. This time Lepke keeps his word.

Allie "Tick-Tock" Tannenbaum, Lepke's Catskill connection, happens to be in his boss's midtown office reporting on his latest little chore when Max Rubin makes it a threesome. Allie, who looks more like an uninspired accountant than a guy whose job is to enforce Lepke's orders, has great respect for the cool, calculating mind of his boss, who never loses his grasp of a situation. So he does his very best to act as though he is witnessing a commonplace, everyday occurrence when Lepke turns from sly fox into maddened bull, snorting and ranting about that sonuvabitch Rosen and how he'll never get the chance to talk. Max Rubin tries to calm Lepke down and convince him that Rosen is a harmless little guy who is just blustering from desperation. Either Lepke is deaf or else he chooses to ignore Max.

Allie Tannenbaum sighs with relief when he leaves Lepke's office, but he is thinking that he would be much happier if he hadn't heard what he heard.

Boomy was actually looking forward to his road work lately. It used to be the worst part of training for him, but Movietone newsreels of the Berlin Olympics, which just ended a few weeks ago, have made track a real glamour sport to him and a lot of other guys. With his basketball sneakers laced up and a towel tucked into his sweatshirt, he bounds down the steps of his building in the early morning darkness and heads down the street at a fast trot.

As he reaches Sutter Avenue, he sees a small crowd of policemen and pedestrians gathered in front of a candy store. He starts to cross the street to avoid them, but for some reason, perhaps because candy stores hold a personal interest for him, he changes his mind and jogs over to the group of five or six onlookers. They are all shaking their heads in pity as a policeman tries to restrain a small middle-aged woman, still in her nightgown, who is holding her arms out to something on the ground.

"Yussy, Yussy," she cries, tears streaming down her lined face. "Why, why, why?"

Boomy has no trouble moving close enough to get a good look at the sorrowful expression on Joseph Rosen's face. He thinks of Willie Shapiro; he thinks of Piggy Schechter; he takes a final glance at Joseph Rosen, kicks the sidewalk with the toe of his sneaker, and continues on his run. By the time he gets to Howard Avenue, he feels his heart pounding. When you cross Howard, you are out of Brownsville. Boomy jogs in place, waiting for a break in the traffic, then turns and runs back in the direction he came from.

Lying there on the small piece of pavement in front of the candy store, Joseph Rosen has no privacy. The police make no effort to hold back curious passersby. After all, what's so special? This is Brownsville. A woman is crying. A man is dead.

A few days after the murder of Joseph Rosen, the High Holy Days begin. Albert Davidoff, three months shy of his seventeenth birthday, is on his way to shul out of respect for his father, who wants the comfort of knowing that at least one of his sons will someday say kaddish for him. Garfinkel the tailor, a pious man, is also on his way to shul, to pray and repent his sins. Pittsburgh Phil Strauss is on his way to nowhere in particular, to repent nothing.

Among the things that Pep does not get too much of in his life are surprises and lectures. As he crosses Georgia Avenue he gets a little of each from a short, chubby guy crossing from the other direction. Probably it's a combination of Pep having such good hearing from always listening for the click of a pistol hammer or the snap of a switchblade, and the chubby guy wanting to get something off his chest but not quite so far off. He is already about five steps past Strauss when he mutters, "For you praying won't be enough. You're a disgrace to your parents and a curse on the world." Garfinkel's very good friend Stamler, who has a tailor shop and lives on Sutter Avenue, was the one who called the police when Rosen was murdered. He heard the shots and saw two men leave the store. Afraid for his life, he wouldn't tell the police who they were, but he confides in his friend Garfinkel. Even without hearing it from Stamler, almost everyone in Brownsville, including the police, is thinking Pittsburgh Phil anyhow.

Pittsburgh Phil induces Garfinkel to begin praying a little sooner than he intended by lugging him back across Georgia Avenue and bracing him against a building. "Who do you think you're talking to, you little fart?"

People slow down to look from the corners of their eyes, and although they do not stop and they do not stare, Pep realizes he is in a dilemma. He wants to stick this guy, but it is no simple proposition in broad daylight on a crowded street. Looney as he may be, he still knows that you do not whack a guy in the middle of the street with a couple dozen people looking on and expect to be around to buy the funnies on Sunday. So when he feels the tap on his shoulder, it is almost with a sense of relief that he turns his head, keeping a firm grip on the squirming tailor, and finds himself looking at Boomy Davidoff.

Pep doesn't say a word, which means it is up to Boomy to start the conversation. "You're gonna make my brother Willie look very bad, you know that?"

"Is that a fact," Pep says with a big smile as Garfinkel's complexion shades toward blue. "How'm I gonna make your brother look bad, Baby Gangy?"

Even Garfinkel, from up above, seems interested in hearing this.

"Come on, you gotta be kiddin' me. You know this creep is a longtime client of Willie's, a fully paid-up insurance protection policy. Anything happens to him, whaddya think happens to my brother's reputation, which is very important to Lepke?" Boomy is proud of himself for thinking of throwing in Lepke's name.

Pep's arm is getting tired, and the street is getting more crowded. "Tell Willie he owes me one, kid," he says, and slowly lowers Garfinkel to the ground.

That afternoon in shul, Max Davidoff is very impressed at the way his son davens, though Boomy has nothing on Garfinkel.

. . .

Dorothy Walsh knew how to make the best of things. At least that's what she thought until Al Anastasia talked her into having a roomer. She wouldn't have said no to Al under any circumstances because he and the rest of the guys made sure her rent was covered and there was always food on the table—that was her widow's pension. But it was more than five years since her husband, Tom "Fatty" Walsh, was cut down by his former boss, Legs Diamond, and she was looking forward to having a little companionship. No heavy stuff, of course, more along the lines of gin rummy and crossword puzzles—the ones from the *Daily News*, not *The New York Times*. It could really turn out to be interesting, she thought, because this Lepke was supposed to be quite a brain.

It did not take too long for Dorothy to realize that she thought wrong. Her grumpy, surly pipsqueak of a boarder was not interested in gin rummy or crossword puzzles. He wanted three-minute eggs, dry toast, and his underwear ironed along with his shirts and trousers.

Louis Buchalter was many things. Without question, he was a man of means: he controlled the New York garment center and called the shots on everything from narcotics to prostitution. He was the chief executioner: all it took was a nod of his head to seal someone's doom. He was "the Judge": it was his wisdom that the Board of Directors relied upon for all their important decisions. And he was a man on the run who didn't have to look behind him because he knew Tom Dewey was closing in. After Dewey put Lucky Luciano behind bars in May 1936, the High Lord of Crime knew it was time to become invisible.

With crosswords and gin rummy out of the question, Dorothy Walsh settled for solitaire. Lepke's game was eenie-meenie-minie-moe. There were a lot of moes out there, each of whom was someone Lepke was sure was out to get him. He would make selection after selection and turn it over to Anastasia, who would bring in Reles and his crew for the execution. So while Fatty Walsh's widow turned over card after card trying to build on her aces, on the other side of the apartment a joker was wild.

. . .

It is ten after three in the afternoon when Dr. Alter Helzeiger reaches the door to the Davidoff apartment on an emergency call from a neighbor. Because there is not a sound inside, he is certain that even with all his rushing he is too late. He knocks, and to his great surprise he hears a woman's voice call out softly, "Give a push, it's not locked."

At eleven minutes after three Dr. Helzeiger is standing in the doorway watching Albert Davidoff eat a Yankee Doodle cupcake and wash it down with a quart bottle of Hegeman's milk while Rose Davidoff stands over him beaming.

"The kidnaper-cantor!" wheezes the doctor.

"Nu?" Rose asks, never for a second turning her gaze away from her son.

Dr. Helzeiger gives a tug on his earlobe. "Is everybody okay? I got a call from a neighbor that someone was maybe having a slight heart problem."

Patting Al lovingly on the head, Rose sighs. "If you call a heart bursting from naches a problem, who could help it with such a son?"

That is what Dr. Alter Helzeiger hears at thirteen minutes after three. What he doesn't hear is what took place an hour and ten minutes earlier.

Rose Davidoff could not believe the time. It was after two and Vrumeleh was still in bed. As soon as she heard that Willie was arranging a little birthday celebration for Albert yesterday, she knew she should worry.

Wiping her hands with a dish towel, she pushed open the bedroom door. First she gagged at the smell of beer and whiskey that seemed to be oozing from her son's pores. Next she slapped her hand to her forehead and shut her eyes when she saw the pink panties held in place on his head by a red garter. This, although she did not approve, she could handle, as being part of a generation that dances lindy hops and sings "Flatfoot Floogie with a Floy-Floy," but when she pulls up the shade and permits sunlight to infiltrate the room, what she sees next is beyond human endurance.

"Oy! Oy gevalt! Tootahs! Tootahs on a yiddisher mensh!"

It isn't so much that Boomy wakes up as that he is frightened out of his sleep and almost out of his skin. "Whatsa matter, Ma? What's wrong? What're you yellin' about?"

"Oy! Vay iz mir! My heart! My heart!" she cries, pounding her chest. "What did you do to yourself? Tootahs! A Jewish boy with tootahs?"

Boomy leaps out of bed, so bleary and confused he doesn't even notice that his head is pounding like a triphammer. "What're you talkin' about, Ma? What the hell are tootahs?"

"Hell?" Rose wails. "Those pictures! The scribbling on your arms! That is hell! What are you, an oysvorf, a bum?"

Light dawns. "Tattoos? You mean the tattoos? But Willie and Heshy have tattoos."

"I said—for bums," she cries. "You're not a bum. God in heaven! You want to kill your father? Me, I'm already dead! What makes you do such a shandeh?"

"Ma, calm down, it's nothing. It was a birthday present from Willie."

"Bums!" she shouts again. "Goyishe bums paint pictures of knives and naked girls on their bodies!"

Boomy takes his mother by the shoulders and looks into her eyes. "Ma, I don't have no pictures of knives or naked girls. It was my birthday present, and I wanted it to be the best present possible, so I think and I think and I decide that what I want is a picture of my best girl that I can always have with me."

"You got a best girl?" Rose steps back and gasps. "Seventeen and you got a best girl?"

Boomy lowers his arm and holds it out to his mother. She stares, then touches one at a time the blue letters M-O-M etched above a pinkish rose. There isn't any cake or pie in the house, but she remembers how her little Vrumeleh always loved Yankee Doodles. Thank God she picked up a package at the grocery store the day before.

Among the things that can always bring a smile of joy to Bronislaw's face are a good chunk of kielbasa, hot or cold, a bottle of slivovitz to wash it down, boiled potatoes with sour cream, and a fat wife to burrow into every night. All of this he has, and that is why Zelke cannot understand what a living misery his brother-in-law is lately. One day he's a hardworking but happy peddler who calls out his wares in a loud, clear voice, and the next he turns into a stone.

It is more than two years since Bronislaw takes over the Davidoff kid's pushcart. In that time he becomes a real Yankee, living the good life with a steady job and a day off every week—even if that day is the wrong Sabbath—and he gets along with all the Yid peddlers on the street just like his brother-in-law. Now he talks to no one. He sits on an orange crate all day staring down at the sidewalk like he's waiting for it to open up and swallow him. His business dwindles, because on Blake Avenue if you don't holler out what you got, you wind up keeping what you got.

Label, who has the pushcart directly across from Zelke's, is highly respected among his colleagues and is known to be a thinker, so when he comes across the street making circles in the air with his pointing finger, Zelke listens.

"Vitout a qvestion, your brodder-in-law got poison blood. The answer is bonkes." Label explains how the small heated cups are placed on the skin to suck out the bad blood like leeches. That night Zelke spent in jail. Not knowing where to get bonkes or how to use them but understanding the principle involved, he tiptoes into the sound-asleep Bronislaw's bedroom and quickly sticks him four or five times with a sharpened knitting needle. Bronislaw, not realizing that he is receiving medical treatment, reacts in a manner that can be considered unappreciative and results in screams of "Murder!" accompanied by a lot of broken furniture, shattered glass, and a general free-for-all among the family.

Probably, as none of the neighbors had telephones, the police must have heard the commotion all the way to the stationhouse. Anyhow, Zelke is not too upset when they come to haul him off because everyone in his family is screaming and pounding him with their fists. Besides, he is not a complete stranger to the holding cells at the Seventy-fifth Precinct, which he considers a very fine place to sleep off the effects of a bottle or two of plum brandy. Eventually, with the help of Label as a mediator, Bronislaw understands that his brother-in-law has very strange ways of being helpful. His wounds heal very quickly but not so his depression. Zelke can only keep wondering what's wrong with Bronislaw and hope that it isn't contagious.

When Boomy comes around a few days later to get some apples, Zelke, who has a problem figuring out the total when adding up the cost of more than three items, suddenly puts two and two together. He remembers the last time he saw the kid, about a month ago, the day after Boomy fights this guy Johnny Williams, who is a lot older and more experienced. All in all, Boomy's amateur career is pretty good, but every once in a while the kid takes a shellacking. Froike tells him it is a learning experience, and it looks to Zelke like last night Boomy earned his diploma. The problem is, it seems Boomy is having second thoughts about continuing his education. Everybody tells him he's a natural and asks what else would he do anyway, and Boomy answers that he can always peddle fruits and vegetables on Blake Avenue again. That's when Bronislaw goes into his deep freeze.

Zelke is very glad to see that Boomy's face is back to normal now. All the bumps and bruises are gone, and he is able to smile again, something he's doing a lot of as he greets his peddler friends. Bronislaw isn't smiling, he's shivering as though he has a fever. Label is the one who asks Boomy what everyone is wondering. He asks him if he thought things over, what is he going to do with his life, is he going to be a peddler, is he going to be a fighter, what did he decide? That's what he asks, but not in so many words.

"Nu?"

Boomy tells Label that he's made up his mind. He wants to fight Johnny Williams again; if he wins he turns pro—if he's going to get beat up he may as well be paid for it—and if he loses, there's always Blake Avenue. Zelke sees a light in Bronislaw's eyes.

Boomy has four sisters, two brothers, a father, and a couple hundred wild friends from Brownsville cheering him on at Ridgewood Grove the night of the rematch against Johnny Williams. They are all drowned out by a raving maniac in the fourth row bellowing for Boomy Davidoff in Polish and broken English. Boomy expends a lot of energy chasing Williams around the ring, banging him from pillar to post. Bronislaw the peddler expends even more. They both come out big winners.

Ridgewood Grove Arena was one of the dozen or so active fight clubs peppered throughout the city and cynically but lovingly known as the buckets of blood. Here, youngsters learned to ply their trade by waging all-out war with their hearts, their souls, and whatever physical equipment they were endowed with, all for the privilege of hearing the crowd roar for blood and being paid the amateur's wages of bloodletting—a five-dollar watch. For the kids who performed well enough, graduation didn't change things much—they continued throwing punches, they continued catching punches, noses still got broken, eyes still swelled shut—but now they were professionals. Sometimes with new, better-sounding names. Instead of fighting three rounds they fought four rounds, then six, and for those who made the grade, eventually eight and ten, and for that rare master of his trade, the dream come true—fifteen rounds for the championship. And instead of watches, money!

May 22, 1937, was graduation day for Al Davis, a.k.a. Boomy Davidoff—his first professional fight. As he walked to the arena with Shorty and Froike, he jammed his hands into his pockets and shuffled his feet nervously. He had enough watches from his amateur bouts to open a jewelry store on Pitkin Avenue, and he had fought at Ridgewood Grove so many times before that it felt like home turf, but even so, he knew he was in a different league now.

As soon as they reached the arena, the nervousness vanished. There is no room for shock and nervousness in the same body. Boomy bolted through the front door and headed directly to the promoter's office, followed by Froike. Shorty stood outside, staring at the fight poster in disbelief.

Johnny Attell was seated behind his desk, chewing on a cigar and reading *Ring* magazine, when Boomy came storming into the office with Froike hanging on to him, trying to calm him down. Attell looked like everybody's idea of a fight promoter. He was a short, fleshy man whose gold key chain, resting on his stomach, preceded the rest of his body by about three inches. His full lips extended from one set of jowls to another, and his pale skin looked like it had never seen the light of day.

"What did ya do that for, Mr. Attell?" Boomy cried, waving his hands wildly. "I can't believe you'd do such a thing."

"What are you doing here so early, Albert?" the promoter said calmly. "You're not going on until eight-thirty."

"What is this Al 'Bummy' Davis? Who put that bullshit on the poster? That ain't my name and I ain't no bum."

"Kid, look at me. Look me in the eye. Would I ever do anything to hurt you? We need each other. If I hurt you, I hurt myself."

Shorty was now standing beside his friend. "You shouldn't get so upset before a fight, Vroomy," he said softly in his ear. Froike joined in, "He's right. Please, kid, calm down now."

Al ignored both. "I want that poster down. That way you won't hurt me so you won't be hurt either."

The smile was now gone from Johnny Attell's face. He stared icily at the youngster but Al Davis didn't flinch. The promoter thought to himself that this was one tough young kid. "Albert, what are you?" he asked, shaking his hand for emphasis. "What are you?"

Johnny Attell knew that this change-of-pace tactic would throw the boy off stride. "What do you mean, who am I? I'm Al Davis, that's who I am."

"No. I didn't ask who you are—I asked 'What are you?' What do you do? Are you a shoemaker? Are you a doctor?"

"I'm a fighter," Vroomy answered.

"Right, you're a fighter." The promoter beamed, sensing that the trap was sprung. "You're a fighter and I'm a promoter."

"But that don't make me a bum," the kid shot back.

"Kid, you're not a bum. You know that. We all know that. You're a fighter. And as a fighter it is your job to fight—to get in there and throw punches, knock the other guy out and climb up the ladder of success." Johnny Attell believed what he was saying. Therefore, he smiled. "You're a fighter and I am a promoter. "My job is to sell tickets. I have to try and put a tuchis in every seat. Now when a kid named Al Davis fights on one of my cards I can count on his father, maybe a couple of brothers and sisters, his mother probably won't want to see him fight. So from family maybe I can count on four. If I'm lucky, a half dozen. Double it with friends—wow! If I'm lucky I sell a dozen tickets because Al Davis is fighting. But if people look up at a fight poster and see a name like 'Bummy,' they don't have to be family or friends—it's a name that sells. It's pure show business, kid."

The promoter pushed his way out from behind his desk and walked around to where Al Davis, Froike, and Shorty were standing. With a great smile creasing his face he placed his arm around the young fighter's shoulder. "Albert, the important thing is that you and all the people who know and love you are aware of who you are—you are a good young man—you are not a bum! Now go out and get some rest before the fight."

At eight o'clock Frankie Reese was getting ready to celebrate. He sat on the rubbing table in the blue corner locker room with a porkpie hat on his head, a towel draped around his shoulders, and his hands taped waiting for the gloves to be laced on as soon as the deputy commissioner came in to check them. No reason for a guy who trains at Stillman's against the toughest cookies in the city to worry about a green kid without one pro fight under his belt. So Frankie Reese is thinking party time is right around the corner. He doesn't even bother going through the motions of loosening up.

Next door, in the red corner locker room, the kid who just learned his name is Bummy is glistening with a fine film of sweat. It is not nervous sweat, it is good sweat; sweat that he made while thwacking away at Froike's moving palm, sweat that lubricates the muscles and joints and lets you know that the body is tuned up and ready to go.

Froike is like a mother hen. He is kneading the kid's biceps. Willie is smoking a cigarette and showing the kid with all kinds of graphic motions how he should steamroll this guy. Max, pacing nervously, walks over to Boomy every thirty seconds or so to pat him on the back. There are seven prelim fighters sharing this locker room. None of them are as nervous as Max. He turns to Willie and snaps, "Put out the goddamn cigarette. You want him to choke to death before he has a chance to fight?" Willie looks at his father, then throws the cigarette to the floor. Froike bends down and picks it up, tamps it out with his fingers, and throws it in the wastebasket. He is very big on sanitary conditions.

"Davis, you're on!" comes a call from the locker room door. The opening four-rounder is ready to go. Vic Zimet, who has rushed to the arena straight from his last class at City College and has just finished taping over the laces on Boomy's gloves, winks at him, and says, "All you have to do is the same thing you do in the gym. Listen to what Froike tells you."

The kid smiles. He is the calmest person in the room. "See you back here in a few minutes, Vic."

The crowd at Ridgewood Grove does not exactly do things according to Robert's Rules of Order. They are stamping their feet and whistling to show their unhappiness that the fight is now five minutes late in starting. It is a frame of mind that a few good punches and a few sprays of blood change very quickly. The punches are mostly Boomy's and the blood mostly Reese's.

There is a good crowd from Brownsville, and they are whooping it up for Boomy. There is no cheering section for Reese, which is just as well as there is not much to cheer about. Frankie is surprised. He expects a seventeen-year-old kid with no pro experience, and this is what he gets. He hears that the kid can take a lot of punishment, yeah, but this he never has the chance to find out. Whatever Reese tries, the kid has an answer for. He takes his time like Froike tells him and does not go crazy trying for a knockout. When the bell sounds ending the fight it is like music to Frankie's ears. His jaw is swollen, his ribs ache, and even his behind hurts from when he was dumped on it twice by those zinging left hooks the kid throws. Instead of partying, Frankie Reese spends the rest of the night soaking in a hot bathtub.

Willie and Max give the kid more of a beating than he takes in the ring from Frankie. They can't stop pounding him on the back. The crowd is happy too. They saw a guy named Bummy. He snarls and snorts and punches hard. He comes to fight. He fits the name. They cheer loud and long. Also happy is Froike. Back in the locker room he congratulates the kid and tells him he is going to talk to Mr. Attell about handling his future. Boomy seems to be the only one who is not greatly impressed. Stepping out of the shower with a towel wrapped around his waist, he wonders what was really different besides fighting four rounds instead of three.

Then he remembers. He is going to be paid twenty-five dollars for twelve minutes' work. Things are very different. Before tonight there was a kid called Boomy who was a pushcart peddler on Blake Avenue. Walking out of Ridgewood Grove in a few minutes will be a guy called Al "Bummy" Davis, professional prizefighter.

9

Abe "Pretty" Levine gets his nickname for a very different reason than Louis Amberg. He is a handsome young man with wavy black hair and a ready smile for everyone. When he walks down the street hand in hand with his wife, Helen, a stunning blond, people think they are in a movie theater looking at a screen. It is extremely difficult to dislike a guy who looks like Abe Levine, but it becomes much easier when you remember that he is one of Reles's boys.

When Abe shattered the wineglass under his shoe to consecrate his marriage to Helen, he made two vows. One was to love, honor, and cherish this girl whom he adored with every fiber of his being. This vow he made for all to hear in the presence of God. The other vow was a silent one, made to himself, but it was just as solemn and just as sincere. So far Abe had been only a nibbler at the mob banquet table. The real feast lay ahead, but Abe would not partake. It was time to leave the table. Whatever he had wanted from life before his marriage no longer mattered, because Helen *was* life. Abe Levine chose beauty, purity, and honor over gluttony, greed, and carnage.

Without a word to anyone, Abe and Helen moved from Brownsville. He bought a truck and shifted his life into reverse gear. No job was too difficult or tedious. A guy who never got dirt under his fingernails before he found himself hauling garbage, working from morning till night, and coming home exhausted, caked with grime—but loving it because he was coming home to Helen and he was coming home clean.

You don't just kiss off guys like Kid Twist, Pittsburgh Phil, and Buggsy Goldstein with a "So long, nice knowing you," because this is a marriage of another kind, also till death do us part, but somehow when Abe Levine walks out no one seems to notice he is gone. Things are going along fine when the most wonderful miracle of all happens for Abe and Helen. They are going to have a family. Helen is pregnant, and they joyously prepare to pay the hundred dollars the hospital will charge for the delivery. Abe dips into the fruits of his labor, but even with all the backbreaking hours he's put in, the money is not there. He turns to family and friends, to people who have outstanding bills for his services, but they are all in the same boat as he is, a boat still foundering in a sea of Depression.

When he pulls his truck to a stop on Stone Avenue across from Moe Bradie's station, he sees Pep standing in front of the office catching some fresh air. Pep just looks at him, saying nothing about his not being around. Abe figures there's no point beating around the bush, so he goes up to Pep and tells him straight out that he needs a hundred bucks. It is strictly business. He does not ask a favor. "You know, I'll take it on a six-for-five." He does not get a favor.

Pittsburgh Phil smiles, lights up a Camel, and blows smoke in Abe's face. "Got any collateral, Pretty? You should know you need collateral to get an approval."

Abe jerks his thumb toward his truck.

"That pile of shit? That's a liability, not collateral. You're gonna have to get hold of a couple of cosigners, Pretty, my boy."

Abe felt like two cents, which was about what he had to his name. With nowhere else to turn, he reluctantly went back to his family, and in spite of past differences about how a man should lead his life, blood did prove thicker than water. Pretty got his cosigners and his money, together with a lesson he should already have learned: five never catches up to six. Bills kept tumbling in, and Pretty couldn't keep up with them, much less with his Shylock payments. Nobody knew better than Pretty Levine what happened to guys who drowned in the vigorish. He'd chauffeured more of them on their final automobile ride than he cared to remember. And with a sense of honor that was completely alien to him before he married Helen, he thought about the relatives who had stood up for him.

Pretty and Helen Levine moved back to Brownsville.

Five days after the Reese fight, Pretty drives his car up to the back of Moe Bradie's gas station, checks to see that no one is watching, and does a full-scale cleanup job. He doesn't see Moe because Moe is working in a bay in the garage, but Moe sees him, and Moe is disappointed. It's been months since he's seen Pretty, so he's been thinking maybe the kid decided to clear out and maybe there's hope for him. Moe got to know Pretty a while back, when Reles's office opens next to the station. Reles is still in the can, and Moe figures that Pretty and this other kid he's always hanging around with, Dukey Maffetore, are just gofers, so whenever Pretty waves a hello, Moe waves back. They even have little talks every now and then, and the kid complains how hard it is to make a buck, which reinforces Moe's feeling that Pretty runs odd jobs to pick up a couple bucks here and there. But when Pretty takes a rolled mat from the trunk, drops it in an oil drum that serves as a trash barrel, and drives off, it becomes obvious that he is running errands to places other than the candy store.

That night Moe removes the mat from the drum and finds that it is covered with blotches of a dried red liquid that does not smell like ketchup. He manages to read the papers in snatches between customers, so he knows that a small-time hood named George "Whitey" Rudnick was whacked with a meat cleaver and ice pick a couple days ago, just a few blocks away. Moe, who thinks often of Lester Collins and how he was killed with an ice pick, stores the mat away for safekeeping and decides that Pretty Levine does not have the brains to go with his good looks.

Another guy who reads the papers is Lepke, but he has plenty of time for it. He reads every newspaper that Dorothy Walsh brings up for him after doing her morning shopping. It is one of his two major activities each and every day, because there is not too much else he can do after he brushes his teeth and shaves.

The much-rejected Mrs. Walsh can understand her guest's interest in the newspapers, especially the *Daily Mirror*, where Walter Winchell keeps inviting Lepke to turn himself in, repeating the invitation on his Sunday night radio show. With a machine gun for a mouth, Winchell makes and breaks social and political royalty with the ease of a kid blowing soap bubbles, and now he's targeting mob royalty. He urges Lepke to surrender, he pleads, he threatens, warning that if Dewey gets him first he'll rot in jail for the rest of his life. Winchell promises to turn him over to J. Edgar Hoover personally. Although Lepke makes a big show of cursing Winchell, Dorothy Walsh knows that he never misses the gadfly journalist's broadcasts and columns.

Lepke also has other ways of keeping up with the news. Al Anastasia and Abe Reles are still his loyal subjects and drop in on him a few times a week to keep him abreast of things. Though he's been forced into hiding, Lepke has no intention of loosening his grip as head of the Syndicate, and his other major activity each and every day is to make sure that everyone is his friend, a goal he achieves by the simple process of eliminating his enemies.

Feeling he has to get away from it all and breathe in some fresh air, Pretty treats himself to a weekend in the Catskills, with Helen's approval. He is standing in front of the mirror dabbing Vaseline hair tonic on his pompadour when Pep walks in without knocking and tells him he is needed at the Evans Hotel.

Meanwhile, at that same establishment, Walter Sage feels as though he is floating on a cloud because the boys are driving all the way up from Brooklyn to spend a Saturday night with him. Sure, it's a hot summer and they want to get away from their furnace of a city, but they could pick any one of a million places and they choose the Evans, his base of operations. Walter handles all the Catskills gambling operations for Lepke as repayment for his show of loyalty four years ago when he sets up his buddy Red Alpert for execution by Reles, Strauss, and Goldstein. For a while Walter feels a little guilty—after all, the kid was only nineteen—but now he knows he did the right thing. Hotheaded street rats like Red never grow up to become grandfathers anyway.

Waiting for Walter in the Evans lobby with Pittsburgh Phil, Pretty reflects that this is not how he intended spending his one Saturday night in the mountains, driving from the hotel to Loch Sheldrake with a carload of three and coming back with two. Besides which, his stomach is gurgling from hunger and he misses Helen terribly. Pep, on the other hand, is so happy that he is cooing to the little steel ball in the pinball machine he's playing. What better way to spend a Saturday night? What better way to spend any night?

Except for Pep, Pretty, a sleeping bellhop, and the night clerk, the lobby is empty when Walter Sage walks in, because on Saturday night everyone runs straight from the dining room to the casino for the big weekend show.

"What're you usin' your nickels for? I'da given you slugs." Walter smiles at Pep, who is slapping away at the machine, trying to make the ball go where it doesn't want to go.

"What's a few nickels in the overall scheme of things?" Pep does not move his eyes from the machine.

Walter tells Pep and Pretty that he has a big night planned for them. He's going to drive them into Monticello, treat them to corned beef and pastrami at Kaplan's Delicatessen, and top it all off with a night at Queenie's, the best cathouse in the Catskills. But when he takes them out to his car, it turns out that he has a flat tire.

"I don't believe it! These goddamn country roads. If they don't ruin your shocks, they ruin your tires. I'll get one of the bellboys to change it."

"Don't bother. We'll use Pretty's car," Pep offers. "Anyhow, Pretty's only comfortable when he drives. You sit next to him so you can give him directions, Wally. Go ahead, tell me about the broads they got here."

"The best, Pep. The very best. But if you don't have rubbers, we'll stop in town and get some. There is a very transient element up here." Walter Sage feels a twinge of remorse. He cannot get over what a great bunch of guys he hobnobs with, and he's thinking maybe it is about time he mentions a certain business decision he had to make, regarding the divvying of the profits from the gambling machines, while Lepke was somewhat incommunicado.

Pretty puts on his brights. He can't believe how dark the country nights can be, especially when it's cloudy.

"You'll go about three-quarters of a mile to the highway, but take it easy on this road. It'll turn your kishkas inside out," says Walter.

They do not drive three-quarters of a mile, and they do not have to worry about their kishkas—at least Pep and Pretty do not have to worry. Less than two hundred yards down the road they come to a lake.

"Do me a favor," Walter says as he turns to Pep in the backseat. "I been meanin' to tell Lep—" At this precise moment Walter Sage realizes that Lepke already knows.

Pep deftly loops his piano wire around Sage's neck and gives a couple of tugs. For a fleeting instant Walter Sage is mesmerized, seeing his old buddy Red Alpert having one hell of a laugh. It is Walter Sage's last vision, but not his last action. In his seat, he is doing what looks a lot like Saint Vitus' dance as Pep perforates his gut with an ice pick about thirty times.

Pretty Levine struggles under the weight of an upside-down pinball machine as he and Pep set it atop a blanket on the roof of the car and tie it down, being careful not to make any sounds that might draw attention to them. Pretty is wondering what Pep would have done if the clerk and bellhop hadn't been sound asleep on the job when they strolled off with the machine. He chooses not to think about it. He has learned that you do not say no to Pittsburgh Phil, although that doesn't mean he can't recognize that he is working with a lunatic.

Back at the lake, Pep finishes lashing the very inert body of Walter Sage to the pinball machine, explaining to Pretty how puncturing the gut allows the gases to escape and thus permits the corpse to sink but there's no harm in having additional insurance. As they row their flat-bottomed boat to the center of the lake a few things still bother Pretty. Number one is that he is getting fat water blisters on the palms of both hands, as only he is doing the rowing. Next, he finds it inconceivable that at a time like this Pep chooses to rifle the pinball machine and pocket all the nickels.

Walter Sage was no longer floating on a cloud, but Walter Sage was floating! When two eight-year-old kids came running to the Loch Sheldrake chief of police and told him they saw a guy playing pinball in the middle of the lake, he laughed them off at first. Loch Sheldrake wasn't Loch Ness, there was nothing in it but fish, and fish didn't play pinball. The chief learned otherwise. Pittsburgh Phil also had a learning experience. What he learned was that perforating a belly while the body is still alive does not vent the body's gases, because the heart is still pumping blood, which seals the puncture wounds.

Charlie Beecher has no expectations of ever becoming a wealthy man. If the ticket he buys on the Irish Sweepstakes each year should ever come in, he wouldn't see the money because he would die first of shock. Even so, his chance of making it that way is a heck of a lot better than his chance of making a buck from the gym he runs with his brother. He doesn't even think of running a gym and training fighters as a business. To Charlie Beecher the gym is home, and the fighters, trainers, and managers are his family.

That is why Charlie is disappointed at first when Willie Davidoff and Johnny Attell bring in Lew Burston to take over as manager after Al Davis's fifth pro fight. It's not that Charlie has anything against Lew, but for four years Froike, young Vic Zimet, and Charlie bring the kid along, watching him develop under their guidance from a wild-swinging, left-handed, know-nothing street fighter to one of the fastest-rising stars in the fight game. Charlie Beecher is an old-school kind of guy who has these strange ideas about loyalty and showing appreciation.

Lew Burston is an educated man. He is smart enough to know that one is never so smart that there isn't something else he can learn. Willie Davidoff doesn't have Lew's formal education, but he knows that if he manages his kid brother, the biggest fight the kid will ever have will be with him. It is a problem that Lew Burston would call sibling rivalry. Willie Davidoff calls it a fucken predicament, but he quickly realizes that if there's no Willie giving orders to the kid, there's no predicament, which is why he asks Johnny Attell to call his good friend Burston and offer him the chance to manage Al "Bummy" Davis.

Lew, who already knows that you cannot judge a book by its cover, now learns that you cannot judge a kid by his brothers. Expecting to meet someone who's tougher to handle than an alley cat in a fish market, he discovers that his biggest problem is to convince the kid that it's okay to call him Lew instead of "Mr. Boiston," and before long Al Davis is more than just another fighter in his stable. Lew teaches him everything there is to know about table manners, from how to hold silverware properly to drinking from the cup, not the saucer. He enjoys taking him shopping for clothes and teaching him to coordinate colors. It gives him an especially good feeling to bring his protégé home and introduce him to his family. Meanwhile, Charlie Beecher, seeing how Burston is with the kid, decides to include him as one of the family too.

After a particularly grueling session in the gym one day, Charlie is sitting in Alpert's Deli with Al, Lew, and Froike when Lew tells his young fighter how pleased he is with his attitude and his progress. "All this hard work pays off, Albert. I'm proud to see you coming along the way you are. It shows me that you're dedicated and you enjoy what you're doing."

"What's not to enjoy about a shot in the kisser?" Al laughs, gnawing at a sour pickle. "But I don't know if I'd like it so much if it wasn't for the dough," he adds with a shrug. "Fightin's good, winnin's better, and gettin' paid is best!"

Lew takes the pickle from Al, puts it on a plate, slices it in quarters, then hands a piece back to the kid on a fork. "The way you're going you'll have enough money to get yourself out of Brownsville before you know it."

Al puts the pickle back on the plate and gives Lew a look. "Get out of Brownsville? Why would I want to get out of Brownsville, Mr. Boiston?"

Pretty Levine, who knows nothing about the fight game and cares even less, is on his way to Beecher's Gym. A couple weeks ago Lepke calls Reles and asks him to do a favor for a friend and associate of his, Frankie Carbo, and get him together with Big Gangy's brother, Bummy Davis. Reles bestows the honor of introducing Carbo to Davis upon Pretty Levine.

Frankie Carbo is a big man in the world of prizefighting and is always looking out for new talent as long as there are buttons he can push. What better kind of pushbutton fighter can there be than one who is the brother of Big Gangy? To those in the know, working as an unlicensed manager and promoter is a mere avocation to Carbo, who is most proficient at dispatching people to the hereafter.

Pretty is told that he will know Davis because he will be the kid with a Jewish star on his trunks. Once they climb the stairs to the gym, he counts fourteen kids sporting the six-pointed Mogen David. After he finds someone to point the kid out, Pretty introduces himself and Carbo, who looks Davis over like an army doc checking a new recruit. Pretty is half expecting him to grab Bummy's balls and ask him to cough. Carbo tells the kid he can make him happy. Bummy tells Carbo he is already happy. Carbo says he can make him even happier. The kid tells Carbo he would not be able to stand so much happiness. Frankie Carbo has an expression on his face like he has just read the funnies in his newspaper but does not find them funny when Willie Davidoff comes walking over with Lew Burston and Bummy gladly bounces off to another part of the gym.

Willie starts to put out his hand but decides not to. He has this feeling that if he did it would just hang out there, one very lonely hand all by itself, with no other hand meeting it to shake it. Instead he shoves both his hands deep into his pockets and looks at Carbo with just the littlest bit of a smile. "I'm Willie Davidoff, the kid's brother . . . and handler," he says as Lew Burston walks away to study dirt smudges on the wall, of which there are enough to keep him occupied for as long as might be necessary.

"Yeah, Lepke told me about you," Carbo says without a smile, a frown, or anything in between.

Willie feels as though he is looking at an ice cube with a nose, a mouth, and two eyes. He knows that Carbo grew up with Lepke on the Lower East Side and does an occasional job for him. He also hears that he likes prizefighters and horses and treats them with the same milk of human kindness, except that there are no glue factories for prizefighters.

"I came to look at your kid brother and have a little talk with him."

"That's nice of you, but like I told you, I handle the kid. Burston's his manager," Willie says, jerking a thumb at Lew over by the wall.

"I can move the kid. You know, big-time."

"We're moving him," Willie says. "He's doing okay. The kid's good."

"I make good kids better. I inspire them, Willie. I am truly an inspirational force."

"With all due respect, Mr. Carbo, the kid's got all the inspiration he needs. It's called a left hook. Don't get me wrong, we're very grateful at your interest, but the kid ain't going to make any changes."

"I know. He cannot deal with all the happiness he is feeling." And Frankie Carbo turns on his heel and heads for the door. Pretty Levine, who almost forgets he is Carbo's escort, has to turn and run after him.

A couple days after giving Carbo the scenic tour of Beecher's, Pretty finds himself back there, this time not as an errand boy for Kid Twist but because he is in a state of confusion he would like very much to get out of. He cannot figure why a kid who is the brother of Big Gangy Davidoff, a kid who should be wearing silk shirts and suede shoes while he swaggers around collecting insurance payments and union dues, instead chooses to gamble on getting his head knocked off in a prize ring. It is a very difficult concept for Abe Levine, who grew up dreaming of becoming what was right there for Bummy Davis to grasp.

After standing in a corner by himself for thirty, forty minutes, listening to the twang of skip ropes slapping the hardwood floor, the unsynchronized rat-a-tat-tats of half a dozen speed bags, each being peppered to a slightly different beat, and the clang of a bell that rings every three minutes, Abe, who hasn't spoken to anyone or moved from his spot, feels a tap on his shoulder.

"Be a good guy, Pretty. Don't tell Reles you seen me."

Abe turns. It's the little nickel bookie Puggy Feinstein, a guy Abe Reles hates with a passion for reasons no one knows.

"Piss off. What makes you think you're so important that anyone's going to the trouble of keeping tabs on you?"

Puggy's face lights up. "Can I getcha a Coke or somethin'? It's a real shvitz bath in here."

Abe shakes his head no, wishing the squirt would get lost.

"Checkin' out the kid for the big fight, huh? Listen to me, Pretty. Davis is gonna walk through Friedkin like Sherman went through Atlanta. Forget the smart money. Don't pay attention to no odds. I'm with the kid a lot. He's somethin' special. Remember, you heard it from me."

"You know the Davis kid?" Suddenly Pretty Levine doesn't want Puggy Feinstein to get lost.

"You gotta be kiddin' me! Do I know the Davis kid? I know the Davis kid before he's the Davis kid. I know him when he's a guinea fightin' in the amateurs. Four years I'm watchin' that kid grow."

. . .

The first time Puggy sees the kid, when Al Davis was still a simon-pure fighting under the name Pesconi, he recognizes in him everything he wanted to be when he was in the ring himself. As his mashed nose attests, Puggy bobbed when he should have weaved and zigged when he should have zagged. When he is completely honest with himself, he admits that he is truly fortunate not to have been blinded from spending so much time lying on his back staring up into the bright overhead ring lights. Actually, since he's nobody's fool, this is how Puggy winds up in his current profession as a small-time bookie. Not that he doesn't give boxing his best effort—he loves it too much to give it less than his best— but seeing the practicality of it, he starts betting on his opponents. So it is with a strange mixture of feelings that he finishes each of his fights: he is very disappointed to lose, but on the other hand he is tickled pink because the five-dollar watches he would get as a winner are nothing to what he's making outside the ring. Unfortunately the flush times do not last, not because he starts winning fights, but because after a while there is no one around willing to bet a nickel on Puggy Feinstein, no matter what the odds are.

Sometimes it takes a loser to know a winner. It's no surprise to Puggy that since the Davis kid turns pro he tears his way through the featherweight and lightweight divisions like a team of horses with their tails on fire. From the first day he lays eyes on Boomy, he knows this kid is something special. Even when he's taking more than he's giving, the kid is always coming on. And that is why Puggy, who is not a hero by any stretch of anyone's imagination, decides to hang around Beecher's to watch the kid's climb and ignore Kid Twist's warning to stay out of Brownsville.

In the weeks leading up to Al Davis's fight with Bernie "Schoolboy" Friedkin—an event that has Brownsville divided down the middle because Friedkin is a local boy too—Abe Levine becomes almost a fixture at Beecher's Gym. At first Puggy Feinstein is understandably nervous when Abe starts shmoozing with him all the time, but soon he senses that this pretty boy is not quite the psycho that Reles's other guys are.

Puggy is beginning to get the idea that Pretty looks at his work with the same enthusiasm as a kid taking his daily spoonful of castor oil.

Bummy is in the ring now, and everyone in Beecher's is watching as Froike shoves the mouth guard between his lips and the bell clangs to start the three-minute round. Willie Davidoff stands at the foot of the ring steps next to Froike, shouting instructions. "Jab with the left—bing! bing!—then throw the right. Bing! Bing! Bang!" Bummy bobs, bounces forward, feints with his right, then lands the left hook under his sparring partner's heart. Both the kid's hands come down, and Bummy doubles up the left hook, this time flush on the wide-open jaw. The kid topples over like he is attached to the canvas by a hinge.

Froike throws down his towel in disgust as he leaps up onto the ring apron to help bring the other kid back to the world. Willie wags his finger at Bummy, who turns and looks the other way, covering his mouth with his gloved right hand. You cannot be sure whether he does that to remove his mouth guard or to hide the little smile playing on his face.

"Goddamn it," Willie shouts, "you ain't going to get away with that shit against Friedkin, wiseass!"

Froike, when he sees the other kid is alive, comes over to Bummy and drapes a towel around his shoulders. He doesn't sponge him off because the workout is not over. "What are you proving, Al? Against four-round prelim boys you can do the job with your hook. We all know that. Friedkin knows it, too, and he'll be ready for it."

Day after day Pretty watches Al Davis work out and listens to the regulars talking about the way the kid has come along in his few short years as a fighter. Someone introduces the kid to his left hand, and he immediately falls head over heels in love. Actually it is a double love affair. The kid falls madly in love with his left hand and Brownsville falls in love with him. Not being a selfish kid, he in turn introduces his left hand to everybody he meets in the ring, but none of them share his affection. As Froike is the one who made the introduction, he is now hoping he did not create a Frankenstein.

Slowly it sinks in on Pretty. Puggy has been trying to tell him, but he only begins to understand the kid by watching him. It is not that Al "Bummy" Davis chooses not to follow in his brothers' path, it is that he has to carve out his own path. The kid is something special.

. . .

For two weeks there has been so much rain in Brownsville that there are those who think maybe God could not help seeing how bad the place needs a cleaning up. But on this day—Thursday, July 21, 1938, the day of the Davis-Friedkin fight—the sun is shining the way it is supposed to in July.

Al "Bummy" Davis and Bernie "Schoolboy" Friedkin are as different as fire and ice and day and night. The press is having a field day comparing Friedkin to Little Lord Fauntleroy and Davis to the Dead End Kids—all of them. They are calling it a fight for the championship of Brownsville, but it's like Brownsville's borders stretch from the Atlantic Ocean to the Hudson River.

Nobody is lukewarm about this brash, cocky Davis kid. It's either love him or hate him. Every weisenheimer in Brownsville loves him, and so do a lot of other people because the kid, at the age of eighteen, is fighting as a pro for fourteen months and is unbeaten in twenty-two fights. He's an exciting street-tough brawler, a natural-born fighter who loves what he does.

Bernie Friedkin loves what he does too. He is a master technician who in his third year as a professional is close to being unbeatable. From the time he is in knee pants Bernie has one dream—to follow in the footsteps of Benny Leonard and Ruby Goldstein and be a championship prizefighter. His father, who is a cutter in the garment center, assures his mother that such a good student like Bernie will soon outgrow the little ring he's put together in the basement of their comfortable house on Alabama Avenue, just a few blocks from the Davidoff's cramped apartment. Bernie's father is right. Bernie does outgrow it, and moves on to bigger and better rings. He gets his nickname because he is the kind of kid that causes other mothers to give their own kid a klop in kop, and scold, "How come you can't be a good boy like Bernie?" He is so well-mannered and polite that when he begins boxing there is a lot of concern that after throwing a punch he will stop to offer apologies.

Neutral is not an option for this fight. A local housewife who knows as much about prizefighting as she does about pit-barbecued pork and collard greens but happens to live around the corner from the Friedkin family switches butchers and bakers she shops at for years when she finds out they're not rooting for Bernie. In the local poolrooms if you aren't for Davis you don't bother picking up a cue stick, because you aren't going to get a table. Every store window carries a fight poster. Homemade signs hang everywhere—on lampposts, on pushcarts, even on horses' rumps—touting one boy or the other. Whenever a Friedkin backer throws in his two cents' worth on Blake Avenue, Zelke starts a major reconstruction of the marketplace.

Like everyone else, Puggy Feinstein is tingling with anticipation. He is shadowboxing in the street, demonstrating how Bummy is going to upset the odds and drop a bomb on Friedkin, as he and Stutz walk to the IRT station to take the train to Madison Square Garden, where the fight is being held—finally. Originally, Johnny Attell booked the fight at Dexter Park for July 7, which was when the monsoons began. He booked it outdoors at Dexter Park because there were too many people clamoring for tickets to fit into Ridgewood Grove. As the rains got heavier, the interest in the fight kept growing. After the fifth postponement, an amazing thing happens. Even though the fight is limited to six rounds because of Davis's age, Mike Jacobs, the Garden's promoter, calls Johnny Attell and offers to put on the Davis-Freidkin fight as the main event.

Waiting for the train to pull in, Stutz watches Puggy bob and weave and tries to figure out whether this little peacock is gutsy or stupid. Abe Reles keeps warning Puggy, who lives in Borough Park, to stay out of Brownsville, but the runt pays as much attention to him as a kid who's ordered to turn off the radio in the middle of *The Lone Ranger*. When the subway platform starts vibrating from the rumble of the approaching train, Stutz looks up and is surprised to see that the entire station has filled with people in a matter of minutes. It seems that all of Brownsville is heading for Madison Square Garden.

Pretty Levine lights up a cigarette as he leaves the storefront office on Stone Avenue and cuts across the gas station. Moe is at the pump, and Pretty gives him a wave and a big smile. "How's everything going, Moe?"

The smile is so genuine that it turns Moe's stomach. "Same as always. A workday is a workday."

"Don't tell me you're not going to the fight?"

"What fight? All I gotta do is turn in any direction and I see a fight."

"Stop bein' such a grouch, Moe." Again, the big smile. "With all the hullabaloo around here"—he turns and points at the fight poster hanging in Moe's own office window—"you gotta be deaf, dumb, and blind not to know that Bummy Davis is fighting Friedkin at the Garden tonight."

"Good for them! Do you think they know that Moe Bradie is pumping gas at the S & R station at Stone and Sutter tonight?"

Pretty laughs. "There'll be no one around to drive up for gas."

"If that's the case," Moe snorts, turning back to the garage, "then I'll have an easier night than Davis or Friedkin." There's a lot more he wants to say, but Moe Bradie is a grease monkey, not a rabbi. He picks up a flat from the pile waiting to be fixed and tosses it to the ground as Pretty Levine heads for the train station and Madison Square Garden.

Looking around the dressing room, Lew Burston is thankful that the kid doesn't invite his whole family. It's bad enough to watch his father pace back and forth, wringing his hands, without having to contend with the mother and sisters. Willie and Duff are smart enough to sit by themselves on a bench at the far end of the room and read the prefight stories in the local papers. Shorty and Mousey are playing a game of gin rummy, but neither is paying any attention to the cards. Froike tapes the kid's hands and talks to him soothingly. All the talk is small talk, about the Dodgers, about the weather, about anything except the game plan for the fight.

Until the Friedkin fight, the plan was always a very simple one: Al throws his left hook and hangs out in a neutral corner for about ten seconds while the referee raises his arm up and down. Against a shrewd, sharp boxer like Friedkin, the consensus is that a new plan is in order. Lew and Froike want Al to work on his right hand and deliver a surprise package in the ring. Al, who usually does as he is told in the gym, obliges by banging away at the heavy bag and his sparring partners with his right, but he is not happy with the strategy. "Mr. Boiston," the kid pleads a few days before the fight, "I don't need no tricks or surprises. I wanna win this one by bein' myself. Any other way and they're gonna say it's a fluke." Lew Burston knows he has to show complete confidence in his fighter. There is no new game plan.

"Remember, son," Burston says now as they get ready for their walk to the ring, "we want this one."

Bummy bangs his gloves together, trying to flatten out the padding, and looks into his manager's eyes. "Hey, Mr. Boiston, nobody wants this one more than me. Peddlin' fruit ain't too bad, but it don't stop people from saying, 'Ain't that Big Gangy's kid brother?' I wanna hear 'em say, 'That's Al Davis, the best prizefighter in all of Brownsville.' "

Referee Billy Cavanaugh, who also happened to be the boxing coach at West Point, could not see the crowd too well through the glare of the ring lights, but the level of noise was at least equivalent to the roar at an Army-Navy football game. Brownsville had taken over the Garden. Candy stores had closed early, and anyone needing aspirin or cough syrup would have to find a drugstore on the other side of Howard Avenue. At the Hebrew Educational Society Community Center there weren't even enough guys to choose up sides for a half-court basketball game.

Garfinkel the tailor squirmed in his seat and covered his ears with his hands because the noise was knifing through his head like lightning and thunder. He had never been to a prizefight before, and the way he was feeling right now he would never go again. Garfinkel had a brother—also Garfinkel—who was a jeweler from Borough Park, and who was sitting next to him right now, unable to believe that his brother continued to live in a jungle like Brownsville. The tailor understood the way the jeweler thought because that was how most people saw Brownsville. When people thought of Brownsville, they thought of the Abe Releses, the Pittsburgh Phils, the Happy Maiones, and Murder, Inc. That was why, to the people living in Brownsville, it was so important to have champions of other kinds. That was why Garfinkel the tailor was at his first prizefight. Up in the ring were two young knights. Instead of shining armor they wore satin shorts and leather gloves with six ounces of padding.

Garfinkel the tailor was hoping that when the bell rang to start the fight there would be less noise. There was more. His brother leaned over and shouted in his ear, "Two Jewish boys fighting each other? It should never be. I hope neither one loses. In such a fight there should be no loser."

"Could you believe how they're hitting each other with both hands?" Garfinkel the tailor asked in awe. "How can you tell who's winning when they both hit so much?"

Garfinkel was no boxing analyst, but he knew what he was seeing. Purpose and desire drove the two fighters to a level of furious action that kept the entire crowd on its feet throughout the first round, shouting themselves hoarse as Davis and Friedkin ripped away at each other with a two-fisted attack, neither willing to give ground. Although Davis was the stronger of the two, Friedkin's determination locked him in a punch-for-punch war. It was Bummy's short left hooks that gave him the slightest of edges.

Neither Garfinkel could tell which fighter the crowd was pulling for because "Bummy" and "Bernie" blended into one deafening sound in the cavern that was Madison Square Garden. They watched as Friedkin sucked in lungfuls of air in his corner, trying to relax, while in the opposite corner Davis leaned forward on his stool, poised like a sprinter awaiting the starter's gun, with Froike doing his best to restrain him.

Both Garfinkels were of the opinion that maybe the two fighters were getting to like each other a little bit in the second round. "When they hug like that they can't be so mad," the jeweler pointed out.

Bernie Friedkin decided to do what he did best, use his head and box. He blunted Bummy's wild charges and smothered his left hooks by clinching, then pushed off, snapped a couple of jabs, and slid to his right, keeping out of range of the left hook. Davis chased and swung away at Friedkin but couldn't make solid contact.

"You don't want to give him another round," Froike warned as Bummy flopped on his stool after the bell.

"I didn't wanna give him that round," Bummy said as he spat out his mouthpiece. He knew what Froike was getting at. Because Bummy was only eighteen, the fight was limited to six rounds, which meant he didn't have too many to give away. He decided to psyche himself by not liking his opponent, so he stared across the ring and scowled.

When the bell rang for the third round, Al "Bummy" Davis was very mad at Bernie "Schoolboy" Friedkin. He charged at him, cutting off the ring and banging away with both hands, and didn't give Friedkin the opportunity to fall into a clinch. Bernie responded by coming right back at him, answering blow for blow. If he didn't have the biggest punch in the world, the Schoolboy made up for it with heart. As the round ended Bummy was having a lot of trouble staying mad at him. How could you dislike such a guy?

Froike sponged his fighter down but didn't say a word between rounds. Seeing the look in Al's eye, he knew there was nothing to say.

In the fourth round, the hunger inside Al Davis exploded into a dynamism that transformed him into a near-demonic instrument of destruction. He tore from his corner and blasted through Friedkin's usually impregnable guard with a devastating barrage of left hooks and uppercuts. Gallantly, Friedkin stood his ground, fighting back against the unstoppable. He never saw the short left hook that crashed into the right side of his head with the speed and impact of a cannon blast. No one in the Garden that night believed there was any way he could get up, but miraculously, in a defining moment of bravery, he pulled himself up at the count of eight. There were gasps all around ringside as he swayed against the ropes, waiting for his opponent to come at him. Cavanaugh was shocked into inaction. He looked at Friedkin and knew that he couldn't permit him to continue, but how could he do that to the kid? He never had to make the decision as Bernie Friedkin slumped to the canvas.

The cheers cascaded down over the arena. Garfinkel the tailor was overjoyed. He couldn't believe that his little Vroomy Davidoff from the shul was the Al Davis that all of Brownsville was hailing as its new hero. At first Garfinkel the jeweler's joy was muted, but as he watched the Davis boy walk over and warmly embrace Friedkin, and as he heard the crowd cheering long and loud for both of them, he realized with a satisfied smile that in such a fight there truly was no loser.

10

The day after the Friedkin fight Lew Burston comes to the gym and hands the kid an envelope. Bummy looks inside and stands with his mouth open like he cannot believe what he sees. He is staring at four pictures of Benjamin Franklin and twenty pictures of Ulysses S. Grant. How a guy like Benjamin Franklin, who was never even a president—a guy who's best known for going out and flying a kite—winds up with his face on a C-note is something Bummy cannot figure out, but he is very quick to figure out that he has just been handed $1,400.

When Bummy gives his mother the first fur coat she has ever owned, Rose Davidoff doesn't know what to say except, "In the middle of the summer who wears a Persian lamb coat?" Her son gently brushes away the moistness under her eyes that she blames on chopping onions and tells her it would be a good idea to wear it when she goes to see her new house.

At first Shorty is upset when Bummy tells him he bought a house, thinking he will be losing his best friend, but the idea of leaving Brownsville never crosses Bummy's mind. The Davidoffs move to a large brick house on Bradford Street, just a few blocks away from the apartment on New Jersey, but owning their own home makes them feel as though they are in another world.

Max Davidoff loves the new house, but he doesn't let his happiness blot out the concerns he has for his son. Together with Willie and Harry, he escorts Al to and from each of his fights, protecting him from whatever there is in Max's mind to protect him from. If he were permitted, without question Max would join him in the ring. He may be Bummy to everyone else, but he is still Max's baby.

Which is part of Max's problem in trying to grasp what Johnny Attell and Willie are telling him. "I don't understand. If a boy is eighteen, why should he be twenty?"

Attell chomps on his cigar. "Because you can fight a ten-rounder when you're twenty, but an eighteen-year-old is limited to six rounds, and Mike Jacobs won't pay as much for six rounds as he will for ten."

"What difference does it make, six rounds, ten rounds? My boy knocks them out in one round or two rounds."

"Pop, it don't matter if the fight lasts ten seconds. If it's scheduled for ten rounds, that's what you're selling, a ten-rounder. There's nothing to discuss no more. Why should the kid get shortchanged when all you gotta do is sign an affidavit that says he's twenty?"

Max has learned that his son Willie gives advice freely but somewhere down the road you usually wind up paying through the nose. Still, he doesn't want to stand in Boomy's way, so he takes a trip to the office of the New York State Athletic Commission and discovers that by signing your name in front of a notary public and giving him a quarter you can change almost anything in the world.

If Pretty Levine has one regret it is that he does not know how to tap-dance or do a jig. Probably it's just as well, because the maternity ward of Beth-El Hospital is very crowded. But there is room for laughing and crying, and he and Helen do a little of each, as they are now the parents of a beautiful baby daughter—how could it be otherwise with a mother as lovely as Helen and a daddy as handsome as Pretty? Most of the laughing is done by Pretty. The tears belong to Helen, whose bliss is somewhat muted by thoughts of what the future will hold for a little girl with a father who does the kind of work Pretty does.

Pretty's smile broadens when he notices the colorful bouquet on the windowsill next to Helen's bed. Since he rejoins Reles's boys he feels as appreciated as a bottle of warm beer, but as he walks over to take a closer look he starts thinking that maybe he's too sensitive. He opens the little card on the flowers and reads it aloud: " 'Dear Abe and Helen, Congratulations and Best Wishes on the birth of your daughter. Your friend, Irving Feinstein.' "

"Who's Irving Feinstein?" Helen asks, caressing the cheek of the infant snuggled in her arms.

Pretty's brows furrow. "I don't know any Irving Feinstein."

A couple days later the proud father stops up at Beecher's to give out cigars, and as he hands one to Puggy, he asks the same question he's been asking everyone. "Say, Puggy, do you know anyone named Feinstein?"

Puggy looks amazed. "You're kiddin' me, Pretty! I don't believe it! My mother's name is Feinstein—my father's, too!"

Pretty breaks into a smile. "Irving? Your name is Irving?"

"You think I was born with this shnoz?" Taking his nose between his thumb and forefinger, he bends the boneless blob left and right. "Puggy isn't born until after Irving is bar mitzvahed."

Pretty chucks the little bantam under the chin. Here's a guy who knows him a few short months, and he's the only one who sends flowers, a card, anything, while the guys he grows up with, works with, and puts his life on the line for—they don't even know he's alive.

A couple days later Pretty gets another gift.

It is almost three months since the Davis-Friedkin fight, which is the last time he has a conversation with Moe Bradie. Actually, it was a few grumbles from Moe, pretty much par for the course. It is obvious to Pretty that Moe is not exactly eager to talk to him, but at a time like this, Pretty wants everyone to share in his happiness, so as he leaves Reles's headquarters and sees Moe stacking bottles of oil on the rack next to the gas pumps, he walks over.

"Hiya doin', Moe?"

"Until now, not too good, and it doesn't look like things are getting better." Moe doesn't stop stacking his bottles.

"Compliments will get you nowhere, Bradie. Hey, how come you got such a hard-on for me?"

Moe Brady turns and looks Abe Levine in the eye. "You're taking too much for granted, kid. I ain't got nothing for you." He does not expect to get shot for this statement, so he is surprised when Pretty reaches for his inside jacket pocket.

"But I got something for you." Pretty beams as he holds out a fat black Cuban cigar.

"What's this for?" Moe asks, taking the cigar and sniffing it.

"It's for you, Moe. Helen gave birth to a little six-pound eight-ounce beauty named Barbara the day before yesterday and made me the happiest father in the world, and I want all my friends to share in my happiness."

Tucking the cigar in his shirt pocket, Moe stares at Pretty and rasps, "You think I'm your friend?"

Pretty returns the stare and answers seriously, "I hope you're my friend."

"Okay. I'm gonna show you what a real friend is." Moe turns and starts walking toward the garage. "No other friend is going to give you a gift like I'm going to give you."

"That's not necessary, Moe," Pretty starts, but Moe Bradie is already returning with what looks like a large brown blanket in his arms.

"It's very necessary. It's a gift in honor of your little girl, and it comes with a message. Don't be a shmuck!" He tosses Pretty the bloodstained mat from the trunk of the car that took Whitey Rudnick on his final ride, the mat that keeps Moe Bradie up for more nights than he cares to remember, trying to decide what to do with it.

All Pretty can do is watch his hands, which tremble as they clutch the mat.

"I got work to do," Moe Bradie says. "Go home to your family."

One of the few things that doesn't get punched at Beecher's is a clock, so Froike doesn't realize that the kid is almost an hour late until he hears, "Geez, I'm really sorry, Froike. I can't believe I forgot to check the time."

"No big deal. Go ahead, change and we'll get started." Then, with a wink, "I don't want to get too personal, but what's her name, Al?"

Bummy laughs as he heads to the locker room. "Lady Be Good."

"Hmm. Doesn't sound Jewish."

"I love her anyhow. She paid twelve to one."

Which is how Froike finds out that the kid and his buddies Shorty
and Mousey have been learning the finer points of horse racing under
the tutelage of Puggy Feinstein. At first Froike does not take to this too
well, but when he learns that the kids and Puggy limit themselves to
pooling five bucks apiece for the betting action and that Bummy is more
interested in figuring out the upkeep of a thoroughbred than in playing
the ponies, he decides it is not too bad. In fact, it is probably a lot better
than hanging out on street corners. Anyhow, he sees that this character
Puggy is really concerned about Bummy, and actually he is a pretty helpful guy around the gym. Once you get to know him, you get to like him.
He grows on people—even people who know it is not too healthy to be
with a guy like Puggy.

Pretty Levine should be one of these people, but since Puggy is the
only one in the whole world not related by blood who sends a gift when
the baby is born, Pretty invites him over. Helen is not exactly thrilled,
since Abe's friends make her nervous, but because of the flowers she
hopes maybe this one is different. She is not disappointed. One of her
favorite memories is of Abie taking her to see *Snow White and the Seven
Dwarves* at the Pitkin last year, and when Puggy walks through the front
door she almost expects him to be followed by Sneezy, Grumpy, Sleepy,
and Doc. Helen and Pretty do not have many visitors, so maybe they do
not have a very good basis of comparison. All they know is that when
the evening comes to an end they are truly sorry, but no more so than
little baby Barbara, who seems to enjoy Puggy's kitchy-coos even more
than her rattle and pacifier.

Charlie Beecher is thinking that with all the people turning out to get
a look at Al "Bummy" Davis, maybe he should charge a dime or a quarter
admission—although it's true that a lot of times you don't have to cough
up a cent to see him fight.

Al and his Brownsville buddies do not wait for World War II or an
Act of Congress to take on the Nazis. When Neville Chamberlain prom-
ises "peace in our time" after breaking bread with Adolf Hitler in Mu-
nich, it is with no knowledge of what happens when a gang of guys from
Brownsville comes together with a bunch of brownshirted German
Bundists from Ridgewood. There are enough Germans living in Ridge-

wood that it might be mistaken for a suburb of Berlin. Most are hard-working, industrious people who consider themselves Americans. Most is not all. The brownshirts sing the Horst Wessel song and spout their "Germany wants peace!" and "Blame it on the Jews!" propaganda every night of the week, but Fight Night at the Grove guarantees a big crowd, so they always set up their soapbox an hour beforehand, and if Bummy Davis is on the card, all hell breaks loose.

"You know Bummy's fighting at the Grove tonight? I got left two tickets," Grabstein shouts from behind his deli counter. Every store in Brownsville between Pennsylvania and Saratoga Avenues sells tickets to Bummy's Ridgewood Grove fights, and they go better than a Dr. Brown's Cel-Ray soda after a hot dog and a knish.

"Who's he fighting?"

"At seven o'clock it's Hitler, at eight it's Petey Vitello."

The kid is just turning nineteen, but he packs in the crowds wherever he fights. He brings the curtain down on 1938 by knocking Jimmy Lancaster out in six rounds at the Grove and is now undefeated in twenty-nine bouts. When he climbs into the ring all the seats fill up, and when he leaves, so does everyone else. At Beecher's, as soon as he gets ready for his sparring session, people seem to come out of the woodwork and scurry for seats.

In order to keep Bummy going all-out, Froike sends in a new sparring partner each round. This not only keeps Bummy on his toes, it keeps the crowd glued to their seats. Nobody wants to get up, so it is surprising, when three guys walk into the gym one day at the beginning of Bummy's second round, to see the occupants of three front-row seats surrender their places after being tapped on the shoulder by one of the newcomers, who happen to be Abe Reles, Buggsy Goldstein, and the tapper, Pittsburgh Phil Strauss.

By the end of the second round, Bummy is really loose and winging away pretty well. He comes back to his corner sweating profusely—almost as much as Puggy Feinstein, who is helping out in Bummy's corner. When the bell rings for the third session, Froike practically has to pry Bummy's mouthpiece out of Puggy's hands and drag him down the ring steps.

In another seven minutes the crowd applauds. Bummy is finished. He will be back tomorrow.

"Hey, Beecher," Reles yells over to Charlie, who is standing on the other side of the gym.

"What can I do for you, Abe?" Charlie calls back, not really wanting to do anything.

Reles hooks his thumb in Puggy's direction. "That scumbag! I don't ever wanna see him here again."

Charlie shrugs. "You know, Abe, It's a free country. What can—"

"You'll see a fucken free country if I ever find out this sonuvabitchin' weasel is back here!" Reles shouts, pounding his fist into the palm of his hand.

Puggy, who has been trying to lose himself in a corner of the gym, steps forward, his whole body shaking. "What did I ever do to you, Reles? Why don't you leave me alone?"

Buggsy and Strauss start toward Puggy, but Reles places a restraining hand on their shoulders. He looks right through Puggy Feinstein, as though he doesn't even exist.

At this moment, Beecher's is a quieter place than anyone ever remembers. Puggy looks around for help, but the floor seems to be the most interesting place in the gym, because that's where everyone's eyes seem to be. Boxers are busy tying and untying their shoelaces. Trainers are adjusting punching bags or checking their equipment. People who came to watch the workout are browsing through their newspapers or stirring containers of cold coffee.

Puggy turns around and sees Bummy. He's never noticed before that the kid has an Adam's apple. It is moving up and down, up and down.

A couple days later Puggy stops Bummy on the street and tells him he's glad he stayed out of it. "I want you to know, kid, that bullshit artist don't scare me. The only reason I'm steerin' clear of the gym is I don't wanna make no trouble for anyone—the Beecher brothers, Froike, you. It ain't worth it. But I'll be at all your fights—there's no way he's gonna keep me from that—and even if I ain't in your corner you know I'll be there rootin' for you."

Bummy smiles and tries to hand Puggy a few bucks.

"Who ya bettin'? The only thing goin' right now is the six-day bike race."

"I ain't bettin' nothin'. It's just somethin' to tide you over."

"Hey, kid, I want you to know, besides good looks I am independently wealthy." He pushes Bummy's hand away. "If you wanna go back to the track and learn more about the nags, just give a holler. I'll be around."

"Even after what Reles said?"

"I'm gonna listen to that Chaim Yankel? You yell, I'll be there."

You can learn a lot from tea leaves, especially if you are a gypsy fortune-teller. This Fat Yerna already knows. In Beecher's Gym there are no tea leaves, but Fat Yerna finds out that there are things you can learn from coffee grinds also. As soon as he takes his first gulp, which he does very carefully, he is surprised. What he is tasting is coffee—good coffee, something that is unheard-of in Beecher's late in the week. It does not taste bitter or burnt, which is the usual taste you get on a Friday night from Monday's grinds. Fat Yerna is no swami, but he knows something is up. The newspaper sitting on the counter next to the coffee urn has a picture of Franklin Delano Roosevelt soaking himself in Warm Springs, Georgia, so Yerna figures that the fresh coffee is not because the president of the United States will be dropping in at Beecher's.

Yerna is right. The coffee is not for the president. It is for all the boxing writers who are coming to see Bummy Davis three days before the Farber fight. *Who knows?* Yerna thinks, *Where there is coffee, there may also be cake!*

Mickey Farber is every bit as big on the Lower East Side as Al Davis is in Brownsville. The upcoming fight is important to both their communities because it is a match-up of local champions at a time when pride counts for a lot. It is important to Davis and Farber because the winner becomes a contender for the lightweight championship. It is a fight that has people talking and reporters coming to Beecher's.

For a change there's a news story about Brownsville that has nobody chopped up with a meat cleaver or pumped full of holes and dumped in the trunk of a car. The cameras keep flashing as the photographers shout for Bummy to strike a pose and smile. He holds up his gloves, but there is no smile. The reporters ask long questions and get short answers.

Over at Rappaport's, on Second Avenue, Mickey Farber is full of smiles and goes into graphic detail about how he's going to send Al Davis back into the fruit peddling business. When a reporter points out that Al Davis is pretty tough, Farber sneers and says, "Tough? The only thing tough about Davis is gonna be his luck. You can quote me." They do.

Froike is making a final inspection of his supplies and putting them in a neat pile for Monday's fight. Charlie and Willie Beecher are straightening up the poolroom next door, and the last couple of kids are zippering up their gym bags. All the lights are turned off except for the one by the lockers and the other near the counter, and they cast long shadows across the gym.

Bummy is sitting in front of his locker, still in his trunks, with a towel draped over his shoulders. In his right hand is a comic book, which he has to squint to read because of the dim lighting; his left hand is dangling in a bucket of ice water, a ritual he goes through after almost every training session. It's the price the kid has to pay for being the banger that he is. Swollen knuckles are the trademark of some fighters, just like cauliflower ears and flattened noses are for others. When bone bludgeons bone, something's gotta give. Bummy knows, though, that as long as he ices it the swelling goes down and by the next morning his knuckles are back to normal.

Froike turns as he hears the gym door open, and is sorry that he forgot to lock it when he sees who the visitors are. Reles's shoes squeak as he walks slowly across the gym, followed by Buggsy Goldstein and Pittsburgh Phil Strauss. Strauss slaps at a speed bag, which makes a thunking sound as it bounces against the platform, then sways on its swivel.

"We're finished for the day, fellas," Froike calls over his shoulder, still puttering with his bottles and sponges. "Just closing up."

"Yeah, yeah, I see," Reles says. "Do me a favor. Check in the poolroom. I think I left a pair of gloves there the other day." He points to the doorway.

Froike looks over at Bummy, who raises his head from the comic book and nods for him to leave the gym. Froike feels a sour taste rising from his stomach to his mouth as he reluctantly goes to the poolroom.

"Must be a really good story, kid," Reles says as Bummy returns his attention to the comic book.

"Looks like your hand is hurtin', huh?"

Bummy shrugs, looks at his hand in the bucket of ice water, and shrugs again.

"It's a shame, kid." Reles turns to Buggsy and Strauss. "Ain't that a shame, guys?"

"A real shame," Buggsy agrees. Pittsburgh Phil nods his head, totally in accord with the fact that it is a shame.

"I'm tellin' you, kid," says Reles slowly, making sure he is clearly understood, "nobody can expect a fighter with a bad hand to be at his best. Everyone'll still be proud of you if you fight the good fight . . . and lose. Then you get a rematch, your hand is better, and you turn it around. Fahrshtay'n what I'm sayin'?" He starts to place a hand on Bummy's shoulder, but the kid draws back, raises his head, looks into Reles's eyes, and smiles broadly. Not a word has passed his lips.

As Reles, Buggsy, and Strauss turn to leave, the last thing Bummy hears is Reles muttering, "Tsk, tsk. What a fucken shame."

Froike comes back into the gym and looks at his young fighter but asks no questions. Bummy dries his hand with a towel and says, "I'm gonna change and meet Shorty in front of the Supreme. See ya Monday, Froike."

Froike is a guy who cannot just stand around and not give advice. "Meet him in the lobby. It's bitter cold out."

When Bummy steps out onto the street he gets hit with an icy gust of wind. He shivers, pulls his collar up around his neck, and turns onto Georgia Avenue, where he shivers again when a hand grips his shoulder from behind. He drops his gym bag and whirls around with his fists raised.

"Don'tcha like me no more, Boomy?" Chotchke Charlie is wide-eyed and cringing, shocked that his one and only friend is about to hit him.

"Jesus H. Christ! Don't sneak up on a guy like that, Charlie!"

"I don' sneak up. I been waitin' a long time for you."

Bummy notices that Charlie, in his usual short pants and just a thin, frayed sweater, is shivering a lot more than he is. "What's the matter with you, Charlie? Don't you know you can freeze to death out here? Where've you been waiting?"

Charlie points to the cardboard carton in the doorway of Alpert's Deli, which is closed for Shabbes.

"Come on, let's get out of the cold." Bummy grabs Charlie's arm and pulls him across Livonia Avenue. He drags him into Fortunoff's Department Store and stands him next to a radiator.

"What are you doin' out in this kind of weather, Charlie?"

"I tol' ya, Boomy, I'm waitin' for you."

Bummy shakes his head and grins. "You're somethin' else, Charlie."

"I am?" There is wonder all over Charlie's face. "What I am?"

Bummy can't help laughing as he puts his arm around Charlie's shoulders. "Forget it. You're you. You're Chotchke Charlie and that's good. But I can't get you a chocolate soda now. The candy store is closed till tomorrow."

"I don' wan' a chocolate soda."

"You don't? Then what're you freezing your ass off for, just to say hello?"

Now Chotchke Charlie laughs. "You're sumpin' else, Boomy." Charlie finds this most amusing. It's not unusual for Chotchke Charlie to say something funny. It happens all the time, but this time he does it intentionally.

Bummy arches his eyebrows. "I am? What am I?"

"You're a punch-fighter."

"I'm a what?"

"You're a punch-fighter. I see your picture all over, an' your poppa, he tells me you're a punch-fighter, an' I know alla kids go watch you an' I wanna go too. Please, Boomy, can I go too? Please?"

Until this moment Bummy doesn't appreciate how uncomplicated it is to make Charlie happy by giving him a chocolate soda. He tries explaining to him that Manhattan is a place so far away that Charlie has never been there before, but Charlie has no conception of distance, and no fear of traveling because it has no meaning to him. As hard as he tries, Bummy learns a lesson that so far he's never learned in the ring: you cannot win them all.

Charlie follows Bummy to the Supreme, where he is meeting Shorty. All the way he begs and pleads, "Ain't I your friend, huh, Boomy, ain't

I your friend?" It turns out that maybe Mickey Farber is right when he says that Al "Bummy" Davis is not so tough. It is a frigid February night, but Al melts like a pat of butter on a sizzling grill. He arranges for Shorty and Mousey to take Charlie along with them to the Saint Nicholas Arena on Monday night, which turns Charlie into something resembling a kangaroo as he bounces around Sutter Avenue. Shorty is somewhat more subdued.

A few days after Reles chases him from Beecher's, Helen insists that Puggy be with them for Barbara's three-month birthday party, truly a milestone occasion. Nobody has to point out to Puggy or Pretty that their friendship is something you do not advertise. So, after the party Puggy drops Pretty a block and a half from the gang's office.

When Puggy starts leaving, he looks at the fuel gauge and figures if he doesn't gas up he will never make it back to Borough Park so he pulls up to the gas pumps closest to Reles's office. While his car is being filled he steps out to stretch, then walks over to the soda cooler, takes out a Nehi on which he almost chokes taking the first swallow when he hears a voice from behind him, "Hey, runt, weren't you told to stay the fuck outta here?" Puggy answers by squirting a stream of orange soda through his nostrils, some of which makes a stain on the lapels of Buggsy Goldstein's jacket. Reles's crony slowly and deliberately brushes off the flecks of liquid, staring at Puggy all the while. "If you got one fucken brain in your head you should know to get your ass outta here while you can still do it under your own power."

Puggy Feinstein is convinced that he is not afraid of Buggsy Goldstein. He is prepared to tell him where to shove his threats but unfortunately his mouth does not work. It is like it is broken. Moe Bradie's is not. "Hey, on this station nobody bothers any of my customers," he barks, but in a most casual way as he walks past them, wiping his hands with a bubble-gum colored rag that he pulls out of his back pocket.

Buggsy turns and looks toward Moe. "Hey, what're you, kiddin' me?"

"I don't kid. Jack Benny kids. I sell gas and grease cars. An' if somebody bothers one of my customers an' chases him away, then I can't sell him anymore gas and I'm losin' money."

Buggsy snorts a short laugh through his nose. "Remember, Bradie,

I'm your customer, too. Also your next-door neighbor. What do you got to say about that?"

"I won't let nobody bother you, either. I promise." Moe walks back to where Puggy and Buggsy are standing and takes Puggy by the arm. "Come on into the office. You wanted to check over your bill, right?" It is not right, but Puggy is very happy to follow Moe into his office. He has this great urge to stick his tongue out at Buggsy Goldstein but manages to show great self-control.

So, Moe Bradie winds up with a new steady customer and Puggy Feinstein finds a gas station where the extras are a lot more than just wiping the windshield and checking the oil. When Puggy asks Moe to buy his car, Moe has no interest. "What am I gonna do with this jalopy? I ain't a car dealer." But as soon as Puggy tells him he wants to use the money to place a bet against Reles, Moe Bradie expands his business.

The night before the Davis-Farber fight Puggy Feinstein falls asleep with a big smile on his face in the backseat of his ex-car which Moe very graciously moves into the garage to shield it from the February wind.

The two happiest people in maybe all of New York City are Shorty and Mousey when they get off the IRT train and climb the steps to Sixty-sixth Street, each having a firm hold on one of Chotchke Charlie's arms. The trip goes fine at first, once they explain to Charlie that nobody gets gum balls or Indian nuts when they put a nickel in the turnstile—at least the trip goes fine for the next five minutes, which is how long it takes before the elevated tracks sink below the ground into momentary pitch-blackness as the train enters the subway system. Charlie, who until then is enjoying his first train ride, jumps from his seat and starts trying to pry open the car door while crying at the top of his lungs. Shorty and Mousey drag him back to his seat and attempt to convince him that the world is still going to be around tomorrow and the day after. With a string of snot hanging from his nose, Charlie sits between his two chaperons, his body convulsing as he tries to control himself, but each time the train pulls into a station he bolts from his seat and heads for the door. By the time the train gets to Times Square, Shorty and Mousey have perfected the art of tackling him, one hitting him high, the other low. At the corner of Broadway and sixty-sixth they stagger out of the subway and walk to the arena, holding on tight to Chotchke Charlie, who takes in all the sights as he skips along, the subway ride now a fading bad dream.

Inside the old fight club Mousey and Shorty flop into their seats, believing that nothing can be worse than that hour on the train. It is a belief, just like some people believe in genies and trolls. Charlie is socked in between them like a prisoner between two deputies, but he is so hypnotized by everything he sees that he wouldn't have cared if they were sitting on him. As the prelims get under way he keeps saying, "Where's Boomy? That's not Boomy!" Over and over again they keep explaining to him that Boomy will be up there soon. That is how things go until Nature taps on Charlie's shoulder. Charlie, in turn, taps on Shorty's shoulder.

"I gotta go."

"You don't wanna go now," Shorty says. "Didn't you come to see Al fight?"

"I wanna see Boomy, but I gotta go now." Charlie grimaces, squirming in his seat.

"Oh." Shorty realizes what Charlie is saying. He looks at Mousey. "You wanna take him to the john?"

"He ain't no baby," Mousey says. "You can go by yourself, can't you, Charlie?"

"I can hol' my own shmecker an' I can pee by myself, but I don' know where to do it."

"Remember where we came in?" Mousey asks.

"Uh-huh! Uh-huh! That's where Boomy's picture was."

"Right. You go to Bummy's picture and you just walk a little past it"— Mousey turns and points for Charlie—"and that's where the bathroom is. You'll see other guys going in. Just follow them, okay?"

"Okay, Mousey."

Chotchke Charlie always tries hard to do as he's told. He goes back to Boomy's picture and walks a little past it, only he does not turn down the corridor that takes you to the bathroom. He continues walking straight, which takes you to West Sixty-sixth Street.

It's a little ironic that the fight they're calling the Jewish Lightweight Championship is being held in a place called Saint Nicholas Arena. The stuffy cigar box of a club is packed with an overflow crowd of 6,500, and about a third as many are milling around outside trying to buy their way in, so it is not a polite or contented group that Chotchke Charlie encounters when he blunders out of the arena. He's sure he has found the bathroom, because Mousey told him there would be other guys going in, but he didn't tell him there would be so many. Charlie looks in every direction but doesn't see anything resembling a bathroom door, so he pushes his way through the mob back to the entrance of Saint Nick's, where he cannot go any farther because of this guy whose job it is not to let anyone in without a ticket.

" 'Scuse me," Charlie whimpers with his legs crossed. "I gotta go back to Mousey 'cause I can't find no bathroom."

"Come on, kid, don't bother me."

"Okay." With which Charlie starts walking past the ticket taker into the arena.

"Whoa, shorty! Where d'ya think you're going?"

Charlie looks at him strangely, then giggles. "You call me Shorty! I'm Charlie, not Shorty. Shorty's saving my seat while I pee." Again he tries to slide past.

This time the guy grabs Charlie by the shoulders, spins him around roughly, and shoves him toward the street. "Okay! Enough's enough! Nobody gets in without a ticket."

Charlie's lips start quivering, and he runs his finger under his nose. "I gotta go back. Shorty and Mousey are gonna be mad on me, and on you too! . . . Ooh, I gotta do pee-pee! Where can I do pee-pee?"

"Take a piss on the roof for all I care."

Bummy doesn't have to look around to know that his gang is there because you can probably hear them all the way back to Brownsville. They shout his name, they yell, they whistle, they stamp their feet and honk on bicycle horns. But Bummy looks around anyhow. It's his crowd and he wants to see them. He punches his fist at the ceiling, and the answering roar seems to raise the roof. He sees his father and brothers, some guys from the Cowboys, a lot of his street-corner buddies, and even a few of the girls he kids around with in the candy store. He sees Stutz, then Shorty and Mousey—and then the empty seat between them.

Froike waves a towel in front of Bummy, trying to disperse the heavy cloud of cigarette smoke. He doesn't know what to grumble about more, how his kids choke from these blue blankets of tobacco fumes or how they lose the good sweat they work up in the dressing room by having to stand around while other fighters in the audience are introduced. Bummy keeps turning to catch Shorty's eye. Finally he realizes Shorty does not want him to catch his eye. He doesn't want to think about where Chotchke Charlie is—he knows it's not good to think about anything but Mickey Farber—but he can't help it.

He feels Froike give him a gentle shove and sees that the referee, Arthur Donovan, has been motioning for him to come to the center of the ring. The crowd noise quiets as Bummy Davis and Mickey Farber stand facing each other.

"Gentlemen, I want a good, clean fight. . . ." Bummy tries very hard to concentrate on the referee's words, not to learn something new and informative but to get his head into the fight. "When I order you to break, step back. . . ."

They shake hands. It is like a signal to turn on the crowd again and nothing can be heard except thunderous shouting and cheering. The forlorn wail, "Boo-omy," is completely drowned out.

Chotchke Charlie was happy because he did not wet his pants. As he climbs up the fire escape he thinks, "Oh, oh, I can't hold it in," so he has every right to be happy when he reaches the roof just in time to pee there like the man downstairs told him he should. He was supposed to see Boomy punch-fight, only the man wouldn't let him go back in . . . that's when Chotchke Charlie sees the big skylight in the center of the roof. Very carefully, because the roof is slippery with a thin coat of ice, he steps over to it and squats, looking down into the arena and sees Boomy. He taps on the skylight glass and calls out his friend's name.

When the bell rings for the first round, Mickey Farber bounces from his corner. Bummy Davis doesn't move. He is convinced it's just his imagination. However, Bummy thinks he must have a pretty vivid imagination to imagine the very urgent-sounding cry of "Boo-oomy" that gets his attention. At the same time, a flurry of five or six glove-encased fists bouncing off his head and ribs also gets his attention.

The first round is not a good one for Bummy. Lew Burston is not too upset. Of course, he is not the one getting hit. After the second round, Burston pleads, reminding Bummy of the big-name fights out there if he beats Farber. Froike remains silent, thinking of the Saturday night visitors to the gym and believing that is the reason for the kid's sleepwalking performance.

Farber, surprised at the ease with which he is handling Davis, is filling up with confidence. Behind Davis's corner, Puggy Feinstein is explaining to all the guys that Bummy was just toying with Farber. But there are large bands of perspiration around his armpits.

Shorty wanted to ask Mousey what was wrong with Bummy and Mousey wanted to ask Shorty but as Shorty and Mousey were no longer talking to each other because of Chotchke Charlie, neither one asked the other. Anyhow, they each had a pretty good idea of what was wrong with their friend.

At the end of the third round, Burston looks over at Froike, expecting his trainer, in some way, to light a fire under their fighter. Froike remains silent, running a cotton swab through Bummy's nostrils to clear the mucus from his nasal passages. Finally, Burston pleads softly, "Son, you're not concentrating." To Bummy, this was not exactly a revelation.

Meanwhile, Mickey Farber is feeling good. It is an eight-round fight and Farber already has three rounds in the bank. As the bell rings to start the fourth round, Farber stands up and announces to his cornermen, "I'm ready to take him out." And that is when the roof falls in on Mickey Farber!

Pittsburgh Phil had his druthers. He couldn't see going to a fight that was a foregone conclusion when he had the option of staying home and playing strip poker with Evelyn Mittleman—with his deck of cards. So with the morning sun slanting through the venetian blinds and Evelyn unable to get out of bed as she has lost her panties to a straight to the jack and isn't going to get them back so quickly, Harry Strauss bounces down the stairs to pick up coffee, danish, and the morning papers at the candy store.

Harry is hungry when he sits down at the kitchen table, spreads out all the newspapers, and starts reading in Jack Singer's column in the *Journal-American* that Davis *"looked like a rank amateur and even his hysterical supporters, armed with fish horns, agreed that he should have had Major Bowes working in his corner."* He raises the danish to his mouth but stops as his eyes shift to Murray Lewin's article in the *Daily Mirror*.

> A serious accident was averted when a spectator perched on the roof of the arena suddenly crashed through the glass ceiling. Fortunately for him, he managed to grasp a cross beam as his legs dangled between it. It appeared as though the lad would lose his grip and come tumbling down into the crowd, but he managed to pull himself through the glass encasement and escape before the police could apprehend him.

Pittsburgh Phil put the danish down as he continued reading from the *Daily Mirror*. Then his eyes caught the headline he'd missed in the *Journal-American*: "Rally Brings Davis Win Over Farber."

Evelyn ate the two pieces of danish quietly. She knew when to leave her man alone.

Lew Burston had no idea what woke his fighter up. Froike's heart was bursting with pride. When referee Arthur Donovan gave the signal to resume fighting, Lew and Froike immediately noticed the change in their boxer. Bummy's eyes were narrowed, his nostrils flared, his lip curled. He went after Farber with murderous left hooks. He pounded him, beat him, bloodied him—he taught the East Sider what "tough" is all about. The crowd, the judges, the referee, and Mickey Farber could not believe the turnaround the fight took. On the scorecards it was a close but unanimous decision for Davis, but in an overview of the fight, it was total destruction dealt out by the Brownsville warrior.

Puggy Feinstein accepted all the slaps on the back from his friends with a smile and a "What'd ya expect? I told ya so," but the perspiration patches now covered half his body.

Shorty and Mousey did not see the end of the fight. They listened to everyone talking about it on the train back to Brooklyn. After Charlie miraculously gathered the strength to pull himself up and scramble back through the skylight opening on the roof, they bolted from their seats and found him huddled in a doorway on Broadway. He gave them no problem on the train ride home. It was very difficult to run around with two guys sitting on you.

The knish man was having a pretty good day. Usually he would park his wagon outside the schoolyard, but this afternoon all the kids were hanging out on Livonia Avenue in front of Beecher's Gym, waiting around for a chance to catch a glimpse, and maybe even feel the muscle, of Al Davis, Brownsville's number-one celebrity.

After reading all the morning and afternoon papers, Bummy wanted to be with his crowd. He wanted to hear their cheers and good wishes. He wanted to taste the fruits of his victory. He visited his pushcart peddler buddies on Blake Avenue and dropped in at all his haunts and hangouts. His last stop was Beecher's, where Al "Bummy" Davis had become the guy in whose footsteps all the young fighters wanted to follow. For ten, fifteen minutes training came to a halt as the whining of skip-ropes and the thunking of fists against bags was replaced by calls of "Atta way, Al, baby!" and "That's showin' 'em champ!"

Bummy knew that it was a moment to cherish, a dream come to life. He would have loved to freeze that moment in time, to luxuriate in its glow. Pretty Levine was another guy who would have loved to see time come to a screeching halt, to see the whole world hang motionless, to see everything remain as it was. But it doesn't happen. Not for Bummy Davis, who, as the gym returns to life, fills his gym bag with workout clothes for his mother to launder and waves his good-byes. Not for Pretty Levine, who heads slowly for the door when Abe Reles barks for him to get the car because they're taking a drive to Beecher's.

At three-thirty in the afternoon of February 21, 1939, the people of Brownsville were going about their normal routines. Housewives were bustling from grocer to butcher to fruit store. Deliverymen were making their rounds, peddlers were selling from their wagons, kids were absorbed in their street games. Specialty shoppers from other neighborhoods were looking for buys on lighting fixtures, appliances, and furniture. Every ten or fifteen minutes a train rumbled overhead, drowning out the street noise. It is a typical afternoon in Brownsville in 1939 until Al "Bummy" Davis bounces down the stairs from Beecher's Gym to Livonia Avenue the day after winning a very important fight.

Outside the gym, Puggy Feinstein is wolfing down his third knish. He's been so busy picking up his winnings on the bets his friends placed for him that he has simply forgotten to eat. He hasn't been up to Beecher's since the day Reles chased him out, but he decides to chance hanging around for a while because he wants to congratulate the kid— and also thank him for all the green mattress stuffing he now has.

Puggy spots Al right away, but he can't get through the crowd of kids mobbing him. They all love him, and they all want a chance to touch him or get a wave of greeting from him. Al grins as he rumples their hair and they take turns feeling his biceps. They giggle as he squares off against one of them.

Suddenly all the shouting and cheering stops, like water when you turn off a faucet. It stops even before the large black Packard pulls up at the curb on the other side of Livonia Avenue. Eyes turn from Bummy and stare at the car. The kids' laughter fades, the crowd slowly backs off, and the knish man moves his wagon from the curb to the shadows of the building.

The doors of the Packard open. Abe Reles, Buggsy Goldstein, Pittsburgh Phil Strauss, and Happy Maione step out. Buggsy raises his hand. Traffic stops as they cross Livonia Avenue. Inside the car Pretty Levine's knuckles turn white from gripping the steering wheel so hard. Like everyone else on the avenue, he feels himself shriveling and tries to avoid looking at what is about to happen, but his eyes refuse to follow his command. He wishes he'd tried harder to make a go of it with his truck.

Al grips his gym bag tightly. He feels like a spotlight is on him, and he has no desire for a spotlight performance. However, the stage is set and the show must go on. Standing in front of him is the main cast of Murder, Inc., and they are not in a jovial mood.

"You played fuckaround with us, Bummy," Reles says, pointing his finger and biting off every word.

The kid says nothing, just stares at Reles. Pep, Buggsy, and Happy stand there silently, twitching a little, like snakes ready to strike.

"Who do you think you're screwin' around with? You got a bum hand and you're gonna lose the fight. You think you're a smart-ass wiseguy?"

Al is still looking Kid Twist straight in the eye. "G'wan. I didn't tell you nothin', Reles. And get your finger outta my face."

"Don't bullshit me, you fucken punk. I wasn't there by myself." He jerks his thumb in the direction of Strauss and Goldstein. "We plunged pretty deep on your word, Davis, you hear me? You don't pull that kinda crap on us. Nobody gets away with that!"

Among Abe Reles's imperfections, pushing people around and threatening them are at the top of the list. Al Davis is also an imperfect person: he is unable to handle being pushed around and threatened. So to those who know him best, like Shorty and Mousey, who are there in the crowd with their hearts in their throats, what happens next is inevitable. To them, it is not exactly a shock when Bummy drops his gym bag to the ground. To everyone else, it is like a bolt of lightning strikes Livonia Avenue. To everyone there in a place they'd rather not be on this chilly February afternoon, it is as though Al Davis finally does make time stand still. No one makes a sound, nothing seems to move— no cars, no trucks, no trains on the overhead tracks. And it is within this small universe of motionlessness and silence that the impossible becomes reality, fear becomes joy, and the fabric of Murder, Inc. begins to unravel.

By the time the gym bag hits the pavement, Al Davis is squared off eyeball to eyeball with Abe Reles and his three top goons. Legs spread wide and lips parted in a snarl, he is motioning with both hands for all four of them to come at him. This is not Al "Bummy" Davis, main-event prizefighter, striking his professional stance. What the crowd sees is a street-tough Brownsville scrapper, Albert "Boomy" Davidoff, doing what comes naturally.

"You want me? You want me? I'm right here." Bummy's hands beckon almost pleadingly. "Come on, alla ya, whatcha waitin' for? Where's all the big talk now?!"

Like everyone in the crowd, Reles and his boys see what's happening, but they can't believe it. They look at the wild-eyed Al Davis, they look at each other, they look back at Davis. After an endless moment, Abe Reles, Buggsy Goldstein, Pittsburgh Phil Strauss, and Happy Maione turn and walk back to the Packard. Even though they're all wearing suits and topcoats, they might as well be naked, because one of Brownsville's own has stripped away the mantle of invincibility they've worn with such impudence for so long. As they climb into the car, they see the people on the avenue stepping forward, no longer averting their eyes and trying to fade into the shadows. Instead they are staring—and smiling. For one brief second, Reles catches a glimpse of the guy with the biggest smile of all, Puggy Feinstein.

The kid does not move from where he is anchored until the Packard takes off, turning at the first corner and fading from sight. Then he picks up his gym bag, looks around, and starts walking down Livonia Avenue with Shorty and Mousey at his side. Hands reach out to touch him and pat him on the back, and Al "Bummy" Davis does not understand what all the commotion is about. After all, he's just a guy who doesn't like to be pushed around.

Even though no more than fifty or sixty people actually see how Al chases off the big boys from Murder, Inc., the way word gets around you'd think Walter Winchell broadcasts it to Mr. and Mrs. North America on the radio. Suddenly the boogeyman is not as scary as he was.

Harry Rudolph is a guy who does not have wings or plays the harp, which is why he winds up doing time and nursing his grudges at Riker's. It's five years now since Abe Reles and Buggsy Goldstein knock off Harry's pal Red Alpert with the help of the late Walter Sage and Reles puts a slug in Harry's gut as a sort of notice of intent. Ever since then the only thing Harry wishes for more than to see Kid Twist fry is to throw the switch himself. But wishing is not doing, and for Harry Rudolph, the crescent-shaped scar decorating his stomach is all he needs as a reminder that nobody stands up to Abe Reles and lives to tell about it. Then one day they bring in this very poorly tutored purse-snatcher who has the misfortune of grabbing at the pocketbook of a most possessive bubbe. Not only does the old lady refuse to let go of her pocketbook; she wraps its long strap around the neck of her attacker while she screams "Police!" and proceeds to pull and tug until he is purple from choking and as happy as anyone can possibly be when he is cuffed and hauled away in a squad car, eventually winding up sharing a spot in the sun of the Riker's exercise yard with Harry

Rudolph, to whom he relates all the latest happenings and occurrences in Brownsville.

When Harry hears about the showdown on Livonia Avenue, he feels a surge of red blood rushing through his veins and decides that if Bummy Davis can stand up to Reles, so can he. Harry Rudolph is a guy who does not exactly have a deep acquaintance with pen and paper, but he sits down and writes a letter to the Brooklyn DA.

Bummy is carrying a looseleaf notebook in his right hand and a pencil in his left as he, Puggy, Shorty, and Mousey step gingerly through the stable area at Belmont. With them is Pretty Levine. He's still thinking about Bummy standing up to Reles that way, and what confuses him is that he feels good about it.

"Just wait'll you and Helen meet her," Puggy is saying to Pretty, his smile running from one ear to the other. "You're gonna wonder what she sees in a squirt like me."

Pretty gives him a punch in the arm. "Don't sell yourself short. She's gettin' herself a hell of a good guy."

The "she" in question is Zelda Plotkin, a very prim and proper young lady from a very prim and proper Flatbush family. Zelda becomes somewhat smitten with Puggy through a shiddach made by his mother at a Hadassah meeting, where, out of desperation, she describes her nearly thirty-year-old trombenik son as "an ambitious young man who puts his money out on the street." To a respectable family from Flatbush, what better a catch could there be than a Wall Street investor? By the time Puggy confesses to Zelda what kind of an "investor" he is, love has entered the picture. Zelda accepts him anyway, and Puggy vows to turn over a new leaf and get a legitimate job for the first time in his life. And although he convinces himself that he has no fear of Reles, especially after seeing him back down to Bummy, he feels it is for the best that he stay out of Brownsville altogether.

"I still can't get over it, that such a terrific girl should be in love with me." Puggy sighs dreamily. "Could you believe I even got a real job? In a doll factory, no less, and I start tomorrow, so you won't be seein' me around much from now on." He turns to Al. "But whenever you fight, I'll be there, kid. Could you believe me workin' six days a week?"

"What about poolin' our money and buyin' that gelding?" Although Bummy gets a kick out of placing an occasional bet, what he really wants to learn is the business end of horseracing. The kid who always had the cleanest notebook in elementary school because he never took a note has filled his looseleaf cover to cover with everything Puggy's taught him.

"I wasn't kiddin', Al, I meant it, but it's different now. I'm usin' that money to buy furniture and put down on an apartment. Ya see, kid, it's a new me. No more gamblin', no more makin' book. If her family knew what a bum I am, forget about it. They don't know from such shit. From now on, Puggy Feinstein is on the straight and narrow. Anyhow, you don't need me. You got enough dough on your own."

"I couldn't do it without you, Puggy. I don't know the first thing about ownin' a racehorse."

"Come on, kid," Puggy says, "what's to know? You buy the horse, you pay the entry fees, and you pocket the winnings. When you win the title you'll buy the whole goddamn track."

With Bummy scribbling furiously in his looseleaf notebook, Puggy finishes his last lesson on how to invest in a thoroughbred, thinking how much he's going to miss being part of Al's life and his climb to the top. On the other hand, he admits, but only to himself, what a relief it will be not having to look over his shoulder anymore for Abe Reles. He feels so relieved about this as they walk toward the track to watch an exercise boy put his horse through its morning workout that he's not looking under his feet either.

"Oh, no!" Puggy groans, raising his left shoe warily to inspect the sole.

"Hey, take it easy." Shorty laughs. "Stepping in shit is good luck, ain't it?"

"I think that's dog shit," Mousey says. "It don't apply to horse shit."

A few days after the trip to Belmont, Pretty Levine is sitting next to Duke Maffetore at the counter in Midnight Rose's candy store, wishing he could lose himself in a comic book the way Dukey does. Dukey's mouth is hanging open as his eyes dart from panel to panel. Once he gets between the covers of a comic, forget Brownsville, forget Brooklyn—he takes up residence in a ten-cent fantasy world.

"Hey, Pretty, how far is Metropolis from Brownsville?"

Pretty, who is Dukey's friend and has looked after him since they're kids, knows by now how his mind works. What's bothering Dukey is whether Superman will drop in on them, and if he does, will he consider them bad guys? What's bothering Pretty is whether he's been living in a fantasy world too. All he ever wanted was to be like Reles and Pittsburgh Phil. When he and Duke were brought into the gang he felt like a million bucks. But once he gets to where he always wanted to be he's not sure he wants to be there anymore. There's nothing daring or fearless about breaking the bones of helpless old men or slicing someone's throat from behind with a piano wire.

Pretty Levine has no illusions about who he is or what he is. He's been packing a rod since his bar mitzvah. But somewhere along the way he comes up with this notion that there is a code of ethics, certain rules of fair play, and that friendship counts. These are his thoughts, but that's all they are, just thoughts, until he marries Helen and tries to go straight. He gives it his best shot, not just for Helen but for himself also, but as it turns out, his best shot isn't good enough. So Pretty and Dukey sit at a candy store counter because they are told to sit there and wait for instructions from Reles, Buggsy, or Pep, who, in turn wait for instructions from the big boss, Lepke, who is being hunted by J. Edgar Hoover, Thomas Dewey, and maybe even Superman.

Thinking back to the first three and a half rounds of his first fight with Bummy Davis, Mickey Farber is convinced that that's the way the whole thing would have gone if he'd just stayed with his game plan, so when he bounces into the ring at Madison Square Garden on Saint Patrick's Day, he is brimming with confidence. The bouncing continues throughout the rematch: Bummy bouncing his left hook off Mickey, and Mickey bouncing off the canvas. Some people who hear about Davis's face-off with Reles come to the Garden wondering if the kid might be a little too busy looking over his shoulder. When the bell sounds to end the fight, there is no question in anyone's mind that Al "Bummy" Davis is afraid of no one, inside the ring or out.

Chotchke Charlie is not there to see Al's victory in the second Farber fight. He is much happier indulging his newest passion, rolling the silver foil linings from empty cigarette packs into a great big ball. Charlie has no desire ever to attend another prizefight. He would much rather see his friend Boomy on the street or in the candy store. He gets absolutely no argument from Bummy regarding this decision.

Two other guys who do not attend the fight are Abe Reles and Buggsy Goldstein. True, it's a Friday night fight, but nobody thinks they do not go because they are shoymer Shabbes. Also, just because they don't go see the kid, that doesn't mean they aren't thinking about him. Al "Bummy" Davis is very much in their thoughts. Reles begins to wonder whether he should convert the storefront office into a social club, because with all the traffic they are getting lately it is beginning to feel like one. One day Sergeant William Schroeder drops in, and the next day it's Willie Davidoff.

When Bill Schroeder hears about Al Davis's street scene with Kid Twist, he smiles, thinking of the day he was sent to arrest ten-year-old Boomy on kidnaping charges, but he doesn't jump up and shout hallelujah like everyone else. He knows Abe Reles, and he knows how his mind works. Schroeder is the kind of cop who is liked and respected by everyone in the neighborhood, the kind who never plucks an apple off the fruit stand and always drops his change on the luncheonette counter—with a tip—when he stops for a cup of coffee and a doughnut. Schroeder plays by the rules, but with Abe Reles, that's like a matador confronting a bull with a butter knife. So Schroeder decides to forget the rules, something he's never done before. He walks into Reles's office without a warrant and says that although he is not there on official business, he is doing Reles and his boys a big favor by pointing out that if the whole world doesn't know about the "misunderstanding" between them and Al Davis, enough of it does. If anything happens to anyone— well, they are already under a magnifying glass, and he reminds them that a magnifying glass can burn whatever's under it to extinction.

The next day Willie Davidoff storms in, mad as hell. "You ever try to move in on my kid brother again," he tells Reles, "and there will be one very major problem. I never made a move on anything of yours, and I expect the same respect from you." Willie is relieved when Reles explodes, "Are you threatening me, you sonuvabitch?" He knows Abe well enough to know that if he intended to hurt the kid he'd be extremely cordial and reassuring. What Willie doesn't know is that by the time he walks through the door, Reles has already decided that it is best to leave Bummy Davis as a thought.

11

By the summer of 1939, by virtue of a snarling, raging style punctuated by a thunderous left hook, Al "Bummy" Davis is sitting on top of the world. It is true that Bummy's world is somewhat limited. When he knocks out Gene Gregory in one round on July 22, running his unbeaten streak to thirty-five, he broadens his horizons considerably as the fight is held in Long Beach, Long Island, nearly twenty miles from Brownsville, the farthest the kid has ever traveled. All his previous fights were either in Brooklyn or Manhattan. But a world is a world, and to Bummy the one he's sitting on top of is the only one that matters. Brownsville loves him, and all the papers are saying he is destined to be champion of the world.

The way Al sees it, the next stepping stone to his destiny is Tony Canzoneri. No matter how many different ways Lew Burston tries to explain why fighting Canzoneri is a no-win situation, the kid has a mind-set—and when Al "Bummy" Davis has a mind-set, neither logic nor force will make him come around.

"Come on, Mr. Boiston. I beat Canzoneri and I'm there."

"You beat him—and I know you can—they're all going to say you caught an old man on a bad night. Canzoneri is a legend. Everybody loves this guy. Kid, when Corbett beat Sullivan, it was Sullivan they cheered for. Legends never really lose, Al. Never."

"But Corbett wins the title, right? That's what counts in the end."

"Yeah, but you beat Canzoneri, you still have no title," says the exasperated manager. "All it's going to mean to the crowd is that you picked on a grand old ex-champ on the comeback trail."

"I want Canzoneri. For once, let me call the shot. Come on." Al grins with the devil's twinkle in his eye. "I'll be so good you'll wanna adopt me."

The kid's charm is more potent than his left hook. "Go on, take your shower and go home. I'll call Mike Jacobs and set it up."

The top of the world is a precarious and slippery place to be, and the slide down can be pretty painful. Louis "Lepke" Buchalter, who was sitting on top of the world for so long, is now holding on for dear life. When he hears that Lucky Luciano's pal Thomas "Three-Finger Brown" Lucchese is trying to move in on his garment unions, the teacup he's holding in his hand crashes into Dorothy Walsh's wall, followed by its matching saucer. For a long minute he paces the living room, and then he whirls around and points his finger at Big Al Anastasia.

"You let these sonsabitches know that I have not laid down and died. I want the respect that I am entitled to."

Anastasia's loyalty to Lepke is unwavering—a rare quality in his line of work—and he obviously delivers the message most eloquently, because Lucchese and Luciano back off. But now Big Al is worried that too many people know where Lepke is holed up, so he finds another hideout. Lepke agrees to the change even though the new quarters—a dingy one-room basement apartment on Third Street in south Brooklyn—are nowhere near as comfortable as Dorothy Walsh's Ocean Parkway apartment. They are a lot more comfortable than the eight-by-ten cell where Lepke's partner, Jake "Gurrah" Shapiro, is spending the rest of his life since Dewey put him away in 1938. Lepke has been running ever since.

Dorothy Walsh, who would like to have her cup and saucer back, doesn't receive so much as a thank-you when Lepke leaves. Instead he turns at the door and tells her, "I have some underwear and white shirts in the hamper. You'll have them washed and ironed and send them over with Al or Reles."

Anastasia and Lepke decide upon a list of three visitors to the new hideout, the only people Lepke figures he can trust—the only people who are not potential additions to his ever-growing hit list, at least for the time being. They are Anastasia, Reles, and Moe "Dimples" Wolinsky, Lepke's closest associate, the manager of his business affairs and an old friend. Nobody else is to know where Lepke is. Anastasia's loyalty to Lepke is as strong as it is because he is in awe of the person who has united all the "families" and restructured crime, elevating it to a level bordering on respectability. Reles's loyalty has much to do with the fact that it is Lepke who supplies him and his boys with 95 percent of their workload. Such a person should live and be well. As for Dimples Wolinsky—well, he and Lepke go back a very long way.

After his second week at the doll factory in downtown Brooklyn, Puggy decides to splurge. When he picks up his pay envelope on Friday evening he hops on the Fulton Street trolley car and gets off at the Abraham and Strauss Department Store, where he buys a brown calfskin wallet. It is the first wallet he ever owns, as never before does he see a need for one. After all, his pants have four pockets, more than enough for whatever bills and change come his way. Having enough pockets was never his problem. Although that is a thing of the past now that Puggy Feinstein is a full-time assembly-line worker, he knows that he will continue shoving his money into his pockets. That is not why he buys the wallet. Puggy is so proud to have a girlfriend like Zelda Plotkin that he wants to carry her photograph around so that he can look at it whenever he wants and show her off to his friends and co-workers. The wallet has two photograph sleeves. In one he places a picture of Zelda sitting on her front stoop. The other he leaves empty, saving it for their wedding picture. His mother warns him that it is bad luck to leave a picture frame empty, but Puggy is not one to pay attention to old wives' tales.

Ever since Zelda agrees to marry him, Puggy is floating on a cloud. His only problem is that having been called a punk, a squirt, and a bum so many times by so many people, he finds it difficult to think of himself as anything else. In his mind he isn't even fully qualified in any of these not-so-desirable roles, as he is usually called a two-bit punk, squirt, or bum. So it is no great wonder that he still cannot understand what a nice girl like Zelda Plotkin sees in a bum like him. It is a question he asks himself again and again. "I ain't good enough for her," he tells his friends over and over. Usually they are quick to disagree.

Puggy does have one agreeable friend, though, a guy named Arnold—as in Benedict Arnold. He agrees with Puggy about everything. When Puggy shows him Zelda's picture, Arnold agrees that she is a most attractive girl. When Puggy tells him that he is one lucky stiff to have her, Arnold agrees. And when Puggy says that he is not good enough for her, Arnold agrees with that too. He agrees to such an extent that he takes a trip over to Zelda's house in Flatbush, where he introduces himself to her parents and apprises them that Irving Feinstein, former professional bookie, gambler, and all-around lowlife, is definitely not good enough for their daughter, and that he, Arnold Levy, will be most happy to help Zelda get through this difficult period.

Puggy Feinstein should have listened to his mother. As it turns out, he throws his wallet in the garbage and never buys another one.

The door hardly closes behind him when Moe "Dimples" Wolinsky clasps his friend's shoulders. For one nervous second Lepke is afraid Dimples is going kiss him.

"Lep, the deal is in!" Moe gushes. "You hear me, boychik, the deal is in!"

Big Al watches Moey Dimples talk. His arms are waving like an orchestra conductor's, and his whole body is swaying from side to side. Al cannot help thinking of the elephants prancing and dancing at the circus.

"Louis, listen, everything is set. Hoover agrees to go for only the narcotics rap. Ten to twelve, at most. In two or three years you're out on parole. And the best part is, you take the federal rap and Hoover guarantees that Dewey and the state cannot touch you."

Lepke does not even try to hide his excitement. It's a whole different ball game now. It's almost as good as being home free. "This is an absolute, Moe?"

"Lep, the boys wanted to tell you themselves, but they gotta hang low, so I am the messenger. It is a done deal."

"It ain't worth taking the chance." Anastasia, who has remained silent until now, speaks up. "Nobody's come close to finding you so far, and believe me, Lep, I can keep you hidden away forever. Why gamble when you don't have to?"

Lepke looks at his chief lieutenant, knowing he can trust him with his life, but his is a lone voice of dissent. This is too good a deal to pass up. "I have to think about it, Albert. I've got to give it a lot of thought," he says, but his mind is already made up because his dear friend Dimples Wolinsky croons the melody he wants to hear—a melody composed by Thomas "Three-Finger Brown" Lucchese with lyrics by Lucky Luciano.

Kid Twist has a strong vested interest in Lepke's well-being, but it is not like he goes on home relief if there are no more enforcement contracts from the Syndicate head. Reles has accumulated quite a variety of sources of additional income. Besides the "protection insurance" he collects from many of the store owners in Brownsville and East New York, his major endeavor is the six-for-five loan sharking that is run from Midnight Rose's candy store. He also has his inheritance from the Shapiro brothers—the houses of prostitution sprinkled throughout Brownsville—and his cut from the slot machine and gambling operation in the Catskills. For each of these projects, Reles is dependent upon a hands-on operative.

Reles's favorite form of gambling is to win every roll of the dice, so it is only natural for him to run the biggest crap game in Brooklyn, where every pot includes a cut for the house. Here his hands-on operative is Tiny Benson, whose job it is not only to see that the game runs smoothly but even more important to help out the poor, unfortunate fish who get cleaned out by a run of bad luck by offering them six-for-five money and a chance to reverse their fortunes. The corner of Court Street and State Street, where Reles's game is held in a second-story loft every Friday night, is in the heart of downtown Brooklyn, three short blocks from the office buildings housing many of Brooklyn's most prestigious law firms, real estate brokerages, and insurance companies. The string of taverns sprinkled strategically along Court Street offers one way of unwinding after a week of stress and business pressure; Kid Twist offers another. High rollers and born losers swarm to his game from every corner of the city.

Puggy Feinstein comes from Borough Park and would like to be a high roller, but he doesn't have the bankroll for it. He is thankful that he has any bankroll at all, and that is only because Mr. and Mrs. Plotkin, the in-laws he is never to have, are kind and considerate people, certain to be appreciated by their future son-in-law. Although they take back their daughter Zelda, they also replace all the money Puggy paid for furniture and an apartment, which may not mend his broken heart but does fill his empty pockets with something other than keys and a comb.

Puggy is not the first guy to be stabbed in the back by a friend and dumped on the garbage heap by a girl, but everyone reacts differently to misfortune. Some guys would take a dive from the top of the Empire State Building. Others would decide to tear apart the sonuvabitch who caused the misfortune. As Puggy is a guy who does not like heights, and as Arnold Levy is a lot bigger than he is, he deals with it in his own way. He decides to show the whole world that Puggy Feinstein can take it on the chin and come back doing his own thing bigger and better than ever. When he hears about the big bucks floating around at this Court Street crap game, he is determined to turn adversity into prosperity, relying on the adage "Lucky in cards, unlucky in love."

He has all kinds of good feelings when he gets a parking space on the corner of Court and State, right in front of the building where the game is held. Truthfully, luck does not play such a large role, as most people, even in this crowd, do not park in front of fire hydrants, but Puggy knows Lady Luck is with him. She stays with him until he gets the dice in his hands.

Puggy Feinstein has had cold dice before, but this is the first time he worries about frostbite. Although he is not a quitter, all his recently reacquired furniture and apartment money is soon gone, and it appears he will have to leave the table. Puggy looks around the big green-carpeted room and notices Tiny Benson coming toward him—it is very difficult not to notice Tiny Benson. Puggy has never had any dealings with Tiny, but he knows he's a Brownsville shylock who works with Abe

Reles. This does not bother Puggy, as he is not in Brownsville. Anyhow, the post-Zelda Puggy Feinstein does not scare easy.

"I gotta tell you something," Tiny says as his stomach keeps Puggy hemmed in at the table. "I have seen streaks of bad luck, but yours takes the cake. I mean, it is obvious just watching you that you are one astute player."

There is nothing in what Tiny says that Puggy can in any way dispute, so he just nods his head and tries to see how he can maneuver around the island known as Tiny Benson.

"You ain't lookin' to leave just when it should be your time, are you? It'll be a crying shame. I mean, the law of averages, it's there for you."

Puggy shrugs. "I know, but that's the breaks. If I'm dumb enough to leave my money home, there's nothin' I can do about it," he lies.

As one good lie deserves another, Tiny sighs. "I guess I am just one great big sentimental slob, but it tears me apart seeing you in a situation like this." Then he takes a closer look at Puggy. "You know, I think I seen you around. You from Brownsville?"

"No, I live in Borough Park, but I do some work in Brownsville. I worked with the Davis kid in Beecher's for a while."

"I don't believe it! Bummy Davis? Jesus Christ! We are almost like family! What's your name?"

"Irving. Irving Feinstein."

"Irving, listen to me. It'll break my heart if you blow your chance. Let me help you."

Not wishing to see a big guy like Tiny Benson cry, and also because he is sure he is ready for a big roll, Puggy takes Tiny up on his offer. Sure enough, the law of averages comes through, and he wins back all his money plus a little extra. He tries to repay his loan, but Tiny shakes his head.

"Irving, I don't think it's fair to place such a burden of guilt on my conscience. I would be committing a crime if I take back the money when you are on such a run. If you don't take advantage of such a hot hand, then you don't deserve it. Neither one of us is going anywhere. Use the money for another two, three weeks. You pull in a real stake, then you pay me. You know where to find me. The candy store on Saratoga and Livonia."

Puggy is a guy who has been around the corner and back; he knows the score. He knows that every time Tiny Benson puts a buck out on the street he is doing business. But he also knows that Tiny Benson is telling it like it is: you do not walk away when Lady Luck is at your side. When he finally leaves Reles's club that night, he bounces down the stairs whistling "Happy Days Are Here Again," although he is not a registered Democrat. And when he opens the door and walks out onto Court Street, there on his windshield is a ticket.

It is not so much that he is a big fan of bocci, or even likes the game. In fact, it is only a couple of months ago that he saw it played for the first time, but when there is nothing else around to watch, it beats counting flyspecks on the kitchen wall. Nobody knows who he is and nobody bothers talking to him, because they are all too busy yelling instructions and cursing at the round wooden ball as it rolls toward the small stone on the dirt court, but every day, unless it rains, the stranger with the brown beard who is always dressed too warmly for August stands there by himself for half an hour, then sits down at a bench and reads his newspaper.

On this day, August 24, it is different. Instead of sitting down with the newspaper, he watches them play all morning and decides that even though it is not a prizefight or a baseball game, it is pretty interesting after all. He knows he will miss it. Just like he will miss egg salad sandwiches on pumpernickel bread at Ratner's, the morning papers from the corner newsstand, and even the clanging of the trolley car as it clatters down Seventh Avenue. He knows there are also things that he will not miss, but for some reason he cannot think of any.

When he gets back to his room, the first thing Lepke does is remove his jacket and hat, then carefully pull off the fake beard that is already causing him a rash in this weather. To Lepke, every move in life is a strategy, including the telephone call he has Al Anastasia make to Walter Winchell. For almost two years now he's been listening to Winchell on the radio, reading him in the papers, and ignoring him no matter where he is, but now that Lucchese and the boys have put the fix in, it's a different story.

Lepke has two reasons for turning himself over to Winchell, neither of which is to save cab fare. First, in his mind he is not surrendering; he is making a wise move that knocks Dewey and his life sentence out of the box. That leaves a short-term sentence to deal with, but in order to serve a short-term sentence, you must be around to do it. Lepke figures that with Winchell there will be no mysterious accidents occurring in a dark alley, because with Winchell the spotlight is always on you.

Albert Anastasia, Abe Reles, and Mendy Weiss spend the afternoon with him. They sit around silently, sipping bottles of Coke, not knowing what to say. To Lepke, there is no time or place that is not suitable for attending to business, so while they mope he double-checks his list of things—and people—to be taken care of by Mendy, who will be running things while he is gone. At 6:00 P.M. Big Al looks at his watch. "You still got time to change your mind, Louis." For a moment Lepke gives serious thought to what Anastasia says, but there is no turning back now, not with Dewey reaching out for him.

Anastasia heaves a deep sigh and says it is time to leave. Winchell has offered to pick Lepke up, but Anastasia arranges for them to meet at Madison Square Park. Without traffic, the drive from south Brooklyn to Madison Square Park is twenty or twenty-five minutes. There is no traffic, but it takes Big Al about an hour. It's as though he hopes that everyone will get tired of waiting and just forget about it and go home. He has very strong feelings about knocking on a jailhouse door and asking to be let in, even if he's not the one doing the knocking.

Anastasia circles the block twice, making sure that no one else is around. Then he parks behind the black sedan with the license plate he was told to look for and asks Lepke to stay in the car while he checks things out. He returns a minute later and gently opens the car door for Lepke, who steps out carrying a small overnight bag, a few magazines, and the newspaper. Silently they walk to the other car. The driver's door opens, and Walter Winchell gets out. Lepke doesn't know why, but he's glad to see that Winchell is shorter than he is. They stand looking at each other awkwardly, as though they're both contemplating shaking hands but deciding it's inappropriate.

Winchell speaks first. "You're doing the right thing. I want you to know that."

"Where's Hoover?"

"He's just a few blocks from here. We're going to meet him now." He turns to Big Al. "Mr. Anastasia, I'm sorry. No one else can go along."

"You think I wanna meet Mr. G-Man?" He wants to say the right kind of good-bye to Lepke, but he can't get any words to come out. He tries to smile, but it's as though his face is paralyzed. He looks at this little guy whom he admires with all his heart and can do or say nothing to show how he feels.

As he watches Anastasia drive off, Lepke is thinking that he probably would have been better off turning himself in that morning rather than at night. Then he'd have a whole day to get organized and settled in. He's debating whether to ask about staying in a hotel for the night and getting started in the morning when a question creeps into his mind. Why wasn't Dimples there to say good-bye?

Winchell drives to Fifth Avenue and Nineteenth Street and pulls over to the curb. A stocky guy in a trench coat steps out of the shadows of a doorway. As Lepke gets out of Winchell's car he sees that there is another car parked at the curb, with three or four guys sitting in it. By the slouch hats they're wearing, they can only be hit men or G-men. It seems that time skips a beat, because the next thing Lepke knows is that Winchell is standing between him and the guy in the trench coat, with one hand resting on each of their shoulders, and the four guys in slouch hats are in a semicircle around them.

"Mr. Hoover," Winchell announces with a flourish, "Mr. Louis 'Lepke' Buchalter."

When Hoover extends his right hand, Lepke is somewhat surprised, as he didn't expect a handshake. When Hoover's left hand reaches into the inner pocket of his coat and comes out with a pair of handcuffs, which he deftly slaps on Lepke's wrists, surprise changes to realization. Lepke doesn't bother to ask about staying over in a hotel for the night, because by the time they stop for their first red light at Fifth Avenue and Twenty-third Street, he has figured out why Moey Dimples didn't say good-bye.

As for Winchell, he's bursting with his big scoop and doesn't want to wait until he gets back to the offices of the *Daily Mirror*, so he pulls up in front of the Automat on Fourteenth Street and makes a dash for the alcove where the telephone booths are located. He fumbles in his pocket, fishes out a nickel, plunks it in the telephone, and tries to dial the number, but his fingers are playing games with him. Finally he gets through to the city editor. As he shouts "Hold the presses!" into the mouthpiece, he learns firsthand what a sonuvabitch Adolf Hitler really is. With his story of a lifetime conjuring up visions of a front-page banner headline—"Winchell Brings in Lepke!!"—he hears above the clattering of teletype machines and the scraping of chairs, "We'll squeeze it in somehow, Walter, but I don't know. With Hitler and Stalin signing a pact . . . I just don't know."

Puggy Feinstein is not only a great big bluffer at a poker game, he's a bluffer at everything lately. He laughs, he tells everyone what a great time he's having, but even his run of good luck at the tables and the track does not bring a real smile to his face. So on Labor Day weekend, when his pals Paulie and Lou see him in front of Dubrow's wiping down his brand-new shiny blue Plymouth and ask him if he wants to go out looking for girls, Puggy is all for it. He's for anything that'll keep him from going to bed and dreaming the dreams of Zelda Plotkin that make him feel so bad.

"Whadja do, rob a bank?" Lou asks, eyeing the car like if it was a cupcake he would eat it.

"Actually, I discover dogs are not man's best friend. Horses are. All you do is put a few bucks on the nose and away the horsie goes."

"Yeah, and so does the few bucks."

"Hey, how about we drive out to the World's Fair?" Paulie cuts in. "We'll chip in for the gas. Whaddya say?"

This sounds like a good idea to everybody, so with the sun still up in the sky they pile into the Plymouth. Puggy sets off on the route he's most familiar with, through Brownsville to the Interboro Parkway, but when they get to Pennsylvania Avenue he remembers that it's time to pay back a debt. Maybe it's just an excuse he makes to himself to tempt fate and revisit his old forbidden haunts, or maybe it's that he turns the radio to WMCA and hears Jimmy Powers announce on the sports news that Al "Bummy" Davis and Tony Canzoneri have signed to fight at the Garden. Whatever it is, he makes a sudden sharp turn onto Livonia Avenue, causing Paulie and Lou to hang on for dear life.

"Sorry, guys, there's this shylock I'm into who's only a few blocks from here. It just dawns on me because we're so close by."

"Come on," Lou grumbles, "take care of it another day."

"Another day I may not have the bread. Today I got it. It'll only take me a few minutes. Anyhow, I betcha he's not even there."

It seems that Puggy is still on his run of good luck, because when he parks his car on Livonia near Saratoga and walks around the corner to Midnight Rose's candy store, Tiny Benson is indeed not there. Aside from the old hag picking her nose behind the counter, the only other person in the store is this squirt with his black hair slicked down, reading a comic book at a table in the back with his mouth hanging open.

When Puggy asks for Tiny, Rose takes a look at his mashed-in face and is about to tell him to piss off, but something makes her hold back. "And just who's looking for Tiny?" she says.

"Irv. Irv Feinstein. But if he ain't around I'll come back another day." Suddenly Puggy knows he doesn't want to be here.

The name Feinstein rings the bell for Rose immediately, maybe because she used to have a Boston terrier named Puggy. She remembers Abe Reles's reaction when he went over the "client list" with Tiny the other day. How could she forget? It's not too often that you see someone crush a metal malted milk container with one hand, but that's just what Abie did when he realized from Tiny's description that the Irving Feinstein on his list is actually this guy Puggy, who it seems is quite an obsession with Kid Twist.

"Tiny'll be right back. He just went around the corner for a pack of cigarettes."

"Don't you sell cigarettes here?" Puggy points to the shelves of them behind the counter.

"He smokes a brand I don't carry."

There is no question in Puggy's mind. He wants to go right now. He wants to go anywhere that is not in Brownsville. He turns and calls back over his shoulder, "It's okay, I'll catch him another day."

"What's the big rush?" Rose says. "Tiny'll be very upset."

Puggy reaches for the door handle, but the door opens before he grabs it, and there, standing right in front of him, is Pittsburgh Phil Strauss. At this moment Puggy would like very much to be a turtle and pull himself completely inside his shell.

246

"Harry," Midnight Rose croaks with a meaningful smile, "I want you should meet Puggy Feinstein, who is a real gentleman because he stops on a Labor Day weekend to pay Tiny back his loan."

Puggy is a short step from Pukesville. He is sure he did not give her the name Puggy.

"I know him. How ya doin', Pug?" There is a sly smile on a very nattily dressed Strauss, who looks down at the perspiring little squirt while doing a very good job of blocking the door.

Puggy puts his hands out in front of him, as if to hold off an invading army. "I know you guys don't want me in Brownsville, but I'm only here because this is where Tiny told me to come to pay off a loan. I got it all, interest and everything."

"We appreciate when a guy honors his obligations," Strauss says, and then he calls to the kid sitting at the back table. "Hey, Dukey, be a good guy. Drive my pal Puggy here over to Tiny. I'll tell you where he is."

"Aw, Harry, come on." Duke Maffetore is engaged in serious literary pursuits.

"No, no, that's okay, the lady told me he's just around the corner, but I gotta go anyhow. Ya see, I got these two friends waitin' outside for me." Never before does Puggy want to be at the World's Fair so badly.

Strauss crinkles his brow and laughs. "That's no lady, that's Rose. Yeah, Tiny was around the corner. I was with him, and he had to make a stop. We'll get you over to him."

"I told ya, I got these two buddies. I gotta run over and tell them. In fact, lemme just give you the money, Harry." Puggy's face lights up as he reaches into his pocket.

"Tiny'd be pissin' mad. He don't like nobody messing with his end of the business. Come on, loosen up, whatcha so nervous for, Puggy?" Strauss places his arm around Puggy's shoulder and gives him a squeeze. "Ya come here like a real gentleman—I'm glad to see you."

Four-year-old Buddy Reles, giggling in his cowboy pajamas, is doing a pretty good Lone Ranger even though he has no mask and the horse he's riding around the living room floor looks more like Buggsy Goldstein than Silver. Uncle Marty always makes little Buddy laugh. He is his daddy's very funniest friend.

"Hi-yo, Silver, hoo-way! We gonna catch the bad guys!"

"Come on, Buddy. There are no bad guys. Time for beddy-bye." Kitty Reles and Betty Goldstein are rushing to clear the dishes from the dining room table so they can go to the movies with Abe and Buggsy. Kitty really believes what she tells Buddy about the bad guys. She isn't trying to fool her son—just herself.

The phone rings. "Abie, it's for you," Kitty's mother calls from the bedroom.

When Abe comes back into the living room, Kitty can tell from his face that there will be no movies tonight. She is half right.

"You go with Betty," her husband says. "We got some business to take care of."

Puggy is feeling a lot better. Strauss tells one funny story after another about all the girls he tries banging, and it doesn't even matter if they're true or not because they make Puggy realize that the guy is human after all. When they pull up to what Strauss says is Tiny's building, Puggy goes along with him into the vestibule, and sure enough, the name on the bell plate is "Benson." Strauss rings the bell, and when there is no answer he shrugs and says, "Sorry I wasted your time, Puggy. We may as well go back. You'll catch him another day. In fact, I'll make sure he don't charge you no more vig after today."

Things have a way of working themselves out, Puggy thinks to himself as he climbs back into the car, in a better mood than he has been in a long, long time.

As Duke pulls away from the curb, Strauss snaps his fingers and calls out, "I bet I know where that sonuvagun is! One more shot, okay, pal?"

Puggy smiles. "It's okay with me. You'd think a guy that size would be easy to find." He is very pleased with himself for saying something that is actually a little bit funny.

"Dukey, drive over to Avenue A and East Ninety-first."

There is a look in Duke Maffetore's eyes that Puggy is fortunate not to see.

Once in a while Midnight Rose finds herself in a situation where she has to lean over, reach into the freezer below the counter, and scrape out scoops of ice cream. This is what most people who run candy stores look forward to and enjoy because it is the backbone of their business. Rose Gold is not most people. If ice cream would burn, she would light a match to it. Saturday night is the worst, because that's when the Ambassador Theater across the street draws its biggest crowd, which is made up mostly of young people. As soon as the movie is over, the normal ones are content to sit in the back of a car and neck, but then there are the ones who just have to go out for ice cream.

Rose is not in the best of moods when Paulie and Lou walk into a candy store packed with kids eating frappes and moaning about the fact that this is their last week of freedom since school starts in a couple of days. Somehow Paulie is able to make himself heard over the din at the counter.

"Excuse me."

"I suppose you want ice cream too," she snaps.

"Well, actually, ya see . . . I got a friend . . ."

"That's nice." Hearing that Paulie isn't there for ice cream immediately puts Rose in a better frame of mind. "And why shouldn't you have a friend? I've seen a lot worse come in here."

Paulie smiles. "Yeah, my mother likes me, too. This friend"—he presses his finger against his nostril—"he's a little guy with a nose like this. He went to see someone around here, and he's gone an awful long time. I wonder if he happened to be in here or was—"

"Does this look like the Lost and Found?"

Paulie might as well have bought ice cream, considering the way Rose is now treating him. It is beginning to dawn on Paulie and Lou that there is a good chance they do not make it to the World's Fair.

The second the front door opens at 9102 Avenue A, Puggy Feinstein has a lot more to worry about than getting to the World's Fair. When Duke first pulls over in front of the house, Puggy has no worries because they are on a pretty tree-lined street in a nice middle-class neighborhood called East Flatbush, and also because Pittsburgh Phil is not a bad guy when you get to know him. Dukey is strictly a wheelman, but one thing he knows for sure is that this Puggy has no reason for looking as unruffled as he does. When Strauss and Puggy get out of the car, Duke gets out also. He's always ordered to stay behind the wheel, but this time no one says anything, and he is very curious to see what's going to happen inside his boss's new house.

As the door swings open, the light from the living room makes it seem as though a spotlight has been turned on, and there in the center of the spotlight is the one—the only—Abe "Kid Twist" Reles! Undoubtedly the star of the show. As he bends from the waist, bowing, and gives Puggy a greeting much like the cat gives the canary, it is pretty obvious who the co-star will be.

Puggy Feinstein feels as though he is encased in a cake of ice. He is unable to move or speak, and the images spinning and whirling in his head are like a kaleidoscope. He sees himself in the ocean, struggling to stay afloat. He remembers hearing somewhere that a drowning person goes under three times and then it is all over. He watches himself going under for the first time.

"Come in, punk." A huge grin creases Reles's face. "How come you're not laughin' now? Where's that great sense of humor?"

Puggy doesn't answer. This is not by choice alone but in part because Pittsburgh Phil is no longer as nice as he was. He has Puggy in a stranglehold and is dragging him to the center of the living room, which is no easy job in spite of the little guy's size. Puggy kicks and squirms as drool and phlegm drip down his chin onto the hand Strauss is pressing against his windpipe.

"Yech!" Strauss whines, taking his hand from Puggy's throat and wiping it on his pants. "What a disgusting sonuvabitch!" This gives Buggsy Goldstein, who is sitting on the couch eating sunflower seeds, a big laugh. He remains there, taking in the show. Duke watches from the sidelines in amazement, because he has never seen the big guys in operation before. They sure do enjoy what they do. No matter how much Puggy cries and pleads for his life, they go right on with their work.

Forcing Puggy to the floor, Strauss asks Reles for some rope.

"Where am I gonna get rope from?" Reles asks.

"How the fuck do I know! It's your house, not mine!"

"Shit," Reles grumbles as he heads to the back of the house, calling out, "Ma! Ma!" It dawns on Dukey that Reles's mother-in-law is in one of the bedrooms with his kid.

Lying on the floor with Strauss's foot on his neck, Puggy feels like his lungs are ready to burst. Strauss eases up on the pressure for a brief second, Puggy gulps air, Strauss bears down again, and Puggy feels himself sinking for the second time. He knows that he must not go under a third.

In the bedroom, Rose Kirsch rubs her eyes and looks at her son-in-law's silhouette framed in the doorway. "What's all the tumult? The baby's sleeping. Didn't you go to the movies?"

"No. We got a business meeting. Kitty went with Betty. Listen, I need some rope. We're tyin' up a large package. Do you know where Kitty keeps the clothesline?"

"It's in the garage, next to the hose. Could you at least turn the radio down? What kind of business meeting needs a radio blasting like that?"

"Soon, Ma, soon. The guys need it to stay awake. I may need the icepick too."

"It's in the ice cube tray in the freezer. Now could I please go to sleep?"

When Reles returns with the rope, Buggsy finally gets up from the couch like it's audience-participation time. The three of them struggle to turn Puggy over, but he fights back with all his might, kicking and flailing his arms, and when Strauss shoves his hand in Puggy's face to push him down, the little gamecock clamps his teeth together, producing a "Yeow!" from Strauss that rattles the dishes in the kitchen pantry and brings an exasperated cry from the bedroom. "Finish your meeting already! A bunch of lunatics!"

"Hey, will you morons keep it down?" Reles growls, shoving a cushion under Puggy's face to muffle his cries.

"It's bleedin'," Strauss moans, examining his finger with a shocked expression "The little fucker bit me till it's bleedin'."

Buggsy looks at the wound and shakes his head. "I knew a guy once who got bit by a woman. He died from rabies. They say a human bite is much worse than from a dog." Again he shakes his head sadly at Strauss, who is now looking at his finger in horror.

"I need some Mercurochrome, Abie!"

"Whaddya, kiddin' me?"

"Take a look at this. You wanna see me die?"

Dukey Maffetore can't believe that Pittsburgh Phil Strauss, who has produced enough buckets of blood to create his own Red Sea, is moaning and groaning at the sight of a couple of drops of his own blood. Reles is muttering to himself on the way to the bathroom, but he finds the Mercurochrome, brings it back, and dabs it on Strauss's finger. Strauss blows on the wound until it dries, then stares down at Puggy with a look that makes Dukey press himself into the wall. With Strauss instructing, they begin bending little Puggy like a pretzel. They force him to kneel on the floor, then make him sit on his heels and bring his chest down to his thighs until he is a compact letter Z.

"Hey, come on, guys! Please, cut it out!" Puggy can't stop himself from crying. His entire body starts betraying him. From the corner of his eye he sees Reles standing over him with a coiled length of rope.

"Go on and laugh now, you rotten little sonuvabitch."

Puggy knows immediately what Reles is talking about—the day he and everyone else in Brownsville cheered as Bummy Davis stood up to Reles and his dogs. He closes his eyes and sees it again. It is a good moment, and he knows that if the clock is turned back he would do it the same way.

Strauss loops one end of the rope around Puggy's ankles and runs the other end in a short, tight line through his tucked thighs to his neck, where he expertly fashions it into a noose. He leaves no play in the line, so that any move Puggy makes to relax that terrible, unnatural position only tightens the noose. Dukey, who is accustomed to the devious forms of torture employed by such evil geniuses as Fu Man Chu and the Claw, feels sick as he watches Puggy bite his lips in agony. After tonight he may never read another comic book.

As the pain knifes through him, Puggy clenches his eyes tightly shut, trying to blot out what's happening. He feels his body writhing and heaving. He hears his own choked cries for mercy. He hears the radio blaring in the background, and it's his mother's favorite program, *The Hit Parade*, and they're probably both listening to Lanny Ross crooning "Deep Purple" at the same time. He sees his mother comforting him when he was a little boy and he was hurt or in trouble, and he wants his mother now.

Suddenly Puggy stops struggling. He knows his mother isn't coming, he knows that time has run out, and in that knowledge he finds his strength. There are no more strangled pleas, no more tears. He raises his head as far as the rope will allow and looks up at Reles, his eyes clear and his body still. He sees that even though he draws a bad hand he has a chance to do what most people cannot; he can choose the way he dies. He knows he didn't choose too well when it came to living, and he isn't sure he can make up for it now, but he can try. You gotta play with what you draw.

Reles is sitting on the couch with Buggsy and Strauss, eating peanuts and drinking cold milk straight from the bottle, but he is not enjoying the show as much as he expected to. Watching the little rat squirm and gasp for air is okay, but without the screaming and begging it lacks pizzazz. Reles, who likes to have things completely his way, is getting angry.

It's not that Puggy, who is not on anyone's list of heroic role models or shtarkers, is able to tolerate the pain, and it's not that he's ignoring it. It's that the pain and Puggy are not exactly in the same place. Puggy's mind camouflages it and carries him away on a journey. While the pain continues to invade and torment his body, he is on an express train racing madly through the tunnel of his life, brightly lighted stations flashing by.

He sees Zelda, sobbing as she clasps a framed photograph of him to her breast, wishing she could undo her great mistake. Oh, how she misses Puggy!

He sees a cowering Arnie Levy lying on the ground, deposited there by Puggy's slashing fists, pleading with Puggy not to hit him again. With the cheers of a big crowd of friends behind him, Puggy turns and walks away, realizing Arnie is not worth the effort.

He is in the ring as the trainer and adviser of Bummy Davis, who is being hailed as the new champion. The kid embraces Puggy and thanks him for all he taught him.

Dukey cannot hide his look of astonishment as he sees a smile play across Puggy's face. Reles flies into a rage. He jumps to his feet and stands over the contorted body, shouting, "I'll give ya somethin' to grin about, you fucken stupid baboon!" And then he aims a hard kick just under Puggy's rib cage, causing even Strauss and Buggsy to grimace.

But not Puggy. He turns a street corner, and there is Reles, pointing a gun at him and warning him to stay out of Brownsville. Puggy laughs, knocks the gun out of his hand with a backhand swipe, and calls out a warning, loud and clear.

Abe Reles turns an ashen gray and shudders in disbelief as there before his eyes Puggy Feinstein bolts to an almost upright position, straining against the ropes and tightening the noose for the last time, and rasps out, "I'm going to get you, Reles! I'm going to get you!"

Moe Bradie just sits down at his desk to look through the early edition of the *News* when Buggsy Goldstein, who comes very close to making Moe's list of his favorite five thousand customers, drives up and orders a half gallon of gasoline.

"You sure you want to buy this all at one time? Maybe you wanna buy half now and half in a week or two."

"Come on, cut the crap, Bradie. My friend's car ran out of gas on Linden Boulevard, and I'm doing him a favor."

"Who would expect less from you? It'll be thirteen cents for the gas and a three-dollar deposit for the can."

"Whaddya need a deposit for? You know me."

"That's why I need the deposit. Okay, go on, but remember to bring the can back."

Although Martin "Buggsy" Goldstein has certain talents—he makes an excellent Silver for little Buddy Reles, and no one disputes that he is good with a rod—he would not be considered an asset at a scouting jamboree.

Buggsy has no idea where Paedergat Basin is even though he has been there enough times on similar excursions to stake a claim. He considers asking Dukey, but it's obvious that the kid doesn't even know what world he's in. So Buggsy gives up looking to deposit Puggy in the swamps and directs Dukey to pull over when they come to Flatlands and Ralph, where there is a picturesque vacant lot overrun with garbage and weeds. It is here that Duke Maffetore discovers that Buggsy is no better at making a fire than he is at navigation. And it is here that Puggy Feinstein begins making good his final promise.

254

After they deposit the lifeless body in the middle of the lot, where it is pretty well hidden from the street by tall ragweed, Buggsy unscrews the cap on the gas can and pours gasoline over Puggy's chest and face, then bends down and pulls out a book of matches. This rings an alarm bell for Dukey. Just a few days ago he is reading how one of Ming the Merciless's soldiers tries to destroy Flash Gordon's damaged rocket ship by lighting up some rocket fuel and it explodes right in his face, but before he can say anything there is a great *poof!*

"Holy shit!" Buggsy bellows, fingering his face. "Am I burnt?"

Dukey steps closer, holding his nose, because Buggsy stinks like a singed chicken. "Naw, ya look a little dirty, and . . . ya useta have eyebrows, didn't ya?"

"Whaddya mean, I useta have eyebrows. Everybody got eyebrows."

"You ain't, Buggsy. Not no more, anyhow. And the little wave in the front of your hair, it don't wave no more."

"Come on, let's scram before someone sees the fire," Buggsy says to change the subject, and they head back to the car.

Poor Puggy Feinstein. His life was incomplete, and now even his cremation is incomplete.

Moe Bradie is not an Albert Einstein, but he manages to total up the station's daily sales, figure out the gallons of gasoline sold from each pump, correlate them with the sales receipts, and handle the bank deposits, all without ever making an error. However, it takes him a while to put two and two together after he finds himself working around the clock because his night man has this unique way of celebrating Labor Day by not laboring.

Moe is sitting in his office taking a load off when Buggsy comes in and gives him three bucks. He says he lost the gas can. Moe looks at him and sees that something is different but can't put his finger on it.

"How do you lose a gas can?" Moe asks. "I mean, you lose a key or a dollar bill, I understand, but a gas can?"

It's not until he is reading the paper a few hours later that Moe adds it all up. Once again he makes no mistake.

12

If Bummy had his way every copy of the *Daily Mirror* on his father's newsstand would be in the garbage. Max shares his son's feeling, but you can only be a martyr if it costs you nothing. At two cents a paper you're a shmuck.

The day before, the *Mirror*'s flamboyant sports columnist, Dan Parker, whose eloquent arrogance makes and breaks reputations at the back of the paper the same way Walter Winchell's does at the front, visits Beecher's strictly to interview Al "Bummy" Davis. There's plenty of ink in the papers about Bummy, so it's not such a big deal to catch his name in print anymore, but to be in Dan Parker's column—that's something special. Al finds out how special as soon as he walks into the candy store and his father says, "What do you want to read from such a pencil pusher? Don't waste your time. Read Lester Bromberg or Meyer Ackerman."

Parker writes that the tag "Bummy" tells the whole story. He writes about a bully who terrorizes the neighborhood. He writes that there are three brothers, one worse than the next. It is a tale that reads so well that the name "Bummy" becomes like a prophecy by Johnny Attell— who has recently been appointed matchmaker at the Garden, one of his main qualifications being the crowds he can generate with an Al Davis fight.

It's no mystery to Vic Zimet why Parker was using poison instead of ink. The kid puts on a terrific show yesterday, and everyone has to be impressed with the way he's throwing that left in rapid-fire series of five, six, seven punches. When he finishes his workout he gets a standing ovation from the crowd, and Parker shakes his head in approval. After Bummy showers, Parker asks him some questions and seems visibly impressed at the kid's sense of humor and all-around good nature. Then Willie invites all the guys to join him at Alpert's for a bite to eat.

Everyone's sitting around laughing and kibitzing while they wait for their orders. Willie's dipping into the pickle bowl, taking turns between the sour pickles and the hot cherry peppers and washing it all down with celery soda.

Parker is curious about the cherry peppers. "I'm used to gherkins and dill pickles, but the red things—"

"Ooh, they're good. You gotta try one." Willie winks.

"Are they hot?"

"You can give 'em to a baby with a bottle of milk."

Vic and a few of the other guys are looking a little bit bug-eyed right now, but nobody says anything. Parker picks up a cherry pepper and sniffs at it. Willie pops another one in his mouth and swallows it in one gulp with a big smile. When Dan Parker tries to do it just like Willie, he ends up proving that man is 98 percent water, because buckets start pouring out of every part of him, streaming from his eyes, his nose, his scalp. Also, he is a human rainbow. He turns every color, from yellow to purple to red. It looks like smoke is coming from his ears, and it seems that his eyes do not want to have anything to do with the rest of him as they are making a tremendous effort to leave his head. Strange rumblings are heard. All in all, Dan Parker is doing one of the greatest imitations of Mount Vesuvius anyone has ever seen, and no one appreciates it more than Big Gangy, who is laughing so hard that he is almost as red as Parker. Everybody, including Bummy, is laughing at the newsman's suffering, not realizing the seriousness of his condition. It turns out that Dan Parker has acute stomach ulcers. He also has the last laugh.

When Bummy reads Parker's column the next morning he is caught with his guard down. He doesn't read any further, but then again, he hardly ever makes it to the front of the paper, so he doesn't see the article about the guy whose body was found torched in a lot on Flatlands Avenue.

"I don't think ya wanna go in there, Abie," Duke Maffetore whispers, grabbing at Pretty Levine's arm and pulling him away from the store-front headquarters on Stone Avenue.

"Hey, come on, Dukey, what're you doing?"

"Strauss is having a fit because we didn't clean out this guy we burn the other day."

"What the hell are you babblin' about?"

"Jeez, Pretty, you shoulda been there. You wouldn't believe how they torture this guy—and you know what? They let me go along. No shit, Pretty, I'm right there for the whole thing. But now Strauss is blamin' Buggsy for burnin' up a few hundred bucks that he says was in the guy's pockets."

"Okay, slow down, Dukey. Congratulations! You're finally in on a job."

"Yeah, but not really. I was watchin' mostly, except I went along with Buggsy to torch the guy. And you know what? It's in the papers, Abie. No shit, on page three."

Pretty shrugs. He's been on too many of these jobs. Not that it's old hat, but he just doesn't like thinking about it.

Duke is too wound up to let it go. "We take the guy to Reles's house, the new one. And I'll tell you somethin' "—he can't help snickering— "Reles almost shits a brick because this is one tough little fucker. Just before he croaks, he gives a jump—you shoulda seen, he's all tied up and chokin', but he gives a jump and a yell and scares the shit outta everyone."

"No kidding!" Pretty can't help being impressed. "Who was the guy, a welcher?"

Dukey shakes his head. "I don't think so, because he comes to the candy store to pay off, but it's like they don't care about the money. That's why Strauss is so pissed off. I never seen the guy before. He says his name is Irv, but they call him Puggy."

Pretty Levine takes off running, leaving Dukey standing there with his mouth hanging open. On a side street somewhere near Howard Avenue, he sits down on the curb and throws up his guts.

As soon as Al walks into the gym he knows something's wrong. Froike, Charlie and Willie Beecher, and all the other guys are standing around in clusters, listening to the radio.

"... Feinstein's older brother, Hyman, a clerk in the Law Department of the City of New York, said the deceased had no enemies that he knew of and was unemployed at the time of his death, having recently left his job at a doll factory in downtown Brooklyn in hopes of bettering himself. At present, the police have no leads in the murder of twenty-nine-year-old Irving Feinstein, although it has been determined that the cause of death was strangulation and that he was already dead when his body was set afire."

Froike puts his hand on Al's shoulder. "If you want to take the day off, it's okay," he says.

"No. Let's get to work." Bummy feels that's what Puggy Feinstein would want. He thinks back to when Reles bounced the little guy out of Beecher's and wonders if things would have been any different if he'd stood up for Puggy that day.

It's a tiny gathering in the Levines' kitchen to celebrate little Barbara's first birthday. There's Helen, there's Abe, and there's the birthday girl. That's it, there's no one else. Abe's parents won't set foot in the apartment because their son married a shiksa. Helen's parents stay away because their daughter married a gangster.

In the center of the table is a small Ebinger's cake with one candle in the middle. Pretty puts his arm around Helen's shoulder, and the two of them smile adoringly at their little girl. Helen's smile is a mixture of joy and sadness: joy for being blessed with such a precious child, sadness for having no one to share the proud moment with.

"I can't believe that Puggy didn't remember Barbara's birthday," she sighs. "He sends her a card every month. How does he forget her first birthday?"

Abe turns his head away because he can't look Helen in the eye. "You know, a single guy and all that, he's got more things on his mind than a baby's birthday."

Pretty is careful not to bring a newspaper into the house since Puggy's rubout, and as far as the radio, Helen listens to *Big Sister, Our Gal Sunday,* and *One Man's Family,* not the news. He doesn't see any reason for her to know about Puggy because she just won't be able to understand why anyone would do such a thing and Pretty won't be able to explain it to her. He doesn't know the answer, not anymore.

Al Davis is another guy who learns that yesterday's answers may not be today's. On October 31, or anytime before that, if you ask the kid how important is his fight against Tony Canzoneri, his answer, without hesitation, is "Big!" A win will put him right at the top and in line for a crack at the title, and from there the sky's the limit. But on November 1, 1939, Al Davis finds out that the easy answers are not always the right answers.

Walking into the Garden that night, Al "Bummy" Davis is a guy who is adored by quite a few people living in the two-square-mile patch of land known as Brownsville. Tony Canzoneri, the former featherweight and lightweight champion, is a guy who is adored, idolized, and loved by almost everyone in America and quite a few outside. It doesn't bother Bummy that the crowd goes wild when Canzoneri is introduced—he almost slaps his gloves together in applause himself—but when it's his turn he probably gets a bigger hand walking past the corner candy store. All Bummy hears is how Canzoneri is not just a great fighter but also a great person. Bummy doesn't doubt it, but to him Tony is also a thirty-four-year-old ex-champ who can't let go of his days of glory, and a stepping-stone to a title shot.

When the ring announcer, Harry Balogh, finishes the introductions, Bummy looks out at his crowd. There's Shorty, Mousey, Snake, and Stutz, some of the candy store, poolroom and barbershop gang, and of course his father and Willie. Harry, who's still fighting even though his little brother outstrips him so fast, is in his dressing room after an earlier four-rounder. The rest of the Brownsville crowd is up in the balcony to cheer Bummy on. He smiles, because even with the noise and cheers of more than twelve thousand Canzoneri supporters, Bummy's Legions cannot be drowned out.

The smart money makes Bummy a three-to-one favorite, and for a while you have to wonder how smart the smart money really is. There's a lot of talk about how Canzoneri is just a ghost of himself, and for most of two rounds that's exactly what the kid is throwing punches at—a ghost! Left hook after left hook whistles through the air with breathtaking velocity. Canzoneri is standing in front of Bummy when he starts the punch, but now he's there, now he isn't. The Bummy Davis who swings away but hits nothing and gets popped by left jabs in return is greatly appreciated by the crowd, which gives him a big hand at the end of the first round.

The cheering continues until just before the end of the second round, which is when Tony Canzoneri learns a lesson that almost any Brownsville school kid could have taught him: Time and tide wait for no man, and neither does Al Davis's left hook. It is a lesson filled with pain and humiliation for the former titleholder, who is battered and driven to the canvas twice by the ferocity of the younger fighter's onslaught. Only a courageous heart and the protective arms of referee Arthur Donovan, who calls it a third-round technical knockout, save him from being counted out.

Bummy Davis also learns a lesson that night: winning does not always make you a winner, and losing does not always make you a loser. There is no question that Bummy wins the fight, and wins it in most convincing fashion, but when Harry Balogh calls out his name as "the winner," the boos and catcalls flood the Garden and the kid starts drowning in them. Lew Burston, sadly seeing his prediction come true, drapes Al's robe around his shoulders and feels his body stiffen. As they make their way through the hissing crowd to the dressing room, following the passageway under the loge seats, they hear a swelling crescendo of cheers for the loser but still champion, Tony Canzoneri.

Later that night, Shorty and Mousey want to celebrate what they and a lot of other people feel is their friend's best fight ever, but Al Davis doesn't see what there is to celebrate, so he goes home with his father, Willie, and Harry. Instead of a cold beer or a soda, he finishes the night with a glass of milk, which his mother tells him is very good for you.

Unfortunately the milk has turned sour, so Bummy goes to bed with a bad taste in his mouth.

Frankie Carbo, who spends most of his time on the West Coast running errands for Bugsy Siegel, is there in the Garden that night because Lepke asks him to come to New York. Even in the lockup, Lepke is a guy you don't say no to. When the bout ends, Carbo nods to his companion, Al Anastasia, and the two of them get up and head for the Eighth Avenue exit, then walk a block east to Jack Dempsey's.

Until they finish their roast beef sandwiches and a couple of Johnny Walkers, there is no conversation. When they finally do speak, after lighting up their cigarettes, it is very softly, because what they have to say is not meant for anyone else's ears.

"Lep wants this fat prick Harry Greenberg muzzled, Frank. The slob's been shakin' him down by threatenin' to do a little singin' if he's not taken care of. So Lep wants to see that he *is* taken care of, and he's counting on you. We hear Greenberg's in Hollywood, and Lepke wants you and Allie to do him."

"I gotta go to Seattle next week. Give Tannenbaum all the dope and have him get in touch with me. And tell Louie that he can do me a favor too."

"Name it."

"Let him have someone talk to Gangy about me takin' a piece of Bummy. I spoke with them a year or so ago, but it cut no ice."

When Happy Maione goes up to Beecher's Gym on instructions from Big Al Anastasia, he does not go up as a fan of Al "Bummy" Davis. First, he still remembers that day after the Farber fight when they go to have a talk with the kid for two-timing them and the little shit puts on a show for all of Livonia Avenue. Second, like almost everyone else in Ocean Hill, the Maiones have Tony Canzoneri's picture hanging on the living room wall between a crucifix and a bottle of Chianti. And like almost everyone else in the neighborhood, for this fight Happy doesn't bet with his head but with his heart, which immediately puts him at a tremendous disadvantage. But it isn't the five C's he drops on Canzoneri that has him so upset after the Slaughter on Eighth Avenue. "What kinda fucken animal gets off on beating up on an old-timer like Canzoneri?" Happy fumes to his pal Dasher Abbandando. "You gotta be some sadistic sonuvabitch." Why Frankie Carbo wants anything to do with this punk Happy cannot figure out. He hopes Carbo just wants to get close enough to put a shiv in his gut.

A dozen or so guys are working out in Beecher's, but Happy doesn't see Davis, so he asks a kid who's peppering a speed bag where he is.

"Ya see that guy with the Everlast sweater? Ask him. That's Froike, his trainer."

Froike feels a tap on his shoulder and turns around to see a short, chubby guy who asks, "Are you Freakie?"

"I'm Froike."

"I wanna talk to the Davis kid. Alone. In private."

Froike doesn't know who this sawed-off runt is, but he knows he doesn't like him. "He's in the middle of a workout. I'd appreciate your leaving this area right now."

Happy looks Froike in the eye and puts his hand to his forehead like he's having a major headache. "We are missing a very important point here. I didn't say 'May I?' I wanna talk to the Davis kid right now, capish?"

Maybe if Happy Maione is half a foot taller no problem ever arises, but it's hard to be a strong-arm man who can just about walk under a subway turnstile without bending. Happy is still six inches from respect as Froike looks him over carefully, returning his stare. "I asked you in a nice way. Now please move to the other side of the gym."

"You fucken kike! Who do you think you're talkin' to?" Before Froike has a chance to react, Happy grabs him by the shirtfront and backhands him in the face just as Bummy is coming out of the locker room.

Happy never knows what hits him. Bummy grabs him by the hair and rabbit-punches him in the neck, then hauls off with a booming kick to the backside. As there are no goal posts in Beecher's, nobody knows for sure whether Bummy makes the point after touchdown, but one thing everybody does know is that Bummy makes his point.

. . .

In the back room of Midnight Rose's candy store, after Happy graphically relates his tale, it is unanimously voted that this world should have one lightweight contender less, but democracy does not prevail. From his jailhouse quarters, Lepke exercises his veto. It is not an act of mercy nor a softening of his attitude. Louis Buchalter is quick to hand out a contract on anyone who is a direct threat to him, anyone he believes might talk to Hoover or Dewey. But aside from the fact that Davis presents no danger to him, he has several reasons for not agreeing to a hit on the kid. First, he does not wish to have Willie Davidoff as an enemy; second, a high-profile hit like the kid would only draw unwelcome attention; and third, there is the promise to Carbo.

One of the qualities that elevates Lepke to the head of the Syndicate's table is his ability to anticipate, and it is this that enables him to foresee that Reles and his boys, especially Maione, will not be doing handsprings around Brownsville when they receive his edict. So when Al Anastasia delivers the message, he tacks on the painkiller: they can punish Bummy Davis financially, not physically.

Bummy has just cleaned the table of all his striped balls and is lining the cue ball up with the eight ball, which will lighten Stutz by a deuce if he sinks it. Shorty is waiting to take on the winner. Bummy draws back on his stick to explode it into the cue ball, but it doesn't move. He turns to see Frank Carbo holding the end of it in his right hand.

"A friendly word of advice." There is no "friendly" in Carbo's face. "Be careful. You don't ever want to wind up behind the eight ball."

"I ain't. I'm in front of it."

"Maybe now you are, but the other day with Maione, that put you behind the eight ball. Bad move, kid, bad move."

"You weren't there to see it, so how do you know?"

"Like I said, just a friendly word of advice." Carbo shrugs and lets go of the stick.

Bummy measures his shot again and coolly sinks the eight ball in the corner pocket. Stutz drops two crumpled singles on the felt top, and Bummy pushes them back to him. "Get everybody coffee, will ya, Stutz? How do ya take yours, Mr. Carbo?"

"I didn't come here for coffee. You got a good memory, kid. I didn't think you'd remember me."

"How could I forget a guy who makes me such a generous offer?" Al turns to Shorty. "Go on, Shorty, rack 'em."

As Shorty moves toward the table with the triangle rack, Carbo reaches out and puts a cold hand on his wrist. "The offer stands. In fact, I got a better offer. You know what the future is, Al?"

Bummy grins. "Sure, I seen the General Motors exhibit at the World's Fair. A two-hour wait, but we seen the future, ain't that right, Shorty?"

"Don't wise off. I asked you a question. The future, kid. Either you got one or you don't."

"I know you're sayin' somethin', and I'm not too sure what it is, but I'm gonna assume it's still friendly advice."

"Look, kid, I ain't gonna talk myself hoarse with you. You got some people pretty mad. I can smooth things over, and like I told you before, I can move you like nobody else can." Carbo waits for an answer that doesn't come. "I'm leaving for Seattle tomorrow. You decide you wanna be smart, leave a message for me with Rose at the candy store on Saratoga."

Bummy turns his back on Carbo and takes the rack from Shorty. "Yeah, and if you don't hear from me right away, you have a good trip."

Willie Davidoff stands in front of the mirror in the men's room of the Concord Cafeteria, thinking to himself that with a kid like Al for a brother it's a miracle of nature that every hair on his head isn't gray. He goes back to his table and is just about to get started on his scrambled eggs and hash browns when Abe Reles walk in and sits down across from him.

"I don't have to tell you, Willie," he says without so much as a hello, "that anyone who pulls the kind of shit your little brother pulls with Maione has celebrated his last birthday."

Big Gangy knows all about what happened in the gym. He may be mad at Al, but he's more afraid for him—afraid that the the kid's temper will get him killed one day. Willie has to figure out a way to get him off the hook.

"Hey, back off, Abe. You know I got a problem with the kid too. Lemme talk to him."

"What's to talk? This is the second time he pulls shit that nobody gets away with."

Willie's mind is working overtime. He's thinking that he's got to get to Lepke somehow and plead with him for the kid's life when the next words out of Reles's mouth save him a long train ride.

"It's only because it's you that I have a talk with Lepke and we decide for old times' sake and past services rendered that the kid doesn't pay the full price. But he's gotta be taught a lesson, so here's the deal. He gives us twenty thousand cash in two weeks, and Frank Carbo comes in to put the reins on him. You don't know how lucky the kid is, Willie."

Willie Davidoff feels like he just spent two solid weeks in a steambath. "I'll talk to the kid," he says in a weak voice, and then he gets up, walks to the cashier, and plunks down his check with some change. As he goes through the revolving door, he turns back and sees Reles wolfing down his untouched breakfast. His silent prayer that he choke on it goes unanswered.

When Willie gets to the house on Bradford Street, he finds Bummy sprawled out on his bed, singing along with a Cantor Moishe Oysher record like he doesn't have a worry in the world. Willie starts right in telling him about his conversation with Reles, but the kid shushes him until the record is finished.

"Christ, Al, what were you thinkin'?" Willie says after he's finally allowed to fill the kid in.

"Hey, come on, Willie, I see a guy slappin' Froike around, what am I supposed to do?"

"That depends on who the guy doin' the slappin' is."

"Yeah, that makes a lotta sense. I guess before I pull him off of Froike I shoulda asked him to show me his driver's license. Anyhow, who cares what these bums say?"

"Who cares? You should, and there's a lot of guys planted in Canarsie who'd tell you why if they could."

"Bullshit! These punks are only tough when they're packin' a rod."

Willie grunts out a half laugh. "That accounts for twenty-four hours a day, which should be enough, huh? Al, you don't slap a guy like Maione around and get away with it. It ain't done."

"Whadda they want me to do, say I'm sorry? I'll tell ya what. Let that little butterball say I'm sorry to Froike and I'll say I'm sorry to him."

"They're not interested in apologies!" Willie yells. "What they want is twenty thousand cash to smooth things over, and I can't help you with that, kid. I just don't have it. Besides that, Lepke wants Carbo to come in for a piece of the action."

"Fuck 'em where they breathe." It is as though a light goes on in Bummy's head. "That's what it's all about. That's why that little prick Maione was there in the first place, Willie. Listen to me. Carbo comes up yesterday and sings the same song as last time. You know, how he's gonna move me and all that garbage. And he tells me I'm in a lotta trouble and he's the guy who can fix it. I'm tellin' you, Willie, that's how come Maione came to see me. You tell 'em they can go jump in a fucken lake for all I care."

"You tell 'em yourself," Willie says, but his tone is different now. He knows his kid brother has it figured right. Those sonsabitches are trying to move in on them. Still, he doesn't want to take a chance with the kid's life. "I know these guys, Al. I deal with them. It's not a game. They're too tough and too crazy to fuck around with."

"Tough? Shit! They're all a bunch of pussies, Carbo included. I'd like to see how tough they are without their guns."

Harry Greenberg would have liked to see that too, but he never has the chance, because Frankie Carbo slips out of the shadows on a dark Los Angeles street and puts five bullets in the back of his head while he sits in his car reading a newspaper. Big Greenie never even has the chance to see the sports section.

Shorty is sitting with Al and Mousey in the Famous Dairy Restaurant on Eastern Parkway on a Sunday morning. Mousey is going through his whole routine of jokes he cops from *Can You Top This?* without getting a single smile—forget about a laugh—from Al. Shorty's best friend, who should be floating on a cloud because he is the biggest draw in New York next to Joe Louis, looks like a guy who has just read his own obituary, which is not too far from what Dan Parker's column is intended to be.

It's not that Parker hits on Bummy all the time—probably only when he has gastritis or a sinus attack. Unfortunately, he is not a guy bursting with good health. Parker's potshots get so much attention and create such a strong reaction that other writers like Jack Miley and Stanley Frank hop on the bandwagon, and as they are not bound by the rules of the Marquis of Queensbury, there is nothing to keep them from going below the belt or hitting a guy when he is down.

As they get up to leave, Shorty takes the newspaper and drops it in the wastebasket. All the people who hang out with his friend and work with him know the real Al Davis, and to them these stories are about as believable and true to life as Li'l Abner or Joe Palooka, who are only a few pages removed from Parker's column. But to a lot of other people— those to whom Al is just someone they hear about and read about—this newspaper creation of a bully and a gang-connected punk becomes the real Bummy Davis, and Shorty knows how deep the hurt goes.

One way to deal with hurt is to spread it around. Tippy Larkin probably would have had a much nicer Christmas without Al Davis's willingness to share.

On December 15 more than seventeen thousand people, the biggest crowd of the winter season, jam Madison Square Garden, most of them hoping to see Larkin avenge Tony Canzoneri's loss to Davis six weeks earlier. Tippy, who is called the Garfield Gunner partly because he comes from Garfield, New Jersey, and also because he is quick on the draw when it comes to throwing his left or his right hand, is a top-ranked contender for the lightweight championship—which title he eventually captures—so rooting for him is far from being an unwise bet.

There's no greater adrenaline boost for an athlete than hearing the crowd cheer him on—except maybe hearing the crowd cheer the other guy on. What happens between Al Davis and Tippy Larkin is more than a prizefight—it is all-out warfare! For most of the fight, Larkin eludes Bummy's big punches while banging away with his rapid-fire left. When Bummy does get inside and loads up with his cannon of a left hook, Larkin cleverly ties him up, smothering the big blows. Finally, in the fourth round, Davis starts landing his power punch and has Larkin staggering, seemingly ready to go, until Larkin storms back with a two-fisted bombardment and tears open a cut above Bummy's right eye just before the bell.

Froike applies pressure to the cut, swabs it clean, and dresses it with a thick salve, hoping to stem the flow. Al tries to pay attention as Froike pleads for more head movement, but he is listening to the sounds of the crowd, trying to search out familiar voices and encouragement from his friends. The bell rings, and Froike puts his mouth guard in place. Al clamps down on it and moves toward the center of the ring.

Larkin is there to greet him with a left jab—and another left jab— and another. Al knows what he has to do, but he can't get into gear. The Garfield Gunner is zeroing in on the left eye, shooting from the hip now. Al tries to bob and weave, move into range, but Larkin is snapping out that left jab like a snake. The crowd loves it and cheers wildly as he continues banging away for more than a minute.

Al "Bummy" Davis hears the cheering too. With a growl in his throat and blood streaming down his face, the street fighter from Brownsville plants his feet and throws the left hook with all his fury and force, directing it not at Tippy Larkin but at the crowd. It is Larkin who takes it, though, right in the gut. As the blow crunches home, he crumbles and falls on his back, and Davis stands over him, arms outstretched, lording it over the stunned fans. It is only then, as a gasping Tippy Larkin is counted out by Referee Eddie Joseph, that Bummy is finally able to hear Shorty, Mousey, and the rest of his gang.

Standing before the bench in federal court, Louis "Lepke" Buchalter closes his eyes. Sometimes you see better when you shut out the illusory glare of reality and leave things up to your mind. Lepke sees Thomas Lucchese, Lucky Luciano, and Joe Adonis, the architects of the deal that never was, toasting their guile and good fortune. Even as the judge is sentencing him to fourteen years for narcotics smuggling, he sees consoling visions of getting even. What he doesn't see is the thirty-to-life he gets for union racketeering when J. Edgar Hoover softens in his tug of war with New York State and turns Lepke over to Dewey.

After the verdict, he's turned back over to the feds to begin serving his fourteen-year sentence in Leavenworth, which will just be a warmup, a practice run for the big one in Sing Sing. Before starting his journey he's given a few minutes to visit with his wife and friends. Albert Anastasia cannot believe that it is almost business as usual with his boss.

"Make sure you get Dimples. That no-good bastard—he was my friend, he ate at my table."

"It's done, Lep."

Al Anastasia is a man of his word. It takes three years, but one night in a neighborhood restaurant Moe "Dimples" Wolinsky is thinking of finishing his dinner with a blueberry cobbler when he finishes it with two .22-caliber bullets to the forehead instead.

It's not so much that Abe Levine minds spending New Year's Eve at home with just Helen and the baby. It's the reason that they do not go out for the second straight year that bothers him. Last year it was because little Barbara was just two months old and they would not leave her with a baby-sitter. This year the reason has a lot to do with the fact that Helen eats fish, a food that Pretty never touches ever since he sees Great-uncle Herschel drop dead in a restaurant in Coney Island with a carp bone stuck in his throat.

Even though Pretty tells her there will be plenty of food at the gang's big bash at the Old Roumania, Helen wants to have an early dinner at home because New Year's Eve parties always start so late. That afternoon, when she hears the fish peddler's cry, she runs down the two flights of stairs and buys a small flounder. A few hours later Pretty decides to get ready for the party instead of waiting and having to battle Helen for the bathroom. When he comes into the kitchen patting a final splash of cologne on his face, he finds out that Helen will not be having dinner after all because her flounder is burnt to a crisp and she is sitting at the kitchen table staring at a crumpled, fish-oil-stained newspaper. If the peddler is to wrap his fish in a cost-effective manner, he cannot be expected to use today's paper. What Helen is looking at is the paper from four months ago. It is old news, but not to Helen, who seems to be in a trance, unable to move her eyes from the picture of Puggy Feinstein.

No matter what Abe tells her, it does not lessen the hurt or the shock. She knows that Abe himself would never have harmed Puggy, but instinct makes her believe he knows who did this horrible thing. It is more than just instinct that makes her believe she knows who did it too.

When the super's wife, Mrs. Stone, rings the bell and finds out that they are canceling their plans because Helen isn't feeling well, she is disappointed. The dollar or two she gets for baby-sitting is a big help. But when Pretty hands her a five-dollar bill she is all smiles and says the next time they go out it is on the house. Pretty undoes his tie and sits back, thinking he will tell Reles that the baby was sick. Of course he can't tell him that Helen would not spend New Year's Eve with the people who killed Puggy Feinstein.

Pretty Levine celebrates New Year's Eve listening to the radio in his kitchen because he is locked out of his bedroom for the first time in his marriage. Helen celebrates it crying herself to sleep.

The Old Roumania is filled with good cheer and merrymaking as Reles's boys salute the fond memories of the past few years. The fiddlers fiddle, the liquor flows, they gorge themselves on a seemingly endless glut of food, which does not stop Reles and Buggsy and Strauss and the rest of them from whirling their women around the dance floor. When the women are tired, Reles jumps up on a table and does a kazotzka to howls and cheers.

As the minute hand nears midnight, they all gather around with glasses held high, and a more than slightly tipsy Buggsy Goldstein takes center stage. "Let us toast to a new beginning, an even bigger and better 1940, and many more years of health and happiness. L'chaim!" Buggsy then decides to observe a "tradition" that he probably saw in a movie, because nobody, including himself, knows anything about it, but he feels that throwing his glass against the mirror on the wall is a very good touch. The gesture seems to fit the occasion, so Reles and Strauss follow suit with equal enthusiasm.

The big shots of Murder, Inc. celebrate the New Year by laughing at a very expensive toast and forgetting that a broken mirror brings seven years' bad luck—which there is no question they would gladly have settled for.

Bill O'Dwyer, the newly elected Brooklyn district attorney, and his chief assistant, Burton Turkus, do not take office until January, but New Year's Eve finds them sitting in Gage and Tollner's on Fulton Street, talking business. Their two-inch-thick steaks are cold, having been pushed aside in favor of two-foot-high stacks of files. The steaks are tempting and definitely make the juices flow, but so do the files.

Bill O'Dwyer and Burton Turkus celebrate the New Year by planning their assault on Murder, Inc.

"Nobody goes to sleep on New Year's Eve!" declares Rose Davidoff. "Go with your friends, have a good time."

"Come on, Al," Shorty pleads. "You know Mother knows best." He's concerned about his friend, but his deeper concern is that most of the girls coming to the party are coming because they hear Al Davis will be there. Just like at Madison Square Garden, Bummy Davis is the big draw.

"Nah, I ain't in the mood for a party. I got a lotta things on my mind."

"Who stays in on a night like tonight?" Rose can't imagine what's wrong with her son. "You're going to be home, you'll be home alone. Poppa and me are going to Yetta's. Even your teacher, that Mr. Burston, is going out tonight. That's why you can't call him back until tomorrow, and he said not too early."

Al looks at his mother. "What're ya talkin' about, Ma? Lew Boiston called? Why didn't ya tell me?"

"I told you, he's not home, so what's the rush?"

"What'd he say? Did he leave a message?"

"Could anyone understand him? He said something about getting you loose hampers. I told him you don't need any loose hampers because in our house we have a built-in one in the bathroom. Still, he wants you should know."

Over the years one of the things Al becomes pretty good at is transposing what his mother hears into understandable language. "Lou Ambers? Is that what he said? Lou Ambers?" His voice surges with excitement.

"If I tell you one thing and you want to hear another, why ask me in the first place?"

"That's okay, Ma, that's okay." Al turns to Shorty, who for the first time in quite a while sees a full-fledged smile on Bummy's face. "Ya hear that, Shorty? Me and Lou Ambers! For the title!"

That night the Davidoff house is empty. Max and Rose celebrate the

New Year with Aunt Yetta. Shorty celebrates the New Year eating peanuts, pretzels, and potato chips, listening to Vincent Lopez and Guy Lombardo on the radio, and watching girls gush over Al "Bummy" Davis. Bummy celebrates the New Year by dreaming of being the lightweight champion of the world.

13

The first thing Burton Turkus does after reading Harry Rudolph's letter is look at the postmark. The next thing he does is look at the postmark again, because he cannot believe anyone would let such a letter lie around for nearly ten months. He can only conclude that the former district attorney, the Honorable William F. X. Geoghan, was a very busy individual.

When Harry Rudolph raises his shirt and shows off his magnificent bullet wound, Bill O'Dwyer knows he has a living, breathing witness ready to swear he saw Abe Reles commit murder. Because Harry Rudolph is Harry Rudolph and not Abe Lincoln or George Washington, it is far from an open-and-shut case, but O'Dwyer feels he has enough to get an indictment from a grand jury, which will keep Reles under lock and key until he goes to trial. With the strains of "Auld Lang Syne" barely faded away, O'Dwyer goes to work fulfilling his campaign promise of running the mob off the streets. The order is given to bring in every one of Reles's boys on any charge from vagrancy to loitering—misdemeanors that are subject to extremely loose interpretation.

Abe Reles and Buggsy Goldstein do not seem at all concerned when on the night of January 14 they drop by Dubrow's Cafeteria for a late snack and are told that Sergeant William Schroeder was in a couple hours earlier and left word that he wants to see them at the Seventy-fifth Precinct. The next morning they cheerfully stop in at the station-house, expecting things to go the way they always do. Sergeant Schroeder is a gracious host. They are quite appreciative when he offers them fresh coffee and rolls, as they have not yet had breakfast, and they laugh as he tells them a couple of the latest Hitler jokes. They do not laugh when he gives them lodging.

Later that same day, Duke Maffetore, who is also fingered by Rudolph, is picked up in front of his house on Lott Avenue. Although Maffetore was only the driver for the Alpert hit, he is the guy O'Dwyer and Turkus are happiest to have. In their minds there is no chance that Reles and Goldstein will crack, but with Dukey . . .

There is no letup by O'Dwyer. He packs Reles off to the Tombs in downtown Manhattan, ships Buggsy to Staten Island, and sends Dukey to the Bronx House of Detention. Unless these three guys can yell louder than any other three guys that ever were, communication is out.

When Pretty Levine walks through the front door, he shakes his head, and says, "It's not important," before Helen even has a chance to ask who called. A few minutes ago the bell rings three times, which is the signal that there is a telephone call for them at the candy store a few doors away. Pretty avoids Helen's eyes and bends down to pick up his little daughter, who is going "dada, dada" as she sways and totters, trying to master the art of walking.

"Don't touch the baby, please," Helen says. "You're dripping with sweat. How do you perspire like that in the middle of the winter?"

Pretty doesn't answer, nor does he argue. He gets up and heads straight for the bathroom, where he locks the door, braces himself against the pedestal sink, and splashes his face with cold water. There are so many things he can't share with Helen. Certainly not the call he just got from Dukey's wife, who was crying hysterically. The police pulled Dukey right off the street and threw him in the can, she says, and not just him but Reles and Goldstein too. When Pretty tells her that they'll have him out in no time, just like always, she cries all the harder. This time it's different, she wails. They can't get them out on bail.

Pretty looks in the mirror, and he doesn't like what he sees.

. . .

"Whaddya mean, it ain't for the title? He's the champ, right? And I'm the challenger."

"It's an over-the-weight match," Burston explains to Al. "From the beginning his manager made it clear that's the only way they make the fight: nontitle."

"So I beat his ass, it ain't gonna mean a thing. Then I have to go out and do it all over again."

"Why don't you worry about doing it once. Let's cross each bridge as we come to it."

Lew Burston forgets to tell his unbeaten young fighter that for some bridges you have to pay a much higher toll than for others.

With the Ambers fight still more than a month away, Al finishes a light workout and tells Froike he's taking a few days off to go up to the country with Shorty and Stutz, "the country" being anyplace above the Bronx or west of the Hudson. This time it happens to be Red Bank, New Jersey, where Stutz has a friend with a big cabin where they go every once in a while to relax and play poker.

Froike thinks for a moment. "Just do your road work and sit-ups. Monday we start for serious."

If Stutz can live with Chesterfields, which is what Shorty smokes, everything is okay, but no, Stutz needs Lucky Strikes. By the time they finally leave for Red Bank, Stutz winds up with a carton of Luckies, Shorty winds up thinking he should have stayed in bed, Morris, the owner of the candy store around the corner from Beecher's, winds up staying open much later than usual cleaning up the mess, some guy who sells suits on Pitkin Avenue winds up in the emergency room at Beth-El Hospital, Lew Burston winds up being awakened by a phone call at two in the morning, and Bummy winds up wishing he'd never left Brownsville.

As soon as they walk into the candy store, Stutz is sorry that he didn't settle for Chesterfields, because standing by the candy counter is this guy Mersky, who measured Al for a suit a couple years ago which he decided not to buy. Ever since then, whenever Mersky sees him, which fortunately is not very often, he gets on Al's case.

When Morris sees Al, his eyes light up, and not knowing the dynamics between his customers, he unintentionally becomes Mersky's straight man.

"Hallo, chemp! You know the chemp, Mersky? Al Davis. Right from here."

"The champ? Oh, you mean the champ of the zaydes and the midgets. When are you gonna fight someone your own size or your own age, Dummy?"

"Well, you sure ain't nobody's zayde, and lookin' at your gut I'd say you got me by fifty pounds at least. Maybe you fit the bill, huh, Mushky?"

"Boyis, boyis," Morris pleads from behind the counter. "Enough, already."

Shorty takes a careful look and is relieved when he sees no sparks in Bummy's eyes and no muscles twitching in his jaw. Talk is talk. That's okay. His friend is in control. It looks like everything is back to normal when Bummy, who is thumbing through a *Police Gazette* at the magazine rack, gets plunked by a jellybean. He turns around. All he sees are four innocent faces.

Shorty gives his friend's elbow an urgent tug, but Bummy has picked up another magazine, which Shorty believes he is not really interested in as he has never seen Bummy read *Good Housekeeping* before. That is when another jellybean takes a bounce off Bummy's head. He carefully closes the magazine, puts it back on the rack, and walks over to the candy counter, where Mersky is standing with a big grin on his face and both hands balled up.

"What're you, some kind of a nut job?"

"I don't know what you're talkin' about, Davis." Mersky turns away and mumbles something about Bummy's "gangster family."

The first "Ooh!" is from Shorty, who knows what's coming next. A whole bunch of "Oohs!" follow. They are all from Mersky. It is hard to believe that so much happens in so little time. It starts with Bummy's fist going *splat!* into Mersky's face, which opens up a lovely cut under Mersky's right eye. It also opens up his fists, which release a cascade of jellybeans that go clattering all over the place. When it is over there are two big messes, Morris's floor and Mersky's face. It is much easier to fix up Morris's floor.

Bummy looks around. "I'm really sorry, Morris," he says, and hands him a twenty."

Morris looks around too, sighing. "Go, it's okay. I'll clean up and throw the junk out."

As they head for the car, Shorty wonders if that includes Mersky, who is lying in a heap in a corner of the store.

Hearing Charlie Beecher on the other end of the phone in the middle of the night, Lew Burston wonders if maybe he's been in a coma and slept through the Ambers fight.

"What do you mean, the kid gets another knockout? What're you, crazy, Charlie? What kind of a knockout?" Burston gropes in the dark for his glasses and puts them on like they'll make him hear better.

"This one's in a candy store, and the kid's in a jam. The cops just woke me up looking for him."

It takes a couple of days, but Burston finds out about "the country" from Froike, and then he finds out from Stutz's boss about his friend with the cabin in New Jersey, and then he and Willie Davidoff drive up there together.

"You guys gotta be kiddin'," Bummy grumbles from the backseat. "I'm sittin' there with kings over jacks and you don't let me finish the hand."

"Not when you got a joker playing against you," Willie tells him.

"The guy's an asshole. He had it comin' to him."

"He told the police you started picking on him and Shorty and Stutz held him while you beat him up."

"Who's gonna believe that shit?" Bummy laughs.

Even though the charges against him are eventually dismissed, the press has a field day pumping up the image of a bully and a wild-eyed street punk. It is all headline material, plugged in with the major news items or in the sports section's lead stories. When the charges are dropped in March, the story is buried somewhere next to the answers to yesterday's crossword puzzle.

It's pretty much accepted as fact that nobody picks Rikers Island for their summer vacation. Actually, this holds true for all seasons. For Harry

Rudolph the food alone is enough to turn his stomach, and although some days a guy is definitely better off not getting out of bed, this option is not available. So when he turns around to see who's poking him while watching his breakfast grow hair he realizes this is definitely a big day in the nausea department.

"You want some more eggs, Harry?"

"Eggs? So that's what they are. Thanks, Frosch. I was tryin' to figure out what this shit was all morning." If anything is more unwholesome to Harry than the powdered eggs in front of him, it is the balding, jowl-cheeked lump of pasty flesh sitting at his side, pushing his tray toward him. "Hey, what the fuck do I want your eggs for? Did ya see me touch my own?"

Harry heard somewhere that before Adam and Eve were suckered into biting into the wrong kind of apple, snakes had legs. He is convinced that when all the other snakes are turned into crawlers as punishment for setting up the applenappers, somehow, Frosch is overlooked.

He is surprised to see Frosch vacationing in the same spa that he is and his first thought is that this slimeball, who has a shingle in front of his Liberty Avenue office advertising him as a bailbondsman, established a branch office right here on Rikers. But seeing him dressed in the identical vacationer's outfit as everyone else, Harry Rudolph realizes that this assumption is one of the many mistakes he makes in his life.

Frosch has a reputation for fixing more things than a roomful of carpenters, the major difference being that a carpenter takes something that is broken and fixes it, while what Frosch fixes is usually broken afterwards. He hammers away at everything from cops to judges, and that is why he doesn't need any more clients, because all he needs to keep him busy around the clock is what he's got—Murder, Incorporated!

Still, it comes as a great shock to Rudolph that he is offered a lot more than powdered eggs.

When a guy who scrounges his way through life, dipping his fingers into pockets other than his own, thumbs his nose at a gift of crisp bills totaling 5G's, it's gotta raise some eyebrows—and it does. Bill O'Dwyer calls together a meeting of his entire staff after reading Harry Rudolph's latest letter. He drops it right on the conference table, maybe because it is hot enough to burn his fingers. What Rudolph says is that he is offered five grand by Frosch to swear that it was Duke Maffetore who killed Alpert, not Reles or Goldstein. Although, when Rudolph speaks now, everyone listens; everyone also wonders. However, the entire conversation between Rudolph and Frosch is overheard by a professional stoolie, who is planted at Rikers Island for a completely different matter but winds up at the right spot at the right time. Also, Turkus points out that there is no personal gain for Rudolph as far as trading information for time because he is a short-timer anyhow. Still, the entire staff of William O'Dwyer is amazed that a guy like Harry Rudolph would turn his back on five thousand dollars. They are all introduced to a rather unfamiliar equation—hate equals honor.

What makes this letter so important is that until now they have been able to make Duke Maffetore whine, snivel, and cry, but they haven't been able to make him talk. Nobody reads this as loyalty. It is fear—fear bordering on abject terror. Harry Rudolph's letter turns terror from an enemy to an ally.

Tuesday's 35¢ lunch special at Grabstein's is stuffed cabbage that is so good Moe Bradie can never pass it up. He also cannot tell his wife, Rose, how good it is, because she is convinced that nobody in the world can make a stuffed cabbage like hers, so it happens on more than just an occasional Tuesday that Moe winds up having stuffed cabbage at every meal except breakfast.

On Tuesday, February 20, Moe is in the middle of a brake job under the garage floor in bay number one, which is the bay nearest the wall facing the office. He has no intention of passing up his Tuesday special, so he calls Grabstein's and orders a takeout lunch, which comes complete with a chopped liver appetizer and rice pudding for dessert. When the delivery boy gets there, Moe has the kid lower the bag to him, hands him up two quarters, and tells him to keep the change.

He just finishes wiping the grime from his hands when he hears something that nearly causes him to lose his appetite—the approaching voices of Harry Strauss and Happy Maione. Ever since O'Dwyer started applying the pressure, they spend a lot of time at his garage using the public phone, as there is no doubt in their minds that their own phones are tapped. Moe sees no reason to jump up and greet them.

There is the clunking sound of a nickel dropping into the coin box, followed by seven clicks of the rotary dial.

"Got your signal, Al. What's up?" Strauss is talking in a low voice, but not low enough.

Moe Bradie does not like to feel like an eavesdropper, so he sticks his finger in his left ear. His right ear he leaves alone as he sees no need to go overboard.

"That no-good fuck Rudolph! He turned Frosch down cold. Reles shoulda finished him when he had the chance. If Rudolph rats and it gets back to that mushbrain Maffetore, he'll sing like Kate Smith can only dream about."

There is a long silence.

"If you can get the word to him that he better worry about his family, do it, but do it quick. Meanwhile, we'll take care of his buddy Pretty. He's the guy I'm really worried about. I'm not even sure you know this, Al, but he tried cutting out a couple years ago, so we're gonna stop the song before the music begins. You know, we're gonna have a very pretty widow to take care of."

Suddenly Moe's heart is pounding like a drum, but there is nothing he can do about it.

"Okay, we'll talk tomorrow. Dubrow's at noon."

There is the sound of the phone being put back on the cradle. As their footsteps fade, Moe hears Happy say, "Where is everyone anyway? What is this, a fucken self-service station?"

Moe Bradie remains sitting in the shadows of the underground bay. He thinks of Lester Collins, he thinks of Puggy Feinstein, and he thinks what bullshit it is to be angry and sit around stewing in it. He gets to his feet and picks up a crowbar, then laughs and flings it against the wall. He doesn't touch his stuffed cabbage but feeds it to a stray mutt who thanks him by taking a crap right in the middle of his station.

· · ·

Dasher Abbandando pulls the car to the curb at the corner of Malta and Hegeman and leaves the motor running so he can keep the heater on. Happy Maione gets out of the back, jams his hands in his coat pockets, and walks along Hegeman. He stops in front of 408 and looks up to make sure the lights in Levines' apartment are on. They are, as he was sure they would be. Who wants to go out on a cold February night? The plan is a simple one. He rings their bell three times and ducks into the alley next to the building. Pretty should be down in less than a minute to take his phone call at the candy store. Meanwhile, Strauss, who elects himself the "doer," comes up behind him and does it, with Happy in the alley just for good measure. Then Dasher pulls up in the car and they're off to get something to eat.

Helen is bathing the baby in the kitchen sink when the bell sounds three times. Pretty, who is standing at her side holding a towel to wrap around little Barbara as soon as Helen plucks her from the suds, shrugs his shoulders and grunts.

"I'll go see who it is. Be back in five minutes." He drapes the towel over Helen's arm and heads for the door.

"Put a coat on," she calls after him. "All I need is for you to come down with pneumonia."

Pretty turns and grins. "It's nice to know I'm still loved."

"Who said anything about love? I just don't want to have to nurse you." But there's a smile on her face, and seeing it makes Pretty Levine glow inside and out. He goes to the hall closet and takes out his green plaid lumber jacket. Before he leaves, he walks over to the kitchen sink to kiss Helen on the nape of her neck and the baby on her foam-covered head.

Outside, Pretty stands in front of the wrought-iron door to his building and pulls his collar up around his neck. The night air is colder than he expected. As he turns to head to the candy store and Strauss gets ready to make his move, a long beam of light washes the street. Seconds later a Chevy coupé pulls up to the curb right next to Pretty Levine. In the alley, Happy Maione presses up against the wall, not believing what he sees.

"Hey, do you know where—uh, let's see—where an Axelrod lives?" a gravelly voice barks from the lowered driver's window.

Pretty walks over to the car, squinting into the window. "Moe? Is that you?"

"Oh, hiya. Levine, right? One of my neighbors." Moe Bradie is not in the same league as Clark Gable or even Andy Devine, but his stellar performance does get the full, undivided attention of the two unseen spectators it is intended for. "I'm driving around here half the night looking for this guy Axelrod. He's a first-time customer, and I promised to have his car back today, so I go and lose his address but I can swear I remember he lives on Hegeman. Meanwhile, I got no one watchin' the station because I thought I'll be right back."

"Look, I'm sorry I can't help you right now, Moe. I got a call waiting at—"

The thought enters Strauss's mind that he should take them both, but it is a thought that dies a quick death as a squad car screeches up to the curb, a spotlight swinging in an arc from its roof. Two plainclothesmen step out, walk over to Pretty, and flash a piece of paper at him.

"Abe Levine, we have a warrant to bring you in for questioning."

"What for?"

"We've got a list for you, Mr. Levine, a big list."

The cops cuff Pretty and slide him into the backseat. One of them gets in next to him, and as the other opens the driver's door, Moe, squeezing all he can from his role, walks over and asks loud enough for anyone on the top floor of any building on the block to hear, "You happen to know a guy named Axelrod around here?"

That night Moe Bradie feels better about himself than he has in a long time. Everything works out fine, and he doesn't even need a crowbar, just a nickel for an anonymous phone call and a big pair of balls. He parks the Chevy coupé in the garage and places the work slip back on the dashboard: "Check axle rod and drive shaft." Then he goes out to the middle of the station, remembering that there's another mess to clean up.

Al Davis never thought the day would come when he would have a reason to thank Abe Reles for anything. Well, the day does come, because Reles's last arrest, in early February, is instrumental in keeping the overblown story of his candy store escapade with this jerk Mersky off the front page. But no matter how far back the story gets pushed, it seems like enough people read their way through the whole paper, because on the night of the Ambers fight Madison Square Garden draws a record crowd of 20,586, of whom it seems like only the six are there to root for Al.

Many fighters, when they take a solid punch and are really hurt, smile. On Friday night, February 23, when Al "Bummy" Davis walks into the Garden to the jeers of the crowd, he is wearing a big smile. As all other sounds are drowned out by the boos and catcalls from the balcony, the smile gets bigger.

One thing Froike always tells Al is that every time you climb into the ring it is a learning experience. On this night Al Davis could earn a doctorate with all the knowledge he absorbs. He enters the ring with the confidence of a fighter who has never been licked. Unfortunately, he catches Ambers on what is probably the best night he ever has. Ambers is inspired, a knight on a mission to avenge the thrashing of his good friend Tony Canzoneri at the hands of the brash young villain from the gutters of Brownsville.

For the first four rounds, Davis's booming left keeps him in the fight, and a couple of times it looks as though he has Ambers on the way out. But sometime during the sixty-second break after the fourth round, Ambers is transformed into a flashing, slashing whirling dervish. Bummy doesn't stop trying. He lumbers after the champ for the full ten rounds, taking blow after blow for his efforts and unable to connect in return. Ambers draws blood, but Bummy can handle that. What hurts him more than any punch Lou Ambers can ever dream of throwing is the taunting and derision that bombards him from every corner of the cavernous arena.

Froike spreads the top and middle strands of rope for the kid to step through, but Bummy just stands there, turning his head slowly in bewilderment as the boos and the obscenities come tumbling down in torrents. In the opposite corner, Lou Ambers also stops and stares at the crowd in disbelief. What he and Bummy did to each other was done with their fists inside the ring. It was fair. This isn't.

Froike tugs at Bummy's arm. "Come on, kid," he says, almost apologetically, "don't pay them no attention. They cough up a quarter to sit in the balcony and they think that gives them the right to do whatever they want."

"Fuck 'em." Bummy steps through the ropes and trots down the aisle with Froike and Willie serving as front and rear guards, hoots and insults bouncing off him like hailstones in a summer storm. They shove through the crowd of reporters in the tunnel and push their way into the dressing room, keeping the press out. Bummy, who doesn't land too much in the ring, is now doing much better. He caves in a green locker with a left hook and kicks Froike's water bucket halfway to the Hudson River, and when he finishes with the rubbing table, *it* needs a place to lie down.

"Forget them, kid," Johnny Attell says, tapping his cigar lightly with his chubby index finger and dropping the ash to the floor. "Next time out they'll love you. Right now they're still remembering Canzoneri."

"Bullshit, next time," the kid snaps, tugging his hands roughly out of the six-ounce gloves as Froike tugs back. "There ain't no next time. I'm out of it. You can take the whole friggin' fight racket and shove it!"

Attell starts to say something, but Lew Burston winks and tactfully eases him away from Bummy. "He'll get over it all by himself. Just leave him stew for a while."

Johnny Attell hears every word Bummy says that night of the Ambers fight. He hears but he doesn't listen. He signs up what he believes to be a natural crowd-pleaser of a fight for the Garden, Bummy Davis going against Tony Marteliano. Mike Jacobs, although he is tied up with Mr. Joe Louis at the time, loves the match-up and gives Johnny an approving slap on the back.

The fight crowd loves it as these two guys are scrappers who give it their all, and the Garden box-office boys are working overtime. Tony Marteliano loves it and starts training with gusto since this is his big chance and he has every intention of making the most of it. Bummy Davis does not love it and he is not training at all.

Bummy Davis is not training because if you are not a pugilist there is no reason to train, and Bummy Davis is no longer a pugilist. Willie is very aware of this fact and lets Johnny Attell know that there is a fly in the ointment, and Johnny, who is a very shrewd article, has his chauffeur drive him to Bradford Street so he can change the kid's mind. Never before is such eloquence displayed in the Davidoff kitchen. Johnny Attell is at his best. He uses the whole alphabet in explaining to Bummy why a young man cannot possibly turn his back on such an opportunity as is in front of him. Twenty-seven good reasons he gives him, starting with Ambition and finishing with a flourish on Zealous (he doubles on F with Fame and Fortune).

Bummy is impressed—anyone would have been—but not enough to change his mind. Johnny Attell cannot believe it. His $45 Three Gee suit from Abe Stark's is getting a workout under the armpits every time he thinks about the posters all over town for a fight he can't deliver.

The Sunday after Johnny Attell's visit, Lew Burston learns one of life's important lessons. When you are strolling down Pitkin Avenue, you do not rest your hand on top of the sweet potato vendor's pushcart. Even with all the traffic and the crowd noise, everyone within two blocks hears Lew's howl of pain. Bummy runs to the ice truck parked for a delivery halfway down the street, scoops up a few loose slivers, and uses Lew's handkerchief to tie the ice over the blister that now covers half his palm. Because Lew is such a classy guy, Bummy thinks he'll be out of place anywhere in Brownsville except Pitkin Avenue, but for his own well-being Bummy decides to bring him to his father's candy store, where the chances of an accident are remote. The kid watches in amazement as Lew has his first egg cream ever. He doesn't want to embarrass his manager by telling him only girls drink egg creams with a straw, even though Lew taught him such things as not eating green peas with your knife and bringing your fork up to your mouth, not your mouth down to the table.

Lew Burston is like a second father to Bummy. The kid looks up to him, and when Lew tells him to do something the kid listens. But even Lew cannot convince him to go back into the ring.

"Hey, Lew, I had it! I ain't fightin' no more. Not in the ring, that is. Marteliano wants to fight me, I'll fight him on the fucken street corner.

I don't need that shit no more, all those shmucks callin' me names and pickin' on me."

Lew tries to calm the kid down, and Max Davidoff, who's behind the counter, chimes in, but it's like teaching a mule to tap-dance.

"Where else are you going to make the same kind of money doing something you're good at and enjoy?" Lew asks.

"Enjoy? Come on, Lew, gimme a break. All I was ever in this for was to get a nice house for my mom and pop. I got that now. You think it's fun doin' road work every day and workin' out in the gym, and then on top of that I get treated like crap whenever I climb into the ring? I got news for you. I'd much rather be shmoozin' around with the guys and havin' some laughs. And another thing, Lew, don't take this wrong, but you don't drink an egg cream with a straw unless you wear bloomers."

Either Johnny Attell is deaf, dumb, and blind or else he is the world's greatest optimist, because one day Bummy sees the fight posters advertising the Davis-Marteliano bout popping up in every store window in Brownsville. He immediately pulls from his pocket a slipcover grommet, which just so happens to be the same size as a buffalo nickel, and therefore, if you are not making a slipcover, you can use it to make telephone calls.

"You know another guy named Al 'Bummy' Davis, Mr. Attell? I sure hope you do."

"Al, I am so glad you called." Attell lies through his teeth because Mike Jacobs, who does not know that Bummy has no intention of fighting, is seated right next to him.

Jacobs enjoys kibitzing with the brash kid who always calls him Uncle Mike, so he snatches the phone from Attell and says, "So, boychik, ready for the big night?"

Johnny Attell cannot hear the conversation. He does hear some loud, unpleasant words coming from the phone, and the louder and more unpleasant they become, the whiter and angrier Mike Jacobs's face becomes, until he drops the receiver. Attell never finds out exactly what Bummy says to Mike Jacobs, but he does know that he is no longer the matchmaker at Madison Square Garden.

. . .

Al Davis makes a discovery. A kid with a pink Spaldeen and a sidewalk is set for the day, but when a guy turns twenty he is saddled with an aura of maturity and sophistication that limits his scope to such stimulating activities as standing, sitting, stretching, and yawning. So when Shorty invites Al to join him for a car ride somewhere in the middle of his second week of retirement from the ring, it is an option to be considered.

"Where ya takin' me, Shorty?"

"I gotta visit a sick friend in the hospital."

"What friend? And why the hell should I go? Lemme outta here."

Shorty grabs his shirtsleeve as he pulls away from the curb. "You don't visit someone in the hospital empty-handed. I ain't got no candy, so I'm bringin' you instead."

Al does a little grumbling, but it is not from the heart, because a week and a half of hanging out is more than he can handle. So, whether by some great master plan of Shorty's or whether he is really just there in lieu of candy, Albert Abraham Davidoff finds Esther Barbara Kovsky recovering from an appendectomy in room 324 of the Kings County Hospital.

Al does not exude the same animal magnetism with nice young girls as he does with the gum-chewing, heavily rouged, frizzy-haired broads who hang out under the lampposts on Pitkin Avenue and are always available for a basement party at any hour of the day or night. He does manage to utter three words during the visit—"Hi" and "So long."

On the drive back to Brownsville the spell that is cast upon Al is not yet broken. When Shorty says, "Nice kid, huh, Al?" he answers with a question: "Is she a girlfriend?"

Shorty looks at him and smiles. "She ain't a boy."

The following morning Rose Davidoff hears her son coming out of his bedroom singing, "Mazel, mazel, mazel tov, a-yidee, yidee, yidee mazel tov . . ." The next thing she hears is her son muttering to himself in the bathroom, where he is giving himself a big lecture on what does he need with a nice Jewish girl at this time in his life? He tells himself that she is not yet seventeen, but the importance of this diminishes when he realizes that when he is ninety-nine she will be approaching ninety-six.

Next, he wonders why he should want to be with a girl who is so pretty that all he can do is stare at her. He knows the answer without even thinking—no other girl makes his pulse race the way she does. Also, Bobbie Kovsky is a Jewish model, something previously as unthinkable to Al as a bacon-and-matzo sandwich. The clincher, though, is that suddenly he can't wait to get back in the ring and show her what he can do.

Actually, Al has already decided to cut short his retirement; he simply hasn't made a public statement to that effect yet. But when he hears that Mike Jacobs bounces Johnny Attell from his job as matchmaker at the Garden, he knows immediately it's because of him, so he calls Johnny and tells him he changes his mind and will fight Tony Marteliano or anyone else. He may be "Bummy" to a lot of people, but to Attell, the guy who gives him the tag, the name doesn't fit. Now Bobbie Kovsky gives Al a reason even more powerful than loyalty to fight again.

The next day Al is back in the gym, wrapped up in a rubber sweat suit trying to work off two weeks of hot dogs, ice cream, and candy. When he gets off the scale Froike walks over, puts a wet sponge to the back of his neck. "Forget it, Al. You're never going to see one thirty-five again, not unless you cut off an arm or a leg. You drained yourself trying to make weight against Ambers. Forget the lightweights. Forget Ambers. That's what happens to growing boys."

When Al gets out of the shower, Shorty is waiting with a bouquet of flowers.

"For me? Jeez, Shorty, I didn't know you felt that way." But Al is holding his breath, hoping the flowers are for who he thinks they are.

"Actually, I thought I'd go back to the hospital. You know, the kid's gettin' out in a couple of days, and . . ."

Al is now breaking his personal best record for breath holding.

". . . and the truth is, they told me to hold these flowers straight up because there's water at the bottom, but it's pretty hard to do that and drive, so I was thinkin' if maybe—"

"Hey, come on, friends gotta take care of friends!"

When they get to the hospital, Al cannot believe that Bobbie Kovsky looks even better today than she did yesterday. She's propped up with her hair swept back and the faintest touch of a pinkish lipstick. Anything more would be hiding her beauty, not enhancing it.

Shorty walks over with a big smile and hands her the bouquet. "How ya doin', sugar? These are from my friend Al."

Once Bobbie is out of the hospital, Shorty recommends taking long rides to get fresh air and drinking plenty of milkshakes to regain her strength and energy. It is surprising, considering that Shorty has never even taken a first-aid course, how quickly Bobbie accepts his advice and Al agrees. It becomes a regular routine for the three of them to take daily drives to Coney Island, Sheepshead Bay, or Rockaway. Before long the color is back in Bobbie's cheeks and the bounce is back in Al's step.

The week before Al's first fight since his loss to Ambers, they are all sitting at the edge of a pier at Sheepshead Bay washing down hero sandwiches with medicinal chocolate shakes when Shorty gets tired of waiting for Nature to take its course. He turns to Bobbie, who is taking a bite of her sandwich and attempting the impossible task of chewing the hard Italian roll daintily. A trickle of mayonnaise appears at the corner of her mouth, and she smiles as she dabs it away with her napkin. Al tears off a small piece of bread and drops it into the water, watching as the gulls converge on it, winner take all.

"You know, Bobbie," says Shorty, caught up in the beauty of the moment, "I been wonderin' . . . aw, let me get to the point. Whaddya think of gettin' married?"

Al Davis feels like someone just took a club and swung it right into his stomach. Bobbie coughs her mouthful of sandwich right up and catches it daintily in her napkin.

"I . . . I just . . ." Bobbie takes a deep breath. "I just never thought about you, Shorty. I mean, it's—"

Shorty holds up his hand. "Not me. I'm your friend," he says, and points his finger at Al. "Him. I'm talkin' about him. I'm tellin' ya, you two are wearing me out. You have any idea how much I'm spendin' on gas chaperonin' ya, for Chrissake?"

There are two casualties of Shorty's proposal. The first is Al's sandwich, which drops right out of his hand into Sheepshead Bay. The second is poor Teddy Baldwin, his "comeback" opponent, who never stands a chance against the rejuvenated Al "Bummy" Davis.

In Brownsville it should be the best of times. By March 1, it's a clean sweep for O'Dwyer and Turkus. Reles and his boys have all been locked up on charges ranging from vagrancy to loitering. Their headquarters on Stone Avenue is padlocked, and the only customers in Midnight Rose's candy store are there to buy newspapers, candy, cigarettes, and for those who have never watched Rose wash her glassware, egg creams and lime rickeys. With the streets free of the warlords of crime, with shopkeepers able to go about their business free from worries about an unwanted "partner" dipping into the till, with no one cringing in fear of a heavy-handed "collector," it should be a time of joy and elation. Instead, almost everyone in Brownsville chooses to watch and wait. From years of hard experience, no one is ready to place any bets that Murder, Inc. is down for the count.

As important as Harry Rudolph's testimony is, it needs backup, because Harry Rudolph, in a court of law, comes across about as straight and tall as a humpbacked midget. As for Reles, Goldstein, Strauss, Maione, and Abbandando, the idea of any of them opening up and talking borders on fantasy. What the DA needs is a weak link. And that's what he gets when Dukey Maffetore breaks down under questioning, but pleads that he doesn't really know much of anything. "Why don'tcha talk to my friend Pretty?" he suggests. "He's real smart and understands better'n me."

But even after he finds out that he was marked for a rubout, Pretty Levine won't talk. He is questioned, cajoled, and tempted, but he is so tightlipped that he doesn't even ask for a glass of water. For the DA's staff it is difficult to understand being loyal to guys who are out to kill you, and they begin to wonder—is it loyalty, or is it something else? O'Dwyer and Turkus decide to keep working on Levine because there is the general feeling that he is different. They sense from the look of anguish in his eyes, from the way he buries his face in his hands when he is alone, that Abe "Pretty" Levine has a conscience.

They hear he has a beautiful young wife, which they find out is no exaggeration when they bring her in, hoping she will help loosen his tongue. And what they see then reinforces their belief that Pretty Levine is not like the others.

Mrs. Abe Levine arrives with her little daughter in tow, as there is nowhere to leave her on such short notice. Pretty is so overjoyed to see his wife that he can't control the break in his voice when he cries out her name—"Helen!" He almost crushes her in a one-armed embrace as he hugs the baby tight with his other arm. Helen needs no prompting as she begs her husband to tell what he knows for the sake of their small family, tears streaming down her face. Baby Barbara wraps her arms around her father's leg and tugs at his pants.

Abe caresses his wife's cheek and gently kisses away the tears. He lifts Barbara from the floor and presses his face against hers, cradling her in his arms and shutting his eyes against the sobs threatening to tear him apart. With all eyes upon him, he sets his child down and bows his head.

"I got nothin' to say," he mumbles. "I don't know nothin'." Then he looks up into Helen's blue eyes, and at that moment Burt Turkus understands the quality of Pretty Levine's loyalty. It is a deep and true loyalty, and it is not to Abe Reles and the mob.

Sometimes you have to play a little dirty to get things to come out clean. When O'Dwyer tells Pretty that they're sending Helen to the Women's House of Detention because she is a material witness, he goes into a table-pounding frenzy. "You ain't got no right! You do what you want with me, but leave my wife alone! She's got nothin' to do with this!" But O'Dwyer thinks he has a strong hand, and sure enough, by playing the queen he hits the jackpot. Pretty breaks when they put Helen behind bars, and he breaks with a vengeance. He remembers the humiliation of Pittsburgh Phil telling him he wasn't good enough to borrow six-for-five without cosigners. He remembers the Davis kid ready to take on the whole mob under the el on Livonia Avenue. He remembers Puggy Feinstein.

"Fuck those bastards! What did they ever do for me? My wife ain't stayin' in jail to save their asses!"

. . .

In all probability it is just a quirk of the calendar, but on the third Sunday in March of 1940, Saint Patrick's Day gets together with Palm Sunday and Bill O'Dwyer gets together with the press to announce that he has confessions from Abe Levine and Duke Maffetore. It is a good five hundred years ago that Saint Patrick got rid of the snakes in Ireland. Now another son of the old sod is getting rid of another bunch of snakes an ocean away. And it is nearly two thousand years ago that the people of Jerusalem honored Jesus by spreading palm leaves in his path. There are no palm leaves in Brownsville, Brooklyn, and Bill O'Dwyer is no Jesus Christ, but on March 17, 1940, if palm leaves were to be had, they would have been strewn wherever he walked.

Bill O'Dwyer no longer has the time to sit in on his Friday night "dealer's choice" poker game, where seven-card stud was always his favorite because with each draw you have a chance to improve your hand. He is somewhat consoled by the hand he now holds against Murder, Inc. Hidden away in the hole is Harry Rudolph, and things really start looking up when he draws two knaves in Duke Maffetore and Abe Levine. He is ready to go with this hand when Kitty Reles deals him the wild card.

On March 22, Kitty visits Kid Twist in jail, then heads directly to the office of the district attorney. She is the mother of a boy going on six, she's expecting her second child in June, and she has a husband who may well be on his way to the electric chair. She tells O'Dwyer that her husband is conscience-stricken because of all the terrible things the gang does, and that he regrets how he permitted Harry Strauss and Buggsy Goldstein to influence him. At first O'Dwyer thinks he hears the strains of "Hearts and Flowers" in the background, until Mrs. Reles says that her husband's remorse is so great that he's ready to tell all he knows—as long as he can cut a deal to save his life.

Enrico Caruso, singing his greatest arias, never received such rapt, undivided attention from his audiences as Abe "Kid Twist" Reles is accorded once he begins singing. It is true that when it comes to range and resonance Caruso has the edge, but when it comes to execution Reles is second to no one.

. . .

Of all the guys in the mob, Buggsy Goldstein has the best sense of humor. Nobody loves a good joke more than the pudgy, happy-go-lucky Clown Prince of Murder, Inc. So when his wife, Betty, whom he adores most in this world next to Abe Reles, tells him in the visitor's pen that the word is going around that Reles is turning state's evidence, he almost splits his sides laughing. And as laughing is contagious, Harry Strauss, Happy Maione, and Frank Abbandando join in, not yet realizing that the joke is on them.

Abe Reles sits across the table from Bill O'Dwyer and his staff, his thick lips twisted in a taunting smirk, his thumbs hooked under his armpits. Burton Turkus has an overwhelming desire to grab a bat, a hammer, anything he can get his hands on, and smash it into the leering face.

Reles knows how badly they need him, and he's making the most of it. In New York State you cannot get a conviction on the testimony of an accomplice without further corroboration, so Reles points out that they don't have a strong enough case against him either in the hit on Red Alpert or in the murder of Puggy Feinstein; and without his testimony the case against the rest of Murder, Inc. is questionable. After two days of offers and counteroffers, Reles and O'Dwyer go behind closed doors. When they come out, Reles has full immunity on any testimony he gives before the grand jury, and O'Dwyer has a docketful of almost airtight cases against almost everyone else.

Once Reles starts talking, there is no stopping him. He amazes everyone with his ability to recall every detail of some two hundred murders, sparing no one, including himself. Then again, there is no reason to spare himself. Abe Reles is to stool pigeons what the Atlantic Ocean is to a puddle of water—though that isn't how he sees himself, of course. "All these guys were ready to talk and bury me. I don't believe in bein' polite and bowing and saying, 'You first.' Me, a stool pigeon? Shit, I just beat them to the punch."

Pittsburgh Phil Strauss makes an offer of his own when he and Buggsy are indicted on April 12. "Put me in with my good friend Abe

Reles for ten minutes and I will tell you anything you want to know."
When his request for visitation rights is ignored, he tries to save his skin
by forgoing shaving and bathing and acting like he's crazy, but a madman acting like a madman simply is not an attention-getter.

Not only is Abe Reles an accomplished singer, he is a skilled medium
who is able to call forth all the old ghosts. He brings back the ghost of
Whitey Rudnick to return the favor of a meat cleaver in the head to
Happy Maione and Frank Abbandando; he summons the ghost of Puggy
Feinstein, who wants to see Harry Strauss and Buggsy Goldstein burn
the way they made him burn, and who will never rest in peace until he
fulfills his final promise: 'I'm going to get you, Reles!"

Louis Buchalter, who lives in a world of logic and reason, does not
believe in ghosts—not until he hears that Kid Twist, his trusted executioner, is holding a seance with O'Dwyer. When he finds the next forty-
four years of his life accounted for by the federal government and New
York State, he is certain that's as bad as things can possibly get. It takes
the ghost of Joseph Rosen to show him how wrong he is.

Until Brooklyn District Attorney William O'Dwyer told the world on
Saint Patrick's Day 1940 about the crime syndicate whose operations
extended from coast to coast, and about the band of cold-blooded killers
from Brownsville who served as its enforcement arm, Brownsville was
just a couple of square miles crowded with immigrants from Eastern
Europe whose shops provided a bargain-hunter's paradise. By Easter
Sunday, Brownsville rivaled the Island of Dr. Moreau as a place that
conjured up images of horror and bloodletting. Almost every major
newspaper ran banner headlines and serialized features about this community that served as the incubator for a subspecies of demented, par-
anoid killers, and when Herb Feeney of the *New York World Telegram*
coined the name Murder, Inc., Brownsville was immortalized alongside
Sodom and Gomorrah. Now Brownsville meant gangsters and bullies,
coarseness, depravity, and corruption. And in the minds of many, Al
"Bummy" Davis was Brownsville.

14

Malachy Walker hadn't missed a fight at the Garden since it opened. He loved the sound of the crowd, whether they were cheering or booing or calling for blood. He loved the jostling on the way to his seat and the barking of the vendors: "*Pro*-grams!" "Cold beer!" "Getcha red hots!" Most of all he loved hearing the *thwack-thwack* of a clean one-two finding its mark. No matter who was fighting, Malachy wanted to be there to savor the flavor of the event, but he did have certain favorites. One of them was Al Davis, because whenever Bummy fought there was always electricity in the air.

Malachy Walker had never actually seen an Al Davis fight. The last fight he did see was at the Argonne some twenty-two years ago, when a mustard-gas canister exploded yards away from him and robbed him of his eyesight. But Malachy's philosophy was the Lord giveth, the Lord taketh away, and his belief was so strong that his other senses were enhanced to an acute degree, so that Malachy's vision was transformed, not lost. Malachy knew all Bummy's moves, from the hammering left hooks to the dark scowl that descended on his face the moment the first bell rang.

Malachy had a Popeye-lookalike friend named Roscoe, a smallish guy who stuck to him like his shadow. They drank at Downey's together every night, they played dominoes and checkers together, they went everywhere together. Roscoe was Malachy's second set of eyes. He would describe to Malachy all the things going on around him, and when it came to the fights, he was Bill Stern, Sam Taub, and Clem McCarthy wrapped into one neat package.

Tapping his cane as they walked to their seats on the night of November 15, Malachy could already feel the excitement building up inside him. He still tingled every time he thought of Davis's last fight, exactly eight weeks ago right here at the Garden, against this kid from Little Italy, Tony Marteliano. It was a back-and-forth war, with neither boy giving an inch. Going into the tenth round, the fight was dead even, but then Marteliano started beating Davis to the punch, and the crowd was cheering him on so loudly that Malachy had to lean over to hear Roscoe relate what was happening. Just as the ten-second warning buzzer sounded and he started to relax, a roar from Roscoe almost catapulted him from his seat as a left hook from Bummy felled Marteliano like a tree. Marteliano was saved by the bell, but the punch swung the fight to Davis, and then there were a lot more cheers than boos.

Malachy stretched and leaned back in his seat as Roscoe described the pounding that Terry Young was dishing out to this kid "Texas" Lee Harper in a six-rounder that really got Malachy's juices flowing for the main event.

When Fritzie Zivic upsets Henry Armstrong for the welterweight championship, they offer the kid a nontitle match with Zivic, with the promise that win, lose, or draw, a title fight follows. The kid wants the fight, and Lew Burston goes along, even though he feels that Zivic is the wrong opponent for Al at this stage of his career. This feeling has nothing to do with Zivic's ability as a fighter because Zivic, strictly as a fighter, is pretty much like a Mississippi riverboat gambler without a longsleeved jacket or shirt, playing with an unmarked deck of cards. This Zivic doesn't worry Lew. His concern is for the riverboat gambler who comes to the table wearing his longsleeved jacket and carrying his own deck of cards.

Sitting on the edge of the rubbing table, Bummy feels a little nervous.

It has nothing to do with Zivic; in fact, he can't wait to get in the ring with him. People wearing boxing gloves do not make Bummy Davis nervous. It takes people without boxing gloves to do that, and there are seventeen thousand of them in the Garden tonight. Bummy wonders what kind of reception they'll give him. Even though Zivic is the welterweight champ, he's not a big crowd favorite, which has a lot to do with his reputation as a fighter who uses more parts of his body than the Marquis of Queensberry ever intended. Also, the Garden is Bummy's backyard, not Zivic's, so maybe there's hope. When Froike holds out his robe for him to slip into, the kid bounds down from the table thinking how nice it would be if they cheered for him tonight.

From the sound of the crowd Malachy can tell that one of the main-event fighters is approaching the ring. From the booing with a few cheers mixed in, it might be either one of them. By tradition the champion always enters the ring last, so Malachy assumes it's Bummy, and Roscoe corroborates.

"Davis just entered the ring. Looks like they're never going to forgive him for Canzoneri."

"Roscoe, I don't think they would forgive the lad if he belched and said 'Excuse me.'"

Malachy sits back and listens as the fighters are introduced. He likes Zivic because he appreciates tried-and-true fighters. Zivic's whole background is "fighter": five brothers who all fight, and a nose that only a fighter could have, the way Roscoe describes it. True, Zivic doesn't always do things according to Hoyle, but any guy that can beat Henry Armstrong is Malachy Walker's kind of fighter. Also, Malachy can't help being influenced by all the things they say and write about Davis. He tries to be fair-minded, but where there's smoke, isn't there fire?

". . . in this corner, the newly crowned Welterweight Champion of the World, from Pittsburgh, Pennsylvania, weighing one hundred forty-seven and a half pounds, wearing black trunks, Fritzie Zivic!"

There is a smattering of polite applause, nothing more—no champion's welcome.

"Since when do you introduce the champion first?" Malachy snaps.

"What's wrong with that?"

"It's tradition, Roscoe. I like things the way they're supposed to be, that's all."

"Also weighing one hundred forty-seven and a half pounds, from Brownsville, Brooklyn, wearing purple trunks, Al Davis!"

There is no smattering of anything from the crowd now. An avalanche of catcalls and jeers drowns out the crescendo of devotion from the Brownsville faithful. For Al Davis there is no in-between.

As the bell rings, Malachy leans toward Roscoe to get a better "view" of the fight. Roscoe sets the stage for him: Zivic answering the echo of the bell with a left jab to Davis's face, Zivic throwing lots of jabs, then sneaking in the overhand right. "Now Davis bangs him with a solid left hook and drives him into the ropes. Zivic bounces off and falls in close, and . . . oh!"

"Yeah, what?"

"Davis is rubbin' his eye. The referee is warning Zivic, I'm not sure for what. They were in close. . . . Zivic is peppering him—left, left again, right to the side of the head. Davis is chargin' in, and Zivic drops him with a right to the jaw! Davis bounces right up, no count at all. Now Davis is chargin' in again, bangin' that left hook, and I'll tell you, Zivic gotta feel those shots. He falls into a clinch with Davis, and—oh, wow!"

"What?"

"Davis is shakin' his head. His eye is really red. The referee, Cavanaugh, is warning Zivic again. Holy shit! He goes right behind the ref's back and potshots Davis!"

"What the hell is Cavanaugh doing?"

"He didn't see it!"

There's a lot that Roscoe doesn't see either. Some of it even Davis doesn't see—but what he doesn't see, he feels. His right eye is tearing and his vision is blurry; his face feels like it was massaged with sandpaper. Every time Zivic gets in close he does damage, most of it not with his fists. If the referee is behind him on his right, Zivic blocks his view so he can't see him working the left glove, jamming the thumb at Davis's eye, sliding the laces of both gloves along Davis's face. With his eyes blinking in a reflexive effort to soothe the searing pain, with blood oozing from his nose and his face beginning to resemble something you'd find in the window of a butcher shop, Al Davis knows he can turn to Billy Cavanaugh and cry foul, but that's not his way. Instead he goes after Zivic with more fury than he's ever felt in the ring before.

"Davis is bangin' with that left hook like he wants to break Zivic in half. . . . Zivic's hurt!" Roscoe is now on his feet with the rest of the crowd. There's no reason for Malachy to stand up, but he does anyhow, caught up in the action like everybody else.

"Zivic grabs Davis and falls into a clinch. Jesus Christ! Davis's head snaps back—but I don't see Zivic throw a punch. He has Davis pushed up against the ropes with both his gloves on the kid's shoulders, and Davis's head just whips back. He's covering his face with his gloves . . . and now Cavanaugh is pointing his finger at Zivic and warning him again!"

"That's the third time!" Malachy roars, pounding his fist into his palm. "What the hell is wrong with that Cavanaugh?"

"I thought you were for Zivic."

"I came to see a prizefight, goddamn it!"

In Davis's corner, Froike is screaming at Billy Cavanaugh. "You're lettin' him get away with murder! Why don't you just give him a hatchet in there?" Lew Burston has enough on his hands keeping Willie Davidoff from climbing into the ring to get after Cavanaugh himself.

Meanwhile, game plans and strategy are out the window. Bummy Davis is now fueled strictly by rage. He blasts his way through Zivic's fists, slamming his opponent into the ropes with his left hook, guttural snarls coming from his throat as the bell rings and Billy Cavanaugh pries the two fighters apart.

"Davis is so mad the referee has to drag him back to his corner," Roscoe rasps.

"Why the hell shouldn't he be mad?" Malachy is jumping up and down and waving his hands like a lunatic. "Three warnings in one round—"

"And there was a lot more he pulled that he didn't get warned for. I think Cavanaugh is just lettin' them settle it their own way."

"So what the hell do they need a referee for, Roscoe? Davis has to be thinking payback."

Al Davis isn't thinking, period. In his corner he is all emotion, and the emotion is not love. Froike has to hold him down on his stool as the kid coils, ready to spring. Willie bends down close to his ear.

"The ref ain't doin' shit, so you be the ref, Al."

Froike moves in with the ice pack. "Let me get somethin' on that eye."

"Forget it," Bummy spits, shoving Froike's hand away. "I don't need nothin'. I'm gonna kill that dirty sonuvabitch."

Burston is leaning over the ropes, calling to Cavanaugh. "You see what he pulled there, Billy. You going to let him gouge his eyes out? He's using his thumbs, his laces, his elbows—what's the matter with you?"

The referee doesn't look up as he continues to mark his scorecard. "Let the boys work it out themselves."

Burston ducks his head between the ropes next to Bummy's stool. "You heard what he said, Al. Go ahead and work it out yourself."

Froike seconds Lew. "Go ahead, Al," he mutters, "you do it your way now. Teach that bastard a lesson. Whatever it takes."

"What a look on Davis's face! Jesus, if looks could kill . . ." Roscoe tries his best, but he is frustrated because there's no way he can adequately describe to his friend the contorted face, the quivering nostrils, the eyes narrowed to slits that seem to spit sparks of anger.

But Malachy Walker knows. Imagination, instinct, and reality bring it all to him. He "sees" the look on Al Davis's face, and shudders. Zivic sees the look too as Davis charges toward him at the bell for the second round.

First the roar of the crowd is one of anticipation as the two battlers come together in the center of the ring, but Malachy picks up on the change immediately. The decibel level doesn't decrease, but the tone shifts to an outcry of shock, disbelief!

Bummy gets straight to the point with a left hook and a sweeping right cross, which Zivic takes on his shoulder and arm. He starts a counterpunch that goes nowhere when Davis launches a left hook that misses Zivic's kneecap by a good twelve inches. It does not land anywhere near the ankle. Zivic gives out with a sound that might easily be confused with the five o'clock whistle at a factory.

Roscoe grimaces. "Oooh, Zivic takes one right in the nuts! The ref's motioning with his hand for Davis to keep 'em up. Zivic misses with a jab and tries another jab. It's partially blocked, and-oh! Davis, low again . . .

and another one! Zivic is complaining to Cavanaugh, and Cavanaugh is warning Davis to keep 'em up. Davis is like a madman in there!"

Nobody in Madison Square Garden could believe what was taking place before their eyes, because nobody had ever seen anything quite like this before. There were some scattered calls of encouragement for Bummy, from the few who realized that when the kid came out of a clinch dabbing at inflamed, watery eyes, it wasn't because of an allergy attack; this was one Garden where ragweed and goldenrod did not grow. But most of the fight crowd howled at this guy called Bummy with all the venom of a lynch mob. Even many of the jaded reporters at ringside were standing and shouting for someone to drag Davis out of the ring. Lew Burston stared in disbelief from the ring apron near Davis's corner. His original fear had come true—the riverboat gambler was caught dealing from the bottom of the deck and the kid from Brownsville was calling him on it.

Foulproof Taylor, a legendary character in the annals of boxing lore, often lamented the fact that he was born too late. He missed out on the lightbulb and the motion picture projector because Thomas Alva Edison got there first. So the fat little man from Brooklyn with the big convoluted brain turned his energies to areas where Edison feared to tread. The invention that brought him everlasting fame and bears his name like a true offspring is the Foulproof Taylor cup, which is to jockstraps what an armored tank is to an infantry mule. Foulproof Taylor traveled far and wide, from gym to gym, training camp to training camp, bearing his cup with him. Wherever he went, he would don his hardware over his software and challenge anyone in the house to take his best shot. There are many stories of big tough guys hauling off and sending the little guy flying head over heels, but he would always pick himself up and brush himself off unharmed. The Foulproof Taylor cup is mandatory equipment in the prize ring, and with its adoption it was deemed that since it was now impossible to be injured by a low punch, fighters crying foul and referees disqualifying violators would be a thing of the past. Foulproof Taylor never stood up against Al "Bummy" Davis. Fritzie Zivic did.

Some people at ringside counted a total of thirteen low blows, others counted nine. Whatever the number, Al wasn't finished yet. He was on a mission to destroy, consequences be damned. His onslaught could not be abated, not by himself, not by referee Billy Cavanaugh, and certainly not by Fritzie Zivic, who was now probably able to audition for a soprano role at the Met. Cavanaugh tried to pull him away from Zivic as he signaled that Davis was disqualified, but Bummy kept tearing into his opponent. Six policemen swarmed into the ring, and both corners jumped in, some to pull their men apart, some to join in the fracas. Bummy lashed out at everyone, flailing away blindly, and six policemen became five as he clobbered one of them and knocked him into dreamland. When the others grabbed his arms from behind, he couldn't punch so he kicked, and he caught Billy Cavanaugh in the shins. Luke Carney, Zivic's manager, took a punch at Davis while his arms were pinned. Lew Burston found out that his fighter had learned his lessons pretty well when even he got belted as he tried to calm Al down and the fight spilled over to the crowd.

Malachy Walker found out that his cane could be used for more than just walking when a fan behind him yelled, "T'row dat dirty bum Davis out! Looka what he started!" When Malachy corrected him—"Davis finished it. Zivic started it!"—the guy gave him a hard poke in the back, snapping, "Ya dumb jerk. Ya don't know what the hell you're talkin' about!" Malachy, who believed strongly in free speech, did not feel the same way about free potshots, so he raised his cane and deftly plunked the big-mouth right in the gut—above the belt.

"Ladies and gentlemen. Please, please, I beg of you . . . please," Harry Balogh shouted as the bedlam outside the ring continued. "The time, two minutes thirty-four seconds of the first round."

"Hey, what's wrong with that guy?" Roscoe said to Malachy. "It's the second round. Did he forget about the first one?"

"That's the problem!" Malachy fumed. "Everyone forgot about the first round!"

"The referee disqualifies Al Davis. The winner is Zivic!" Harry Balogh wiped his brow, glad that it was all over. But for Al Davis it was just beginning.

As the fans slowly made their way to the exits, with hooting and calls for the banning of Al Davis echoing throughout the Garden, Malachy Walker clutched the shoulder of his good friend and shook his head.

"You know what, Roscoe? I wasn't the only blind person in the Garden tonight. Not by a long shot."

In the dressing room after the fight, Jack Mahon of the *Daily News* told Lew Burston that as soon as Cavanaugh disqualified Bummy, Bill Brown of the New York State Athletic Commission, without waiting to consult with any of the other commissioners, declared, "Davis will never be allowed to fight in New York State again." At that moment it looked as though whatever Bummy had was contagious, because suddenly Lew, who was generally a pretty even-tempered sort of a guy, had the same wild-eyed look as his fighter did in the ring.

Before it was popular to "promise her anything, but give her Arpege," Al "Bummy" Davis also heard a lot of promises but what they gave him was bubkes. Not that he would have been happy with Arpege, but translating bupkes from Yiddish to English, you get nothing, which is exactly what Bummy gets from his hearing with the New York State Athletic Commission. In fact nothing would have been preferable to what Bummy gets.

Lew Burston had promised him that if he showed remorse and explained how he was provoked by Zivic, they would let him go with a warning, like "Okay, Davis, you hit him in the balls about a dozen times and another one or two shots for good luck. Please do not do it again." Johnny Attell promised him that the guy who would really get a dressing down would be the referee, Billy Cavanaugh, for standing by and not stopping the fouling in the first round. Even Froike assured him that the worst he'd get would be a slap on the wrist because everyone knew about Zivic's tactics in the ring. Fritzie Zivic was boxing's version of Mandrake the Magician. He could hold up his hands, and say, "Pick a thumb, any thumb." After all, he had fifty-two of them, or at least a lot of guys he tangled with in the ring would swear that he did. "Don't tell me which one, just remember it"—like anyone could ever forget Zivic's thumb. "Okay, now don't look. Guess where that thumb is?" It was always in the same place—right in the eye! Like any good magician, Zivic fooled a lot of people. Among those who chose to look the other way as the magician displayed his entire bag of tricks were some who were privy to the secrets of his trade—or at least they should have been as members of the New York State Athletic Commission. But they were also guys who heard tales of Brownsville and Murder, Inc., of Big Gangy and his brother Bummy. As far as they were concerned, Al "Bummy" Davis fought his last prizefight on November 15, 1940, at Madison Square Garden, where he not only desecrated the Manly Art of Self-Defense but greatly mistreated, abused, and very nearly crippled Fritzie Zivic, the welterweight champion of the whole civilized world, in a most uncivilized manner. Four days after the Zivic fight, Al Davis put on a dark blue suit and a pair of sunglasses to hide his eyes, which happened to be the same color as the suit, and went to Beecher's Gym to meet Irving Rudd, the press agent for Madison Square Garden. Mike Jacobs felt it was a good idea to have Rudd, who lived only a few blocks away on Powell Street, go along with Davis to his hearing before the New York State Athletic Commission. The train ride to midtown Manhattan took forty minutes, which was ten minutes longer than the hearing. Al Davis was no expert, but he was pretty sure that half an hour was not very long for a hearing. However, that was all the time it took them to revoke his license and fine him $2,500. For the second time in 1940, Al "Bummy" Davis was no longer a prizefighter.

On the day of the hearing, Garfinkel the tailor closed his shop and took the train to the city so that he could present to the commissioners Brownsville's voice: a petition signed by more than a thousand people on behalf of their champion. Al walked over to the stoop-shouldered tailor, who was wringing his hat because he didn't know what to do with his hands. Al had never realized before how small his father's shul neighbor was. He didn't have a lot to feel good about these past few days, but at that moment he was feeling very good. He patted Garfinkel on the shoulder.

"Thank you. You're a very nice man."

Garfinkel looked up at the young man he still remembered as a little boy in short pants who used to try so hard to sit through the holy days services out of respect to his father.

"I told your father a long time ago that you were a son to be proud of. We all are, Albert. We're all proud of you."

As Garfinkel turned and shuffled out of the office, Commissioner Phelan smiled and called out a thank-you, but the petition was never read. Like Al said, it was a hearing where not much was heard.

Al left the hearing flanked by Irving Rudd, Johnny Attell, and Lew Burston. He was glad that he was wearing dark glasses, because the reality of what had just occurred was beginning to sink in. Lew said they were going to the Garden to talk to Mike Jacobs about Al's purse and the fine, but all Al wanted was to be by himself, preferably in the dark, where he could close his eyes and try to blot everything out.

As not too many things are going his way lately, he is walking down the narrow hallway to the elevators with his eyes wide open when he hears a cry of "Al! Al!" Bobbie Kovsky does not do road work, and it shows as she runs up to him swallowing quick gulps of air.

Al cannot stop the flush crawling up his cheeks as he stammers his way through something that can be loosely construed as an introduction.

"Uh, guys, this is a friend of mine, Esther Kovsky, but she's, uh, she's Barbara. Bobbie. That's her maiden name." The flush is suddenly a flame. "I mean middle name." Since he starts training for Zivic, Al hasn't seen much of Bobbie. An occasional movie, hanging out in a candy store—that's about it, except for talking on the telephone.

She nods her head but doesn't take her eyes from his face. "I asked for the rest of the day off. I had to know how it went. Al?"

He shrugs and forces a smile; it's a weak one, but it is a smile. "Well, it coulda been worse. I just haven't figured out how yet."

Bobbie is not wearing dark glasses, so everyone is able to see the tears welling up in her eyes. She raises her hand and puts her fingertips gently to Al's cheek, so gently that it is more like the touch of a summer breeze and Al Davis no longer wants to be alone by himself in a dark place.

If there was any way of having an enjoyable experience on the afternoon of the hearing, Johnny Attell came up with it. The $2,500 fine wouldn't have been so bad by itself, but on top of the suspension it was like salt on an open wound.

"Al, I'm going to show you the power I am endowed with. Remember when I took two years away from you?" Attell is referring to the affidavit he had Max Davidoff sign, stating that his son was born in 1918, not 1920, so that Al would not be restricted to fighting six-rounders.

Al just sits there, and because of the dark glasses nobody can be sure if he is paying attention or staring off into space.

"I'm givin' you back the two years, kid. You're only twenty, not twenty-two." Attell leans back and waits for the kid to ask what that means. He waits some more.

"You know what that means? It means they cannot take money from you. You see, kid, you're a minor. That money doesn't belong to you. It belongs to your mother, who by the grace of God, and of course me, is your guardian."

Attell expects the kid to jump for joy or at least give out with a cheer, but Al's thoughts are not about $2,500 or affidavits or guardians. All Al Davis is thinking about is how he tingled at the touch of Bobbie's fingers.

When the word comes down to Lepke in his not-too-spacious quarters at Leavenworth to throw a few things together because he is going on a trip, it presents no problem at all. The once-upon-a-time brains of the Syndicate becomes most adept at packing in his years of moving from hideout to hideout. However, this particular trip is one that Louis Buchalter is not looking forward to, even though it is to Brooklyn, which is as close to home as he could ever hope to be. It is also not too far from Ossining, the home of the electric chair.

Lepke has not been pleased at the prospect of spending his next forty-four years reading magazines and newspapers behind prison walls, but he has known for months that it is just a matter of time before he becomes a chorus in Abe Reles's seemingly endless song. That is the reason now for his command performance in front of the Brooklyn DA, and suddenly, with all the options laid out in front of him, forty-four years of reading magazines and newspapers anywhere does not sound too bad.

While Lepke is packing to go to Brooklyn, Al Davis is packing to leave. Maybe his predicament is not as critical as Lepke's, but his heart, too, is not exactly bursting with joy. He loves Brownsville, and for the first twenty years of his life he has hardly slept anywhere but in his own bed. However, Johnny Attell and Lew Burston realize that something has to be done about improving their young fighter's public image, and everybody loves a soldier.

Although not thrilled with the idea at first, when Shorty and Mousey show their allegiance to God, country, and Bummy by telling him they'll enlist with him and go off as the Three Musketeers, it becomes much more appealing—a real adventure, just like going camping at Bear Mountain, which they always talk about but never get around to doing.

Lew Burston drives them to the recruiting station on Livingston Street in downtown Brooklyn. He is heartbroken at how things have been going for Al lately. He can't count how many nights he's spent tossing around in his bed, unable to sleep, wondering how such a respectful, good-natured kid can be so misunderstood. He blames Johnny Attell, he blames Mike Jacobs, he blames the kid's brother Willie, he even blames himself for how they all go about making a box-office hit out of a guy called "Bummy." He's watched the kid force himself to smile as he bounces down the aisle toward the ring with the boos and catcalls raining down on him, and he knows that on the inside the kid is crying. So when Johnny Attell suggests that having the kid enlist in the army would be a very good move, Lew doesn't have to think too long. He doesn't remember anyone ever booing a soldier.

When they get before the recruiting sergeant, Lew is very impressed. The guy is Mr. Congeniality himself. He assures Al, Shorty, and Mousey that it is the army's business to keep their soldiers happy, because a happy soldier is a good soldier, and there will be no problem about the three of them staying together. "As a matter of fact, it makes for good teamwork," the sergeant says as he rubber-stamps their papers.

Al's first day in the army, February 13, 1941, is as close as he ever comes to a ticker-tape parade. At seven in the morning, he is marching through the streets of Brownsville to the local draft board at P.S. 72 on New Lots Avenue, followed by his entire family, as well as Shorty's and Mousey's families and assorted friends. What some neighbors mistake for a bugler accompanying them is Max Davidoff blowing his nose rhythmically; when his eyes fill up, which is every few seconds, his nose fills up too. The chairman of the draft board has his picture taken with Brownsville's premier suspended fighter, after which he makes Al the leader of the group, handing him a package containing his, Shorty's and Mousey's records. As they board the bus taking them to Camp Upton on Long Island, it is Albert Davidoff's opinion that army life can't be all that bad.

For three weeks Al grumbles to Mousey and Shorty about waiting on long lines and walking around the grounds of Camp Upton picking up cigarette butts and scraps of paper. He is pretty confused about the way this army does things. No breakfast is worth getting up at four in the morning and waiting on line freezing your ass off for two hours, which is how long it takes to reach what is known as the consolidated mess. Al tries to figure out how they expect to win a war by training you to stand on line and pick up garbage. Someone explains to him that this is "pre-basic," which is not the real thing.

At the end of the third week, when Private Albert Davidoff sees the list posted on the bulletin board in the dayroom, he realizes that in an organization as big as the army mistakes are bound to happen, so he marches into the office and tries to explain that it's okay to send him to Camp Hulen in Texas but his two friends have to go with him. That is the deal. Al finds out more things in the next ten seconds than he would have believed possible to learn in a week. He finds out that he is not allowed just to walk into the company office, that you do not call a noncom "sir," that the United States Army is not a democratic institution, and that the first sergeant has halitosis, the recruiting sergeant lied, and he, Shorty, and Mousey are being split up. As it turns out, it is still the best three weeks he spends in the army.

When the winter wind is howling down a frost-coated Saratoga Avenue, carrying stinging pellets that attack like an army of glacial hornets, but instead of being there you're walking down Collins Avenue in Miami Beach getting hit in the face with a sun-drenched eighty-degree breeze, there's no better way of expressing how you feel than what Sam Gold says to Tiny Benson as he closes his eyes and spreads his arms wide. "A mechaieh! A real mechaieh!"

For Sam and Tiny, Miami Beach is not just a haven from bitter weather but also from the grasp of William O'Dwyer, who has made Brooklyn a most inhospitable town. At first Sam and Tiny think they're safe when their boss, Abe Reles, starts pointing his finger at everyone in every direction; after all, Sam's mother, Midnight Rose Gold, is not only Reles's partner in the loan-shark business but is also the one who always raises the bail money for the boys. Before long, though, it looks like Rose's grandchildren will have to get their ice cream cones at a new candy store, but they will also be able to brag that they have the only bubbe in Brooklyn doing time, because the sixty-nine-year-old Rose pleads guilty to eight counts of perjury in bail bond frauds. Not anxious to find out how far O'Dwyer's crusade will go, Sam wishes his mother well and follows the migratory birds south, while Tiny makes the same trip following the whales.

At present, Tiny Benson is not thinking about Midnight Rose, William O'Dwyer, or anything except the platter of challah French toast and scrambled eggs with onions and lox that he will momentarily be devouring at Wolfie's. Reaching the corner of Collins and Twenty-third, he and Sam are greeted with a line extending into the street, which is enough to bring a great big man like Tiny close to tears. Just as he is trying to condition himself to waiting another half hour for breakfast, there is a tap on his shoulder—"Louis Benson?"—and his first thought is that now that they are regular customers they're being moved to the front of the line. When he turns and looks at the face under the snap-brimmed, pulled-down hat, he sees the map of Ireland and knows that instead of eating breakfast he and Sam will be heading back to the cold winds of New York and in no time their suntans will be gone.

Sunshine and warm breezes are not much of a mechaieh for Private Albert Davidoff either. He doesn't mind leaving the cold behind, but he finds that southern hospitality does not extend to Texas or to the United States Army. At least everyone at Camp Upton spoke pretty much the same way he does, and it made him feel secure to know that it was the same time at home as it was there. And even though telephone calls were long-distance, they weren't very long-distance.

It took three weeks for trouble to find him at Camp Upton. At Camp Hulen it is waiting for him. He gets off the bus that brings the recruits from the railroad station to the company quadrangle in the section of the camp called the Heights, which is the basic training area. They are a tired, bedraggled group of Irish, Italian, and Jewish kids from New York City thrown deep in the heart of Texas. What they want most of all is to lie down and rest for an hour and then take a shower to wash off the road dust. What they get is an order to stand at attention under a broiling midday sun as Sergeant Leonard Fast, who lets them know right off the bat that he will inject as much misery into their lives as he can, introduces the officers and noncoms assigned to get Company A through basic training. Al listens but doesn't pay attention because he is thinking of his farewell weekend at Camp Upton, when Bobbie came to say good-bye along with Willie, Harry, and his parents. It was the first time his parents ever saw him hold a girl's hand and slow down for her when he walked so she could keep up with him. Poor Max must have wound up with a bruised arm for sure, the way Rose kept poking him with her elbow and whispering, "Lookit, lookit. See, this is special."

Knowing it will be a long time before he sees Bobbie or his family again, Al squeezes as much from this daydream as he can. He feels too good to let the sergeant's harangue or anything else bother him—except for the pesky fly that lands on his nose and starts tickling it.

"What are you doing, soldier? Just—what—are—you—doing?" Each word is a booming, separate roar, which is not at all necessary as the red-faced sergeant is standing right next to him.

Bobbie is gone, his parents are gone, and so is the fly. Bobbie and his parents are gone because—just like popping a soap bubble—Sergeant Fast made them go. Al looks the sergeant in the eye but says nothing because he has no idea what he's talking about.

"Are you deaf or just plain dumb? I am waiting for an answer. Do you know what 'Attention!' means?"

Al knows he cannot do things the way he would on Blake Avenue. Anyhow, he can't make up his mind whether this is just a big joke or not. "Yessir, I do."

"I am not a 'sir.' I work for a living. You do not address a noncommissioned officer as 'sir.' Ever. Now, soldier, and I use the term loosely, if you know what 'Attention!' means"—at which point he leans right into Al's face and bellows—"why were you scratching your nose?"

As this is not too tough a question, Al does not hesitate to respond with an honest answer. "It itched." Even though he makes no attempt to be funny, the soft undercurrent of snickering from the other men is like a lighted fuse on a dynamite stick.

Sergeant Fast slowly takes two steps back, slapping his palm with his swagger stick. "Are you one of those New Yawk wiseguys? What's your name, soldier?"

With Al it is instinctive. He is already measuring this guy, and he feels his muscles twitching. "Davidoff. Private Albert Davidoff. I am from New York, and I'm not trying to be a wiseguy." He is upset as he hears a break in his voice.

Two more slaps of swagger stick on palm. "Davidoff . . . mmm-hmm. Yes, that's a real New Yawk name. I know a troublemaker when I see one, Private Davidoff, but I am going to nip you in the bud."

There is no more snickering. Everyone can feel the tension in the air.

"Pick up your duffel bag, Private Davidoff, and with both hands raise it above your head and stand at attention. You will not move. I do not care if a fly tickles you, a bee bites you, or a bird shits in your face. You do not move!"

Al is smoldering. He can't believe that he's letting this happen. As he hoists the khaki duffel bag over his head, he thinks that Zivic wouldn't believe it either.

While he's standing there like a statue, Sergeant Fast walks over and picks up a small satchel called an AWOL bag in army vernacular. It is Al's, and it contains the made-to-order snow globe Bobbie gave him at Upton, with a scene of a little cottage and a tiny Bobbie and Al sitting on a bench.

"This, Davidowitz, is a test of how well you stand at attention," Fast drawls, lifting the AWOL bag to place it on top of the duffel. "This bag had best remain balanced."

"Don't do that." Al speaks softly but firmly. "There's glass in there and it's important—"

"You do not speak without permission, soldier!" Fast rages, pulling back to glare at Al. As he does so, the bag topples to the ground and the sound of breaking glass can be heard all the way back to Brownsville. At least that's the way it seems to Private Albert Davidoff, who has held himself in check longer than anyone who knows him would ever believe.

All at once, the lips draw back, the nostrils flare, and Bummy heaves the duffel bag into the chest of Sergeant Fast. Everyone joins in a spontaneous gasp.

Before Fast can react, the piercing command "Ten-hut!" sounds throughout the quadrangle, and Captain Harper, the company commander, strides forward. "I'll take over now, Sergeant. Thank you."

"Yessir!" Fast salutes smartly, about-faces, and steps back with the rest of the cadre.

When the company is dismissed, Al picks up his AWOL bag, which is sopping with water from the broken snow globe. Texas may be tougher to take than Lou Ambers and Fritzie Zivic.

Hardly anyone knew his real name because everybody called him Frank DeBarber and that's what they thought his name was. And that was because Frank DeTomi's father told him, "A barber, he's-a never hungry. No matta what happen, still you gotta getta you hair cut." So Frank followed his father's advice, not because he was such a good son and not because his father was such a wise man but because there were no options; in the DeTomi family, when the father spoke everyone listened. From the time he was fifteen Frank was cutting hair in his father's shop on Sackett Street near the Brooklyn docks.

Now, for the first time, he had his own shop, in the latrine of A Company's Third and Fourth Platoon barracks. Being the unofficial company barber had its advantages. At a dollar a haircut, he was making a lot more as a barber than as a soldier, even with Sergeant Fast taking a 50 percent cut. Also, Frank never pulled KP, and he was excused from a lot of the routine exercises and drills as a perk for having the right business partner. Frank would have been happy to cut his bunkmates' hair for nothing. It was Sergeant Fast who set the price, as there was no percentage in being a partner in an on-the-house enterprise.

Private DeTomi did not have the latrine all to himself. Even when the rest of A Company was out training and learning the skills of soldiering, Private Albert Davidoff was usually there with him. All the guys knew who Davidoff was—the dirty fighter from Brownsville, Al "Bummy" Davis, a real well known guy, a celebrity. He wasn't such a celebrity anymore, though. A poor slob crawling around a shithouse on his hands and knees, scrubbing floor tiles and fixtures day after day, cannot be regarded as a person of note. Still, Frankie and all the other GI's had to admit that he was a pretty decent guy. In fact, Frankie couldn't help feeling a little guilty about the deal each of them drew. Here he was, goofing off every day, sitting around reading girlie magazines or making believe he was straightening out his combs and scissors and razors, while Davidoff finished each day with a crick in his back and his knees scraped raw.

From the minute they got to Camp Hulen, this guy Fast seemed to single Davidoff out for his own brand of special treatment. He went out of his way to torment him. At morning inspections, he'd pass everyone's bunk with barely a glance until he got to Davidoff's. One morning he'd look at his cot, tell him it wasn't tight enough, and rip it apart with his swagger stick. The next morning he'd dump all the toiletries in his foot locker out on the floor, saying they were a sloppy mess. Hardly a day went by without his making an example of Davidoff for one thing or another. But the special punishment, which was really not so special anymore as it was doled out on an almost daily basis, was the latrine detail. It wasn't just a matter of cleaning and mopping the place. Sergeant Fast wanted the cracks between the tiles scrubbed with a toothbrush. He would step up to Davidoff, jutting his jaw into the kid's face as though he were daring him to take a poke at him, and sneer, "Okay, soldier, you are trying my patience!" No matter what was happening, he could always find a reason to fault Al.

They all waited to see Al "Bummy" Davis explode, but Private Davidoff just clenched his teeth and did as he was ordered. Not that any of them would have done differently, but they were disappointed. Everyone wanted to see Sergeant Leonard Fast get what was coming to him.

The Lone Ranger clippety-clopping down Fifth Avenue on Silver would not have been as out of place as Willie Davidoff was walking down the main drag of Palacios, Texas. It's not that no Texan ever wears a navy blue pinstripe suit or slicks his hair back with Vaseline Hair Tonic or wears a slouch hat with the brim turned down to cover his eyes. It's not that no Texan ever has a cigarette dangling almost straight down from his lower lip, and it's not that no Texan's eyelids droop like he's looking at his shoe tips while he's talking to you. But the Texan has not been born and probably never will be—nor would he want to be—who puts all the parts together like Big Gangy.

He walks from the hotel called Hotel to the saloon called Saloon, which he quickly realizes is the major commercial enterprise in this town. The reason he goes to the saloon is not to have a drink or to socialize but because the clerk in the hotel told him he could find a taxi there.

In town for only three hours, Willie has already learned that the big local sport is tobacco-juice spitting and the most difficult thing to come by is a seat on the wooden bench in front of the barbershop. As he enters the saloon, realizing that every eye of every bench warmer is on him, Willie Davidoff comes to the startling conclusion that he is in a town filled with cowboy yentas.

Willie is still having a problem accepting the fact that his kid brother is getting married. When he gets the call last week from Al asking him to come to Texas with Barbara, he tries his best to convince him to wait. He can't picture the kid taking care of a family, not when Willie feels that he still has to take care of the kid.

"Willie, cut the lectures. My mind is made up. I got to get married."

"Why, kid? Whatsa matter, you pregnant?"

"Come on, Willie. I think of her day and night. She's the only girl I ever felt like this about. You know, I just wanna take care of her, walk with her, hold her in my arms."

"I'll get you a cocker spaniel."

Willie knows it before the words are out of his mouth. The kid slams the phone down on him. That makes Willie feel better. When you're two thousand miles away, slamming the phone down takes the place of throwing a punch. And if the kid would take a sock at him, then he must really be in love with this girl. He passes the test. Willie calls the long-distance operator and tells her he was cut off.

When the cab pulls up to the front gate, the MP gives him a pass to the visitors' center. At the visitors' center they ask him what he's doing there; he should be at the Heights, where the basic trainees are. So they give him a pass to the visitors' center at the Heights, where they give him a pass to the headquarters office of the Seventy-second Quarter-master Battalion. As the taxi is not permitted on the base, Willie covers all this ground by foot, and he's beginning to wonder if basic training is any tougher than what he's doing.

He's on his way to the headquarters office when he sees this cluster of long, rectangular wooden buildings with the Seventy-second Quartermaster Battalion logo, and beneath it a company plaque. Two of the buildings in the group are Company A barracks. Willie pulls out a paper with Al's army address and sees that that's the kid's company. Although his pass states in big bold letters that "all areas other than the designated Headquarters Office are unauthorized and off-limits," he shoves it in his pocket with all the other passes and decides he has had enough of army routine. He heads to the closest building, the one that lists Third and Fourth Platoons under Company A.

Frank DeTomi is sweeping up hair from the latrine floor when the screen door opens and in walks this guy who looks more like George Raft than George Raft. It's not that Frankie hasn't seen muscle before— the south Brooklyn waterfront isn't exactly known for its social teas— but he realizes that this guy is a cowboy from Palacios like Frankie is the Barber of Seville.

"You know Albert Davidoff?"

"Yeah. He's cleaning out the grease trap behind the mess hall."

Immediately Willie knows things are not going the way they're supposed to. Al told him he had a three day pass starting Friday night and he was going to be waiting for Willie and Bobbie at the hotel.

"What the hell is he doing cleaning a grease pit? The kid's supposed to be getting married."

"Yeah, I know. We're in the same platoon."

At first Frankie tells himself it wouldn't be a bad idea to mind his own business, but after thinking it over for three and a half seconds he decides it is his business. In the next ten minutes, Big Gangy hears how this Sergeant Fast goes out of his way to make life miserable for his kid brother, how he punishes him by giving him every dirty detail, how he intentionally mispronounces his name—Davidowitz, Davinsky, David-the-jerkoff, anything to embarrass him—how he shoves his face right in Al's, like he's daring him to hit him. As he listens, the color slowly drains from Willie's face.

Then Frankie tells him how Al gets showered and dressed before reveille this morning and shows everyone pictures of his girlfriend. "All

317

the guys, even Corporal O'Sullivan, our barracks noncom in charge, wish him luck. Then, just as he's walkin' out, Sergeant Fast, who's standin' around watchin' Al get ready without sayin' a word, gives out with a 'Hold on, soldier. Just where do you think you're going?' Al says, 'I got a weekend pass. I'm going into Palacios.' The sarge says, 'I didn't issue you any pass,' and Al tells him that Captain Harper did. Fast accuses him of going over his head, and Al tells him the truth. 'I don't go to you for nothin' because you and me don't get along too good. Anyhow, my name is listed on the pass list all week, so it's no surprise to you.'"

Willie's face is an expressionless mask.

"Fast calls him a real wiseguy and tells him that Captain Harper didn't know how he was screwin' up all week and that he's going to be pulling KP because of it. Al is about to explode. A few of the guys have to pull him back and try to calm him down. But Fast, he ain't finished yet. 'You're just itching to take a punch at me, soldier. You are just two steps from the stockade.' Then Corporal O'Sullivan—he's not the brightest guy around, but he's pretty decent—he goes over to Fast and whispers to him for a minute, then he comes back to where the guys are holding Al and tells him to hang tough for today and he'll have his pass for tomorrow. Al tells him his girl is in the hotel in Palacios and she'll be worried sick, so O'Sullivan promises he'll go over personally and let her know she'll see him tomorrow, that somethin' special came up on the post today. Right now a couple of the boys are hangin' around by Al to make sure he don't do anything crazy."

"I want you to do me a favor and take me to this Sergeant Fast."

The look on Willie's face makes Frankie feel sick to his stomach, and he swears to himself that starting tomorrow he practices keeping his mouth shut. But this is still today. "Hey, you don't wanna meet this guy."

"Believe me, I do wanna meet this guy, so bad it hurts."

Frankie is wishing himself as far away from Camp Hulen as he can possibly get when he looks out the window and sees Sergeant Leonard Fast walking down the path to the barracks.

This was not the wedding Barbara Kovsky had dreamed of having. She had pictured herself walking down the aisle of an elegant flower-bedecked chapel in a flowing traditional bridal gown, escorted by her parents, in a ceremony conducted by a rabbi to the accompaniment of the golden voice of a magnificent cantor. Neither was Al Davis the groom her parents had dreamed of having as their son-in-law.

Standing before the medicine cabinet mirror, which was the only mirror in her hotel room, Bobbie stared at what the Texas humidity had done to her $5.95 wedding-special hairdo from Elsie's Beauty Salon on Rockaway Avenue, and tried her best to refurbish it by brushing out the frizzy little curls. She gazed at her image, and like the teenager she was, she wondered what Albert Davis saw in her. Sure, there was the pretty oval face with full lips and doe-like hazel eyes, but there were plenty of pretty girls in Brownsville. Was a pretty face enough to make someone fall in love?

Al Davis had much better vision than Barbara Kovsky gave him credit for. Besides seeing the beauty of her face, he saw the beauty inside her. He liked the way she always had a smile for shop owners and clerks. She never laughed so loud that people took notice, but she always had that smile. Then there was the way she was with Chotchke Charlie. She had him beaming from ear to ear when she asked him on a walk to Lincoln Terrace Park, and when she got him a bag of peanuts to feed the pigeons, he was so ecstatic Al was afraid he would fly off with them. Some of the things he loved and appreciated were things that would have made his buddies run the other way. "Bobbie Kovsky? Nobody gets to first base with her," one of the guys warned. And Al couldn't picture Stutz being happy if his date told him she had an eleven o'clock curfew.

At the age of seventeen, Bobbie Kovsky had already received two marriage proposals, enough to make any young lady blush with pride. True, both were from Al, but on the other hand, neither was from Al. First it was Shorty who proposed for Al on the docks at Sheepshead Bay. Then, last week, Al calls and starts stammering and stuttering his way through a whole prologue, explaining how the army is okay but it's not what it's cracked up to be, how he misses all his friends, his family, and most of all her, how happy and proud he is about guys not getting to first base. The more he goes on the more nervous he sounds and the more nervous Bobbie feels, but she knows this is leading to somewhere, and she is determined to stick it out. Just when she is sure that the critical moment has arrived, Fate intervenes in the form of static.

Al can't believe it. He's finally, painfully, worked his way up to where he wanted to be, and now Bobbie can't hear him. He starts clicking the receiver furiously.

This does not bring an end to the static, but it does bring results.

"This is the operator. May I be of service?"

"Operator, this is a very important call, and all of a sudden we can't hear each other."

"There is a temporary disturbance on the line due to weather conditions. Would you wish to make your call later?"

"No, I am in the army. I do not know when I will be able to get to a phone again. I would like you to please fix the phone."

"I cannot do that. Can you hear me clearly, Texas?"

"Yeah, I can hear you, but I can't hear my girl."

"Can you hear me clearly, New York?"

"Yes, I can."

"But you cannot hear each other. Is that the problem?"

"Of course that's the problem!"

"Would you like a refund, sir. I will take—"

"No, I don't want no refund. I wanna talk to my girl. Look, do me a favor. Tell her somethin', will ya? It's an emergency. Tell her she's the only girl for me and I want to marry her."

"Miss, the party in Texas says you are the only girl for him and he wants to marry you."

"He does?"

"I will verify that. Sir, the party in New York inquires whether you do."

"Whether I do what?"

Although she does not wish to seem rude, Bobbie feels it is time to interrupt. "No, no, operator—"

"Sir, she said 'No, no.' "

Al can barely be heard. "She did?"

"Operator, please tell him yes, I want to marry him."

"Sir, the party in New York now says, 'Yes, I want to marry him.' "

"Wow! Great! Terrific! I love both of you!"

"Thank you, sir, but that will be an additional seventy-five cents."

That was Al for you. Nothing about him was ordinary. From the first moment she saw him, looking up from her bed at Kings County Hospital, Bobbie knew he was going to be someone special in her life. The Al Davis she knew wasn't the tough, bullying wiseguy she'd read about in the papers. The Al Davis she knew was a guy who would buy a carload of presents for the neighborhood kids just because he wanted to see them have a good time. Shorty told her that you couldn't have a better, more loyal friend than Al. On the few occasions when she went up to the gym, she saw how respectful he was to the managers and trainers. Mr. Burston smiled when he told her he only wished his own children showed him the respect that Albert did. When she asked him how good a prizefighter Al was, he laughed, and said, "Not bad, but you should see him sell fruit from his pushcart. The best, the very best."

But to Bobbie, the most revealing things about Al were his secret desires. Two or three times he took her to a small luncheonette on Amboy Street just so he could be around the actors from the Yiddish theater who hung out there. That was when he confessed to her that he used to dream of being a great cantor. Later he showed her his record collection of cantorials and Jewish folk music, but she couldn't get him to sing for her—not yet. And when she saw how Chotchke Charlie adored him, she knew that her boyfriend was a very special and complex person.

Bobbie's biggest problem was convincing her parents of that, but she knew it was just a matter of time. Her mother would ask, "A nice boy?" And she would answer, "Yes, Momma, a very nice boy." Her father would sit and read his newspaper.

Then, a day or so later, "The same boy again? What's his name?"

"Albert, Momma. Albert Davidoff."

"Davidoff? It's a nice name. Did you hear, Poppa? The boy that Barbara is going out with so much, his name is Davidoff. Herbert Davidoff."

"No, Momma, Albert, not Herbert."

"Davidoff?" Her father puts his paper down and gets up from his chair. "Is his father a cutter?"

"He has a candy store, Poppa. A very nice candy store."

"And this Albert, he goes to school with you?"

At first she wishes there were another newspaper she could give her father, but she knows the moment of truth had arrived. "No, Poppa, he works. He's twenty."

"Twenty. That's not so bad. He works with his father in the candy store?"

"Well, he helps out there sometimes, but he has his own job. He's a sportsman, Poppa, an athlete."

Her father cups his chin in his hand, and the shadow of a frown forms. "That's a job? A sportsman is a job?"

"He does very well, Poppa. He earns a lot of money. He even bought his parents a house."

At this her father nods his head in approval, and she thinks that maybe it won't be so bad after all.

"What is he, a baseballer like Hank Greenberg?"

"No, Poppa." Her eyes light up. "He's a prizefighter like Benny Leonard." One thing she knows, Benny Leonard is everybody's hero. As she watches the frown return to her father's face, she knows that Benny Leonard is almost everybody's hero.

"Did he fight Joe Louis?" Poppa asks.

Momma clasps her hands and looks at her husband with newfound admiration. "Oy, would you believe the man? First a Hank Greenberg, now a Joe Louis. Who has so much knowledge in one head?"

"No, Poppa. Joe Louis is too big. He's a heavyweight, and Al . . . Albert is a welterweight."

"Too big?" Poppa shakes his head. "If David said that about Goliath we'd all be scrubbing floors in Persia."

"He's really very good, Poppa. His picture is in the newspapers a lot, and next month he's fighting the champion, the week before Thanksgiving." Barbara decides there is no point in postponing the inevitable. "Would you like to see a picture of him from the paper?"

"Such a celebrity you're going out with?" Momma marvels.

Poppa looks at the picture for a good couple of minutes. "Davis . . . Davis . . . Davis is not Davidoff. This boyfriend, he got a bunch of names?"

"No, Poppa. Davis is the name he uses for prizefighting."

Seeing the lines in his forehead turn into furrows, Barbara knows her father is deep in thought. She holds her breath and waits. It is not a long wait.

"This is the one who's Big Gangy's brother? This is the one they call Bummy?"

"He's not like that, Poppa. He's a fine person."

" 'He's a fine person.' Listen to her, Momma. 'He's a fine person.' He's such a fine person, he's from a family of gangsters!"

"It's not true. People make up stories. You can't believe everything you read in a newspaper, Poppa."

"I don't read it in the newspaper. I hear it from people, people I trust."

"And they hear it from people you don't know."

"It is not open for discussion. You are not to see him anymore."

"Poppa, I love you and I've always listened to you, but now I'm old enough to know what I'm doing."

"You're old enough to know what you're doing? I got news for you. Seventeen is still a child."

"A child? I have news for *you*, Poppa. I've been wearing a brassiere for four years now. I am not a child."

"How dare you use such language in this house! Did we bring you up to talk filth?"

"Filth? What kind of filth? You mean brassiere? That's filth?"

"Again? After I tell you, you use such a word again?"

Barbara doesn't question that her parents love her and want to protect her, but the old ways of the shtetl don't always make sense to her. Fortunately, her mother, who usually plays a silent role except when it comes to housekeeping, knows when to intervene.

"Poppa, we got to understand. It's a different world. Here they're so modern it's okay to talk about underwear." Turning to her daughter, she smiles and pats her cheek, sighing. "My precious shainkeit. Don't you know how much we love you? For you we want the best because you deserve the best. We always have this dream of you finding a wonderful young man. That will be our one true joy and happiness."

Bobbie embraces her mother and father and kisses them each on the cheek. "Then you've found your happiness, because I've found a wonderful young man."

What do you do when you're all alone in a small, dusty Texas army town on a Saturday night? That's what Barbara Kovsky was asking herself after this Corporal O'Sullivan, who just left about ten minutes ago, told her that Albert wouldn't be getting off until tomorrow because something unexpected came up at the base.

She flopped down on the edge of the bed, as there was no place else to flop. She wanted to cry, but she knew it was bad luck to cry on your wedding day. Adding to her misery was the discovery that the scarred Bakelite Philco radio on the chest of drawers played only two stations. The one from San Antonio had cowboys singing to cows, and the one from Houston sounded like cows singing to cowboys. Remembering that it wasn't going to be her wedding day after all, she pulled out a tissue and permitted the tears to flow from her eyelids and roll down her cheeks.

It would have been understandable if at a time of such despair Bobbie chose to make a wish, which was exactly what she was contemplating. Not being a self-seeking person, she was willing to settle for a very simple wish, such as getting one single New York station like WEAF on the Philco radio. When she closed her eyes, as much to blot away the tears as to make her wish, there was another knock at the front door, and she wondered if there was going to be a minor miracle in the form of a bellhop bringing her a shortwave radio. She opened her eyes and ran to the door.

"Al! I don't believe it!" she cried as Private Albert Davidoff hugged her and whirled her around. It was a major miracle.

Frankie DeTomi is busy cleaning his tools of the trade so he can close up for the day when the screen door opens and George Raft walks in. "Kid," he says, "don't put your stuff away, I need a trim. I'm going to a wedding."

15

Nineteen forty-one becomes the year of "Chinky shows" in Brownsville. In many street games and debates where there was no official referee, "Chinky shows" was the preferred and peaceful way of resolving disputes. Opposing participants would interlock pinkies and call out "Chinky shows," which simply meant "another chance," "do-over." The general belief is that the expression evolved from a Confucian-like cartoon character in the *Daily News* called Ching Chow who each day stated a wise proverb.

It was "Chinky shows" time for Happy Maione, Frank "Dasher" Abbandando, Pittsburgh Phil Strauss and Buggsy Goldstein—and, also, for Al "Bummy" Davis. When their conviction for the murder of Whitey Rudnick was overturned on a technicality, Happy and Dasher went to trial a second time. Happy very eloquently explained how it was impossible for him to have been involved because he was at his grandmother's deathbed and no one can be at two places at the same time. And as Dasher's lawyer informed the court, "Ballplayers don't kill people," Dasher nodded in agreement. The jury didn't. They were found guilty again.

Buggsy Goldstein and Harry Strauss appealed their conviction for the murder of Puggy Feinstein. On April 25, 1941, the Court of Appeals upheld the original murder-one verdict and Buggsy had a message. "Just tell that rat Reles I'll be waiting for him. Maybe it'll be in Hell!"

Al Davis wasn't facing the electric chair like the other four. He drew a life sentence from the New York State Athletic Commission and he, too, wanted a chance to do it over again. He already had his second chance in the United States Army when, right after the wedding, Sergeant Leonard Fast requested a transfer to another company and Private Albert Davidoff was promoted from permanent KP to an assistant boxing instructor for the post. But when Lew Burston calls and asks him if he would like a rematch with Fritzie Zivic at the Polo Grounds for the Army Relief Fund, this was the second chance he dared not even dream about.

On Bradford Street you'd think the war was over, only it hadn't even started yet. But that didn't matter because the conquering hero was returning. There were no punchball games, no stickball games, because all the kids were out on the street waving flags and waiting for Private Al Davis to come home.

Inside 756 Bradford, as the smell of potato pancakes drifted through the open window, the two Mrs. Davidoffs were running around the kitchen like kids playing hide-and-seek. Bobbie was chasing her mother-in-law, pleading with her to get dressed, but Rose Davidoff insisted she had to make sure the latkes came out right.

"Al will be here any second now. He's not going to care about food. It's you he'll want to see. Now go freshen up. Make yourself even more beautiful than you are."

Hands on hips, Rose smiled at her daughter-in-law. "Barbara, darling, you be the beauty. I'll be the cook."

Just then the honking of car horns and the ting-a-ling of bicycle bells signaled that Rose Davidoff would be greeting her son just the way she was. Al strode into the kitchen a few minutes later and dropped his duffel bag to the floor as Bobbie threw herself into his arms. Rose beamed.

"That uniform is hanging from you! They don't feed you? Come, sit down. I happen to have your favorite. Latkes!"

"No, I can't, Ma. No fried foods. I'm in training."

"You're in training? That's what I want to talk to you about. What do you need him for, that Zivic? You need his fingers in your eye again?"

Barbara nodded as she listened to her mother-in-law saying things she still didn't have the courage to say. Al ignored Rose's question and popped two latkes into his mouth even though he knew he shouldn't. He did a lot of things he shouldn't, but the return bout against Zivic wasn't one of them. He was sure it was right for him.

Because of his suspension, Al didn't think he'd ever get another crack at Zivic, but Johnny Attell kept pushing the idea of a Zivic-Davis rematch with a big chunk of the proceeds going to the Army Relief Fund, which was why the army was willing to give Al the time to train. The Boxing Commission gave its approval, knowing they would be put in a bad light if they refused, but they stipulated that the only way Davis's corner men from the first fight would get into this one was by buying a ticket. In addition to sidelining Froike and Burston, they handpicked trainer Ray Arcel. When a fighter had Ray in his corner it was like having his mother, his father, and a Saint Bernard. Ray Arcel was the standard by which all other trainers were measured.

When Arcel gets the call from Lew Burston asking him to join Al Davis's team, he doesn't want any part of it. The first thing he does is tell Burston that his schedule is too heavy for him to handle Davis, and the next thing he tells him is that with the kid trying to scrape off almost eight months of rust in just thirty days they may as well have him fighting windmills with a switchblade as put him in against a slick article like Zivic, who's been fighting regularly. Burston, who knows a thing or two about human nature, tells Ray that the kid wants this fight no matter what, and asks him to just meet the kid.

That's all it takes, a face-to-face meeting with Al Davis, for Ray to learn what so many other people have learned: that all the stories about a dirty fighter and a mob-connected bum, all the barbs in the columns of Dan Parker, Jack Miley, and Stanley Frank, are no more real than the exploits of Joe Palooka. Ray and Al don't talk too much about the fight. Al tells him how proud he is to wear the uniform of the U.S. Army and how he's learning to take orders and what teamwork is all about. They talk about selling fruit and vegetables from a pushcart and how it feels to take on the responsibilities of a married man. Al tells Ray what a great place Brownsville is and how he wants to raise a family there and how he worries about his parents and wants to take care of them. Suddenly Ray Arcel's schedule gets a little lighter and he decides it's time to get down to work.

There's a lot to be done, but first Ray has to work on the undoing. Marching ten miles with a sixty-pound backpack while you're singing "I got a girl in Kansas City" may strengthen the legs and build stamina for guys used to sitting around pushing a pencil all day, but a fighter needs elasticity and spring in his legs; Al would have been better off hitching a ride. And when it came to diet, Ray tried not to think of chipped beef in cream gravy, chicken-fried steak, or even the healthier supplements, such as green salad with bacon-dripping dressing.

Ray didn't waste any time in packing Al off to the country to train. Al couldn't get over how the roosters woke up and started their cock-a-doodle-dooing at exactly five-fifteen each morning. There was no question in his mind about the time, because he'd already been out running the country roads for half an hour and as soon as he heard the crowing he would look at his watch. He looked at his watch a lot because he was not enjoying these morning runs, which seemed to be uphill all the way. Not that they were any worse than pushups and situps.

Still, Al enjoyed the time he spent at Billy West's small training facility in Woodstock, New York, for the simple reason that people liked him. Woodstock was a small Catskills town where the rent was cheap and the scenery beautiful. It wasn't much bigger than Palacios, and the people were almost as strange, but not in the same way. There was no tobacco-juice spitting in Woodstock, and the men didn't sit around on benches watching the grass grow. Instead, they drew pictures of the grass growing. With its live-and-let-live philosophy, Woodstock was an ideal place for struggling artists, sculptors, and writers to call home. It was probably the only town in New York State where the art supply store raked in more than the tavern.

In the late afternoon, between the end of his workout and supper, Al liked to walk into Woodstock with Ray or Lew. He had a natural gift for shmoozing that captivated his bohemian neighbors. In a very short time this unschooled roughneck from Brownsville, whose favorite artist was Hype Igoe, was sporting a beret and turning into Woodstock's most ardent admirer of the arts. Ray and Lew would stare in wonder as whoever they passed in town had a wave and a few friendly words for the kid. Sometimes artists called him over to take a look at their paintings and ask his opinion, knowing there would be a "Wow!" or a "Jeez, you really captured that!" They knew he meant it, and they loved him for it.

A couple of weeks into his training, Al came back from his run one day accompanied by a shaggy brown dog that was maybe hoping for a scrap of food or maybe just enjoyed Al's company, like everyone else in town. Sadly, Ray saw, the dog was breathing a lot easier than his fighter. While the mutt jumped all over Al, showering him with saliva, Al told Ray how a few miles into the run a big German shepherd hurdles a five-foot stone fence and goes for him.

"Ya had to see it. I'm thinkin' I'm dog meat when this little sonuva-gun darts up between us and starts clawin' and snappin' until the shepherd turns tail and runs off." Al bent down to pat the ecstatic dog. "Could you believe it? The little guy really likes me."

Ray Arcel could believe it.

On the last day of his life, Martin Goldstein made the tears flow. This time, though, the tearstained cheeks were those of his aged father, Jacob Goldstein, his wife, Betty, and his brother, Karl. They wept as they left the prison that afternoon. They wept because he refused to see them, and they wept for a person they could not believe was the same person the whole world knew as Buggsy Goldstein. The jaunty funnyman who wisecracked all through his trial and his stay at Sing Sing had suddenly forgotten his punch lines.

When the guards told him that his family was there, he grabbed the bars of his cell door and screamed, "Send them away! I don't wanna see anybody." Then he started throwing himself around the cell, tearing off his clothes and pounding his head against the hard stone walls. As the guards raced in to restrain him, he flung himself onto his cot, crying about how Governor Lehman "won't even gimme a break." Buggsy Goldstein, who never once commuted a sentence that was imposed by Abe Reles or himself, expected a lot more than he ever granted.

Martin "Buggsy" Goldstein walked his last mile, which in reality was only about twenty yards, without an ounce of the swagger and arrogance of his walks through the streets of Brownsville. The switch was thrown at exactly 11:00 P.M., and Buggsy became a bad memory.

Harry Strauss had a much quieter day than his partner. His sanity recently restored, he spent the afternoon with his girlfriend, Evelyn Mittleman, undoubtedly reminiscing, because there was not much to discuss about the future. At nine minutes after eleven, Harry Strauss was pronounced dead at the age of thirty-three. He never did get to see Pittsburgh.

It was not unusual for stomachs to do flip-flops when people went to Coney Island. The Cyclone, the Parachute Jump, and Steeplechase Park could all produce intestinal acrobatics. But Kitty Reles didn't visit any of these attractions. She got the same results just by entering the lobby of the Half Moon Hotel. It was Coney Island's largest hotel, situated on the boardwalk at West Twenty-eighth Street, and with Abe Reles, Allie "Tick-Tock" Tannenbaum, and a couple of other cooperative members of Murder, Inc. housed there as guests of the state, it rivaled the Chambers of Horror or any of the freak shows on Surf Avenue, the Midway of Coney Island.

It was Kitty's first visit since the day after Buggsy and Pittsburgh Phil were electrocuted. She had come that day, nearly three weeks ago, expecting to have to comfort Abe over the deaths of his friends, but when she got to his room he couldn't stop gloating and laughing about how Buggsy came apart at the end. That was when she realized that she couldn't stomach that laugh, or his smugness or his sneer, or the way he gloried in his role as O'Dwyer's star stool pigeon. And he walked like a duck! What had been so attractive to her as a teenager was repulsive to her now, a mother in her early thirties with two small children to consider. She had done a lot of serious thinking since then. She had decided that her children deserved better. And so did she.

Now she got off the elevator at the sixth floor and waited for the guard to open the steel door to the east wing. That section of the Half Moon had been converted into an impregnable fortress, not so much to keep the witnesses in—they weren't going anywhere, not when every hired gun in New York was looking to collect the mob's bounty on them—but to keep the more daring of the hit men out. She followed the guard to Abe's room and found him sprawled on his bed, reading the paper.

Abe had plans to go into the witness protection program. Kitty tried to be tactful. She told him that it wasn't fair to tear the children away from their friends and the life they were accustomed to. "You'll be running and hiding the rest of your life, Abe. Is that what you want for your family?"

Abe Reles understood what was really being said to him, and he didn't like it. "You got the chutzpah to say to me—to me, after all I gave you, after I take you from the slums, from the gutter, and put you in a beautiful house in Flatbush—that you don't wanna stick by me when things get a little tough?"

"After all you gave me? You don't think I earned it? Anyhow, it's not me or you that counts now. Think of what's best for your children." She looked out the window because she couldn't stand looking at him. She could see the crowded beach, people splashing in the ocean and building castles in the sand.

"Go home and think about what you just said. You'll come back to your senses. And next time you come up here, bring me up a couple hot dogs from Nathan's."

There were not many things that aroused Lepke's interest anymore, but he could not mask his look of surprise as he sat down opposite Frankie Carbo in his New York City jail cell. They spoke in soft whispers, keeping an eye on the guard standing at the other end of the long table. If Lepke was impressed when Carbo told him how a little green grease on the guard's palm helped convince him that he was part of Lepke's legal team, he was awestruck when he heard that California had dropped the case against Carbo for the murder of Harry Greenberg.

"You know how it is, Lep. A few jurors get cold feet. Who knows what they're afraid of."

Lepke recovered himself quickly. "Frank, there's a lot of money out there on the street that belongs to us. Anastasia has the list. I don't want those bastards thinking they can get away without paying us."

It was now Carbo's turn to be impressed. He grew up with Lepke, so he knew how tough the bookish-looking mob boss really was, but he still couldn't get over the fact that the most important thing on Lepke's mind was business.

"I'll work with Al. Don't worry, Louie, we'll collect. But what about you?"

"As long as Reles is alive, I'm dead. Can we get Reles?"

"Impossible, unless we make it a bloodbath on the street while they're transferring him."

"Work with Anastasia, Frank. Get our money and don't worry about me."

As Frankie Carbo left, he couldn't imagine what Lepke wanted the money for. Neither could Lepke, but business was business.

Carbo got together with Big Al Anastasia in the back room of a Brooklyn waterfront bar on Columbia Street. He was there only out of loyalty to Lepke, because he had no desire to get involved with strong-arming guys to pay their debts—until he came across the item "Al Davis, 756 Bradford Street—2 G's." There was a notation next to it: "Happy M. will handle."

The $2,000 in question was what remained of the $20,000 "fine" imposed on Bummy for slapping Happy around after the Canzoneri fight. Reles had reduced the amount, perhaps in a moment of magnanimity, or perhaps on orders from Lepke. Either way, it was all the same to Bummy. The way he figured it, Reles was out twenty grand before and now he was only out two grand, so he was eighteen grand ahead.

Carbo raised his shot of Canadian Club. "I'll take care of this one," he said, clinking glasses with Anastasia. "Salud!"

Stutz stood at the dressing room door like Lew Burston asked, making sure no one came in. He thought about the day he'd gone to the city morgue to identify some stiff from the poolroom who wound up with a stiletto in his gut. He'd never been in a quieter place, or a more depressing one. Bummy Davis's dressing room reminded him of that day. He snuck a look at his friend and he wanted to cry. It had nothing to do with the double C-note he'd dropped. He couldn't care less about that. He just felt so damn bad.

Maybe he should have started worrying at the weigh-in, where he expects sparks. Instead Fritzie and Al do everything but the waltz. Fritzie eyes Al's soldier suit and says, "You look pretty good in a uniform, Al." Instead of giving him a shot in the kisser, Al says with a smile, "I got you to thank for it, Fritzie. You put me in it." That is his high point. From there it is all downhill.

The dressing room was like a Turkish bath. Stutz saw that Ray Arcel had taken his shirt off. He watched him bathe Al's puffy, reddened face with a cold washcloth, a Q-tip dangling from his mouth like a toothpick. He cut a gauze pad, soaked it in peroxide, and taped it over the cut on Al's lip. The only sound was of the scissor snipping the gauze.

Ray Arcel was not an I-told-you-so sort of guy, but he had to be thinking that way as he repaired the battered face as best he could. Nobody wanted to listen when he said the kid needed a lot more time than a month. After all, didn't a sledgehammer left hook equalize everything? Just like a home-run hitter could knock the ball out of the park and turn the game around with one mighty swing? But if the bat didn't connect with the ball, it was just a lot of wind, a strike.

For Fritzie Zivic, the fight was target practice. He jabbed Al's head like he was hitting a speed bag hanging on a swivel, he tore left hooks into the kid's rib cage like he was playing a number on a xylophone, and his overhand right turned Al's legs into strands of spaghetti. Through it all, Al Davis was right there, in front of Zivic, lunging at him, throwing punches and bringing the fight to him. Toward the end of the first round, Zivic caught the kid flush on one of those desperate lunges and felled him like a hunter nailing a charging rhino. Al was struggling to pull himself up at the count of seven when the bell rang.

It was Ray's job to patch, to bring Al back to his senses and instruct him. It was a job he had to do, and he did it well. Too well, because the kid went back out believing he could get his fists to follow his commands, but each seemed to have a mind independent of Al Davis. Every round was worse than the round before. Al's face was cut and battered almost beyond recognition. He staggered and reeled, but he kept coming forward, throwing punches and throwing some more. There was something almost insane about his tenacity, how he kept coming after Zivic through it all.

In the crowd there were rumblings of grudging respect. "Is the kid crazy?" "What's holding him up?" They'd come to see Al "Bummy" Davis get a horsewhipping—some things even the uniform of the United

States Army couldn't erase—but now that they were seeing it, it turned their stomachs. Suddenly, they were feeling sorry for the beast. And as the beast stood up under the flogging, holding its ground with honor and determination, pity turned to admiration. In the fifth round, when Al finally landed his left hook and sent Zivic reeling into the ropes, the crowd let out a wild cheer, but he didn't have the strength to follow up.

Somewhere in the middle of the sixth round, Ray caught a glimpse of Al's young wife running from her seat with a handkerchief to her face, unable to watch anymore. He pitied her, but he also envied her. He wished he could run too.

Arcel told Al after the ninth round that he was going to stop the fight, that there would be another, better day. The kid leaned forward on his stool. "Don't do that to me, please. Nobody ever made me quit, and this bum ain't either. I'm gonna catch him, I'm tellin' ya." Ray Arcel was too intelligent and responsible to let himself be swayed by a beaten fighter's prideful pleas, but there was such urgency to Davis's voice— the kid believed what he was saying, he believed in himself, he believed he was going to get Zivic. Referee Arthur Donovan came to the corner. There wasn't a better referee in the business, but even he was persuaded to let the bout go on.

Fighting strictly from memory and instinct, Al Davis came after Zivic with everything he had in the tenth round. Al's punches were slow-motion heaves without their sting, while Zivic's were quick, crisp whip-lashes that hurt Al but couldn't halt his continual barreling forward. Then they both unleashed left hooks, and Al's was still arcing in the air when Zivic's plunged deep into his solar plexus, paralyzing him. It was then that Arthur Donovan stopped the fight, wrapping his arms protectively around Al Davis.

Right after the fight, Bill Corum, who shared the WJZ mike with Don Dunphy, climbed into the ring to interview Zivic and Davis. It was an interview that nobody would have blamed the kid for ducking. Instead, without making any excuses, he apologized through cut and swollen lips. "I'm only sorry that I couldn't do what I really wanted for the army," he said, and went on to hail his once-hated rival. When Corum interrupted to tell him that he fought a great, courageous fight, he shook his head and said, "He's a better fighter. Good luck to him."

. . .

Willie Davidoff had been warned by the Boxing Commission not to go near the ring. He didn't, but he might as well have been right in the middle of it the way each punch that slammed into Bummy registered on him. When the fight ended, he took his father by the elbow and headed for the dressing room.

Stutz always thought that the only difference between Big Gangy and a stone was that a stone never had to go for a haircut, but when he opened the dressing room door for Max and Willie, it was no stone he was looking at. Lips trembling, Willie walked over and patted his brother on the back. The kid looked up at him. Maybe he tried to smile, but his face was so swollen it was impossible to tell.

"Hey, Willie, I feel so friggin' lousy. I let everyone down."

Tenderness was not Willie Davidoff's main suit, but he ran his fingers through the kid's hair and cleared his throat to speak. Arcel beat him to the punch.

"That's the second time you said that tonight, and I don't want to hear it again." Arcel put his hand under the kid's chin and raised his face so that their eyes locked. "You fought a fight tonight that very few other men would have been capable of. It's no special feat to look good when you're throwing punches and landing them. But to do what I saw you do tonight, to stand up under an attack from a world champion and continue fighting back the way you did—Al Davis, that's the mark of a very special prizefighter. I want you to know something, and I mean it. I was proud to work your corner tonight. It was a privilege."

"Thanks, Ray, you're an okay guy." Al turned to Willie. "Where's Bobbie?"

It was Max who answered. "We told her to take a cab and go home. It's better, we thought, she don't see you till tomorrow."

"I'm gonna shower and go home."

"You're going to need some stitches first," Ray told him.

While Al was in the shower, Max walked over to Arcel. "I was so excited with how he was doing as a fighter. Ich k'velen. But now maybe it's enough. Maybe he should stop."

Ray looked at Max. He was hoping that Willie would say something,

but Willie just stood there as though he too wanted to hear what Ray had to say.

"Let me ask you something, Mr. Davis. What do you do? For a living, that is."

"It's Davidoff. What do I do? I got a candy store, and if Al wanted he could come in and take over. I don't think that would be for him, though, to tell the truth."

"I agree with you one hundred per cent. So, do you make a good egg cream?"

"If I made a bad egg cream would I have customers?"

Arcel smiled. "And how do you make a good egg cream?"

"U-Bet chocolate syrup, about an inch and a half, the same amount of milk, and finally, fill up with seltzer and stir."

"Tell me, Mr. Davidoff, suppose you accidentally removed the cap of the seltzer bottle and didn't replace it for a couple days?"

"To this question I think you know the answer. The gas would be gone. It wouldn't be good."

"And if you used it to make an egg cream?"

"I wouldn't."

"Let's say you did because you didn't know it had been sitting around open."

"It would be flat. No fizz."

Ray put down the small satchel he had been packing his equipment in and placed a hand on Max's shoulder. "I don't think you'd close up your candy store because of that. I think you would make sure to use a good bottle of seltzer next time. Right?"

Max just nodded, but the expression on his face showed that he knew this wasn't really about making a soda.

"Max, that's what your son was like tonight—an egg cream with flat seltzer. Next time we'll make sure he has fizz."

It was after 2:00 A.M. when Al got home, because he had to wait for his lip to be stitched up, which was a hell of a lot more painful than any of the punches he took in the fight. Bobbie was sitting at the kitchen table waiting for him. They had a two-room apartment in the basement of

the house he bought for his parents, and as far as he was concerned, he would live there with her forever, but Bobbie wanted them to have their own place when he got out of the army. Al couldn't understand her logic but he didn't argue about it.

As soon as he walked through the door she came to him. Her eyes were red and puffy. His were even redder and puffier. Bobbie raised herself on her toes and cupped her husband's face in her hands and gently tried to kiss away the pain. For the briefest of seconds he pulled back. To Bummy Davis, tenderness meant weakness. Then he leaned forward and pressed his cheek to hers. He didn't want the warm, feathery brushing of her lips ever to stop. He wanted the sweet smell of her body to flood his nostrils. He wanted to feel the steady throbbing of her heart against his chest. He wanted to close his eyes and ears to everything around him and lose himself in the small wonderful universe of his young bride. If it was weakness, it was also his strength, and he craved it.

They slept through the night and most of the next day in each other's arms. The phone rang. They didn't answer it. There were knocks at their door. They didn't answer them. When they finally woke up, Bobbie made her plea.

"But I gotta fight, Bobbie," Al said. "It's what I do. It's what I am."

"You mean it's what you want to do. Nobody is born a prizefighter."

"No, I wasn't born a prizefighter. I became one. But it's like it chose me, not like I chose it." He put his arms around her and pulled her close. "It's my life, Bobbie. It's what I am, what I do, and it's not a matter of do I want to—I got to."

"I love you, Al. I can't stand seeing you hurt like this."

"It never happened before, not like this, and it ain't ever gonna happen again."

"You didn't want it to happen tonight, but it did."

Al smiled at her. "But I said it won't happen again."

Esther Barbara Kovsky Davidoff Davis capitulated. She convinced herself that she fell in love with and married Al Davis, prizefighter, and to try to change him wouldn't be fair. For his part, Al did everything he could to put Bobbie at ease. The only problem was that even if he'd convinced her, he still wasn't convinced himself. The fighter is always the last one to know that he's been betrayed by his body, that he simply isn't in the shape he should be in. All Al Davis knew was that he gave it everything he had and it wasn't enough.

Al looked at the date on the morning edition of the *Daily News* and wondered why that date looked so familiar. Then he remembered. It was the same date that was on his train ticket back to Texas—the ticket that he was thinking of not using. Al had become a pretty conscientious soldier. He knew about AWOL, desertion, and the stockade. But Private Davidoff did not want to go back and face his buddies, the guys who sent him off with such resounding cheers and expected him to come back a winner, just as he'd promised them he would. He wanted the security of Brownsville, the refuge of his own home, the comfort of his mother's voice and Bobbie's devotion.

As he shaved, he looked at himself in the bathroom mirror and was able to recognize himself for the first time since the fight. The swelling had gone down, the bruises and purple blotches had faded, and except for the black threads holding his lip together, it was pretty much the face he was accustomed to seeing. The stitches—they had to be taken out! It was the closest he could come to a reason why he couldn't use that train ticket yet. It wasn't a good reason—stitches could be removed in Texas too—but at least it was a reason.

Al decided to walk to Beth-El Hospital, which was slightly more than a mile away. He felt the walk would clear his head. His route took him to Van Sinderen Avenue, which was just about the halfway point to the hospital from Bradford Street. Van Sinderen was shrouded by the elevated tracks of the BMT Canarsie line, and whatever couldn't fit in someone's garbage pail usually wound up there. As it bisected Brownsville, it had to be passed going east or west, but it was a place most people wanted to avoid.

However, not everyone steered clear of Van Sinderen. To Chotchke Charlie, it was a scavenger's paradise. He would tie a handkerchief over his nose and mouth to cut down on the smell and spend hours picking through the garbage for something to add to his collection of rubber bands, tin foil, and trinkets. Today the July sun was baking the entire area, even though its rays couldn't penetrate the maze of overhead train tracks, and the smell was overpowering. Charlie was just putting all his stuff in one large potato sack when he almost jumped out of his skin at what sounded like a train crashing down from the tracks above him.

The first thought that crossed Al's mind when the guy asked him for some change was that he was dressed too well to be a panhandler, but who was he to make such judgments? He tossed the guy a quarter. "You cheap no-good fuck!" the guy yelled. "You think I'm gonna settle for a two bits? Shove it up your ass!" He flung the quarter at Al and started trotting up Van Sinderen Avenue. Al knew he should just chalk the creep off as a screwball and continue on his way to Beth-El, and if he hadn't been a Davidoff that's what he would have done. Instead, he clenched his fists and raced down Van Sinderen, sidestepping cans and bottles, leaping over cartons and piles of rags, his mind set on teaching a punk a lesson in manners.

He had just passed the corner of New Lots Avenue when six rats popped out of the garbage. Two of them he recognized as members of Happy Maione's Ocean Hill gang. The other four he didn't know, but he felt that no introduction was going to be necessary. For the sake of simplicity, he dubbed them Ugly and Uglier, on up to Ugliest. It was Uglier Still, the one putting on the brass knuckles, who spat out, "Two grand gets you through the turnstile, Davis. You been welchin' long enough."

Al figured that three of these bums against him would be a pretty even fight, so two-to-one odds wasn't so terrible. He didn't bother to factor in the brass knuckles or the bottles and chains they were holding as he threw himself at the one who tossed the quarter back at him.

Chotchke Charlie was greatly relieved to see that no train was tumbling down on him, but he still wondered what was causing all that loud, crashing noise. He was afraid to find out, but he was more afraid not to, because his was a world filled with goblins and monsters of all kinds. He carefully put down the bag containing his day's hoard and scampered over the piles of debris in the direction of the sounds. As he looked down from a high mound just on the north side of New Lots Avenue, Charlie's breath caught in his chest.

Al flew forward, lashing out, tearing flesh and crunching bone. His fury raged through his veins and flooded his brain, stripping it of reason and fear. His two fists inflicted devastating damage, but two fists against six guys with a small arsenal can do only so much. A bottle caught him from behind and he pitched forward. As he fell his fists were still flailing away. Like a pack of hyenas, the Ocean Hill boys pounced on him, swinging at his prone body with whatever they had, no longer thinking of collecting a debt but looking to devour a carcass.

The scream was so sudden, so shrill and piercing, that all six of them felt like an electric current was running from the soles of their feet to their scalps. "Boomy! Boomy!" They thought it was a woman, but what they saw racing toward them was a short, bowlegged madman with his face covered by a white bandanna, so they decided not to think at all and just get the hell away from there as quickly as their feet would take them.

"Boomy? Boomy? Are you dead?"

The question filtered down to Al through a haze, and he couldn't answer it. It was a tough question. Somehow he got his eyes to open into tiny slits imbedded in puffed, swollen lids. The face looking down at him was not Bobbie's or his mother's. A tear from the overhead face dropped into his mouth. It was warm and tasted salty. Al was pretty close to coming up with an answer. He didn't think dead people could taste anything.

"You're not dead, are you, Boomy?" Chotchke Charlie was cradling Al's head in his lap, dabbing at the blood with his bandanna, when his friend passed out.

He awoke in a cubicle in the emergency ward of Beth-El Hospital with no memory of how he got there from Van Sinderen Avenue. When the doctors told him how Charlie came stumbling in with Al's arms locked around his neck, half dragging and half carrying him, it started coming back in flashes. He looked at the exhausted little guy, asleep in a chair next to the bed, and realized that whatever Charlie may have been shortchanged in the thinking department was more than made up for by the size of his heart.

Al wanted to get out of the hospital. He told them he had things to do. They told him they had things to do. There weren't any broken bones, but there was a slight concussion, and the face that looked so good in the mirror that morning was all busted up again, with interest. Compounded. They told Al they wanted him to stay, but as it turned out, they didn't want him to stay very long.

When they asked him what happened, he told them it was from the Zivic fight. They wanted to know who he thought he was kidding, since cuts did not bleed for three days. Was he a hemophiliac? Chotchke Charlie had no idea who or what Zivic was. All he knew was that a bunch of bad guys had just tried to beat up his friend Boomy.

The doctors finally left Al alone because they had to rush off on one of their doctor missions—a cardiac arrest down the hall, the coffee wagon up the hall—and Charlie wandered off to the waiting room to search for treasures. A couple of minutes later he came tearing back, agitated and out of breath.

"It's the Sibics, Boomy! The Sibics are here!"

Al caught what Charlie was saying pretty quickly. The look of panic in the little guy's eyes helped. Since his body was so beat up that he couldn't find a comfortable position in the bed anyhow, he climbed out of it, put on his shoes, and followed Chotchke Charlie to the doorless archway that separated his alcove of a room from the main corridor. What he saw then made him feel better than any of the painkillers the doctors and nurses had given him.

Uglier Still, the one who liked brass knuckles and had demanded the two grand, was sitting on a chair holding his hands to his face, which was swollen even more than Al's, plus the lower part was completely out of line with the upper part. Charlie whispered that a couple of other "Sibics" were here with him, but Al figured they just came to dump him off and left. He watched Uglier Still howl as one of the doctors fingered his jaw, and it made him feel good. Wanting to feel even better, he waited until they left Uglier Still alone for a moment, and then he walked over and smiled, even though smiling hurt. It probably hurt

Uglier Still a lot more, because he didn't smile back. His eyes bugged and he started grunting, most likely because his mouth did not work too well.

"Okay, prick, ya lookin' for two grand? I ain't got it, but here's my IOU." With which he hauled off, mercifully smashing his right hand, not his left, into the plug-ugly's nose, which spread with a bloody splatter across his face. Al's heart was filled with more joy than he'd felt since his wedding, and the emergency room staff of Beth-El Hospital, who had to redo their Treatment Required list completely, decided that it was time to release him after all.

It wasn't Al Davis's style to make lists of things he should do. It wouldn't have mattered anyhow, because he wasn't the kind of guy who would follow a list. And it didn't take a list to tell him that he should get himself back to Texas on the very next train as he already had some big-time explaining to do, but it wasn't going to happen. At first, he was too deflated to face all the guys at Camp Hulen who believed in him. Like a wounded cat, he needed the security of his own lair. But now the cat's back was arched and his hackles were bristling.

Another thing that wasn't Al Davis's style was to turn the other cheek, especially when the other cheek was as banged up as his was. The idea that someone would put the finger on him drew the cat out of his lair, and he was ready to pounce. Rhyme, reason, and intellect went out the window. There were only two guys he could think of who would be after him for that money—Reles and Maione. He couldn't get back at them because they were both out of circulation, but he was willing to settle. There were still five Ocean Hill boys out there who put the hurt on him, and he wanted them. He didn't think about the United States Army, he didn't think of Bobbie, he didn't think of anyone or anything except getting even. No plan, no strategy. He was just going to walk into every bar in Ocean Hill until he found them.

That's what Al Davis was doing on Eastern Parkway near Atlantic Avenue, the hub of Ocean Hill, when the MPs caught up with him and hauled him off to the army hospital on Governors Island, where they checked him out and shipped him back to Texas.

. . .

Allie "Tick-Tock" Tannenbaum was trying to play solitaire, but he couldn't concentrate on the cards. There was too much noise coming from the next room. Kitty Reles had arrived about an hour ago, and it didn't take long before she and Abe got into a shouting match.

Allie Tannenbaum was already quite a celebrity because of some other shouting he happened to overhear. The murder trial of Louis "Lepke" Buchalter had been going on for almost two months, and Allie was one of the state's star witnesses. He was like an industrious elf, busily driving nails into his former boss's coffin as he related how Lepke exploded in front of him and union boss Max Rubin, shouting that he was fed up with that sonuvabitch Joe Rosen and swearing to take care of him. By turning state's evidence in the Lepke case Allie saved his own neck, but the whole experience convinced him that hearing too much was not very healthy, so he turned his radio on with the volume as high as it would go and went back to his cards.

Kitty Reles walked through the door and put a Nathan's hot dog on the table. The hot dog was covered with mustard, which Abe's ulcerated colon and hemorrhoid-plagued rectum could not possibly tolerate. He shouted at her that as his wife she should know how bad spices were for him. Everyone knew of his delicate condition because he made no secret of it. His room smelled like a barnful of rotten eggs, and the officer assigned to bring him his meals generally had no appetite to eat his own. He was still complaining about the mustard when Kitty told him that she'd thought things over very carefully and not only did she not want to go away with him but she wanted out of the marriage.

The night of November 11, 1941, was exceptionally good for sleeping. A little before eleven Allie Tannenbaum heard Abe Reles's door open and close, and was soon drowning the radio out with his snoring. Kitty Reles thought she would be too upset to sleep, but her eyes closed the minute her head touched the pillow. Abe Reles, his stomach rumbling in rebellion at the outrage of his wife walking out on him, passed some gas and fell asleep. Even the pigeons roosting on the parapet of the Half Moon Hotel slept soundly through the night. It was such a good night for sleeping that the three detectives and two patrolmen assigned to guard the turncoat mobsters all dozed off at the same time.

But not everyone was asleep, unless the big guy in the dark topcoat on the boardwalk was sleepwalking. His snap-brimmed black hat was pulled low, shadowing his face. He walked back and forth from West Twenty-eighth Street to West Twenty-ninth Street, ignoring the brisk chill of the November night. He was joined by a second person, of medium build, who came briskly down West Twenty-eighth Street from Surf Avenue. Hands thrust deep in their pockets, the two men headed for the Half Moon Hotel and entered the lobby.

Pigeons have a good sense of direction, but in other respects they are said to be extremely stupid creatures. It may be that they hold the same opinion of people. As the morning light began to erase the darkness of night, one of the first pigeons to wake up took a beady look at the only person it ever saw trying to fly, and cooed, "Flap your arms, dummy." The person paid no attention, and the hungry bird turned its mind to more productive thoughts of breadcrumbs.

About 7:45 A.M., William Nicholson, the commander of the Coney Island Draft Board, got to his second-floor office in the Half Moon Hotel and saw a bed sheet dancing in the morning breeze. He immediately reported it to the night manager, who was upset because the Half Moon was a relatively upscale establishment where the bedding was changed on a daily basis. There was no reason for anyone to be airing out their linens, so the manager sent a porter to check. The porter went to a vacant apartment on the fifth floor and opened the window. Looking up, he saw the sheet dangling from the window above. Then he turned and looked down at the second-story kitchen-annex roof, where Abe Reles was lying on his back, spread-eagled, his face twisted grotesquely in what the porter at first took to be a sneer but quickly recognized as a look of horror, a look you might see on someone who has just awakened from a nightmare only to find that his phantom demons have followed him.

When the authorities notified Kitty Reles that morning, they were impressed by her regal composure. When Lepke was informed in the courtroom about 10:00 A.M., he raised the glass of water in front of him and took a sip; to some it seemed like a toast. It's hard to celebrate with any real enthusiasm on death row, but Happy Maione and Dasher Abbandando would have danced the tarantella if they'd had a tambourine. Only William O'Dwyer and Burton Turkus were grieved by the loss.

In Palacios, Texas, Private Albert Davidoff heard about the end of Kid Twist three days later, from a fellow New Yorker in his platoon who received a salami and copies of the *Daily News* twice a week. It was a strange mixture of emotions that he felt. Reles had turned his stomach ever since he was a kid, and he mistakenly believed that it was Reles who had sicced the Ocean Hill boys on him. Still, he felt a kind of sadness, a sense of melancholy that he couldn't understand, over the death of someone he knew to be a walking affliction. It took him a while to realize that any news at all about Brownsville made him homesick, and that the person he was feeling sorry for was himself.

No witness was forthcoming in the Reles case. According to the police, Reles knotted two sheets together, tied a wire to one end, wrapped the wire around the radiator valve in his room, and was lowering himself to the window of the empty fifth-floor apartment right below him when he fell forty-two feet to the annex roof. One version of what prompted him to do this was that he was trying to escape. Another was that Reles, who was very big on practical jokes, just wanted to get into the empty apartment, then walk up the stairs, knock on the steel door, and go "Boo!" when the guard opened it. Neither version answered the question of how his body wound up twenty feet from the building.

The five guards assigned to watch over the guests of the state in the Half Moon Hotel hated Reles. He complained about everything, snapped orders at them, cursed, ranted, and raved. When he was in a good mood he would torment them with his pranks. His room was a foul-smelling pigsty that nauseated them whenever they entered it. When all five of the guards claimed to have been asleep at the time of

Reles's flight to eternity, eyebrows were raised. Fingers started pointing when the five guards were demoted by Police Commissioner Lewis J. Valentine.

There was no shortage of opinions and theories about what really happened to Reles. The strong assumption among certain sages was that the big guy in the dark topcoat who paced the boardwalk for hours and who bore a remarkable physical resemblance to Big Al Anastasia, together with his medium-sized companion who could have been a double for Frankie Carbo, did not enter the Half Moon Hotel to use the men's room. Ever since that March day in 1940 when William O'Dwyer announced that Abe Reles had become a gangbuster, Anastasia had been in hiding. He knew that no one was more vulnerable to Reles's song than he was as the guy who delivered Lepke's orders to Murder, Inc. And in October 1941 the state of California had filed a new indictment against Frankie Carbo for the murder of Harry "Big Greenie" Greenberg, based solely on the anticipated testimony of Abe Reles.

It was further assumed that the two men took the elevator to the sixth floor, where, by the virtue of a "donation" made by the philanthropic duo of Meyer Lansky and Bugsy Siegel, the massive steel door opened for them. Quietly, they slipped into Reles's room, each stifling a gag. The big guy wanted to wake Reles, who was sound asleep, so that he could have the pleasure of seeing the look of fear upon his face, but his partner waved him off. Instead, they transformed sleep to unconsciousness with a whack of a billy behind the right ear, then poured half a pint of whiskey down Reles's throat to make it appear that he was drunk. They rigged up the sheets and hung them out the window, and then the big guy bent down and gathered Reles in his arms, much as his mother must have done when he was a colicky baby. What happened next was not a maternal act. Abe Reles was heaved from the window. He plummeted, never awaking from his sleep, and landed in a sitting position, his spine shattered.

As the news of his aerial route to the hereafter spread, one of gangdom's more fertile minds made the pronouncement "The canary can sing but he can't fly," the epitaph by which Abe "Kid Twist" Reles would always be remembered. Only three cars were needed to transport his family to Mount Carmel Cemetery for the burial. There were no friends.

. . .

Early on the Sunday morning of December 7, 1941, less than a month after Reles's death, Japanese planes swooped down on a sleeping U.S. naval fleet in Pearl Harbor, and the United States was at war. With an honorable medical discharge for a misdiagnosed skin condition already in the works when war was declared, Private Albert Davidoff, a guy who never walked away from a fight on his own, was going to miss a big one. Al Davis went home.

Back in Brownsville, he breathed in the smells, walked the streets and avenues, went to the moviehouses, and sat in the parks, sharing it all with Bobbie. They got their own apartment on Saint Marks Avenue, about a mile away from his parents' house on Bradford Street. On Sunday mornings he did what he remembered his father doing every Sunday morning as far back as memory would take him: he went to the Appetizing Store on Sutter Avenue for fresh-from-the-oven bagels, cream cheese laced with chives, thick slabs of lox, a sturgeon, and a container of mixed olives and pickles, and on the way home he picked up the Sunday *News* and *Mirror*. As this was a ritual followed by just about every family in Brownsville, the Appetizing Stores were more crowded on Sunday mornings than the IRT train during rush hour, but when Al Davis walked through the door someone would always call out, "Make way for the champ!" A path would open like the parting of the Red Sea as the eager hands of his people propelled him to the counter, no matter how much he protested that he wanted to wait his turn. On the walk back to Saint Marks he always felt a letdown, thinking about how badly he really wanted to be their champ and how the powers that be would never give him the chance.

As soon as he walked through the front door, Bobbie smiled and the letdown was gone. She would put everything on a tray and then they would hop back into bed, nibbling away at their bagel-and-lox sandwiches and taking turns kissing away the cream cheese oozing from the corners of their mouths. As they ate, they laughed their way through the Sunday comics and read each other articles about the war and society and fashions and sports. The Sunday before Washington's birthday they read that Happy Maione and Dasher Abbandando ate huge meals for lunch and dinner the previous Friday before going to their electro-cutions. That was it—they were all gone now, Abe and Buggsy and Pitts-burgh Phil and Happy and the Dasher. Al and Bobbie went back to reading about the antics of Li'l Abner being pursued by Daisy Mae and Dagwood knocking over the mailman on his daily race to catch the bus.

When Bobbie was at work, Al spent his time doing all the things he'd dreamed of doing while he was in Texas. He visited his pushcart pals on Blake Avenue, and sometimes he rolled up his sleeves and pitched in, to the joy of the peddlers and the housecoat-clad baleboostehs who still blushed at his boyish charm. He played stickball with the neighbor-hood kids and walked the streets and avenues, returning waves and smil-ing at everyone he saw. It was the same Brownsville he'd left, the same Brownsville he loved—but something was different. He couldn't put his finger on it for a while, but gradually it sank in. He was no longer Big Gangy's kid brother. He was Al "Bummy" Davis, Brownsville's own.

After Sunday came Monday, and Monday was the real world. That was when Al had to think about what he was going to do. They wouldn't let him fight in New York, and for a guy who never fought outside of New York because he never wanted to, that was a dilemma. Lew Burston kept telling him to get back in the gym and start working out, that there were plenty of worlds to conquer on the other side of the East River and the Hudson, but Al couldn't see the point in fighting if his Browns-ville crowd wasn't there to watch him.

On August 7, 1942, the marines landed on the Japanese-occupied island of Guadalcanal. A couple days later, Al was helping his old friend Zelke on Blake Avenue when he heard some women talking about a wonderful, brilliant young doctor who had died on Guadalcanal. "A real hero, that Carl Packman. Such a pity, he'll never realize all those dreams." Al was stunned. Who had bigger or better dreams than Carlie Packman? That's when Al Davis decided to go after his dream.

Big Gangy knew what he was seeing, but that didn't mean he had to believe it. He was about to rub his eyes when he remembered that he had chalk on his hands, so he put his cue stick down on the table and settled for blinking very hard at Albert Anastasia in the uniform of the United States Army.

"What're you doin' dressed up like that?"

"I'm in the army."

"You gotta be kiddin' me. What the fuck are you doin' in the army?"

"Whaddya mean, what am I doin'? I enlisted, that's what. You know a better place to be when the heat's on?"

"You mean to tell me you're on the lam in the army?"

"I get seasick, Willie. The navy is out."

"Wow, Al! If I'da known I woulda thrown you a farewell party."

"Okay, Willie, shut the fuck up before I change my mind. Now, what I'm tellin' you I'm sure don't mean shit, but I just wanna let you know."

Wille shut up.

"A while back, Lepke gives me a list of guys who owe us money and tells me to collect. That sonuvagun may be facin' the hot seat, but it's business as usual."

"Yeah, so?"

"Well, the kid . . . Bummy is on the list."

"Hold on a second, Al—"

"No, you hold on. I know the whole story, and I had no intention of pushin' on that one, but I was workin' with someone else and he pulls out the kid's name and says he'll handle it. Like I said, I'm sure it's nothin', but I thought I should tell you."

"Who were you workin' with?"

"Frankie Carbo."

On the occasion of his transfer from the Seventy-fifth Precinct, Sergeant William Schroeder received an engraved seventeen-jewel Longines-Wittnauer watch from his fellow officers. With the war draining man-power, police precincts found themselves understaffed as their young officers swapped blue uniforms for khakis, so as part of a program to realign the force, Schroeder was scheduled to be transferred to the sixty-ninth Precinct in Canarsie in November 1942. The assumption was that with no more mob in Brownsville, there should be no more crime in Brownsville. The way Bill Schroeder figured it, with Murder, Inc. dead and buried, things were that much easier for every punk and two-bit hood looking to make a name for himself. Maybe crime didn't pay, but you never had to look in the Help Wanted ads for openings in that profession.

Bill Schroeder wasn't just a good cop, he was a smart cop, but he still couldn't figure out why he was beginning to hear a person here, a person there, lamenting that Reles, Strauss, and Goldstein were gone. The same Reles, Strauss, and Goldstein who caused people to shake in fear just at the sight of them. The same Reles, Strauss, and Goldstein who didn't complain too loudly if they were shortchanged on a contract rubout because they loved their work so much. Not so long ago what he heard on everyone's lips was a fervent prayer for God or whatever power was on hand to rid the world of these remorseless killers who preyed upon everyone, including their own.

But that was before almost every family in Brownsville was touched by a war thousands of miles away, before all the graphic stories of relatives and friends uprooted and brutalized, before the knowledge that everything people had run from not only still existed but was evolving into something more horrible than they could ever have imagined. Now it wasn't really so surprising that Sergeant Schroeder heard people say, "If there were more Releses and Strausses, no one like Hitler could come along and do what he's doing. They made people respect us."

Lew Burston backed his car into the parking spot in front of Circle Sporting Goods on Kingston Avenue, pulled a package out of the trunk, and went inside. Red Sarachek looked up from the uniform orders he was going through behind the counter and tried remembering who the guy was that just came through the door.

"I want to return this. I can't use it."

"I'm sorry, we can't take back sleeping bags once they're used unless there's a defect."

"A defect? My friend, I can't breathe in it. Suffocating is one of the things I don't enjoy."

"What do you mean, you can't breathe in it? That's the first time I ever heard that one."

"I zipper it up, I climb in, and I can't breathe."

"I guess you never went camping before, huh?"

"Camping? Do I look like a lunatic altogether?"

"Let me ask you then, what do you do with the sleeping bag . . . if it's not too personal?" Red Sarachek stared at his customer, finally remembering who the guy was—Burston, Bummy Davis's manager. His boy was really rocking them all to sleep lately.

"It's a long story," Lew said.

"Do me a favor, show me what the problem is."

Lew did.

Suddenly all of boxing was tuned in on Al Davis, who in less than two and a half months had scored seven consecutive knockouts on the road. As Lew Burston would watch the referee count to ten over the out-like-a-light forms of Al's opponents, he was almost envious. After each fight Lew begged to stay over in a hotel so they could get a good night's sleep.

"I'm not a bat. I don't hang upside down in a cave. I sleep at night. I know it's a bad habit, but I can't break it."

"Don't worry. You sleep and I'll drive. We'll be home by three."

"Al, what is it with you?" Burston knew it was pointless to go on. The kid was like a homing pigeon. All he wanted was to get back to his wife, to his own apartment and his own bed. He told Lew that in all their married life his father and mother were never apart for even a single night. Lew wanted to tell him that Max Davidoff never fought in Washington or Philadelphia, but he kept quiet. While Al drove through the night singing his entire repertoire of songs from the Second Avenue Yiddish Theater, Lew Burston stretched out in his sleeping bag on the backseat—with his head sticking out.

World War II—it was a time of shadows and brownouts and dimouts. Store windows were covered, the upper parts of streetlights and automobile headlights were painted so that no light could be seen from above. Necessities became luxuries as many everyday staples were rationed. Lifestyles and lives changed. Al Davis's life changed. It made Bill Schroeder feel good seeing how Brownsville embraced this kid who used to have a race with trouble, a race wherein you could never tell who was chasing whom. Now, wherever he went, people stopped him to shake his hand, to ask about his parents, or just to smile at him. It wasn't only Al Davis the prizefighter who was bowling over everyone in his path, it was Al Davis their neighbor, the same Al Davis who used to sell tomatoes from a pushcart on Blake Avenue and kibitzed with them in the stores. It was this Al Davis who was Brownsville's special kind of hero.

With all that was going on in the world, dropping a single, solitary person with a left hook in a twenty-foot-square enclosure was no longer such a spectacular achievement. As far as heroes went, it was a time when heroism abounded, a time when pilots crash-dove their fighter planes onto the decks of enemy warships, when infantrymen fresh from being grocery clerks, postal workers, and plumbers' apprentices threw themselves into battle against the foe. Their deeds were recited on the radio and replayed in theaters on the Movietone News. It was understandable that whatever Al did in the ring would be overshadowed, because a ten-rounder could not compete with a world war. Schroeder walked along Pitkin Avenue, and there, in a store window, was a newspaper article with picture of Al "Bummy" Davis scoring a knockout in Washington. It was flanked by two large posters: Uncle Sam Wants You! Enlist Today! and Loose Lips Sink Ships!

Still, Al Davis was able to shine. Like everything else in 1942, he glowed softly, but he did glow. Everyone in Brownsville knew him. He was their favorite son.

16

ew Burston was so exhausted from the exertion he put into his
speech that he sat himself down at the curb in front of the New
York State Athletic Commission office and sucked in lungfuls of
the crisp November air. He could tell from the cool breeze sliding up
his backside that the tearing sound he'd heard as he bent down was the
seam of his pants and that his luck was running true to form with the
rest of the day. One thing he knew was that he'd given it his best shot,
not just because he'd promised the kid he would but partly out of pure
self-interest. He didn't think he could survive another fight followed by
a ten-hour car ride.

How could they have turned him down after such an eloquent argument? Lew pulled out all the stops. The kid would be the hottest
drawing card in New York. Wherever he'd fought lately, he'd been a
perfect gentleman. Lew pointed out that Al Davis was now a responsible
family man who had served in the United States Army and received an
honorable discharge. He reminded the commission of how Al fought
for the Army Relief Fund. It was that second Zivic fight that had drawn
an unwritten promise to lift Bummy's suspension.

Lew Burston had a strong sense that he was watching a puppet show.
He just wasn't sure who was pulling the strings. He sat there trying to

figure how to get up without being arrested for indecent exposure and decided there wasn't going to be much to be thankful for on this Thanksgiving weekend of 1942.

At first there was no question in Fat Yerna's mind that the most unfair, despicable regulation ever instituted was the one whereby the government prohibited the eating or selling of meat on Tuesdays for the duration of the war. It was true, Yerna thought, that war was hell. But even Yerna had to concede that Meatless Tuesday was not as unfair as the Boxing Commission's treatment of Bummy Davis.

Willie Davidoff was worried. He tried to call Albert Anastasia, to see if he would ask Frankie Carbo point-blank what he had in mind when he said he would "handle" the Davis matter, but Big Al had already shipped out to Tennessee en route to becoming a self-made war hero. When his unit was sent overseas, Anastasia, with a few well-placed dollars in the right pockets, wound up with a transportation unit strategically located between Germany and Japan, in a place called Town Gap, Pennsylvania. It took a few more dollars to buy a chestful of medals and ribbons at a local pawnshop, with which Sergeant Albert Anastasia paraded around Brooklyn after the war, convincing everyone including the mob goombahs that he was a real-life version of John Wayne.

So Willie decided to talk to the kid about Carbo, but he wasn't surprised when Al just shrugged the whole thing off. "I never crossed the guy or nothin' like that, Willie. He wanted in and I said no. He may not like me, but I don't like him either."

Frankie Carbo didn't bother Al. The only thing that bothered him was the turndown from the Boxing Commission.

They saw it in his walk, in his workouts at the gym; they saw it in his eyes. The flame was growing cold. The commission's decision knocked the wind out of Al Davis.

Bobbie saw it too. Her husband was in a funk. Somehow she managed to convince him that it would be fun to go to the annual Jefferson-

Tilden Thanksgiving Day football game and cheer for her cousin
Sy, who played fullback for Jefferson. They were supposed to join the
caravan of cars that was assembling in front of the school to follow the
team bus to the Tilden High field in East Flatbush, but by the time Al
finished dawdling and moping around, then calling his mother to
check on what time Thanksgiving dinner was going to be, the caravan
had left. Bobbie pouted because half the fun was driving through enemy
territory with horns honking and a bugler blowing the charge from the
lead car.

As they drove from Jefferson toward Linden Boulevard, a bunch of
kids came racing across the street. Al saw them in plenty of time to slow
down without hitting the brakes, but he hit the brakes anyway, hard.

"I don't believe it!" Bobbie gasped.

Chotchke Charlie didn't know much, but he did know that some very
bad people called Nasties, from a place called Nasty Germany, were
trying to hurt the good people—his people.

For the last four years, Charlie had been picking up every scrap of
tinfoil he saw, mostly from cigarette packs. In that time he had rolled
together the biggest silver ball that anyone in Brownsville had ever seen.
There were people who said it belonged in *The Guinness Book of Records*
or *Ripley's "Believe It or Not!"* It was Charlie's pride and joy. He kept it
right next to him when he slept and petted it the way he used to pet
Shvartzie.

Another great joy in Chotchke Charlie's life was fire engines. The
sound of a siren or fire alarm excited him like nothing else could. When
he heard the wail of a fire engine and the clanging of its bell, he would
stop whatever he was doing and take off down the street after it. And
as fire engines always wound up at a firehouse, it was only natural that
so did Charlie, which was how he learned about tinfoil being so important in the fight against the Nasties. Firehouses were the main collection
points for scrap metal, and Charlie's friends, the firemen, explained how
pots and pans, tin cans, aluminum hub caps, and foil could be turned
into bullets and bombs and airplanes.

Chotchke Charlie loved his silver ball, but he was prepared to make
his own supreme sacrifice for his country.

. . .

Al pulled over to the curb. It was a couple of years since he'd seen Charlie's tinfoil ball, before he went in the army. It was big then, but now it looked like a planet. It had to be at least four feet in diameter.

"Where ya goin', Charlie?" he called from the car window.

Puffing from the effort of rolling his ball, Charlie shouted, "Boomy, will you help me? We going to bomb the Nasties. The firemen, they gonna drop this on 'em. They do it with pots an' everything. Maybe we can ride it in the car, 'cause it's hard to push, Boomy."

Al shook his head, and Bobbie laughed. "Charlie, we gotta go some- place now. We got an appointment," Al said. "Wait till tomorrow and I'll give ya a hand, okay?"

But as much as he didn't want to part with his tinfoil ball, Chotchke Charlie had already made up his mind to do the right thing, and he couldn't wait.

Just seconds were left in the game when Bobbie's cousin Sy took a hand- off from the quarterback at the fifteen, came right up the middle, broke two tackles, and crossed the goal line for the winning touchdown with half the Tilden team on his back. Bobbie squealed in delight, and the Jefferson crowd roared.

Now there were two new heroes in Brownsville: Cousin Sy and Chotchke Charlie, who could never remember hearing people call out his name or clap for him before. He was exhausted from pushing the big tinfoil ball, but he knew he was almost there. People came out of stores and patted him on the back, saying, "Atta way, kid!" and "Come on, Charlie, you can do it!" He didn't realize so many people knew him, and he was really glad that he was going to save them because they were very nice people. Some kid thought it would be a great idea to have the fire department give Charlie a special welcome, so he pulled the alarm.

Chotchke Charlie had just crossed Livonia Avenue on his way to En- gine Company 290 on Sheffield when the alarm went off. People were still shouting for him as he used all his strength to push the huge ball those last few feet. He reached the front of the firehouse, and a tingling thrill surged through him as he heard the blast of the siren and the clanging of the bell. For a second he couldn't decide what to do—bring his tinfoil ball into the firehouse or leave it and follow the fire engines— but then he heard them calling his name again, louder and louder, and he knew he had to finish pushing the ball inside so they could make it into a bomb to drop on the Nasties. He grinned because the people were screaming so loud now. It was the happiest and proudest moment of his life. . . .

When Sergeant Schroeder arrived at the firehouse on Sheffield Avenue, on his final day at the seventy-fifth, he didn't make much of an effort to hold the crowd back. Women with swollen red eyes were gently dropping flowers on the blanket-covered body of little Chotchke Charlie. One of the firemen came out with an American flag and draped it on top of the blanket while a rabbi swayed above the crumpled form, intoning prayers and blessings.

In his last report as a Brownsville police officer, Sergeant Schroeder asterisked the Description of Accident paragraph and added, ". . . while performing a patriotic service for his country." It didn't do anything for Charlie, but it made Bill Schroeder feel a little better.

Rose Davidoff had a lot of turkey left over that evening because Al and Max barely touched theirs. Max had gotten so used to the ritual of making chocolate sodas for Charlie that he couldn't believe he wasn't going to see him tomorrow or the next day. Al sat in a stupor. They'd told him it was quick and Charlie never knew what happened, but all he could think about was how he didn't stop to drive Charlie and his tinfoil ball to the firehouse. Bobbie was grieving too, and decided it wasn't the right time to tell Al and the family her big news. Nothing was going to make them feel better just then.

Charlie's father wouldn't claim the body. While his son was being readied for the potter's field, he stayed home and turned the pages of his prayerbook, always the pious man. Bummy paid for the funeral and a cemetery plot. He gathered together a few friends, and with Rabbi Borodkin conducting a graveside service, he said good-bye to his friend.

. . .

The one thing that Al "Bummy" Davis and Louis "Lepke" Buchalter had in common was that both their fates were in the hands of governing bodies. It was the New York State Athletic Commission that was keeping Bummy out of New York. It was New York State that was trying to keep Lepke there, in an absurd jurisdictional tug of war with the federal government.

One day Lepke was reading *The New York Times* when he came across a small notation on the last page of the sports section about a scheduled fight in Pittsburgh between Al Davis and Carmen Notch. He couldn't help smiling as he remembered something that Albert Anastasia had told him some twelve, thirteen years ago. Lepke had sent Willie Davidoff to meet with Cantor Yossele Rosenblatt, who was having some financial problems that the whole garment center wanted to see taken care of. After the meeting Lepke was surprised to hear that Willie had taken care of it without even giving Rosenblatt the money the community had raised for him. Naturally, Lepke was impressed, and he tells this to Anastasia, who then tells Lepke that it was really Willie's little brother who worked it all out. As time goes on, it is brought to Lepke's attention that this ten-year-old negotiator grows up to be Al "Bummy" Davis.

Later that day, when his lawyer came to consult with him, Lepke asked him to get a message to Frankie Carbo: "Drop the matter with Al Davis. The slate is clean."

Lew Burston sat through the ten rounds in Pittsburgh's Duquesne Garden thinking that he didn't have anything against zombies, he just never wanted to manage one. He was under the impression that zombies sleepwalked, ate flesh, and scared the hell out of people, and that might not have been so bad, but Lew's zombie only sleepwalked. He saw it first in the gym—that is, when the kid showed up in the gym, which was a signal in itself. It was bad enough when the commission refused to lift his suspension, but ever since that poor little guy who was like Al's shadow had that terrible accident, there was just no other word for it—the kid was a goddamn zombie.

Fritzie Zivic sat through the same ten rounds not believing what he was seeing. It wasn't that Bummy Davis wasn't fighting—it was how he was fighting. He was going through the motions, doing everything he had to do to stay in the fight and keep it close, but he was like a car that never went into third gear. And another thing—Davis's face never changed expression. He was poker-faced, which was what they always said about Joe Louis, only Bummy Davis was not a poker-faced fighter. Where was the snarl, the curled lip? Where were the eyes narrowed to slits, flashing sparks? This was not the Al "Bummy" Davis Zivic fought. Still, he figured Davis did enough to win, but the referee held up Carmen Notch's hand in victory.

When Zivic walked into Davis's dressing room, the kid was in the shower, so he went over to talk to Lew Burston. Lew wanted to punch him in the balls, for two reasons. One was that it was because of him that Bummy couldn't fight in New York, and the other was that by now Zivic was used to it. Instead, he shook his hand.

"I thought Al won, but he sure didn't fight Notch the way he fought me. I wondered if maybe his hand's hurtin' or something's wrong."

"What's wrong is that Al's not happy about not being able to fight in New York."

Zivic's face reddened a little. "Yeah, they sorta came down too heavy on him."

Al Davis came out of the shower and stopped when he saw Zivic in his army uniform. "Wow! Look who's wearin' a monkey suit now! You don't look bad in a uniform, Fritzie."

"And you don't look bad in skin," Zivic said as Al stood there naked with beads of water still dripping from him. "I mean, I've seen better-hung guys in a kindergarten bathroom, but . . ." Zivic pulled Bummy aside and lowered his voice so that only the two of them could hear. "I had it scored for you, but I know you can fight better. You seemed to be holding back."

"Nah, I wasn't holdin' back. Truth is, I'm tired of the racket, Fritzie. They won't let me get a crack at the title, I gotta stay on the road—"

"What do you mean, they won't let you get a crack at the title? Who won't let you get a crack at the title?"

"I fought you twice, and it wasn't for the title. I ain't blamin' you. It was the commission that went along with 'no title,' and that's the way it is with the suspension. They just won't let me wear a belt. So you know what I say? Screw 'em. I go out to make a night's pay, and that's it, no more, no less."

By the time Fritzie Zivic left Duquesne Garden, he was taking a worse licking from his conscience than he'd ever taken in the ring. And when his conscience got finished with him, he went up to the New York State Athletic Commission and let them in on a secret that the whole world already knew. He admitted that he started the fireworks by roughing Davis up in a way that was not prescribed by the the rules and regulations of the Marquis of Queensberry. "So I guess it's my fault that Bummy lost his temper," Zivic said, "and maybe you should reconsider his suspension." His army uniform with its brass buttons all shined added to the nobility of his confession and made the likelihood of any punishment almost nil.

When Fat Yerna heard about Zivic's visit to the commission, he was quite impressed. "Cheez, the fucken Polack is another George Washington, even better. He squealed on himself without no one even askin'."

Bummy's suspension was lifted in August 1943, but the New York State Athletic Commission was upstaged in the gift-giving department. They gave Al Davis a license to box; Bobbie gave him immortality—a son to carry on his name.

Al and Bobbie named the baby Charles Floyd Davis and hoped that somewhere Chotchke Charlie was beaming with happiness and dancing on a cloud. They dreamed of raising a son who was tall and handsome in a world of springtime and sunshine. They dreamed of their joy as they watched him go to grade school, then high school, and of how they would cheer for him as he led the baseball team and the football team to victory. They dreamed of how proud they would be when he went off to college to become a doctor or an engineer or a statesman. But dreaming was easy. Al Davis was going to make the dreams come true.

That's when Lew Burston saw his zombie come back to life.

The crack in the Liberty Bell was about the only thing in Philadelphia that could not be blamed on Blinky Palermo. That is not to say that Blinky did not do any cracking, just that bells were not his interest. Wherever there is cracking and breaking, it is comforting to find a person with the ability to fix, and when it came to fixers, none were more highly thought of than Blinky Palermo.

When Blinky takes a sudden interest in Al "Bummy" Davis it is not on a humanitarian basis. He is looking for a credible opponent for Bob Montgomery, the lightweight champion of the world. Montgomery, a South Carolinian who lives in and fights out of Philadelphia, is managed by Joe Gramby, a pretty decent guy who cares about his fighters. Over the years, Blinky watches Montgomery, just as he keeps an eye on all the fighters in Philly, and now and then he helps Gramby out, like when Gramby asks what time it is, Blinky will tell him right down to the minute. Of course, he also fills Joe in with information about other fighters, and he even gives him advice, asked for or not, but when Blinky Palermo does a favor he keeps it in a mental ledger where payback is always expected.

And right now that's what Blinky is thinking—time to balance the ledger. That is why he is looking for a credible opponent—credible enough to warrant a title shot, but not so credible that he won't come in a big underdog. Since Davis's license is reinstated, permitting him to fight in New York again, he celebrates by wading through five consecutive opponents, which qualifies him in the credible department. On the other hand, he is known as a one-handed fighter, besides which, the word is out that he no longer spends much time in the gym as he is somewhat disillusioned with the fight game. The kid seems to have all the ingredients to be a big underdog against the champ, and to Blinky Palermo, big underdogs are the stuff of which dreams are made.

He puts the bug in Gramby's ear that Davis would be a very good opponent for Montgomery because he always draws a big crowd, which means a big payday for Gramby and his fighter. For Blinky, the only big paydays that count for anything are big paydays for Blinky Palermo, which is the reason he is so anxious to see this fight come off. He is convinced that Al "Bummy" Davis will sweat off a few pounds to make the weight and become the new lightweight champion, not because he believes that Davis is a better fighter than Montgomery, but because he believes that besides his money clip and a handkerchief, he also has Joe Gramby in his hip pocket. Blinky figures that if the fight is signed he and his pal Frankie Carbo will see how the odds open, and if they're as high as he thinks they'll be, then they will plunge pretty heavily on Davis.

Blinky doesn't know anything about Carbo's history with Davis. He doesn't know how Carbo exerts a great deal of energy and influence whenever and wherever he can to stymie Davis's career and keep him from fighting for the title. He just knows that Carbo is a guy he can play with because they use the same playground—the prize ring. And when Carbo hears what Blinky is planning, it is true that the idea of Bummy Davis as champ is pretty painful to him, but when he thinks of how much money they can pick up on a heavy underdog, he decides a little pain never killed anyone.

Meanwhile, Gramby is not too sure of Davis as an opponent. His fighter has a tough challenger in Beau Jack at the end of November, so Gramby wants a soft touch for Montgomery's next defense. He decides it would not be a bad idea to check Bummy Davis out, so he takes a drive up to the Broadway Arena in Brooklyn.

About thirty minutes before he's due to go on against Johnny Jones from Pittsburgh, Bummy is sitting on the rubbing table in his dressing room at the Broadway Arena when Willie comes barging in and clears everyone out except for Lew Burston. Willie looks all around like he's checking to make sure there are no holes in the walls where someone could listen in, and then he whispers to Bummy, "Bob Montgomery's manager, Joe Gramby, is sitting in the second row. He came in from Philly to look you over."

Bummy leans forward on the table, his mouth open but no breath passing in or out. He has conditioned himself to accept the fact that he is never going to fight for the title. "Maybe he's visitin' relatives in Brooklyn and this is his evening's entertainment," he finally says.

"I'm tellin' you, he's here to check you out. I know it for a fact."

Willie knows it for a fact because he hears it from Max Joss, the Broadway Arena's promoter. Joss knows it for a fact because Blinky Palermo, who always does his best to make Lady Luck's husband a widower, calls Joss to tell him that Gramby will be there and that Davis has a good chance at a title shot if he doesn't look like too much of a threat.

"Okay. He wants to see a show?" There is a light dancing in Bummy's eyes now. "I'll give him a show he won't forget."

"No, that's just it, kid. What he's looking for is a soft touch. Montgomery's fighting Beau Jack in a few weeks. He figures that's gonna be a tough fight, so he wants to follow it with an easy one. If you look good, you'll be scratched. Just take it easy tonight. Don't scare Gramby off."

"Come on, Willie, that's a crock of shit."

"It's not, Al," Burston cuts in. "We got it straight from Joss."

So Al "Bummy" Davis moves around the ring with a guy named Johnny Jones who came all the way from Pittsburgh for a fight that never really happened. They called it a draw. Bummy considered himself lucky. He was not pleased with the way he fought, but Joe Gramby was, and that was what mattered.

When Montgomery agrees to fight Al Davis and the odds open at ten-to-one on Montgomery, Blinky Palermo wants to get his bets down fast, before there's any chance of the odds dropping. Frankie Carbo asks how much it will cost them to take care of Montgomery and finds out that Blinky hasn't even bothered to talk to Gramby yet.

"I told you I got Gramby in my hip pocket, Frank. He's a pussycat, and he looks up to me because I help the guy out a lot. There's nothing to worry about."

"Talk to him and let him say it out loud."

Two days before the Beau Jack fight, Blinky catches up with Gramby in Stillman's, where Montgomery is finishing up with his final workout. Because it is not too easy to find a quiet corner in the place, he waits until the champ's manager heads for the john and follows him. It's there that Palermo springs his big surprise on Gramby, telling him that he's cutting him and Montgomery in on a small fortune for lying down, and noting that there's a return-bout clause in Montgomery's contract.

Joe Gramby is caught so off guard by this proposition that he jerks from the urinal and gives Blinky a better hosing than Blinky is giving him. That is Blinky's first surprise. The second is when Gramby says, "You're barkin' up the wrong tree. My boy don't go in no tank. I won't even ask him. It would be an insult."

Blinky has options. He can dangle Gramby from a window, always a very convincing mind-changer, but as Lou Stillman seems to have something against fresh air, keeping his windows tightly shut, it is not an option that Blinky can easily exercise, at least not at the moment. Blinky looks at his wet shoes and decides on another option. After all, what's the harm in waiting a few days? Gramby is bound to be more receptive after his boy takes care of Beau Jack.

. . .

A funny thing happens on the way to the coronation—someone swipes the crown! On November 19, 1943, Beau Jack, the battling shoeshine boy from Augusta, Georgia, tiptoes into the Garden ring with a big grin and walks out with a bigger grin—and the lightweight championship.

As Blinky Palermo has so thoughtfully pointed out to Joe Gramby, Montgomery has a rematch clause, and the return bout against Beau Jack is signed for March 3, two weeks after his scheduled bout with Al Davis, which changes Bummy's role from "challenger" to "foregone conclusion." Bummy Davis is now just a tune-up opponent, and he doesn't like it.

Blinky Palermo doesn't like it either. He knows that after the shock of Montgomery losing a decision and his title to Beau Jack, there is no way he's going to convince Gramby to have his man drop two in a row. With his faith in human nature diminishing by leaps and bounds, Blinky comes to the conclusion that he can either watch the Montgomery-Davis fight without placing a bet, which is about as appealing as eating a sandwich with nothing between the two slices of bread, or he can switch horses in midstream and bet on Montgomery, even though he's the favorite, as long as Bummy Davis is willing to listen to reason.

Blinky Palermo decides that in this case he is better off dealing directly with the fighter. He knows Lew Burston, and it is an absolute certainty in his mind that they will never be dancing cheek to cheek. With the kid he feels he has a good chance. Having a brother like Big Gangy, about whom Blinky has heard a few things, Bummy Davis is probably more than just a little sophisticated when it comes to dealings that go on under the table.

He waits until Bummy finishes his workout, then follows him from the gym to this street lined on both sides with pushcart peddlers shouting out prices and bragging about how great the quality of their stuff is. As soon as they see Bummy, they act like General Douglas MacArthur trudges out of the Pacific Ocean and honors them with a visit. Instead of "String beans, onions, and cucumbers," now it's "Hey, Bummy!" and "Look, it's the champ!" In a flash Blinky knows that if he's betting Montgomery this is where he has to come to place his bets. He can have everything covered on this one street.

He watches as the kid gently fingers the produce, smells it, and holds some of it up to check it more closely. At some stands he bags and weighs the stuff himself. When the kid finishes his shopping and is about to cross the street, Blinky taps him on the shoulder.

"I'm very impressed with your talent, Davis."

"Nothin' to be impressed about. It's my profession."

"No kidding? And I thought you were a prizefighter."

"That's my night job." Al looks closely at Palermo. "Do I know you?"

"That I can't answer, but I know you, and that's what's important. Can we go someplace quiet?" Kids keep running up to Davis to say hello, and Blinky is not fond of kids.

"This is quiet. You just gotta listen between the noise. Anyhow, I gotta bring this stuff home."

"Just a second. My name's Palermo. I do a little bit of managing, promoting and such."

Bummy takes a close look. "Blinky Palermo? Philadelphia?"

"Nice to know that my fame precedes me. Now, I'm gonna tell you something that you're going to find very interesting, Davis. I have this small group of extremely influential people, and this group has a very, very strong interest in your career."

"So does my mother, my father, my wife, and my kid, not to mention my brothers and sisters."

"Yeah, but they only cheer for you. We . . . well, let me put it this way. We were very instrumental in getting you this fight."

"I got a manager. He gets one-third of my purse for doin' that."

"If we all work together now, someday soon we wind up with the title. Like I said, we got some very influential people, kid. Let me tell you how influential. We worked with Gramby and our friends at the Garden to get you this fight. So if you just show a little appreciation and—"

Bummy takes a step forward and looks Blinky Palermo in the eye. "If and when somebody does somethin' for me I'm the kinda guy who always shows appreciation. But like I said, *if*. First of all, I never asked you to do nothin' for me. Second, I don't know nothin' about you or anyone else being involved in me gettin' this fight, except for what you tell me, which may be and also may not be. But if you did, lemme show my appreciation right now. Thank you." Bummy is finished showing his appreciation.

Although he is unable to convince Bummy Davis to listen to him, Blinky Palermo does manage to convince Frankie Carbo that even without having anyone in the bag they should still put down a few grand on Montgomery, as Davis has no chance.

On February 18, 1944, Willie and Harry met Bummy at the Edison late in the afternoon. "How about something light, like tea and toast?" Willie suggested, but the kid didn't want anything. He didn't want to talk or play cards either. They just sat around the hotel room in silence until seven, when they walked the couple of blocks to the Garden. At the Forty-ninth Street employee's entrance, Bummy said he wanted to go in through the main lobby, so they went around to Eighth Avenue. He stopped on the sidewalk facing the Garden, not wanting anyone to recognize him, at least not yet. His brothers knew when to keep quiet. They watched the kid's eyes travel in a slow arc, from left to right.

Bummy couldn't see the huge, milling crowd clogging the outer lobby or the lines stretching back from the ticket booths on the left side all the way to Eighth Avenue. He couldn't make out the neon lights of the Nedick's hot dog stand in the center of the lobby. He couldn't see much at all, because everything blurred together in bright splashes of color and movement through his moist, glistening eyes. He drank in the distinctive roaring exuberance of the Friday-night fight crowd, and he felt a warm glow on this crisp winter night.

It was almost three and a half years, but Bummy Davis was back. Back at the place where he belonged. There was only one Madison Square Garden, and it was every fighter's dream to shine there. To Bummy, it was home, even when the crowd raged against him, booed and heckled him. He understood now why an alley cat kept returning to the same backyard fence where he was greeted with taunts and threats and curses and flying shoes, because in spite of it all, that backyard fence was where that alley cat wanted to be.

His brothers shielded him as they walked through the crowd. Bummy's collar was pulled high and his cap pulled low. They almost made it to the inner lobby when someone yelled, "Hey! It's Bummy!" He put his head down as his name began echoing throughout the cavernous lobby. He couldn't make out what anyone was saying, but it sounded like music.

As they walked through the bowels of the Garden, Bummy realized how badly he wanted this fight. He could laugh and wisecrack about it to everyone else, but he couldn't fool himself. He was Brownsville's son, and they believed in him; they called him champ. He wanted to make it true. For them. For himself. For Bobbie and their son. The champ's wife—it sounded special. And he knew that this was as close as he might ever come.

Bummy was standing in front of his dressing room door with Lew Burston and trainer Freddie Brown when he turned and saw Blinky Palermo about thirty feet down the corridor, talking with a deputy boxing commissioner. Next to Palermo was Frankie Carbo. Bummy froze, thinking back to that day on Blake Avenue when Palermo said, "We were very instrumental in getting you this fight." Now he knew who the "we" was.

In the dressing room, after Bummy changed into his trunks, Burston looked at his fighter. He had never seen the kid this tight before. He and Freddie Brown tried to get Bummy to loosen up, do some light shadowboxing. Instead, Bummy began winging away with vicious combinations, slicing through the air as though he were out to demolish an army of invisible opponents. Perspiration flew from him, and snarls erupted from his throat. He wouldn't listen as they pleaded with him to stop. Freddie Brown clutched him in a bear hug and dragged him back to the rubbing table.

"What are you doing, Al?" Lew cried.

"The kid's hyperventilating," Freddie whispered to Lew.

Lew Burston had never considered himself a hero or a person of great courage, but neither did he consider himself a coward. However, he was disgusted with himself when he found out that that's what he was, at least at 9:30 on the night of February 18, when the call came from the hallway for the main event with a crowd of eighteen thousand already in their seats. As concerned as he was about Bummy's condition, he opened the door and led his fighter toward the ramp that went to the ring.

As Bummy looked around Madison Square Garden, he performed a marvelous feat. From the eighteen thousand fans, he picked out two thousand—his people. Most were sitting in the balcony. His family and close friends were clustered in one ringside section. They cheered for him, stamped their feet, and whistled, and Bummy's friends were good whistlers—the best. Brownsville was in the Garden. To Bummy there was no one else—until he caught sight of Blinky Palermo and Frankie Carbo at the front of the crowd.

All at once Bummy's prefight moves stopped. No more bouncing lightly on the balls of his feet, no more rotating of his upper body and shoulders to loosen his muscles. Instead, he found himself shaking as he thought about the seven years he spent climbing through these ropes giving it everything, his blood and his sweat, doling out beatings and taking them. Every time he stepped into the ring he was putting his life on the line, and then these sonsabitches came along to tell you when to win or lose, to dictate who could and who couldn't go for a title, while they sat back and grinned through the fight, picking their noses and cleaning their fingernails. He felt his breaths coming in quick, sharp bursts and sweat coursing down his body.

Bob Montgomery stood in his corner waiting for the bell. He felt great, and why not? Even if Davis was a one-punch fighter he could dance circles around, this would be still a good workout for the big fight. In two weeks, he would be back in this same ring to reclaim his title from Beau Jack.

Fat Yerna, who didn't go to many fights because he had to buy two tickets if he wanted enough room to sit down, decided this was one fight he did not want to miss. Even though his heart was for Bummy he did not bet, because his brain was a lot bigger than his heart. But when the bell rang and Yerna saw Bummy go right at his opponent without any pretense of feeling him out or staying out of harm's way, he had to ask himself a question. Didn't Bummy know who he was fighting?

As soon as heard the bell, Bummy moved forward quickly with measured, purposeful steps. From the opposite corner Bob Montgomery glided toward him, his left hand held high, his right ready to pick off or deflect Davis's left hook. Then he caught the look in his opponent's eyes.

Bummy Davis never really saw Bob Montgomery. Burned into his mind's eye were the crowds that taunted and jeered him, the writers whose pens stung and humiliated him, the commissioners who robbed him of more than three of his prime years and drove him into exile, not for what he had done but for who they believed he was. He saw the title shot that was always kept just out of his reach, and he saw the vultures who thought they could push him around, not giving a flying fuck for him as long as they walked away with their pockets jingling. He saw Reles, Goldstein, Strauss, and Maione like they were back from hell, and joining them now were Frankie Carbo and Blinky Palermo, the detonating device that caused Al Davis to explode.

The Madison Square Garden ring became a street under the elevated train tracks, and Bummy Davis dropped his gym bag. This time the army of spiraling, mocking faces—Reles, Carbo, Goldstein, Strauss, the boxing commissioners, Bummy couldn't keep track—didn't run, and he lunged with a roar erupting from his throat. His knees were bent and his right foot turned slightly inward, and at the same time his left foot pivoted along with his hips, sending all his power surging through his body to burst from the short arc of his left fist. The leering faces disintegrated, the street and the train tracks vanished, Madison Square Garden came to life, and Bob Montgomery never knew what hit him.

At sixty-three seconds of the first round, Al "Bummy" Davis scored the quickest knockout in the history of Madison Square Garden.

There was no Equator, no North Pole or South Pole, no sun or moon or planets, no stars or galaxies. For Al Davis there was nothing but this place of pandemonium where an unbelieving, maniacal crowd of eighteen thousand fans—and now Bummy saw and heard each one of them—seemed about to blow the roof off the Garden. As his two brothers paraded him around the ring on their shoulders, the crowd howled and clamored and cheered for him until the thunderous din reverberated from Eighth Avenue to Ninth, from Forty-ninth Street to Fiftieth.

With his brothers and his corner men forming a wedge in front of him, Al made his way to his dressing room through the clutching, fickle, fanatical mob that now adored him. A throng of wall-to-wall reporters awaited him with a reverence usually reserved for royalty. When one of them asked if there was anything comparable to this achievement in his life, Bummy scored another knockout without throwing a punch. He leaned back, a smile playing on his face, and told them how it was to be ten years old and selling tomatoes on Blake Avenue, learning all the tricks of the trade and fighting every peddler on the block to keep his pushcart and his space. He talked and they listened, wondering if he was putting them on, but as he described his days as Prince of the Fruit Peddlers, they realized that Al "Bummy" Davis was speaking from the heart. When he got up to shower, they were all scribbling away filling their notebooks with all they had to say about a fight that barely lasted a minute.

Al Davis woke up the morning after the Montgomery fight with the same feeling as a mountain climber who reaches the top of Mount Everest—first, the sense of euphoria, then, "Where do we go from here?" He knew that for him the answer was "Nowhere," and that was fine, because for Bummy Davis, there weren't any higher peaks.

He looked around and saw that there was life outside the roped-off twenty-foot square that had been his world for so long. Whatever was out there, he was ready to go for it. In the next year and a half he had fifteen fights, but the passion and lust were missing. He was closing out the show and putting his house in order. There was nothing left to prove, because when he knocked out Montgomery he had shown them all, including himself. Bummy Davis was not a guy who kept an impressive wardrobe. He did not need belts or crowns.

On March 3, the same Bob Montgomery who had been flattened by Al Davis in record time two weeks earlier defeated Beau Jack and was once again champion of the world.

The Sunday morning after Bob Montgomery reclaimed his title from Beau Jack, Bobbie was amazed to see that her husband not only didn't say a word about the fight but was actually in a good mood. He was playing with little Charlie, and she couldn't decide who was more of a baby as the two of them crawled around the apartment chasing each other. Bobbie was slicing bagels and putting out the food he had just bought at the Appetizing Store when he shouted from the living room.

"Hey, Bobbie, Chuckie's doin' it again! He turned right to *Little Orphan Annie!*"

"Okay, Al, when he's finished let him do the crossword puzzle."

A few weeks ago, when Bummy laid the Sunday *News* out on the living room floor, the baby opened the comics to *Little Orphan Annie*, and when he did it again the following week, Bummy started his little game about how his genius of a son loved to read about Annie and Sandy and Daddy Warbucks. Bobbie considered pointing out that as *Little Orphan Annie* was on page three of the comics section, all you had to do was to turn one page and you were there, but she let Al have his fun. So what if Bubbe Rose and Zayde Max were drawing strange looks from all their friends and neighbors when they bragged, "Not a year old and he reads the newspapers already!"

While little Charlie tried reading the comics upside down and then tried eating them, Bummy stretched out with the main section. He looked at the banner headline on the front page—"Lepke, 2 Pals Die in Chair at Sing Sing"—and for a brief moment he was haunted by the memory of stopping his morning run to look at the body of Joseph Rosen. He felt a chill. He might have felt more of a chill, except that Bummy never knew Lepke had called for an amnesty on him. But then, he never knew one was needed. What he did know was that Lepke's execution on March 4, 1944, was the final curtain for Murder, Inc. He started to turn to the sports section to read what Jimmy Powers had to say about Beau Jack losing the title two nights ago, but he decided to read *Little Orphan Annie* with Charlie instead.

Bummy would have loved every day to be Sunday when he could walk down a crowded Pitkin Avenue with his wife at his side, pushing the stroller and sharing a charlotte russe with Charlie, who was just learning to call him Pa-Pa. Wherever they went, people stopped to greet them, beaming and shaking their heads, calling them "Bummy and the Bumlet" and saying how the baby was a chip off the old block. Bummy adored his son. People got used to the sight of the little guy perched atop his father's shoulders, proudly overseeing his domain. And little Charlie adored his father. Bobbie couldn't believe it, but he was actually able to recognize Al's footsteps bouncing up the stairs, and he would stop gnawing on the Lionel locomotive he used as a teething ring and start laughing in joyful anticipation.

Bobbie was used to the looks and smiles of friends, neighbors, even strangers; whenever she walked down the street with Al. It had always been that way with him, but lately she was beginning to realize that it wasn't admiration. It was more a sense of pride, a feeling of "We're part of him and he's part of us. We're one and the same." Sure, they were thrilled with what happened in the Montgomery fight, but that wasn't it. It wasn't about winning or losing. It was about standing tall and straight, about puffing out your chest and looking anyone in the eye. To a lot of the uptown swells, Brownsville was the land of the greeners and mockies, the dregs at the bottom of the barrel. Bummy made them feel good about themselves, about who they were and where they were from. He wasn't the only one whose star had risen from the tenements and streets of Brownsville, but most of the others couldn't wait to get out, whereas Bummy stayed to shine among his own.

Flesh and blood are not brick and cement, but Bummy and Brownsville shared a coarseness that was born more of naïveté than of ignorance and was balanced by a natural gentleness and unpretentiousness. Bummy and Brownsville—rough, tough, simple, sincere, unrelenting but openhearted, praised and revered by some, maligned and belittled by others. Bobbie Davis knew that Al was not hers alone.

Everyone agreed: they had never seen Bummy happier. Everything was going so well Rose Davidoff knew it was time to worry. Rose was the kind of person who as soon as she woke up on Wednesday started worrying about Thursday and wishing it were Tuesday. Life was never so good to her before, so why should it be now?

Rose couldn't help worrying. Worrying was a part of a mother's job. Max worked, she worried. She worried while she shopped, she worried while she cooked, and she worried while she slept. First there was Willie, who by a natural process of elimination was now the Number One Big Shot in Brownsville. Maybe he wouldn't win any Mr. Popularity contests, but if he wasn't loved at least he was respected. Then there was Albert, who was treated like a prince in Brownsville. Besides being such a popular prizefighter who knocked out champions, he was only twenty-four years old and already looking for his own business—maybe a bar or a poolroom or even a restaurant. He had a beautiful wife and baby he was crazy about, and in the past year he'd made more money than she and Max could have dreamed of making in five lifetimes. A mother had to take care of her children and nurse them and cook for them, praying that they'd do well in life, and then when they did, of course she had to go crazy worrying that they were doing *too* well. Also, Rose didn't want to sound like one of those old-fashioned yentas who went around grumbling that things were better the way they used to be, but maybe they were, with all the wolf packs of yungatsh roaming the streets thinking the world belonged to them now that the old mobs were gone and half the police force was in the army. God forbid they should start with her boys! She knew her sons' tempers.

Rose knew her husband too, and she knew he had worries of his own, because he told her so—which for him was a minor miracle, maybe even a major one. Albert the businessman—that they both liked. But Bummy the fighter—they were as proud of him as any parents could be of a son, but Max felt maybe it was time to quit. Rose had felt that way from the beginning, but now even more so, mostly from instinct. Max, who understood what she could only sense, explained to her that even though their son was young, for a fighter it wasn't so young and there were ambitious new fighters just coming up, and even though he believed that the fighter wasn't born that Albert couldn't beat, he also believed that the time comes when enough is enough. He didn't want to see Albert take any more punches. Max felt each and every one of them. So when their daughter-in-law told them that Bummy was going to have just a few more fights, then retire, it felt like Chanukah and Purim and every other celebration came at the same time.

For Rose and Max and Bobbie to worry was understandable. That's how it was with parents and mothers. But Lew Burston was worried too. Lew was not a guy who was in it strictly for his thirty-three-and-a-third cut. He'd always had a special feeling for this kid who still called him Mr. Boiston, from the first day he'd met him some seven years ago.

Lew couldn't believe that any one person could take as many hotfoots from Fate as Bummy Davis. If you got a hotfoot and you laughed it off, some people would call you a jerk while others called you a good sport; if you got mad as hell, some people would still call you a jerk, but now others would say, "Don't mess with this guy." As long as the kid was fighting, Lew wanted to see him get mad. "Mad" made Bummy go. But the kid just walked around with a smile, and when Bummy smiled, his manager was not happy. He was not happy because he thought Bummy was not happy. He thought Bummy was laughing on the outside, crying on the inside, as the song went.

Over a tongue sandwich in Alpert's Deli, Lew, who was very big on little lectures, told the kid that he shouldn't be down on himself, that his day would come and so would a crack at the crown. "Who's down?" Bummy wanted to know, and then he enlightened Lew by explaining that his day had already come when he fought Montgomery and as days went it was a pretty good one. And as far as the crown, he'd happily settle for some big purses instead. Bummy Davis was beginning to understand that it was easier being a realist than a dreamer. He looked around and saw the ranks of young fighters thinning out as other opportunities beckoned. Everybody's goal seemed to be Brooklyn College or City College, to become an engineer, a doctor, a dentist, or a school-teacher. It made a lot of Bummy's buddies feel that they were out of synch, that Brownsville—the whole world—was marching to a new tune. But not Bummy. He was hearing a tune of his own and happily marching to it double-time.

Lew almost choked on his celery soda when he found out that the kid's smile was for real and he didn't need any consoling. Bummy was so happy that it was a shame Lew had put on too much weight to do cartwheels, because that's what he wanted to do. There was a whole other world out there for this kid Lew loved like a son. And yet he couldn't help feeling that if Bummy Davis was walking through a field of four-leaf clovers he would probably wind up with poison ivy.

When Shorty was discharged from the army in the spring of '44, he came back to find his best friend almost a different person. He understood that playing punchball and hanging out in a basement clubroom were things of the past, but the sight of Bummy kitchy-cooing a little baby was one for the books.

Sure, Bummy was glad to see him, but Shorty could tell right away that something was missing. Bummy's head seemed to be in a very different place from the rest of him. He was beginning to sound like Buck Rogers. All he talked about was the future—and not his future as a fighter. He was talking about a future as a businessman, and about how his kid was going to grow up learning to punch a cash register, which did not punch back. These were the dreams his friend was chasing.

Sometime in the middle of May, Bummy changed his entire training routine, including the hours and the place. He stepped up in class in the entrepreneurial world, graduating from pushcart peddler to owner, operator, maître d', and chief cook and bottle washer of a bar and grill on Remsen Avenue around the corner from the Brooklyn Terminal Market, where he'd spent so many early morning hours picking up produce to hawk from his pushcart. Bummy did his roadwork running from behind the bar to the back room and the cellar. The rest of his workout consisted of hauling kegs of beer and huge containers of pretzels and nuts. Instead of punching out sparring partners he punched out tunes on the jukebox, because he was the guy who supplied the music too. This training program worked very well for some—like Henry Armstrong, for instance, who on June 15 mopped up Bummy Davis much more thoroughly than Bummy ever mopped up the floor of his tavern.

Bummy fought Armstrong like a guy hauling beer kegs. He walked right into Hammerin' Hank's range of fire, slugging with him toe to toe, which was like trying to turn off the heat by climbing into the furnace. But sometimes even taking a beating has its compensating virtue. As Bummy was in the ring for less than six minutes, and as there was no reason to go out and celebrate, he was in his own bed at a pretty reasonable hour, so he didn't mind—not that he would have minded anyway—when he was awakened early the next morning by a slight pressure on his chest and opened his eyes to see little Charlie sitting on top of him, peering studiously at his father's swollen, purple-hued left eye. Tentatively, he inched his tiny fingers to the eyebrow and patted it, and said in his sweet baby's voice, "Ooh, Poppa boo-boo."

Still, it wasn't the way Bummy wanted to go out, and before long he was having second thoughts about retiring. Bummy breathed and bled like everyone else, but he never realized how human he really was until it looked like the limelight that had bathed him for so long might begin shifting away. When a star leaves the stage, the spotlight doesn't follow him down the aisle. It remains to focus on another performer.

They called Morris Reif the Blond Bomber of Brownsville. A gunner on an LST, he was wounded in a sub attack and discharged by the navy. But if he could no longer fire fifty-five-millimeter shells, he could still fire six-ounce leather gloves, which he did very well upon resuming his ring career early in 1944.

Reif should have been called the Blond Bomber of East Flatbush, because he had moved there from Brownsville just before turning pro in 1940, but that would have lacked the notoriety as well as the alliteration. And even after he moved, Reif kept returning to his old neighborhood and his favorite hangout, the candy store on the corner of Blake and Hinsdale, where he'd met someone special, someone he always spoke of as "one of the prettiest and nicest girls in Brownsville" if anyone asked. One night in the early summer of 1941, Reif drove to the candy store to hang out with his friends. He was sidelined with a broken right hand after winning his first thirteen fights, most of them by knockouts scored with that same right hand. While everyone was signing his cast, Reif asked, "Where's Esther?" and someone told him that she went out to Texas to marry Bummy Davis. Morris said, "Oh," and drove back to East Flatbush.

When Morris Reif returned to the gym he put his right hand in mothballs, changed his style, and became a left-hooker second to none—or second to one. The similarities in style and power punching were almost eerie. Bill Corum, doing the color commentary for Morris Reif's fight against Beau Jack in 1946, called Reif "the road show Al 'Bummy' Davis."

Bummy hired a couple of bartenders so he could spend more time in the gym. Even with the additional payroll expense, the operation immediately became more profitable without him, because he gave away more rounds in his bar than he ever did in the ring. In no time at all, he disproved the theory that absentee management could never be as good as a hands-on approach, but it took him a lot longer to get back in shape. He waited more than five months after the Armstrong fight before climbing back into the ring, and when he did, he still came in over his fighting weight, but with his newfound desire he scored four quick knockouts in a row.

17

Early in the spring of 1945, Lew Burston and Johnny Attell visited Bummy at the bar. It was Lew's first time there. They brought a plant as a good luck present, and Bummy asked his manager if he had hay fever, because his eyes were watering and he kept blowing his nose.

"Kid, I'm bustin' for you, that's how proud I am."

Lew wrapped his arms around his fighter and gave a squeeze. Bummy guessed that Lew had eggs, onions, and lox for breakfast. The eggs and lox were a maybe, but the onions for sure.

"Look at this place!" Lew waved his hand with a flourish. "You think I don't have a good reason to be proud of you? How many young men your age have a business of their own and a head on their shoulders like you do?"

Bummy tried not to show it, but he was glowing. "What is it that Jolson says? 'You ain't seen nothin' yet.' This is just a start, fellas. One or two more big purses and I'm ready to pick up another place or invest in a good solid business."

A smile creased Lew's face, and he winked at Bummy, who had just filled a pitcher with beer from a tap behind the bar and set it before them with three steins.

"As for those big purses, Al, that's one of the reasons we're here. You know this Graziano kid?"

"Yeah, he stiffened Billy Arnold last time out, didn't he?"

"Yeah, the kid's a real caveman. Anyhow, I got a call from Irving Cohen, his manager, and he wants to know if we're interested in fighting Graziano. I'm not particularly crazy about the idea because he's too big. He's got you by ten pounds. But it's my duty to tell you, because the Garden is willing to cough up real numbers for it."

Bummy's eyes lit up. It was evident that in this case the dollar was worth more than the pound.

Before Mousey followed Bummy to the induction center, he had just about memorized all those punch lines he'd been scribbling on toilet paper over the years, and was seriously thinking of giving it a shot as a standup comic on the vaudeville circuit. It beat working, he felt, and if David Kaminsky could make it so big—that kid from Bummy's block who went under the name Danny Kaye now—why couldn't Mousey? After going to a few amateur nights at the Bushwick Theater, he came to the conclusion that no smart, heads-up vaudevillian wants to come on right after the troupe of cute little yapping dogs that jump through hoops or the kid in a sailor suit who tap-dances to "Stars and Stripes Forever." Not when there's a fat soprano on the program. Fat sopranos are accorded much more appreciation at the Metropolitan Opera House than on a vaudeville stage, where they are considered a not-too-tough act to follow. Al "Bummy" Davis and Rocky Graziano did not have the luxury of any fat sopranos in their line of employment, and they were getting ready to follow the toughest acts conceivable.

The stage was a big one that took in the whole world. What occurred on that stage caused emotions to plummet, then skyrocket, to go from anguish and total despair to joy and wild jubilation.

The fight was scheduled for May 25, 1945. On April 12, President Franklin Delano Roosevelt passed away. In Brownsville it was as though everyone had lost a father. Al was just about to climb into the ring at Beecher's when some guy walked in from the poolroom with his cue stick in his hand and tears streaming down his face. "President Roosevelt is dead," he said, and everything stopped. The speed bags came to a halt. The entire gym fell into silence. Bummy took his gloves off, went to his locker and changed, and walked slowly down the stairs to the street. Within fifteen minutes, the gym was empty.

Bummy started to head for home, but he wound up at the Supreme instead. He found a seat in the back row, way off to the side. He didn't know what was playing and he didn't care. Training for a prizefight no longer seemed to matter much. Neither did watching a movie. All he remembered was Bing Crosby singing, " 'You gotta accen-tu-ate the positive, e-lim-i-nate the negative, latch on to the affirm-a-tive, don't mess with Mister In-Between.' " He left the theater with those words stuck in his mind, and when he got home he tried to teach the song to Charlie.

It seemed as though the mourning of a nation would never end, but eighteen days later Hitler took his own life in a bunker, and the mourning was replaced by joy. *You gotta accen-tu-ate the positive.* . . . One week after that Germany surrendered and the world went crazy.

Maybe no two fighters ever had a tougher act to follow, but Bummy and Rocky had something to offer that made the crowds turn out. People were ready for a different kind of war. On May 25 the big bombs were dropped, but nobody ducked for cover. There was explosion after explosion as both fighters staggered and reeled and hit the deck. Davis went down in the first, Graziano in the second, Davis again in the third, but the biggest explosion was yet to come.

Madison Square Garden was a house of hysteria. Bedlam reigned. It was difficult to hear anything above the screaming of the frenzied throng. But it seemed that Bummy's hearing was somewhat more acute than Rocky's, because when the bell rang to end the third round he dropped his hands and turned to his corner. Al Buck described what happened next in the following day's *New York Post*.

> Rocky Graziano knocked out Al (Bummy) Davis with a right to
> the jaw that landed seconds after the bell had sounded ending
> the third round at the Garden last night. Officially, the end came
> in 44 seconds of the fourth, but the blow that did the damage
> came at a time when the ring was full of handlers for both fight-
> ers. It was clearly an illegal punch, but Young Otto, the referee,
> ignored the protests of Lew Burston, Bummy's manager.
>
> "I asked Otto to stop the fight and disqualify Graziano, but

he refused," Burston explained. "Instead, he ordered the fight to continue." Davis, hurt and bleeding, was knocked to his feet and took a count of nine. When he got up Rocky smashed right after right to Bummy's chin. Al was still on his feet when Otto stopped it.

Lew Burston and Bummy Davis didn't have too much trouble accentuating the positive, because almost everyone thought the kid got a raw deal after trading Graziano blow for blow and showing the heart of a lion against a bigger opponent. Even though the fight went down as a knockout in the record book, you had to eliminate the negative as all the guys along Jacobs' Beach and in Brownsville knew Rocky should have been disqualified and Bummy should have been declared the winner. Suddenly he was everybody's darling because he got coldcocked the way he did. Those who'd been for him 50 percent were with him 100 percent, and those who'd been for him 100 percent were with him 200 percent. In Brownsville they loved Al "Bummy" Davis more than ever. So there was plenty of affirmative for him to latch on to until he found out that someone messed with Mister In-Between.

Willie Davidoff wasn't happy when he heard that Bummy was going to fight Graziano. He thought the kid was giving away too much weight and there was much more in it for Graziano than for Bummy, so he decided to balance the scales a little. He wanted to see Bummy wear the crown one day. He wanted to make sure that Bummy got justice, and if he had to, he was willing to pay for justice. Willie Davidoff was no piker when it came to his kid brother.

Willie knew that Rocky Graziano was a guy who could have played one of the Dead End Kids without taking a single acting lesson. To Willie, that meant he was a perfect guy to do business with, but Willie also knew he couldn't handle things personally because he didn't want Bummy involved at all; in fact, he knew better than to even mention it to the kid. He'd heard that Rocky hung out in a poolroom in Little Italy, on Mulberry Street right off Broome. As no one was more at home in a poolroom than Bummy's loyal buddy Stutz, who had worked in one for half his life, he was the ideal choice. Willie told Stutz to offer Rocky an amount double his purse to lie down, on top of which a ten-G bet would be placed for him. Under no circumstances was Rocky to find out that Stutz was a messenger of Willie's or that he knew Bummy. Stutz was to be strictly a gambler looking to make a killing.

In a matter of four or five nights, Stutz became a connoisseur of lasagna and zabaglione, which were much easier to find on Mulberry Street than Rocky Graziano, who was busy training as he was supposed to be. Finally, on the Monday night before the fight, Stutz walked into the poolroom and saw Rocky standing next to a table with his cue stick jammed perpendicular to the floor like a soldier's rifle at parade rest. He was wearing a porkpie hat, pegged pants that looked like something he'd swiped from a harem girl, and a plaid jacket that clashed with everything in the world.

It took a while for Stutz to get Rocky alone in a corner, but not long enough as far as Stutz was concerned. He started off okay, telling Rocky how great he was against Billy Arnold, but from there it was all downhill. Stutz began to feel very uncomfortable about the whole situation when he found Rocky's cue stick jammed against his Adam's apple instead of the floor, a development that transpired somewhere between one and one and a half seconds after he offered Rocky "a small fortune."

"Who do you think you're playin' with, some dumb fucken dago?" Rocky growled.

When Stutz tried to answer, some of the guys at the next table commented on what a great Donald Duck he did.

"You sonuvabitch! You tryin' a set me up or somethin'?" Rocky lowered the cue stick, but only so he could grab Stutz by the collar and shake him like a maraca.

"Take it easy, Rocky, I'm lookin' to do you a favor."

"I oughta bust your fuckin' head open! Who put you up to this shit?"

Stutz noticed that Rocky was getting about as much attention as a guy chewing on a Hershey bar. Everybody just continued shooting pool or doing whatever they were doing before, like Rocky was just being Rocky.

"Nobody put me up to nothin'. I'm talkin' about makin' you more money than you'll make in ten years. Okay, you had a big night against Arnold, but be real, will ya? Harold Green beat you twice—"

Stutz knew he'd said the wrong thing even before he hit the floor, doubled up from taking Rocky's knee in the nuts. Now a few heads were turning their way. Clearly things were becoming a little more interesting. Stutz preferred it when things were duller.

"You oughta thank God I don't wanna hurt my hands. But do me a favor and gimme your address, because after I stomp you flat I'm gonna take you home and slide you under your door. Now, one last time, you gonna tell me who's lookin' to set me up?"

Stutz was a pretty taciturn guy most of the time, but when he was able to read the "Cat's Paw" on Graziano's heel hovering over his face, he suddenly felt an overwhelming need to communicate. "Okay! Nobody's lookin' to set you up! Bummy's brother Willie asked me to work the deal with you. It's all on the up-and-up. You'd make a bundle, and hopefully Bummy gets a shot at the welterweight title down the road."

Rocky looked down with his mouth hanging open. Then he held out his hand to help Stutz up. "Tell Bummy I said if he don't watch his fucken step he'll get us both suspended. And also, he can shove his deal up his ass."

"Bummy don't know nothin' about it. Willie just looks out for the kid's interest, that's all," Stutz said, wincing as he brushed himself off. At the door he turned back and called out, "By the way, nice meetin' you, Rocky."

Rocky was sitting on the edge of a pool table twirling a gold key chain. "Likewise."

Little Charlie Davis looked into his mother's eyes. "Moo-moo heeya," he mumbled halfheartedly as Bobbie smiled and tousled his hair. "A moo-moo here, a moo-moo there, here a moo, there a moo," she sang, trying to imitate Al's voice, but Charlie needed his poppa to work him into "Old McDonald Had a Farm" or any of the other songs from their nightly sing-along sessions. Charlie cocked his head at her and squinted à la Al, and Bobbie read the message. She was there for diaper changing and feeding, but when it came to "Old McDonald" and such, that was strictly man to man.

Bobbie was not exactly in a singing mood anyhow, not since Al called her from the Garden, where he'd gone with Lew to pick up his purse.

He was so flustered she could barely understand what he was saying, but she did get that he'd bumped into Rocky Graziano, who was also there for his money. Then his speech became so garbled that she couldn't make out a word, except for one that sounded a lot like "Willie."

Harry Davidoff was sitting on a seesaw in the children's playground at Betsy Head Park, pushing himself up and down in deep concentration. He knew that the word for children who lost their parents was "orphans," but he wondered if there was a word for parents who lost their children. If there was, he wanted to come up with it fast, because it sure as hell looked like that's what his parents were going to be.

A few minutes ago, Bummy had come storming into the Madison Cafeteria looking for Willie. He was so upset he didn't even let Willie and Harry finish their dessert. As they walked the couple of blocks to Betsy Head, the kid asked Harry to excuse him and Willie while they discussed a personal matter. Seeing how the kid was acting, Harry didn't argue; he felt he was much better off as a spectator rather than a referee. Now, as he watched from the seesaw, it seemed to Harry that his kid brother must have been in the navy, not the army, because he was waving his arms around like semaphores. Willie sat on a bench looking like he was getting ready to play basketball, but there was no ball, just his head, which he was holding in his hands between his knees.

"Jesus, Willie, what's with you? Are you outta your fucken mind?" Bummy was saying in a low, hard voice.

Willie didn't answer. He just sat there leaning forward, his hands cupped over his eyes and his head hanging low.

"How do you think I felt when Graziano accuses me of somethin' I don't even know about? And do you know what happens if he ever says anything to the Commission? I'm finished, Willie! I'm fucken finished!"

"Kid, I'm sorry, I don't know what else to say. I'm sorry."

"Where do you come off? Do you know what it makes me look like? Do you know how I feel? Do you even give a shit, Willie?"

Willie's head came up, and his eyes seemed to glisten in the afternoon sun. "Do I give a shit? Who do you think I did it for? Myself? It was for you, Bummy, not for me—for you! Maybe I was wrong. Maybe

I shoulda spoke to you, but it was tearin' me apart seein' the royal screwin' you were gettin'. What can I tell you? You're my kid brother, and I guess I can't stop tryin' to take care of you."

When Bummy saw the look on Willie's face, all the anger seeped away like wisps of smoke, and only weariness was left. Willie stood up and grasped Bummy's head, drawing him close.

"I'm sorry."

Watching his brothers walk toward him, Harry sighed with relief. He hadn't come up with the word, but he wouldn't need it now.

Bummy didn't sing any songs that night because he had no one to sing with. Charlie was sound asleep when he got home. Bobbie felt terrible because the lamb chops she'd been keeping warm on a low flame were burnt to a crisp, and it didn't make her feel any better when Bummy told her that was how he liked them because that was the way his mother always made them. She knew something was wrong. When she tried to cheer him up by surprising him with one of his favorites, a fresh Ebinger's blackout cake, he smiled, but she knew it was a forced smile.

"I'm thinkin' maybe we should get away on our own," he said, looking at the cake in front of him, not at Bobbie. "You, me, and the baby."

"You mean a vacation, Al?"

"That's not exactly what I had in mind. I'm thinkin' maybe it's time for a change. You know, get out on my own, try somethin' new. It's just somethin' I been tossin' around in my head."

Bobbie couldn't help feeling that whatever had upset Bummy so much when he called from the Garden had a lot to do with what he was saying now. She wasn't looking to stir things up, just to comfort him, so she spoke as carefully as a Hindu fakir walking on a bed of hot coals.

"Did you see Willie today?"

Bummy looked at his wife as though she had just performed an amazing feat of mind reading. "Willie?"

"Willie. Remember? Your brother Willie?"

Bummy smiled that masquerade smile again. "You mean my brother Willie who thinks he's my father?"

"Al, he's your brother. I know he'd never do anything to hurt you," she said, and she meant it, even though the subject of Willie always made her uncomfortable. "Don't let there be any bad blood between you."

"Nah, Willie's a good guy. He means well. But you know somethin'? All my life I get kicked in the ass or spit at in the face for what Willie does. That I can take. I'm used to it. What I can't take is Willie tryin' to help me. If I was drownin', he'd probably throw me a rock."

Bummy sat at the table for a long time, staring at the blackout cake, until Bobbie finally saw the old uneven smile and decided she didn't have to start packing yet. Bummy was just talking off the top of his head after taking an emotional shot in the gut, and in a few days he wouldn't even remember what he'd said.

It was her mother-in-law who made Bobbie start packing.

When Bummy stopped in at Bradford Street to pick up a pot of Rose's gefilte fish the Friday before Passover, she was busily stuffing everything that wasn't bolted down or didn't belong to her into cardboard boxes that were headed for the garbage. Rose Davidoff had a very sensible plan when it came to spring cleaning: whatever you threw out this year you wouldn't have to throw out next year. Where her family was concerned, it was her one sadistic pleasure. But what she did after her son kissed her hello was completely out of character—she offered a chance to salvage.

"Vrumeleh, this is yours?" she asked, holding up a school composition book. "I never saw one of your schoolbooks with so much writing before."

Bummy took the book from her hand and opened it. His eyes widened as though he had uncovered a long-forgotten treasure. The pages were filled with all the notes he had scribbled down six years ago, when Puggy Feinstein was instructing him and Pretty Levine about everything from the basics to the finer points of the horse racing business. Those lessons had stirred something in Bummy, who'd become a regular visitor at the track, two or three times a month, less as bettor than as a continuing-education student or an on-the-job apprentice. That night he dreamed about thoroughbreds and sunshine.

When he woke up the next morning, the dream stayed with him. He went to Mike's Barber Shop for a trim and a shave and wound up with three ponies and a stable in Miami.

There was one customer ahead of Bummy, a friend of Mike's—who wasn't?—and this customer was complaining that he was so deep into the shylocks that his family's jewels were in jeopardy. Not wishing to part with such a personal commodity, he let it be known as Mike lathered his face with a mountain of Burma-Shave that he would be forced to sell his one viable asset, a three-horse stable, at a bargain-basement price. This lament was strictly for the ears of Mike, who spent many more hours at Belmont and Aqueduct than he did snipping hair, but as Mike had his own shylock problems, his ears did not perk up. However, his were not the only pair of ears in the shop.

"Did you get a haircut?" Bobbie called out from the kitchen when Al got home that day.

"Yeah, among other things."

Lew Burston was in a bad mood. First there was no toilet paper in the john, and then the coffee was cold. When Charlie Beecher told him to stop being such a grouch, Lew realized that what was really bothering him was Bummy's plan to move to Miami and race horses. He wanted to advise the kid that you do not go into a business you know nothing about. Instead, he advised Charlie Beecher to make sure that his bathroom had enough toilet paper and his coffee was hot. Lew had always pictured that after the kid's fighting days he and Bummy would hook up and do something together.

One day in the middle of summer, Stanley Joss, Morris Reif's manager and the son of Broadway Arena promoter Max Joss, brought his rising star up to Beecher's, and asked Burston, "How about your boy and my boy sparring today?" Burston was all for it, but Bummy wasn't sure what he wanted to do. Even though he was there at Beecher's almost every day, he was now more of a shmoozer than a boxer. But when some of the guys went, "Wow, Morris Reif! He's some banger!" Bummy's juices started flowing.

So that day everybody in the gym gathered around the ring and yelled their heads off while two of the best left-hookers in the business went at it. Both boxers banged away, showing their stuff without letting things escalate from sparring session to brawl. When it was over, the crowd of fighters, managers, handlers, and hangers-on applauded enthusiastically. Davis and Reif removed their gloves, and Reif, who had a reputation for being a pretty roughneck kid, walked over to Davis, who was never invited to dine at the Queen's table himself, and said with deference, the way you would to someone you felt good about and respected, "Hey, Al, thanks for goin' it with me. You're okay." Bummy shook Reif's hand. "You're okay too, Red."

Lew Burston and Stanley Joss watched as their two fighters left the gym together. Morris told Bummy that he'd known Bobbie since they were kids and asked how she was. Bummy showed him some snapshots of her and Charlie and invited him to stop over and visit sometime soon. Morris said he would be sure to do that.

Bummy went to his stable at the Jamaica Racetrack with a few apples and lumps of sugar to wish his ponies a safe journey to Miami. He promised them he'd be down there with them soon, and he meant it. Maybe he should have paid attention when one of them stamped his hoof and snorted, "Nay! Nay!" But everything was pretty much set. Bobbie had packed most of their stuff into cartons that were sitting in the foyer waiting to be shipped, Max was going to look after the bar on Remsen Avenue, and Bummy was too busy telling himself what a smart move he was making to listen to some good old horse sense.

Lew Burston's bad mood got worse. He was all for it when Bummy opened his bar. He was proud of the kid, and he told him so. But ponies—that was totally different, a subject he knew almost nothing about. If you don't know, you ask, and that was exactly what Lew did.

To find out anything about the sports world, you could go to the third floor of the New York Public Library, where back issues of all the newspapers were stored along with all kinds of informative books, or you could write to Albert Mitchell, the Answer Man, who had a radio program and knew everything because he had a staff that went to the third floor of the New York Public Library, or you could make the rounds of Gallagher's, Toots Shor's, and Lindy's, where all the same information was to be found and the only page you had to turn was that of a menu.

Ron Ross

By asking a lot of questions of a lot of people over such gastronomical delights as rare roast beef with grated horseradish, Irish lamb stew, and rich, creamy cheesecake, Lew Burston learned that owning thoroughbreds was okay if your name was Vanderbilt. He learned a lot more, and none of it made him feel good. If Bummy was the kind of kid who came out rolling sevens, maybe he'd have a chance—but that fell into the same "if" pool as elephants with wings.

Which was why, even though Johnny Attell called him a buttinsky, Mike Jacobs accused him of playing God, and his own wife told him it wasn't his place to tell anyone what to do with his life, Lew Burston, to whom Bummy Davis was not an "anyone," decided he had to do something to keep the kid in Brownsville. It wasn't easy to help a kid who didn't want to be helped and didn't even know he needed help. Lew didn't know where to begin. His first idea was to hire a hit man to knock off the three horses, but one night when he was having dinner with his wife at a local diner, staring down at the blue-plate special in front of him—a whole rainbow trout—it came to him. Dangle the bait.

But Morris Reif was not a worm, and when Stanley Joss told him that he and Bummy Davis were going to have a big payday at the Garden the Friday before Christmas, he wasn't happy. He wasn't surprised either, because ever since they'd brought the house down sparring at Beecher's, all the talk was what a natural this fight would be. It was a fight everyone wanted to see—the fans, the press, the whole boxing community. Everyone but Morris Reif. Maybe it had something to do with Bummy being the guy that Esther Kovsky picked to spend her life with. Maybe it had to do with all the street talk of what a good guy he was. Maybe it had to do with Dan Parker's Bummy Davis, because tough, rugged Morris Reif's heart went out to the kid about the phony image swallowed by people who didn't know the flesh-and-blood Bummy Davis. Or maybe it was just a gut feeling from swapping punches for fifteen minutes, and then a smile and an embrace. Whatever it was, Morris Reif didn't want to fight Bummy Davis, but he was a prizefighter, and that was his job.

It was Bummy's job too, and Lew couldn't believe that the kid would ever walk away from a fight, so he was feeling pretty confident when he told Bummy that the date was set for December 21. "You don't have to

390

make up your mind this minute," he said. "Take a few days and think it over."

"There's nothing to think over. I'm not gonna be here on December twenty-first."

Lately Max Davidoff didn't look strong enough to take care of himself, let alone his son's bar. For the past few months he hadn't been feeling right, but no one knew what the trouble was because Max refused to go to a doctor. When he insisted that it was simply bad blood, which he would clear up by using bonkes, Bummy insisted that he wasn't going to Miami. That's when Max became either a psychologist or a martyr. "So, I guess Momma and me, we'll just have to learn to live without. You know how we were looking to spend some of the winter in the sunshine with you two and Chalkele. I knew it was too good to be true." Miami was back in the ball game, but there was still the problem of what to do about the bar.

It was a problem solved by Art "Dudy" Polansky, who was part of the crowd that had followed Bummy from his days as an amateur. Artie was a regular at the bar, and when he heard that Bummy was heading for Miami, his first thought was that he was losing a friend who made him feel important and a place that had become part of his life. Then he stopped by at Bummy's apartment one day and got up the nerve to ask him what he intended to do with the bar, and pretty soon there they were washing down pound cake with strong coffee in the living room, floating on separate clouds for different reasons. Bobbie felt a glow of pride when she heard Bummy tell Artie that the bar wasn't a big mon-eymaker as he kept giving "a round on the house." Artie only smiled and shook his head. He wasn't just buying a business; he was buying a keepsake, a memento, maybe even a shrine.

The heat generated by the large Rosh Hashanah crowd made the shul uncomfortably warm, but Bummy felt a chill and shivered. He remem-bered how he used to hold his father's hand, half running, half being swept along by Max's strong, swift steps. Now Max shuffled when he walked, hardly able to raise his feet to negotiate a curb.

Bummy looked at the fragile shell of his father, whose hands were twitching slightly but steadily as he held his Siddur and prayed in a barely audible monotone. Still, he seemed like a shtarker next to Garfinkel, who made Bummy think of a snowman beside a bonfire, rapidly melting away before his eyes. The hair protruding from his nose was now as prominent as a beard.

Max leaned close to Garfinkel's ear and told him in Yiddish that his son, with all the money he made as a prizefighter, had bought some racehorses and was moving to Miami Beach, and that he and Rose were going to spend the winters there with Albert, his wife, and their grandson. "No more freezing off of the tuchis up here," he whispered proudly.

Bummy was staring straight ahead, so he never saw the sad, almost pitying look in Garfinkel's eyes. The old tailor said nothing until the service was over and Bummy excused himself to go to the men's room. Then he placed a bony, quivering hand on top of Max's.

"Davidoff, I want to tell you now that I wish your son well, because inside of me I know that after these holidays I won't see him again."

"Don't talk like that, Garfinkel, you're probably going to live to be a hundred."

"That may be, Davidoff," said Garfinkel, "that may be."

The following week was Yom Kippur and it was a good feeling for Max to have his youngest son sitting there next to him. Max knew that Albert, like so many of the other young men, wasn't observant and didn't go to shul to pray and celebrate the holidays. He went out of respect for his father. It was more than a comfort, it was a blessing to have such a son who would always honor his father's memory and say kaddish for him.

They should have put Bummy Davis on the menu, because in just about every restaurant, luncheonette, and coffee shop in Brownsville they were paying more attention to Bummy now than to any lunch special being served. Guys who skipped lunch talked about him on the street, in the shvitz, wherever they happened to be. Everybody knew why Bummy was leaving, only no two people knew it the same way.

Some of the guys who knew Bummy pretty well would sit around and tell everyone else how he was moving on with his life because he was one ambitious sonuvagun but then they would explain that if he just had the chance to do it all again, only do some things differently this time, that's what he would really want . . . maybe ease up a bit against Canzoneri; walk away from this jerk Mersky in the candy store; forget the "this is the way they do it in Brownsville" shit against Zivic; even consider playing a little ball with the boys. . . .

Then there was Shorty and Lew Burston, and there was Bobbie . . . and all they could do was listen politely and laugh silently to themselves. They knew that Al "Bummy" Davis, if given the chance, would do everything over again exactly the same way.

Turkeys didn't do nearly as well in Brownsville as they did elsewhere— from a butcher's point of view, that is. A turkey would have said just the opposite. Thanksgiving found most Brownsville housewives, who were children of the pogroms, not the Pilgrims, busy stuffing kishka, cabbages, peppers, and an occasional roast chicken. This year, though, Bobbie had volunteered to prepare a traditional Thanksgiving dinner for the entire family as a special celebration and sendoff for Bummy, who was going to leave for Miami right afterward. The only compromise on the menu was to be a noodle kugel for Max.

Bummy was in a great mood. Thanksgiving had never been more meaningful to him. He was ready to get started on the best and most exciting years of his life, and he was ready to leave Brownsville, something that had always been unthinkable to him before. Brownsville was in him, it was his foundation. His family, his friends, the way he thought and did things—it was all Brownsville. That would never change, no matter where he went.

The Night Before Thanksgiving has very little in common with the Night Before Christmas. Or at least that was the case on Thanksgiving Eve of 1945, when plenty of creatures were stirring, maybe even a mouse, but definitely a few rats.

Russell Donahue was bad, and he wanted to do bad things. He'd had a lot of practice in his twenty-four years. His kid brother, David, seven years younger, was mostly a follower, and since it was Russell he followed, he was more bad than good. Vinnie Giarraffa was dumb. At twenty-three, he was so dumb that he was dangerous. When Russell decided to form a gang, Vinnie thought that was a good idea. Vinnie thought any idea was a good idea. He even came up with one of his own, which he thought was the best idea ever—a gang had to have a name and an identity to be famous. That is how the Flatbush Cowboys were born.

Like everyone else in the borough of Brooklyn who had ever dreamed of rifling a cash register or swiping a car, Vinnie and the Donahue brothers had heard of Brownsville's Cowboys. They were not unique. Facsimiles sprouted up throughout the city. With Murder, Inc. gone forever and most of the police force gone to war, New York City became Tombstone and the Cowboys were running wild. Every neighborhood had its own stylized pack of wolves.

As Thanksgiving approached, turkey was not on their minds. They were much more interested in devouring the golden goose.

Bobbie almost dropped the bowl of cranberry sauce she was carrying when she heard Bummy shout. She turned around and saw the two crazy men in her life laughing and clapping their hands. Little Charlie was straining to fly out of the straps that held him in his highchair and leap into his papa's arms. Bummy was pumping both his fists in the air. "Sonuvagun! Didja hear him?" he bellowed, bending down to hug his son. Charlie had squealed out, "Limmee neh-neh-neh," which was easily recognizable to everyone in the Davis household as "Eliminate the negative," and he wasn't just parroting what he'd heard. For the first time, all on his own, he'd come up with the line following Al's "Ya gotta accent-chuate the positive."

Bobbie couldn't hold back a smile as she thought of when Al took her to the Roxy a couple of weeks ago to see Tony Canzoneri, who was now a vaudeville star. Tony did a "Sonny Boy" routine with a straight-man "Daddy" that had Bummy so excited she was afraid he was going to jump up on the stage and grab the microphone. All he talked about on the way home was how he and Charlie were going to do that act someday. She knew what he was thinking now: since Charlie had actually picked up a cue line, he was ready for "Sonny Boy."

Bummy reluctantly kissed his son on the cheek and went to get his coat. He had some unfinished business to take care of. He'd told Artie Polansky that he would stop over on Monday night and give him a final rundown of inventory and suppliers, but the heavens had opened with such a steady, drenching downpour that he'd had to postpone the meeting. He didn't have to consult a calendar to check for dates to reschedule. He only had one day left.

Bobbie was putting the cranberry sauce in the refrigerator when she realized she hadn't kissed her husband good-bye. She ran down the steps to catch him, but his car had already pulled away.

When Bummy left the house he didn't take the most direct route to the bar, Howard Avenue into Kings Highway to Remsen Avenue. Instead he took the scenic route, a slow drive through Brownsville, soaking up all the pleasures and memories of the avenues and side streets. Then he remembered that he hadn't kissed Bobbie good-bye. It was a sort of tradition they'd developed, never to leave the house without a kiss, so he stopped at a phone booth on the corner of Hopkinson and Livonia, and for a nickel he made Bobbie and himself feel like a million bucks. Their last kiss was not on the lips, but Bobbie treasured it for a lifetime, Bummy for eternity.

Morris Reif felt the tingle travel up his left arm and knew immediately that Vic Costa was not getting up. The Broadway Arena was stunned into silence. Ever since their last fight two months ago, when Reif squeaked out a close decision, Costa's backers had been squawking about his getting jobbed. Tonight's fight was a real grudge brawl that had packed the rickety old fight club to the rafters, but the fans were quiet now. There wasn't much to make noise about when your guy never got to hear the bell ending the first round.

When someone in Reif's crowd said, "Let's celebrate," it sounded like a good idea to Morris.

"Where do ya wanna go?" another guy said.

"How about Bummy's place in Canarsie?"

They went in two carloads. When they found out Bummy wasn't there, they got back in their cars and drove out to Rockaway. If Morris

Reif had just waited two more rounds before knocking Costa out, Bummy, who drove up about five minutes after they left, would have been surrounded by a whole ripsnorting crowd.

Bummy pulled his car into the empty lot next to the bar and saw that Art Polansky had had Dudy's Bar & Grill stenciled on the front plate glass. There was a crowd of about a dozen people around the bar when he entered, and everyone started calling out, "Hey, Bummy!" and "How's it goin', champ?"

George Miller, the bartender, shouted over to him, "Morris Reif and his crowd stopped in to see you about ten minutes ago. I didn't know you were going to be here, so they left."

Bummy grinned. "Was he lookin' for a fight?"

"Already had one. Knocked out Costa in one."

It took Bummy no more than twenty minutes to explain everything Dudy wanted to know, and he was about to go home when they started talking about the good old days at P.S. 174 and all the laughs at Curly's Poolroom and Mike's Barber Shop. Every once in a while someone would walk over to their table, ask Bummy to sign a napkin or a dollar bill, and start talking to him about his fight with Mickey Farber or this or that fight at the Grove, and every memory reminded Bummy of all the wonderful days of his life. He wasn't ready to leave.

The hands of the clock had moved into the A.M. hours and the crowd had pretty well thinned out when Dudy astounded Al by telling him that he was actually in the temple the day young Boomy Davidoff had infiltrated Cantor Isaac Tepperman's choir. The two of them laughed until they cried, and without too much urging other than a couple of beers, Bummy unbuttoned his collar, sat back in his chair, and sang and sang and sang. And Art Polansky wondered to himself how his friend, whose every fiber was so interwoven with the traditions and heritage of his Brownsville, could possibly survive anywhere else.

George Miller heard the wailing and looked over at the table next to the partition that separated the bar area from the dining area, where the only cooked food served were hard-boiled eggs. There were his two employers, past and present, Al "Bummy" Davis and Arthur "Dudy" Polansky, two okay guys in George's book—although he did wish that

Bummy knew some other songs. "Roumania, Roumania" wasn't too bad, but when he got past that and "Hava Nagila," George was ready to hunt for earmuffs. He tried to shut the singing out as he ran his towel across the top of the bar, even though there was nothing to wipe down. By now there was no one sitting at the bar. A drunk was sleeping it off at the table near the rear door. Eddie Fritz, a cop who'd been in a couple of times before, was sitting next to the jukebox reading the evening editions of the *News* and *Mirror* and nursing the same bottle of beer he'd had for the past hour. These were the two paying customers, one almost dead, the other almost on the wagon. He might as well have been a revivalist in the Salvation Army.

The front door opened, and George knew he wasn't going to be serving any drinks to the four young men who entered.

This had to be a record, Vinnie Giarraffa was sure of it. Al Capone, move over! Six fucken bars in one night! When Russ said to get a car, he probably thought he was dealing with an all-mouth, no-action guy. So when Vinnie pulls up with a Caddy, he does so very calm, cool, and collected, and says, "Okay, here's my end. What now?"

Maybe Russ is afraid of being shown up or maybe he feels he's on the spot, but what a "what now" he delivers. They start in Fort Greene, at a bar on Classon Avenue. The four of them—Russell Donahue, his kid brother, Dave, Johnny Romano, and Vinnie—walk in pointing their rods, and Russ gives out with, "Okay, fuckers, you know what we're here for," and the bartender cleans out the register so fast he must think there's a prize for speed and neatness. From there, they drive down to Franklin Avenue, where the bartender is not nearly so fast; in fact, he is paralyzed, and there is a distinct smell of shit coming from him. Not wishing to stay long in an unhealthy environment, Romano cleans out the register and the Flatbush Cowboys move on. They repeat this four more times, and it's basically the same at each watering hole. Except for the fact that it's so much fun, it's almost boring. The fun part is about two hundred bucks at each stop.

They finally meet disappointment when they pull up to the Beverly Bar & Grill on Ralph Avenue in East Flatbush, only to find that it is already closed. Realizing that even most bars are closed for business by now, Russell says, "Let's go for coffee, my treat." They drive over to the Cobe Diner, which is only five short blocks away, and as Vinnie is about to pull into the parking lot, he spots the bar on the other side of Remsen Avenue about halfway down the street. Its lights are still on.

Bummy was squeezing Art Polansky's hand and wishing him luck when he saw two gun barrels pointing down at them. "Everybody just stay where you are and don't do nothin' stupid. This'll be quick and pain-less," Romano yelled from the bar as Vinnie Giarraffa stood guard at the door.

Eddie Fritz looked up from his newspaper and saw that there were four of them. The one at the door he immediately pegged as an asshole who would probably either piss in his pants or pull his trigger if you said "Boo!" to him. The two guys holding pistols on the owner and his prizefighter friend looked like brothers. The younger one had a baby face that sent the message. "He knows not what he does." The older one sent a much stronger message; he looked like a nasty SOB. Fritz could see the owner's eyes darting nervously from one gun barrel to another while his fingers danced almost spastically in the air. Davis, the prizefighter, was the only one in the place who appeared calm as he looked from one gunman's face to the other's. The guy holding his gun on the bartender looked like the smartest and toughest of the bunch. Fritz decided that it would be suicide to go for his service revolver. The scary part was that these guys weren't pros. He hoped they kept their cool. His pulse was racing and his mouth was parched. He watched as the bartender nervously kept motioning to Romano with little waves of his hand. "All right. Take it easy. I'll give you what's in the register. Just ease off a bit."

Bummy wanted very badly to be home with his wife and son. He wished now that he had left a little earlier. He knew himself, and because he knew himself, he didn't trust himself. Ordinarily, he didn't let punks like this bother him, but he felt something like an obligation, a moral duty, because Dudy was not only his friend but he had bought the place because of him. He remembered how often Willie had shoved his finger into his chest and told him, "Keep your nose clean and stay out of other people's business." He thought of Bobbie and little Charlie, and he knew Willie was right. Then he thought how important it was for the little guy to be proud of his father, and in that moment he decided to do the right thing without losing his self-control. Wasn't that what maturing was all about? Bummy Davis smiled his last smile.

Vinnie stood at the door waving his pistol in excited arcs, watching as the bartender opened the cash register in front of Romano. He couldn't believe how easy it was. Seven hits, seven easy scores. Then he heard the guy at the table.

Bummy called out to the gunman at the bar, but it was for all of them. His voice was steady, calm, and not threatening, as though he was making a plea for decency. "Why don't you leave him alone?" he said, gesturing at Dudy. "The guy just bought this place. Give him a break."

Dudy wanted to clamp a hand over Bummy's mouth, but he couldn't move. He wanted to plead with him not to say anything more, but he couldn't get any words to come out. All Eddie Fritz could do was suck up air. He couldn't believe it. The way Davis spoke, you would think he expected them to apologize and leave.

Vinnie's pistol was now wagging more rapidly, in wider, more erratic arcs. His mouth hung open. Johnny Romano turned from the bar, speechless, and looked at Bummy, while Dave Donahue looked at his brother, who was the only person besides Bummy who hadn't turned into a statue.

"Why don't you mind your own fucken business before I blow your brains out?"

Maybe if Russell Donahue knew who he was talking to . . . maybe if Al "Bummy" Davis knew there was only $150 in the register . . . maybe if he had taken another look at the snapshot of Bobbie and Charlie in his wallet . . . but none of these maybes were so. Bummy flung the table aside, and a left hand that was supposed to be in mothballs lashed out, crashing into Russell Donahue's jaw, sending him reeling across the room to the door.

Even though Fritz saw it, he was sure it didn't happen. George Miller wasn't such a skeptic; he dove behind the bar for cover. Vinnie's gun started spitting as soon as Donahue splattered against the doorframe at his side. The bullets thunked wildly into the floor, ceiling, and walls. Mirrors shattered, bottles exploded. Vinnie started a chain reaction. Romano and Dave Donahue, turning, tripping, and sliding, also began firing wildly.

Finally Dudy unfroze and reached out for Bummy. "Al, please, it ain't worth it," he said, but he was too late. Sounding above the gunfire was the snarl of rage from Bummy's throat as he lunged for all four of them at the same time.

Eddie Fritz heard himself call out, "Kid, don't. You can't do any more." He had never seen such foolhardy, crazy bravery before, and he didn't want to see it now. Two fists against four guns. He knew he couldn't stand by any longer.

The four guns retreated. They ran out the door, still firing. A bullet tore through Bummy's right arm as he raced after them, knocking over tables and chairs. Eyes blazing, he let out a roar of fury as he shoved a handkerchief into the wound and kept running, his right arm dangling uselessly at his side. All Bummy Davis ever needed was his left. Ask anyone.

As the four unbelieving punks stumbled over each other in a frantic dash to their getaway car, Bummy could have stopped. He should have stopped. He was the winner by a million miles. But he was Al "Bummy" Davis, so he didn't stop. He chased them down Remsen Avenue, roaring curses at them and swinging his left hand wildly. In panic they continued firing back at him. Eddie Fritz unholstered his revolver and bolted through the door, trying to get to Bummy's side. He saw Bummy lurch as a bullet tore through his neck, cracking his spine. As he spun around, another bullet ripped through his back into his left lung. Fritz went to catch him, but Bummy didn't fall. He reached into his pocket and pulled out his car key. There was a fire in his eyes as he tried to get to his car and continue the chase. He only knew one way, in the ring or anywhere else, and that was to fight to the end. Bummy had come to the end.

He fell facedown in the sandy patch of lot where his car was parked. Police Officer Eddie Fritz wiped away tears, rested his revolver on his left forearm, and fired it at the fleeing Cadillac until the chamber was empty.

The last thing Al "Bummy" Davis did as he fell to the ground was to swing out with his left hook.

. . .

On Friday, November 23, 1945, Bummy Davis rode through the streets of Brownsville for the last time.

The crowd outside the I. J. Morris Funeral Parlor was many times larger than the crowd inside. They huddled together, collars turned up against the cold. The day had turned itself around as though out of respect for the occasion, the morning sun retreating behind the dark clouds that now seemed to hover in reflection of the somberness below. Mourners had come from all parts of Brownsville and East New York, from the far reaches of the borough and the city, even from other states. They were there for Al "Bummy" Davis because he was always there for them. Some came to say "Thank you." Some came to say "I'm sorry." They all came to say farewell.

Inside, Rabbi Borodkin looked down upon the silent gathering, at all the faces he knew and the many others he didn't know. Fritzie Zivic came from Pittsburgh to salute a tough guy who, as he learned the hard way, couldn't be pushed around. Morris Reif came "as a mark of respect to a good fighter." Lew Burston lost a fighter but cried for a son. Willie and Charlie Beecher closed the gym to spend a last day with Bummy, and if anyone intended to shop on Blake Avenue, they wouldn't have much to choose from, because Zelke and most of the other peddlers closed their pushcarts for the day and came to say good-bye to their little Boomy.

Rabbi Borodkin looked at Esther Barbara Davidoff, whose reddened eyes and occasionally quivering lips belied her otherwise stoic composure. The little one sitting on her lap was no longer restless and seemed almost attentive now. The rabbi's heart ached for them.

Bobbie leaned forward and pressed her cheek against little Charlie's. She remembered the fear that had knifed through her when the phone rang at four in the morning and they said Bummy was "injured." When she arrived at the hospital, they told her he was dead. She thought back to what she had said to the reporter from the *New York Daily News* in those dark hours.

> "I went over to the tavern," Mrs. Davis explained. "It was almost 6 A.M. when I got there. Dudy and the boys told me how Bummy had died, how he died a hero. It was typical of him to rush in like that, take up for a friend. Now he's dead."

401

"If Bummy had to die," she sobbed, "I'm glad he died the way he did, trying to protect his friends. He would have wanted to die that way."

The baby, serious-eyed, patted her cheeks.

"It shows, as they say in Brownsville, that Bummy had guts," Esther Barbara Davis continued. "Going after those gunmen with his bare hands."

As Rabbi Borodkin brought the service to a close, Charles Floyd Davis was borne up on a sea of the memories and thoughts of all those who had known his father and shared moments of his life.

They didn't come just to pay their respects. They came to see Bummy off. You couldn't see from one end of the funeral procession to the other as it drove slowly up Sutter Avenue on an almost direct route to Springfield Boulevard and Montefiore Cemetery. All through Brownsville and East New York they lined up to say good-bye, and from the eyes, the faces, the hearts of this somber, reverent crowd, a soundless roar of love and admiration reverberated.

Bummy would have loved that final drive.

When they passed through the main gate of the cemetery, little Charlie turned around in the limousine and looked at his zayde and bubbe. Max was trembling as he tried to hold back a flood of tears that could not be denied. Rose was slumped in the seat, her head resting on the shoulder of her youngest daughter, Eva.

As they walked from the car to the narrow roadway leading to the freshly turned mound of earth, Bobbie realized that not once in these past two days had Charlie asked where his father was. Perhaps his age would make the loss easier. Then she saw the coffin at the edge of the grave, and for a brief moment the whole world blurred and teetered. She clenched her teeth and drove off the dizziness. She knew that for Charlie's sake she couldn't afford the luxury of weakness.

Rabbi Borodkin waited until everyone in the procession was gathered around the grave. Harry and Willie were on either side of their parents, Harry holding Rose and Willie supporting Max. Their sisters and brothers-in-law stood behind them. Bobbie stood at Harry's side, holding Charlie's hand. As the rabbi raised his hand and was about to say a graveside prayer, Max Davidoff brushed Willie's arm aside, squared his shoulders, and stepped forward with a sure stride.

"It is my son and it is my place."

Max's strength was a loan that would certainly have to be repaid, but for now it was his own. He walked around Rabbi Borodkin to his son's casket. Above him, the branches of the trees swayed in the chill breeze, and the sun still could not find the courage to come out from where it was hiding. Gently, he placed his right hand on the plain pine box. He spoke softly, but everyone in the large gathering heard him clearly.

"It isn't right. This is not the way it is supposed to be, my son. I should not be here and you should not be there." A lone tear trickled from the corner of each eye, but Max Davidoff's voice did not break. "You are my Kaddishel. It is not meant for a father to say kaddish for a son. It is not the way it should be."

Before Bobbie realized what was happening, Charlie slid away from her and skipped over to Max's side. "Zayde . . ."

It wasn't that Max was ignoring Charlie, but to say the kaddish for his son was his only thought at that moment. He swayed, and his voice rang out in such a pitiful wail that even Rabbi Borodkin found it difficult to control himself.

"*Yisgadal v'yiskadash . . .*"

There was a small, high-pitched echo.

"*Yisgal v'yeesgaga . . .*"

It took Max a moment or two to realize where it was coming from. He looked down and saw the same resolve in the eyes of his grandson that he had seen so often when his little Vrumeleh tackled something that no one thought he could possibly do. Max reached down and patted the child's head. He was not alone. All the mourners drew together more closely, the intensity of their silence overwhelming. Bobbie had taken a couple of steps toward her son but stopped. She was as much in awe as everyone else.

Charlie's hand was resting on the casket next to Max's.

"*. . . sh'me rabbo b'olmo deevro chiruseh . . .*" And little Charlie followed along, as near to being perfect as could be expected from any two-and-a-half-year-old.

"*. . . v'yamlich malchuseh b'chayechon uvyemechon . . .*" Max sang out the larger words in two or three separate syllables so that Charlie could follow more easily. "... *uv'chayey d'chol beys yisroel baagolo uvizman koreev, v'imru omain.*"

Max looked down at his grandson again, then turned his eyes skyward. "This is the way it should be." Taking Charlie's small hand in his own, he turned with him to walk back to the others, but Charlie stopped and looked back at the casket. "Poppa," he said.

That night at Madison Square Garden, when they tolled the bell ten times in honor of Al "Bummy" Davis, a few people in the crowd said, "What a shame. That's not the way he shoulda gone." To those who knew Bummy, there was no other way.

EPILOGUE

Eddie Fritz fired six times at the fleeing getaway car. He hit Vinnie Giarraffa and put two bullets in the younger Donahue, who was paralyzed and eventually died. Vinnie was picked up within a week after the shooting, wearing the same bloodstained shirt, and with a .38 slug still floating around in his neck. His biggest fear was that Willie Davidoff would get to him, and his second-biggest fear was of going under the knife to have the slug removed. He was also most disgruntled over the fact that his cut of the $1,500 they'd scooped up that night was $18, so he resigned from the Flatbush Cowboys and turned his cronies in.

On July 10, 1946, Russell Donahue, John Romano, and Vincent Giarraffa stood before the bench for sentencing. "For one super-charged moment," the Associated Press reported the next day,

> Mrs. Barbara Davis, 23, wife of slain boxer Al "Bummy" Davis, held the fate of the trio in her hand after Kings County Court Judge Samuel S. Leibowitz, preparing to sentence the youths, told her: "Mrs. Davis, I have the power to send these men to the chair. What are your wishes?"
>
> Then, with head bowed, Mrs. Davis, mother of a 3-year-old

child, said: "I don't believe in capital punishment. Whatever you decide to do will be all right with me."

This was not the eye-for-an-eye justice the Davidoffs were seeking, and Barbara Davis was no longer considered part of the family. She eventually remarried, moved to New Jersey with her new husband and Charlie and passed away in 1971. Al "Bummy" Davis's headstone reads:

SON

ALBERT DAVIDOFF

DIED NOV. 21 1945

AGE 25 YEARS

There is no mention that he was also a husband and a father.

Max Davidoff never got over the loss of his youngest son. He died about a year and a half after Bummy. Rose Davidoff lived another twenty-one years after Max passed away. Willie Davidoff, unable to take his own advice about staying out of other people's business, got twenty to forty for blowing away some guy in a barroom dispute. Harry Davidoff became president of the Teamsters Union at Kennedy Airport. He never turned his back on his Brownsville associates, and he took care of Wille from the time he was released from prison until he died. Harry retired to South Florida and passed away in March of 2003.

Frankie Carbo continued his strong-arm stranglehold on the boxing world throughout the 1940s and 1950s. The "underworld czar of boxing" was arrested for four murders, but he never went to trial because of a combination of witnesses afraid to testify and one, Abe Reles, unable to after an unscheduled flight from the Half Moon Hotel. Carbo never paid his dues in full, but he did pay something. He was sentenced to two years in 1958 for being an unlicensed manager, and in 1961 he was sentenced to twenty-five years in a federal penitentiary for conspiracy and extortion against welterweight champion Don Jordan. He died in Miami Beach in 1976 after an early release due to ill health.

Vic Zimet, who worked with Froike as Bummy's trainer early in his career, stood straight, tall, and regal almost until the day of his death, on January 13, 2003, at the age of eighty-five. He remained active in amateur boxing up until the end, after an illustrious career in which he served as first president of the Metropolitan Amateur Boxing Federation and assistant ringside manager of the 1984 Olympic Boxing Team. He was named Coach of the Year by the National Amateur Boxing Federation in 1986. He helped launch the careers of numerous headliners, including Al Davis and Bernie Friedkin. "Bummy was as polite and respectful a young man as I ever came across," Vic told me. "He always had a pleasant smile, and even though I was only three years older than he was, it was always 'Mr. Zimet.' And as far as paying attention and his ability to learn, he sopped it up like a sponge."

Bernie "Schoolboy" Friedkin is eighty-five and lives in Brooklyn with his lovely wife, Lenore. Bernie spent hours with me setting the record straight regarding the Al Davis he knew. There were some early articles on Bummy by respected, usually reliable journalists, describing him as a bully who taunted and tormented Bernie at every opportunity. When I showed these articles to Bernie, he laughed. "I guess when you want to sell a newspaper this is what you write. Let me tell you something. We didn't hang out with the same crowd, me and Bummy, but I only got good things to say about him. Anytime we'd bump into each other, it was always a smile and a 'Hiya doin', Bernie?' And everything I ever heard about him from the rest of the guys was if you ever had to have someone to count on, Bummy was the guy. He'd give you the shirt off his back."

Beau Jack lived in a small two-room apartment in Miami's South Beach until his death in February 2000. The place was cluttered with mementos and memorabilia from his years in the ring. Beau told me that the hardest punch he ever took was Bummy Davis's left hook flush on the mouth during their bout in 1944. He said he was reminded of it every time he ate. "I only know Bummy from our fight, but it's the way he smiled to me at the weigh-in. He didn't say nothin', but he just smiled nice. And then the way he is in the fight. He's one tough guy. He fights hard, real hard, but no rough stuff like Zivic. Even when he runs out of gas in the fifth round, all he does is fight hard and clean. You get to know a guy in a fight. I felt real bad when I heard about Bummy."

At my last get-together with Bob Montgomery, at *Ring* magazine's seventy-fifth anniversary celebration in Atlantic City in March 1997, I asked him what he remembered about Bummy Davis. He was brief and to the point, just like their fight. "I only knew the man for sixty-three seconds, and I can't say I enjoyed his company."

More than fifty-seven years after their fight that never was, Morris Reif lives in Tamarack, Florida. He's eighty years old, and his body is still rock hard. He remembers Bummy as "one helluva good guy who wasn't afraid of anyone or anything," and regrets that the whole world didn't know the Bummy Davis he knew instead of the image painted by media hucksters.

Irving Rudd, who was inducted into the International Boxing Hall of Fame in 1999 as one of boxing's all-time great press agents, knew Bummy from two perspectives. They both grew up in Brownsville just a few blocks apart, and by the good graces of Mike Jacobs, Irv had Bummy as a public relations and restoration job in the late '30s and early '40s. He always said that Bummy "was one of the most maligned, misunderstood fighters of all time. To this day there are people who carry such a wrong impression about Bummy, even the way he died. What registers in their minds is the false stereotype some people painted, so when the words 'bar,' 'holdup,' and 'Bummy Davis' roll around in their heads, they put it together that he died holding up a bar, not as the hero that he was. That's the way it always was with poor Bummy. Someday I would love to set the record straight."

Maybe Lew Burston put it best when he said, "The kid had it all, ring smarts, a fighting heart, natural ability, and the big punch. He had it all except for one thing—mazel. Luck. And this was a racket where, if Luck wasn't in your corner, neither should you be."

What Lew didn't consider was that even though Bummy and mazel never traveled the same route, Bummy never depended on luck. He had a left hook.

GLOSSARY OF
YIDDISH WORDS
AND PHRASES

For the spelling and usage of Yiddish words, I have relied on Leo Rosten's *The Joys of Yiddish,* Fred Kogos's *A Dictionary of Yiddish Slang and Idioms,* and the wisdom and patience of my Yiddish-speaking friends, especially Vic Zimet.

Aliyah: special honor given to a respected congregant to recite a blessing over the Torah

baleboosteh: capable homemaker
bimah: reading platform in a synagogue
bobbe-myseh: old wives' tale
bonkes: heated suction cups
boychik: affectionate diminutive of "boy"
Brith Milah: ceremony of the circumcision
bubbe: grandmother
bubkes: something trivial or worthless
bulvon:oaf
burtchen: to grumble or gripe

Chaim Yankel: a nobody
challah: braided loaf of white bread
chazzen: cantor; professional singer in temple
cheder: Hebrew school
chotchke: toy, trinket
chozzer: pig, hog; one who is greedy, ungrateful, cheap
chozzerai: terrible food; junk, trash
chutzpah: gall, nerve, effrontery
cuk: a look

davening: praying
dreck: shit

GLOSSARY

fahrshtay'n: Do you understand?
fahr vuss: why
farblondjet: bewildered, confused
farchadat: confused
farshtinkener: stinking
faygeleh: little bird

gevalt: a cry of fear, amazement, or pro-
test
goldeneh medina: the golden land
golem: clod
gonif: thief, crook, shady character
gontzeh megillah: the whole rigmarole
goyisher kop: Gentile brains, Gentile ways
gozlen: merciless thief
grauber yung: crude, insensitive young
man
gribbenes: crisp pieces of fried chicken
fat and skin

haftorah: a passage from the Prophets,
read in the synagogue after the Torah reading
hund: dog

Ich k'velen: I'm bursting with pride

kaddish: the mourner's prayer
kaddishel: affectionate term for a son
kiddush: the prayer and ceremony sanc-
tifying the Sabbath
kishkas: intestines, innards, guts; sau-
sages
klezmer: Jewish folk musician
klop in kop: a knock in the head
k'nocker: big shot
kop: head
kugel: pudding, usually made with noodles or potatoes
kurveh: prostitute
kvell: to beam with pride

latke: potato pancake
lokshen: noodles
lokshen strap: cat o' nine tails, so called
for its resemblance to noodles on
a stick

mameleh: mom, momma
matzo: unleavened bread
mazik: mischievous child, little devil
mechaieh: a pleasure, a real joy
mensh: human being; decent person
meshugge, meshuggeneh: crazy; crazy person
mikva: ritual bath
minyan: the quorum of ten male Jews
needed for a religious service
mishegoss: craziness, insanity
mohel: circumciser
momzer: bastard; stubborn or untrust-
worthy person; scalawag
moshkeh: whiskey

naches: prideful pleasure, especially in
the achievements of a child
Nisch g' felach: not such a big deal
nu: an all-purpose word meaning
"Well?" "So?" "What's new?" and so
forth

oysvorf: bum

paskudnyak: rotten, contemptible person
payess: sidelocks
pishachs: urine, pee
pisher: young, inexperienced person; in-
significant person, a nobody; bed-
wetter
pupik: navel, belly button
pushke: charity box; savings container
putz: penis, ass, jerk, fool

rachmones: pity, compassion

Shabbes: Sabbath

shainkeit: beauty

shammus: synagogue caretaker

shayner Yid: a man or woman of honor, of whom other Jews are proud

shaytl: the wig worn by Orthodox Jewish women after marriage

shandeh: shame

shiddach: an arranged marriage

shiksa: non-Jewish woman

shtik naches: piece of joy; precious child

shivah: the seven days of mourning for the dead, beginning immediately after the funeral

shmecker: penis

shmendrick: milquetoast, weak person

shmaltz: drippings of chicken fat, considered a delicacy

shmuck: penis; dope, jerk; detestable person

shnorrer: cheapskate

shnozz: nose

shoymer Shabbes: observant Jew

shtarker: strong person

shtik: piece, part; prank or trick; contrived bit of business

shtikl: little piece

shtupping: fornicating

shul: synagogue

shvartzer: black; Negro

Siddur: Jewish prayerbook

tallis (pl. *talaysim*) : prayer shawl

tateleh: dad, poppa

Telyaineh: Italian

trombenik: blowhard; glutton; lazy person; phony

tsuris: troubles, woes, suffering

tuchis: behind, fanny

tzedaka: charity

tzitzit (pl. *tzitziot)*: fringe at the corner of a prayer shawl

vay iz mir: woe is me

vonce: bedbug; nobody, dummy

vos vilst-zu'?: what do you want from me?

yenta: gossipy woman

yeshiva bucher: student at a school for Talumdic study; scholarly, shy type

yungatsch: young punks

zayde: grandfather

AUTHOR'S NOTE

When I began this project in 1994, I intended researching and writing about Al Davis, the Brownsville Bum, a much-maligned prizefighter whose life had always fascinated me. However, I soon learned that the story of Al "Bummy" Davis was not just the story of a person. His life was so intricately intertwined with a time, a place, and a phenomenon in our history that to separate one from the others would be like pulling the thread that unravels the fabric. To chronicle his life was to chronicle the Brownsville of the Prohibition and Depression eras and their inevitable offspring, the notorious band of killers known as Murder, Inc.

I never met Bummy, but I feel as though I've known him most of my life. In 1940 my cousin Irwin Kaye Kaplan, a tough California lightweight, moved to New York. He trained at Beecher's Gym on Livonia Avenue in Brownsville and was greatly impressed by two things: my mother's stuffed peppers and the friendship of Al Davis. At seven years old, I was greatly impressed by one thing: my cousin Irwin. I would sit at the dinner table, listening in wonder as he told my father, grandfather, and uncles about Beecher's and the fight game and how this guy Davis, who didn't know him from a hole in the wall, offered to stake him until he got settled and was earning his keep. Irwin didn't need the help, but that was beside the point. He couldn't get over the fact that Davis offered it.

By the time I was ten I was listening to Davis fights on the radio and reading about him in the newspapers—reading about a very different Al Davis from the one described by my cousin. This Al Davis was a bum, a guttersnipe, a gangster, a bully, and the dirtiest fighter to grace the prize rings of the '30s and '40s. So I left him to rest in the recesses of my mind, but the intrigue never faded. Over the years I became involved in many areas of the boxing community, probably due to my cousin's early influence. I took turns as a participant and then a manager and promoter. It was more like wine-tasting experience than a professional endeavor, but it was through these peripheral involvements that I met Vic Zimet and the mystique of Al Davis was reawakened. Vic was Bummy's assistant trainer during his early career. He opened the door that permitted me to enter a world—a world in step only with itself— where I got to know the real Al Davis. He brought me together with Bummy's friends, neighbors, and ring opponents. And as I learned about Bummy, I learned about Brownsville. The two were inseparable.

As a youngster growing up in East Flatbush, I was not unfamiliar with Brownsville. I could bicycle there in fifteen minutes or take the Kings Highway bus, but my memories are of floating in on an aromatic cloud of roasted chestnuts, baked sweet potatoes, and knishes. I never thought of Brownsville as a place. It was an experience, an adventure. It wasn't very different in appearance from its neighboring communities of Crown Heights, Canarsie, East Flatbush, and Flatbush, but these were places you passed through. There was no reason to visit them. It was different with Brownsville. Brownsville lured you, suckered you, conned you. It was everyone's poor relation, and everyone's invitation from the spider to the fly.

Brownsville was a world of haggles and gaggles. From every part of the city, crowds converged on the overflowing pushcart marketplaces and the Pitkin Avenue haberdashers and the Rockaway Avenue furniture and appliance merchants, hunting for bargains and delighting in being swells on a slumming expedition. Nevertheless, people respected Brownsville. From the outside looking in, it was the land of the bizarre; everyone was a character, from the kibitzer to the comic, and every character was tough. Brownsville was tough, and tough earns respect.

Sometimes respect grows and becomes fear. Brownsville earned that kind of respect too, packaged and wholesaled in the form of the Shapiro brothers and the Ambergs and finally the ultimate gangland killing machine, Murder, Inc.

The headquarters of Murder, Inc. was right next to the Socony gas station on Stone and Sutter Avenues, which was owned by two of my uncles. I heard many frightening inside stories about this gang from Moe Bradie, the station manager, from my cousins Morty Rosen and Alan Rosenwasser, who pumped gas there from time to time, and from other employees who shook hands with or just shook at the sight of the shtarkers. Over the years the stories were told to me conversationally, and then much more purposefully when I began this project. Initially my interest in Murder, Inc. came from natural curiosity, geographic proximity, and the pervasive media coverage at the time. It was while I was traversing the world of Al "Bummy" Davis that curiosity graduated to intense research.

In writing this book, I consulted archival records, authoritative books, and contemporary newspaper accounts. I also talked with neighbors, friends, and relatives of Al Davis, including his brother Harry, and interviewed trainers, managers, opponents Al faced in the ring, boxing historians, and even the guy who gassed up his car.

I pieced together some of the lesser-known characters in Bummy's life from stories and anecdotes I heard over and over, usually from more than one person. For instance, Marvin Dick, a former fighter from Brownsville, told me about Bummy's strange "big brother" friendship with a kid called Chotchke Charlie, and so did two other sources, Al Spieler, who owned Brothers, a popular Brownsville eatery, and Larry Linden, another Brownsville contemporary of Bummy's. Moe Bradie used to tell me about a guy named Mottel who lived across from the station and went to the I. J. Morris Funeral Parlor like other people went to the movies. Dave Smith, another uncle of mine, head of the Sheetrock union and a former fighter, told me stories about a pushcart peddler he called "the big Polack," and Marvin Dick gave a hilarious rendition of Bummy's brothers coming to settle accounts after this peddler bullied the kid. Neither Dave nor Marvin knew the guy's name, so I gave him one, and he appears in these pages as Zelke.

The Al Davis portrayed throughout this book is the Al Davis that I believe he truly was: a young man who couldn't understand a world that shunned him, but who stood up to it eyeball to eyeball, jaw to jaw. It is about a guy born Albert Davidoff fighting to rid himself of the image of a guy dubbed the Brownsville Bum. Because I wasn't there to hear Bummy and my other characters, I've invented much of their dialogue, but the conversations in this book are the conversations I heard a million times in my youth, informed by careful research and interviews. I have been as faithful to everything I know about Al Davis as is humanly possible, and the same goes for the entire cast of Murder, Inc. as well as all the peddlers, shop owners, and baleboostehs of Brownsville and East New York.

ACKNOWLEDGMENTS

My attempt to breathe life into Al Davis and all those who shared his time and place on this earth could never have been carried through without the many wonderful people who joined in to assist me. I want to take this opportunity to thank them.

Besides Vic Zimet who brought me into the world of Al "Bummy" Davis by introducing me to his friends, neighbors, and opponents, and opened up new lines of communication that afforded me insights I would never have had otherwise, I am forever indebted to Hank Kaplan. Acknowledged to be boxing's foremost historian and archivist, Hank's unflagging support and never-ending supply of information were invaluable. To Hank, thanks for being the great and wonderful person that you are—and my treasured friend.

My dear friend Mike Welch, a boxing historian, made his vast library of boxing audiotapes available to me, bringing back to life the voice and the fights of Al "Bummy" Davis. More important to me, though, was the enjoyment and appreciation he expressed for my work.

Stanley Weston, the irrepressible former publisher and editor of *Ring* magazine, helped me tremendously in gathering material and requested in return no more than a bar of halvah.

Gil Clancy, who started out as a schoolteacher in Brownsville and went on to become the legendary trainer of such ring greats as Emile Griffith, George Foreman, and Oscar de la Hoya. Gil urged me on from the opening bell and is still in my corner.

Special kudos to: my wonderful agent, Jill Grinberg. Jill was truly the captain of the ship, and what a great job she did steering a smooth course all the way. Joy Johannessen, my freelance editor, navigated our trip, plotting out a short but exciting route to the end. A true Joy to behold! Alicia Brooks, my editor at St. Martin's Press calmed all the turbulence, never losing sight of our goal while guiding us to safe harbor. You turned work into a pleasurable experience. Thank you all for rounding out a great crew!

Last but not least, I thank all those Brownsville denizens now scattered around the land, those who have lived the life described in these pages, those who were kind enough to share their experiences with me, and those who only know of this period and these events through the stories they've heard from their parents and grandparents. This is your book.

And thanks to those who cared, encouraged, and pointed the way— Eric Miranda, Hy Cohen, my daughters, Lisa Ross and Wendy Woods, Lou DiBella, Mark Davidoff, and so many others too numerous to list here.

The tolling of the Ten-Count for my dear friends and associates who have passed away during the course of the research and writing of this book: Ray Arcel, Marvin Dick, Beau Jack, Bob Montgomery, Mort Rosen, Irving Rudd, Dave Smith, Stanley Weston, and Vic Zimet.

BUMMY DAVIS'S
BOXING RECORD

Career Totals: Al (Bummy) Davis

Won 67 (KOs 48) | Lost 10 | Drawn 4 | Tot 81

date	opponent	location			
1945-09-11	Johnny Jones	Broadway Arena, Brooklyn, NY, USA	W	DQ	6
1945-05-25	Rocky Graziano	Madison Square Garden, New York, NY, USA	L	TKO	4
1945-05-01	Eddie Saunders	Broadway Arena, Brooklyn, NY, USA	W	PTS	8
1945-03-20	Rudy Giscombe	Broadway Arena, Brooklyn, NY, USA	W	KO	6
1945-03-06	Solomon Stewart	Broadway Arena, Brooklyn, NY, USA	W	KO	4
1945-02-16	Roger Marquette	Worcester, MA, USA	W	KO	1
1944-11-21	Frankie Ross	Broadway Arena, Brooklyn, NY, USA	W	KO	2
1944-06-15	Henry Armstrong	Madison Square Garden, New York, NY, USA	L	KO	2
1944-05-23	Charley Sabatelle	Broadway Arena, Brooklyn, NY, USA	W	KO	3
1944-05-15	Julio Gallucci	New Haven, CT, USA	W	KO	2
1944-05-02	Johnny Dougwillow	Broadway Arena, Brooklyn, NY, USA	W	TKO	6
1944-04-04	Oscar Suggs	Broadway Arena, Brooklyn, NY, USA	W	KO	6
1944-03-17	Beau Jack	Madison Square Garden, New York, NY, USA	L	PTS	10
1944-02-18	Bob Montgomery	Madison Square Garden, New York, NY, USA	W	KO	1
1944-01-18	Buster (Charlie) Beaupre	Broadway Arena, Brooklyn, NY, USA	W	KO	1
1943-11-02	Johnny Jones	Broadway Arena, Brooklyn, NY, USA	D	PTS	10
1943-10-12	Phil Enzenga	Broadway Arena, Brooklyn, NY, USA	W	PTS	8

1943-09-28	Tony Reno	Broadway Arena, Brooklyn, NY, USA	W KO	7
1943-08-26	Pete Galiano	Blue Hen Arena, Wilmington, DE, USA	W KO	2
1943-08-19	George (Red) Doty	Fort Hamilton Arena, Brooklyn, NY, USA	D PTS	8
1943-08-11	Ray Rovelli	Elizabeth, NJ, USA	W KO	4
1943-06-28	Al Tribuani	Arena, Philadelphia, PA, USA	L PTS	10
1943-05-17	Al Tribuani	Arena, Philadelphia, PA, USA	L PTS	10
1943-04-16	Tommy James	Stadium, Chicago, IL, USA	W PTS	10
1943-04-10	Carmen Notch	Duquesne Gardens, Pittsburgh, PA, USA	L PTS	10
1943-03-22	Manuel Rosa	Convention Hall, Philadelphia, PA, USA	W KO	2
1943-01-25	Frankie Wills	Washington, DC, USA	L PTS	8
1942-11-20	George (Red) Doty	Mechanics Building, Boston, MA, USA	W KO	8
1942-11-09	Felix Morales	Washington, DC, USA	W KO	1
1942-11-05	Buck Streator	Olympia A.C., Philadelphia, PA, USA	W KO	5
1942-10-19	Ken Stribling	Washington, DC, USA	W KO	4
1942-10-13	Billy Scott	Bridgeport, CT, USA	W KO	1
1942-10-05	Manuel Rosa	Washington, DC, USA	W KO	6
1942-09-07	Harold Gray	Valley Arena, Holyoke, MA, USA	W KO	3
1941-07-02	Fritzie Zivic	Polo Grounds, New York, NY, USA	L TKO	10
1940-11-15	Fritzie Zivic	Madison Square Garden, New York, NY, USA	L DQ	2
1940-10-26	Johnny Rinaldi	Ridgewood Grove, Brooklyn, NY, USA	W TKO	3
1940-09-20	Tony Marteliano	Madison Square Garden, New York, NY, USA	W SD	10
1940-09-07	Joe Ghnouly	Ridgewood Grove Arena, Brooklyn, NY, USA	W TKO	7
1940-08-12	Johnny Rinaldi	Starlight Park, Bronx, NY, USA	W PTS	8
1940-04-25	Teddy Baldwin	Laurel Garden, Newark, NJ, USA	W KO	5
1940-02-23	Lou Ambers	Madison Square Garden, New York, NY, USA	L PTS	10
1939-12-15	Tippy Larkin	Madison Square Garden, New York, NY, USA	W KO	5
1939-11-01	Tony Canzoneri	Madison Square Garden, New York, NY, USA	W TKO	3
1939-07-21	Gene Gregory	Stadium, Long Beach, NY, USA	W KO	1
1939-06-08	Eddie Brink	Madison Square Garden, New York, NY, USA	W PTS	10
1939-03-17	Mickey Farber	Madison Square Garden, New York, NY, USA	W PTS	10
1939-02-20	Mickey Farber	St. Nicholas Palace, New York, NY, USA	W PTS	8
1939-01-28	Johnny Cabello	Ridgewood Grove, Brooklyn, NY, USA	W PTS	8
1939-01-07	Wally Hally	Ridgewood Grove, Brooklyn, NY, USA	W PTS	8
1938-12-17	Jimmy Lancaster	Ridgewood Grove, Brooklyn, NY, USA	W KO	6
1938-12-04	Dom Colan	Brooklyn, NY, USA	W KO	2
1938-10-15	Al Ragone	Brooklyn, NY, USA	W PTS	8
1938-09-16	Jack Sharkey Jr	Madison Square Garden, New York, NY, USA	D PTS	6
1938-08-24	Young Chappie	Madison Square Garden, New York, NY, USA	W KO	3

Date	Opponent	Venue	Result	
1938-08-12	Al Ragone	Stadium, Long Beach, NY, USA	W PTS	6
1938-07-21	Bernie (School Boy) Friedkin	Madison Square Garden, New York, NY, USA	W KO	4
1938-06-20	Jack Sharkey Jr	Dexter Park Arena, Woodhaven, NY, USA	D PTS	6
1938-04-02	Jack Sharkey Jr	Ridgewood Grove, Brooklyn, NY, USA	W PTS	8
1938-03-19	Benny Rubano	Ridgewood Grove, Brooklyn, NY, USA	W KO	2
1938-02-12	George Karkella	Ridgewood Grove, Brooklyn, NY, USA	W KO	4
1938-01-29	Johnny Mirabella	Ridgewood Grove, Brooklyn, NY, USA	W KO	2
1938-01-18	Johnny (Skippy) Allen	Broadway Arena, Brooklyn, NY, USA	W KO	1
1938-01-08	Dominick Zaccolla	Ridgewood Grove, Brooklyn, NY, USA	W KO	1
1937-12-18	Johnny (Skippy) Allen	Ridgewood Grove, Brooklyn, NY, USA	W KO	1
1937-12-08	Dominick Zaccolla	Hippodrome, New York, NY, USA	W KO	1
1937-11-27	Johnny (Skippy) Allen	Ridgewood Grove, Brooklyn, NY, USA	W KO	4
1937-11-06	Ray Garvey	Brooklyn, NY, USA	W KO	4
1937-10-29	Benny Rubano	Madison Square Garden, New York, NY, USA	W PTS	4
1937-10-16	Andre Sarilla	Ridgewood Grove, Brooklyn, NY, USA	W KO	6
1937-10-05	Joe Novellino	Broadway Arena, Brooklyn, NY, USA	W KO	1
1937-09-25	Pete Vitello	Ridgewood Grove, Brooklyn, NY, USA	W KO	1
1937-09-11	Al Lopiano	Ridgewood Grove Arena, Brooklyn, NY, USA	W KO	2
1937-08-31	Willie Bush	Queensboro Arena, Long Island City, NY, USA	W KO	4
1937-08-03	Sammy Rivers	Canarsie Arena, Brooklyn, NY, USA	W PTS	4
1937-07-28	Jim McSweeney	Dyckman Oval, Bronx, NY, USA	W TKO	4
1937-07-20	Tommy Vello	Canarsie Stadium, Brooklyn, NY, USA	W KO	1
1937-06-29	Benny Johnson	Queensboro Arena, Long Island City, NY, USA	W KO	3
1937-06-15	Benny Rubano	Queensboro Arena, Long Island City, NY, USA	W PTS	4
1937-06-01	Benny Rubano	Coney Island Velodrome, Brooklyn, NY, USA	W PTS	4
1937-05-22	Frankie Reese	Ridgewood Grove, Brooklyn, NY, USA	W PTS	4